Robert Crowcroft is Lecturer in Contemporary History at the University of Edinburgh. He completed his Ph.D. at the University of Leeds in 2007. He is the co-editor of *The Philosophy, Politics and Religion of British Democracy* (I.B.Tauris).

ATTLEE'S WAR

WORLD WAR II AND THE
MAKING OF A LABOUR LEADER

ROBERT CROWCROFT

I.B. TAURIS

LONDON · NEW YORK

Published in 2011 by I.B.Tauris & Co Ltd
6 Salem Road, London W2 4BU
175 Fifth Avenue, New York NY 10010
www.ibtauris.com

Distributed in the United States and Canada Exclusively by Palgrave Macmillan,
175 Fifth Avenue, New York, NY 10010

International Library of Twentieth Century History 41

ISBN: 978 1 84885 286 0

A full CIP record for this book is available from the British Library
A full CIP record for this book is available from the Library of Congress

Library of Congress catalog card: available

Camera-ready copy supplied by
Oxford Publishing Services, Oxford
Printed and bound in Great Britain by CPI Antony Rowe, Chippenham

Contents

Abbreviations

AEU	Amalgamated Engineering Union
AHRC	Arts and Humanities Research Council
CPGB	Communist Party of Great Britain
HC	House of Commons
LCC	London County Council
LLP	London Labour Party
LPACR	*Labour Party Annual Conference Report*
LSE	London School of Economics
MFGB	Miners' Federation of Great Britain
NCL	National Council of Labour
NEC	National Executive Committee
NHS	National Health Service
NUDAW	National Union of Shop Distributive and Allied Workers
NUR	National Union of Railwaymen
PLP	Parliamentary Labour Party
RAF	Royal Air Force
TGWU	Transport and General Workers' Union
TUC	Trades Union Congress
USSR	Union of Soviet Socialist Republics
VE Day	Victory in Europe Day (8 May 1945)

Acknowledgements

This book grew out of a Ph.D. on Labour Party politics between 1939 and 1945. In my view, one problem with our impressions of Westminster during the war – and this has solidified into a conviction in the process of adapting the thesis into a book – lies in the *texture* of the previous literature. Most of those works take on a markedly sunny and cheerful hue. Wartime politics comes to appear overly optimistic. To me, the documents convey a very different impression: it is of dark, swirling, forces at work, endless uncertainty and political titans doing battle. The period is at once oppressive and exhilarating. Frankly, it has always felt utterly Wagnerian in its atmospherics. I hope that this monograph captures one aspect of that story – the rise of Clement Attlee to a position of pre-eminence in the British polity.

I take this opportunity to thank the various archivists and library staff who helped to facilitate the research, as well as the bright sparks at the National Archives who put the Cabinet papers for 1939 to 1945 online, a genuinely invaluable resource. Let us all hope that the online national records are expanded further in the years to come. The AHRC generously funded my Ph.D. over three years, for which I express my gratitude. Ms Joanna Godfrey at I.B.Tauris has consistently been a fantastic source of help as my editor. Professor Kevin Theakston and Professor Philip Williamson examined the Ph.D. thesis, and the former gave helpful advice on the adapted version. I am deeply indebted to Professor John Charmley for comments on the manuscript and other acts of generosity. I should also express my affection to students and former students – some of them now good friends – who offered amusement and stimulation, especially Mr Thomas Dawn and Mr David Lyons. Teaching is a unique pleasure (why so many people do not like doing it is baffling to me), and I have always treasured the weekly doses of outrage and the shredding of the liberal and peacenik conscience.

I would like to thank Dr Simon Green, Professor Andrew Thorpe, Dr Jeremy Smith and Ms Maria Di Stefano for various kindnesses. I will always be grateful to my old secondary school History teacher, Mr Paul Allen, for sparking my interest in the subject in the first place through his wonderful classes. Without him, I would not be writing this now. I owe a great deal to Mr Lee Bruce for his unfailing friendship as well as his comments on an earlier draft of the manuscript. By far my largest intellectual debt is to my former supervisors, Dr Owen Hartley and Professor Richard Whiting, who have acted as inspiring mentors and friends. Each also offered insightful suggestions to improve the text.

But my oldest, and deepest, debt is owed to my mother and my grandparents. I can never begin to repay it, but this book is a small token of my affection.

Introduction

In July 1945 the Labour Party secured its first ever majority in Parliament and formed a government that remains, depending on one's perspective, either the finest or the most destructive in the twentieth-century history of these islands. Major reforms – economic, industrial and social – were enacted and the powers of the British state expanded to reflect a new faith in the ability of government to solve problems once believed intractable. The Prime Minister of that government, Labour leader Clement Attlee, became a political legend. His only modern peers in that regard are Winston Churchill and Margaret Thatcher. Attlee was recently voted the most successful Prime Minister of the twentieth-century,[1] and yet he remains the most poorly understood senior politician of the whole era due to his utter lack of charisma, 'diffident' manner and air of a 'bank manager'.[2]

But the position that Labour won in 1945 did not just fall into its lap; the party and its leaders had played a critical role in the Churchill coalition ministry that guided Britain through the Second World War. Previously, nearly all political historians have explored whether the conflict facilitated a policy 'consensus' between Labour and the Conservatives on a mixed economy and an expanded welfare state that lasted until the election of Mrs Thatcher in 1979.[3] Part of this has been an examination of the development within Labour's institutional structure in the years prior to the defeat of Hitler of the policies that would be enacted in the 1945 government.[4] Extensive work has also been conducted on explaining the 1945 general election result.[5]

This book offers a fresh perspective on wartime politics by concentrating attention for the first time on the extent to which the years 1939 to 1945 marked a decisive political shift towards the Labour Party, and the role in that process of Attlee. The shift in question was much more than controversial policies like state intervention in industry coming to be regarded as common sense under the pressures of war. It instead represented a fundamental realignment of British politics. It was,

1

moreover, a transformation driven through by the Labour leaders themselves, particularly the much maligned and misunderstood Attlee. As such, the book poses questions that allow the familiar landmarks of this period to be analysed in new ways. Labour's impact on the political world was fundamental and systemic. Attlee and other colleagues in the Churchill coalition – particularly union boss Ernest Bevin, the wartime Minister of Labour, and Attlee's great rival Herbert Morrison, the Home Secretary – assumed the central role in a reconstruction of the British state and the establishment of new doctrines and practices under which the country was governed. The apparatus and boundaries of government were hugely expanded. The transformation these men wrought had an impact that lasted much longer than just one generation of Labour leaders; the legacy of their wartime activities remained in place until at least 1979 and arguably afterwards. Moreover, Attlee was personally central to achieving this change in his party's fortunes. His leadership style – consistently elusive to historians – enabled Labour to dominate party politics between 1939 and 1945. In fact, Attlee's ascendancy within the government and over his own party was possibly the most significant force in shaping the entire direction of wartime politics. He played the principal role in enhancing Labour's negotiating position for office in the 'phoney war' of September 1939 to May 1940, and secured considerable leverage for the party with the formation of the Churchill coalition. Between 1941 and 1945 Attlee led the way in a revolution in British government and the growth of the state; he helped guide the coalition in the direction of new, and social-democratic, politics; and he was the most energetic figure from either party in seeking to bolster the electoral arrangements that underpinned the structures of cross-party alliance. None of this has been recognized by historians, who have downplayed Attlee's importance during the war. Reassessment of this alters our perception of the period as a whole.

Once within sight of real power, the ineffective Leader of the Opposition of the 1930s gave way to a man who became the key figure in the course, and outcome, of wartime British politics. This book seeks to address the failure to appreciate the significance of Attlee by making the case for a new perspective on politics before 1945. Attlee's impact on British politics was extensive; more than 60 years later, he remains the embodiment of an era. Yet, scholars have still proven unable to grasp his essence as a political operator. The bottom line is that no political history of the war has treated Attlee as central. This book makes the claim not only that he was central, but also that insights gleaned from the war perhaps represent the key to understanding his career as a whole.

Wartime politics and the impact of Labour

In the years before 1939, Labour had always been a minority party; two brief spells in office without a Commons majority seemed to disprove the idea of an inevitable 'march of Labour'. During the war this all changed. Yet, this was neither the result of a convergence of circumstances nor the emergence of a new received wisdom. It was not simply because of blows to the credibility of the Conservative Party, signified by the failure of appeasement, or even about national unity or political necessity. It instead represented fundamental change wrought by deliberate political action.

At a time when cultural history is in the ascendant, and political history is all too often the history of 'political culture', that is an important point.[6] The impact of the Labour leaders on the political system between 1939 and 1945 conveys much to support the argument that I, and others, have mounted for a reassertion of the value of traditional 'elite' studies in political history.[7] It is also clear that most contemporary studies of elite politics are woefully under conceptualized and content merely to tell a story, any story. The case can be made that the war was perhaps the most significant instance of political strategizing and calculated scheming in twentieth-century British politics, and all carried out under the guise of coalition. Yet, the events considered have never been interpreted from this perspective. To be sure, an attempt to retell well-established tales about the war would not be worth writing. This book aims at doing something else. Labour's wartime transformation represented one of the most important political turnarounds of modern history, and the pre-eminent role that the party's senior figures – particularly Attlee – played in achieving this warrants recognition. In its emphasis on strategy and tactics, and in exploring the threads that tie action together, the book's assumptions are largely those of the 'high politics' approach associated with Maurice Cowling.[8] That sits within a larger 'Tory' school of political history, which offers a corrective to triumphalist (translated: liberal and socialist) accounts of developments in British politics since the seventeenth century, where 'public opinion', or the 'people', in different forms, ultimately win out and in which public opinion and the people are usually – and not coincidentally – found to conform to left-wing totems.[9] In the alternative 'Tory' approach, change emanates from the centre.

Something deeper also informs that interpretation of politics – a specific worldview and belief about the nature of man. It is the assumption that at the core of human conduct sits what Augustine labelled *libido dominandi* – a thirst for power and authority, for honour, recognition and to shape the world to reflect one's own outlook – and that this offers powerful insights into politics.[10] Think of the second book of *Institutes of the Christian Religion*, and Calvin's overarching argument that the appetite dominates the intellect.[11] A Christian view of man's conduct offers the conviction that 'The Lord knoweth the thoughts of man, that they are vanity';[12] and 'every imagination of the thoughts of his heart was only evil continually.'[13] Politicians are prideful and intent on reworking the world to satisfy their own desires. I have participated elsewhere in work exploring the merits of a Christian worldview in fashioning an intellectual paradigm quite at odds with more recent, secular, mental tendencies.[14] Of course, most modern thinkers – with their core belief in the potential for human fulfilment – share both a Platonic optimism and a Hegelian concept of progress, and display little sympathy for such ideas. In being that way, however, they miss something important. After all (to take one of the more obvious examples), did not these very same assumptions about the nature of politics – the primacy of individual interest and faction over principle and virtue – provide the whole rationale for the framing of the American Constitution and the contents of *The Federalist*?[15]

Adopting a distinctive view of political practice, this book examines leadership in the raw. It has an analogous method not only to Cowling but also to more recent 'high politics' work of a similar vein by Richard Shannon on the Conservatives under Salisbury, and by Jeremy Smith on the Conservatives and Ireland prior to 1914.[16] In focusing on leadership, it concentrates on how leaders achieve their goals, how they have to face in several directions at once and on the issues that confront them in each.

This is a salient point. Both before and after taking Labour into the coalition, Attlee and his colleagues placed Labour in a political straitjacket. That quickly produced a tide of discontent that tested Attlee's leadership to the limit. Most of their followers simply did not appreciate the tightrope of difficulties that Attlee and other Labour ministers were compelled to walk. What followed were recurrent outbreaks of bitter disillusionment with Attlee's suddenly authoritarian, brook-no-complaints manner. Within the government, Attlee led the way in pursuing a distinctive Labour agenda and engaging in belligerence towards the

Conservatives. Attlee and the Labour ministers thus had to carry out a delicate strategy in highly restrictive conditions. It was an under-appreciated political triumph. Against this backdrop, Herbert Morrison determined to exploit the political tensions of the war to seize Attlee's job. The two decades-long struggle between the pair was at its most intense here. The outcome was a series of high stakes, tactically complex conflicts between Attlee and those who wished to change Labour's course, challenge his strategy of alliance with the Conservatives, or remove him altogether. Morrison exploited the unpopularity of some of Attlee's decisions to fashion a unique credibility for himself as the heir to Labour's soul in a protracted bid to unseat the leader. The importance of these issues in shaping wartime politics, not just in the Labour Party but also across the broader political nation as a whole, has not previously received adequate attention. They were in fact the most significant political conflicts in Britain after the fall of Chamberlain and dominated politics for considerable periods between 1939 and 1945. The Attlee–Morrison rivalry, for instance, terminated in a struggle for the keys to 10 Downing Street in July 1945. Furthermore, the extent to which Attlee was the central player from either party in the attempts to plan for, and mould, the shape of postwar politics – particularly in struggling to create the conditions under which the cross-party alliance could be prolonged after the war – has not been understood.

As already suggested, the book makes the case that the years 1939 to 1945 marked, in effect, a seizure of power by the Labour Party and its leaders. Wartime political history has not previously been studied in quite this way, but the possibility has significant explanatory force. In essence, the present account deals with both Labour and government politics in parallel and as part of addressing the same problem – Labour's growing political dominance. Whereas previous historians have studied 'policies', this book analyses 'politics' and uses it to craft a fresh interpretation of the period, breaking new ground by integrating questions about the upheavals of the era as much within 'parties' and 'personalities' as 'policies'. The intended result is an account that necessitates the larger political dynamics of the era be rethought.

Churchill's shadow looms large and dominates one component of the historiography;[17] the other was best articulated by Paul Addison and is the issue of 'consensus', specifically whether the coalition produced a new set of core agreements between the main parties that was carried into the postwar era – over the welfare state, nationalization of industry, Keynesian economics and a health service – until the advent of Thatcherism.[18] Addison worked in close collaboration with Angus Calder and together the two forged an enduring orthodoxy about the war. Historians have not broken free from the framework they established and have overwhelmingly tended to engage with the consensus question, either for or against the thesis. Kevin Jefferys and Stephen Brooke provided the most persuasive statements of the case against consensus, arguing that fundamental disagreements still remained between the parties during the war.

Addison and Jefferys, despite their conflicting opinions, dealt with the evolution of government policy and the coalition's response to the challenges and pressures – as well as opportunities – it faced. [19] Yet, both paid less attention to the importance of the political parties during the war, placed insufficient emphasis on the interplay between government and party and badly neglected the role of Attlee. In addition, neither noted the extent to which Labour came to dominate British politics between 1939 and 1945 and the endless strategizing conducted to that end by Attlee and the rest of the party's ministers. Jefferys acknowledged that by 1940 there was established 'a pattern of coalition politics in which each side constantly sought to maximize party advantage',[20] but he failed to pursue what that meant in practice; neither he nor Addison charted the war as a Labour-directed reshaping of British politics.

Brooke's work is the only previous treatment of Labour's role in domestic politics during the war. Brooke – unlike Addison and Jefferys – dealt with policymaking and development within the Labour movement itself rather than the government. He showed how Labour evolved the policies that it would implement in the 1945 government, and suggested that Labour was a far from happy party before 1945. Moreover, Brooke sided with Jefferys in challenging the consensus thesis, arguing that tensions within the Labour movement over policy fatally undermine any idea of an overarching agreement with the Conservatives. The party's 1945 general election victory has also generated considerable psephological analysis.[21] Trevor Burridge, meanwhile, offered an epilogue to the debates over rearmament in the 1930s by examining the development of the party's perceptions of foreign affairs after 1939.[22]

The one major exception to the tests of 'consensus' is a quite different, recent, work by Andrew Thorpe on the organizational base of the parties between 1939 and 1945.[23] In it he adopted a perspective that facilitates a fresh understanding of political developments; he suggested much in a methodological sense as well. Importantly, Thorpe highlighted the immovability of 'party' from the political scene, a point that will have ramifications for the closing stages of the account that follows. He also stressed the need to move beyond old frameworks and into fresh interpretative territory.

It is clear that, in seeking to prove or disprove consensus, the rest of these works exist within the analytical paradigm established by Addison and Calder.[24] Moreover, they concentrate overwhelmingly on policy; but what about the role of political strategizing, creative leadership and the purposes behind decision-making? By the same token, to what extent can a reassessment supply a fresh perspective about the degree to which the war represented a deliberate reshaping of the political environment by the Labour Party's most senior figures? The idea that the position the Labour leaders found themselves occupying in 1945 did not just come to them, but had to be made, deserves serious consideration. This book attempts to be the first to transcend the arguments about 'consensus' and place emphasis on alternative ideas in explaining politics before 1945. Disregarding the consensus thesis does not entail questioning its importance or criticizing Addison's work. *The Road to 1945* is one of the best monographs on any era of British history. But it was written more than thirty years ago and the arguments it spawned have been raging for that long. It is a period ripe for reassessment. The book works to address this by integrating the government and the Labour Party together for the first time to give a proper analysis of Labour's trajectory, as well as highlighting elements and events that add fresh themes to our perspective on wartime politics. It seeks to tie together the threads of political action and describe a new structure to politics before 1945.

For instance, each of the standard texts on the period, Addison, Brooke and Jefferys, neglected the approach taken by the Labour Party and its leaders in both the phoney war of 1939 and the first year of the coalition. Addison and Jefferys focus on the erosion of Chamberlain's support in the first period, and then the readjustment of the Conservative Party and the consolidation of Churchill's authority in the second. Even Cowling failed to spot what Labour was up to.[25] This book will address this oversight by concentrating attention on the strategy and tactics of Labour's senior figures in these crucial two years. Then, from 1941, it will show how the Labour ministers and other representatives of the party took the reins of British government in unprecedented ways, their ruthless attitudes towards their own party, the conflict for the Labour leadership between Attlee and Morrison, and how the electoral basis of the coalition became a subject of intense controversy that effectively all senior British politicians hoped could be fashioned into an ongoing alliance *after* victory over Hitler.

What emerges is a quite different sense of politics in the period before 1945 and one that, moreover, serves to answer many longstanding questions about Attlee as a leader. Though it does not engage with the consensus thesis, some parts of the analysis will support it; others will call it into question. Others show how, in some respects, consensus perhaps ran deeper than even Addison suggested. But whatever happened during the war – consensual or otherwise – it did not simply emerge because of the national emergency, and new ideas such as Keynesianism. It came together because the Labour ministers moulded it out of the British state and national politics. The most useful explanations for the momentous political changes of the 1940s are not found in the 1945 election results, so easily reversed six years later. The real story can instead be located here, during the war.

The rise of Attlee

Despite being granted secular sainthood by those sympathetic to 'progress', Clement Richard Attlee was the most puzzling major British politician of the last century. He has given rise to greater misunderstanding than any other leading politician has during that time, and no satisfactory account of his success has ever been established. The longest serving leader of a political party during the century, Attlee was at the head of the Labour Party for two decades, from 1935 to 1955. A Cabinet minister between 1940 and 1951, in the Churchill coalition he played an integral role on the home front and running the machinery of government. His doctrinal instincts were those of Green; his political methods those of the planner; and his temperament that of the military officer. And at the end of the Second World War, after leading Labour to victory in the July 1945 general election, Attlee became Prime Minister of the most famous government of the whole century, attempting to reconstruct Britain in an unprecedented series of economic, social and political reforms. His frontline career extended from the deprivations and turbulence of the interwar period to the beginnings of the affluent, consumer society in the 1950s. Attlee's adult life extended even further, from late Victorian Britain to the trenches in the First World War and finally to the liberalizing society of the 1960s.

His story therefore represents the various faces of twentieth-century Britain, the triumph and tragedy of that period, as well as anyone; yet he is paradoxically more elusive than comparable figures. Attlee has remained stubbornly resistant to enquiry despite decades of intermittent attempts. Scholars have identified few plausible reasons for his remaining atop British politics for so long. Efforts to understand the shy, reticent Attlee have yielded at least as many questions as answers and, despite a sizeable volume of literature of various kinds (biographies, studies of his government and of the Labour Party), the secret of his political leadership and the basis for his remarkable ascendancy remain poorly understood. The difficulties of interpreting Attlee have had consequences for explaining British politics more broadly, for he is central to numerous important fields. These include rebuilding the Labour Party after MacDonald's expulsion; the 'appeasement' and rearmament debates of the 1930s; the strengthening of Labour's credibility during the Second World War; the remaking of government between 1940 and 1945; the forging of the postwar 'consensus'; and Britain's protracted 'decline'.

This book is an effort to address that problem. It is a study of his place in British politics in what was its most important period, the Second World War – a period, moreover, when his personal significance has been consistently overlooked. This was the era when Attlee emerged from isolation and powerlessness to become the key figure in the machinery of government, as well as party politics. The book will explore Attlee's growing dominance over political life during the Second World War. He had been a relatively ineffectual figure since becoming leader in 1935 and was unable to offer his party much in the way of direction or inspiration. Talk of replacing him was constant. Yet, by 1945, Attlee had become the most powerful actor in domestic politics. This account seeks to explain the reasons for that transformation and, in doing so, facilitate a satisfactory analysis of Attlee and his impact on British politics. It is not a biography. Biography abstracts the subject from his surroundings, which in Attlee's case is precisely how he should *not* be studied. His practice of politics and leadership needs to be integrated into the practices of those around him. By placing Attlee in his environment, this book will be the first analysis to focus specifically on, and draw out, the nature of Attlee's leadership.

In locating a centre of gravity in the Second World War, the book makes the case that Attlee can be more productively understood here, where he worked to secure the Labour Party a powerful role in the wartime coalition and then quietly stamped his own seal on Whitehall, extending his influence across the entire field of government, than in the period of his own post-war ministry that has yielded little in the way of explanation for Attlee's success. The same applies to looking at this era rather than at his stints in opposition (1935 to 1939, 1951 to 1955). It is doubly significant because it allows us to challenge the prevailing sense that Attlee did not have a good war, continued to offer little decisive leadership to his party, and did not emerge as one of the period's political 'heavyweights'.[26] Virtually all previous work on this period has been critical of Attlee's role. The idea that the war may offer insights into Attlee's leadership or how to understand him as a politician has not been taken seriously. This misunderstanding is closely linked to those same basic problems of properly interpreting Attlee in the first place.

These were the years when Attlee evolved and began to exert influence on the political world for the first time. It became clear that when in proximity to office Attlee was capable of authoritarianism and a rare tactical astuteness. He played an important part in the downfall of Neville Chamberlain and, between September 1939 and May 1940, prepared the ground for the Labour Party to enter a coalition government in a powerful position. He became the key power broker in Westminster party politics. From mid-1940 in a non-departmental role, Attlee also served as Deputy Prime Minister and used the Whitehall committee system to expand his influence and, eventually, consolidate his authority across the British state. Immediately upon entering office, Attlee began an overhaul of the machinery of government. He dissolved dozens of committees, centralized decision-making, reduced the ability of ministers to evade responsibility and produced a considerable improvement in administrative efficiency. For the next five years, he was central to the rapid expansion in the boundaries of the state and clustered into his hands a unique degree of influence within Whitehall. Attlee also sought to guide the government in the direction of Labour policy and played a role in the emergence of a new way of doing things that was to reshape public life. And through it all, he fought to control the Labour Party and engaged in bitter rivalries with those keen to dislodge him. One reason why this period is so revealing is that it was when the somewhat ramshackle state apparatus that had emerged in the first decades of the twentieth-century – and which had so struggled to cope with the pressures the era unleashed – was finally converted, under the impetus of war, into the modern, powerful state that was to dominate the second half of the century. Attlee was crucial to this change. We see his mastery of political positioning and creative leadership, as well as his advancement and implementation of a distinctive agenda within a government dominated by those viscerally opposed to such ideas. We see him grappling with and devising solutions to the fundamental problems of the state in a condition of deep crisis; and we see the broader context of government and party politics in which Attlee had to function. He was one of the few individuals able to shape the wider political system through his conduct.

This book thus places the story of the rise of Attlee in the context of the broader history of British politics and government during the period. In using the war as a vehicle to enhance historical understanding of Attlee as a political leader – as well as studying the strategic, tactical and doctrinal goals of the party's other senior figures – this, then, is a study in 'leadership'. Paradoxically, political historians rarely examine leadership in its own right but it surely constitutes the principal driving force of political action. I contend that only by seeking out his 'leadership' in this manner can one solve the mystery of Attlee's political practice. In identifying the problem of leadership and analysing one of its foremost yet elusive modern practitioners, the book argues for greater emphasis to be placed on leadership as an activity in itself. It mounts a challenge to the popular image of Attlee as a reticent collegiate and seeks to shed new light on his reputation.

The method employed to study this is worth considering. The connections between the things politicians say, the ideas they espouse and the impact this has on events is how historians usually study the influence of political actors. Such an approach is logical. Where a politician played only a minor role as an exponent of ideas and a similarly small role on the public stage, however, the task of investigation becomes much harder. Attlee's personality has certainly proven a 'besetting handicap' to historians.[27] Perhaps if he had been a 'prima donna' it would be different.[28] Yet, this book contends that just because Attlee possessed an elusive personality does not mean that he has to remain politically elusive. He leaves his imprint elsewhere. In his case, we have to immerse ourselves in the political world, and particularly Attlee's skilful working – and manipulation – of it. By 1945, Attlee already occupied a position atop the political system. The key consideration – and the one that helps to explain him as a political figure – is the story of how he established that position in the first place.

As stated at the outset, this book is fundamentally 'high political' in its orientation and assumptions. This complements ongoing historiographical developments in a number of respects. Bucking the trend, Philip Williamson has recognized the relevance of leadership.[29] I therefore build on both this and a tradition of suggesting that other poorly understood politicians were also canny operators.[30] Recent penetrating work has explored the importance of 'reputation'.[31] Tony Shaw examined political manipulation of the public sphere.[32] Given the reassertion of agency and the extent to which it belongs to politicians as creative actors, it seems sensible to consider this in the context of someone like Attlee. Much of the work that has returned agency to politicians under the aegis of 'the new political history' has done so in the context of exploring popular politics and political culture.[33] As I have argued elsewhere, it is logical to extend this to the study of elite politics as well.[34] Therefore, the book stresses the freedom and creativity open to politicians rather than viewing them as being in hock to social or most other structural pressures, and pays attention to the detection of political purpose and objectives, as well as language.

This approach to observing Attlee – very different from previous ways of studying the Labour leader– represents the best means of getting to grips with him and comprehending him as a politician. Thinking about leadership enables historians to ask fresh questions of the actors in our island story and seek to understand them in new ways. Depicting Attlee as an architect, I make these distinctions in order to integrate both the key components of Attlee's success – his proficiency as an administrator and at running things and his capabilities as a political tactician. His leadership consisted principally of actions within the political world itself (as opposed to, say, personal charisma directed at a broader audience). Yet, during the Second World War he also presided over Labour capturing the political centre ground by becoming aligned – for the first time in its history – with public opinion and particularly the powerful sense of 'national community' that grew over the course of the conflict. In terms of public politics, this was the key to Labour's 1945 election victory. While some may dispute this claim because Attlee was not a central *public* figure, nonetheless it was achieved through the direction in which British government went after 1940. This was firmly in the direction of Labour policy across a number of fronts and which, by 1945, left Labour's proposed postwar reform pro-gramme merely a logical extension of what had come before. And Attlee certainly *was* central to that. There is something else. Unlike many leaders who could be judged similarly important figures – men like Gladstone, Disraeli, Salisbury, Baldwin, Churchill and Thatcher – Attlee's name has never become 'a counter in the currency game of political cult'.[35] From the moment of their political demise, the reputations of prominent leaders frequently become an arena of conflict between those eager to lay claim to their mantle and identify themselves as their 'true' heir. The name of a famous leader carries potent symbolism. This is one of the conventional legacies of important leadership. Yet, no one has fought to lay claim to Attlee's personal reputation, or purported to be his inheritor (however much people may identify themselves as a successor to his *government*). The curious lack of competition over his memory is intriguing.

Attlee: the literature

Only Arthur Balfour and Stanley Baldwin have eluded their pursuers as doggedly as Attlee. Previous interpretations of Attlee's career have been many and varied, and encompassed a number of formats. The core problem of accounting for Attlee's political style and his impact on an era, however, remains unresolved. For decades, many had negative perceptions of Attlee's leadership. This was an impression reinforced by some critical depictions of him in the memoirs of colleagues, particularly Hugh Dalton and Morrison.[36] Both men thought that losing their seats in 1931 enabled Attlee to become leader in their place.[37] Attlee was 'very small'.[38] But many other Labourites and Conservatives poured scorn on him as well. These first impressions lasted and generated an enduring legend of negativity around Attlee. Churchill was said to have commented that Attlee was 'a modest man who has a lot to be modest about', and 'a sheep in sheep's clothing'.[39] That he probably never said it – and doubtless did not believe it – is beside the point. Attlee generated bewilderment, it being assumed that he failed to provide decisive leadership, acquired his job by sheer luck and that Labour's success was primarily the result of those around him. Attlee's own memoir, *As It Happened*, was one of the most unrevealing autobiographies ever written by a British politician.[40] True to form, Attlee painted himself as little more than an observer of larger people and events. This was itself an integral part of his self-image and the identity he cultivated. But historians still understood very little about him. When a different sort of perspective began to be advanced in the 1970s, however, it found favour as a symbol of the party's golden age, particularly against the backdrop of the failure of contemporary Labour governments. It was reinforced by the advent of Thatcherism. The Attlee era now resembled the highpoint of Labour history, as the 'forward march' of the party never really resumed after 1951, and first Wilson and then Callaghan struggled with an economic malaise to which Labour seemed to have no answer. Rather than merely one stage of a Labour-led transformation of Britain, the Attlee era began to seem more of a treasured inheritance that stood fast against the crises of later decades.

The most effective study of Attlee to date remains Kenneth Harris's 1982 biography.[41] Harris provided a well-rounded picture of Labour's famous leader. He began to draw out the fact that, though Attlee was a profoundly shy man with little charisma, he was not dominated or over-whelmed by others and was in fact a capable actor in his own right. Harris's biography made the case that Attlee was a far more significant politician than had previously been recognized. But it left unanswered key questions as to the character of his leadership style, the balance that he struck between political administration and political manipulation, an explanation for his longevity, and the way in which he was able to dominate the Labour Party. These weaknesses were perhaps inherent in the biographical format, for in extracting Attlee from the world in which he functioned the ability to observe that functioning was also lost. As a result, the book did not demonstrate Attlee's ability to drive forward political events through his engagement with the world of party and government and, in doing so, left a picture that was enticing but unsatis-factory.

Another biography, by Trevor Burridge, expanded the body of Attlee literature in 1985,[42] but he neither convincingly established Attlee's cen-trality in the way Harris had nor advanced understanding of how someone with Attlee's personality could have remained at the top for so long. Burridge saw Attlee's success as lying in his 'moral probity' and absolute reliability, and drew out his political views that married socialism with a conservative disposition.[43] While these were certainly significant traits, it

14

again tells us little about Attlee's interaction with the political world. A spate of subsequent studies reflects the now established interest in Attlee. The biographies by Jerry Brookshire, David Howell, Robert Pearce and Nicklaus Thomas-Symonds are generally elusive.[44] A recent comparative study of the 1945 ministry and the roles of Attlee, Bevin, Morrison, Dalton and Stafford Cripps depicted Attlee as the 'tortoise' dependent on the capabilities of the four dynamic 'hares'.[45] The cumulative impact of these separate efforts – some of them very good – to take a hold of Attlee is limited. Howell's was a short study aimed at students; Pearce and Brookshire consider the legislative record of the Attlee era but neglect examining his distinctive political style; Thomas-Symonds offers a narrative overview but fails to come to grips with Attlee as a political animal. Francis Beckett's biography was a perceptive account of Attlee's career that in many respects built on Harris's work, reasserting the notion that Attlee was a central figure in his own right.[46] With the exception of Harris, it represents the best insight into Attlee so far, but, like Harris, Beckett did not concentrate on Attlee's interactions with, and working of, the political system.

What emerges is a sense that Attlee was undoubtedly important but must be analysed within a broader context if the enigma surrounding him is to be resolved. John Swift's study of Attlee's performance between 1931 and 1939 in some respects points the way towards this goal, but, like the other attempts listed above, shows Attlee within the political system without, again, making a clear case for his impact *across* it.[47] Nor does Swift seek to draw out the nuances and character of Attlee's style.

Building on this sense of puzzlement, Attlee's performance during the Second World War, particularly, has been a subject of both neglect and heavy criticism. Harris recognized that Attlee played a 'crucial role' in the success of the Churchill coalition, but still saw 1945 as marking the beginning of his political dominance.[48] His concluding chapter concentrated on Attlee's early life, the 1930s and the postwar ministry; the war years did not receive emphasis.[49] Recently, Richard Whiting endorsed the view that Attlee's experience of the war 'was less dramatic' than it was for other Labour politicians and observed that 'Attlee's behaviour appeared to open up the danger that the war would pass Labour by.'[50] 'He did not emerge as one of the big men of the war.'[51] Burridge supported the thesis that the 'people's war' ushered in major shifts in economic and social policy, but failed to highlight Attlee's importance in this.[52] It was not until 1944 that

Attlee had 'begun to make his mark', and even then, 'only among a few'.[53] Just as he missed out Attlee's role in his own postwar ministry, Ralph Miliband left Attlee conspicuous by his absence in his comments on Labour's war.[54] Elsewhere, Swift took a quite different view, arguing that the 1930s saw Attlee's 'greatest development as a statesman' rather than the period after 1939.[55]

It is clear therefore that Attlee's role, and centrality, in British politics during the war has gone unrecognized. Indeed, Addison is roundly critical of Attlee, and in his account the future Prime Minister is not depicted as one of the war's major players. What is most interesting is how *little* Addison says about Attlee, treating him as a largely peripheral figure. This is instructive, for the failure to recognize his role is indicative of the failure to understand Attlee more broadly. Addison saw him as 'unimpressive' even during the 1931 Parliament, and, still worse, acting as a brake on radicalism and change during the war itself.[56] Addison neither perceived him as one of the big instigators of reform in government during the conflict nor highlighted his dominance over party politics. As this book will show, nothing could be further from the truth. Addison saw Bevin, not Attlee, as the Labour 'leader' with the 'ability and ambition' to reverse the defeat that the failure of the 1926 General Strike had inflicted on Labour.[57] Bevin can hardly be downplayed, but this view certainly under-rates Attlee's significance. Addison argued that Attlee was 'as enigmatic a figure in office as in Opposition ... although he was a competent com-mittee chairman ... he was never among the big men of power in wartime Whitehall'.[58] He felt that there was 'truth' in the view that Attlee was 'worthy, but limited', and it was 'incredible that he should be where he [was]'.[59] 'It very much looks as though Attlee's [range of wartime posts, including Deputy Prime Minister] were designed to disguise the fact that the leader of the Labour Party had very little influence in the government.'[60] Moreover, Attlee is implicitly charged with a fundamental failure of leadership. 'In a sense ... Labour failed to rise to the opportunity Churchill offered in May 1940,' a position only recovered by the good fortune of 'the rise of Bevin and Morrison'.[61] Addison clearly does not rate Attlee nor think much of his performance; but this is a good example of where Attlee's nature has led to his importance being overlooked. Beckett got rather closer to the truth when he noted the political 'iron' in Attlee's 'soul', which became apparent once the war got underway, turning him into the 'greaser of wheels' at 'the heart of the government'.[62]

Burridge observed that Attlee's preference for 'sometimes saying nothing' was in fact 'deceptive' and 'almost certainly the result of deliberate calculation and experience'.[63] What this book seeks to do is to demonstrate the impact of that calculation and experience on the course of events.

Previous attempts to establish a definitive interpretation of Attlee have therefore yielded little success and the man himself remains determinedly elusive. Though historians now take a more positive view of Attlee, bewilderment persists. As yet, no one has convincingly explained either Attlee's leadership style or how he practised his direction of party and state. No one has demonstrated his mastery of the political world or studied him as a political operator. To do this requires a willingness to see things as Attlee encountered them in the 1940s and, furthermore, requires a conscious decision to pursue his leadership across the networks of party and government, literally dozens of committees and a multitude of institutional environments. We must follow his dispatch of memoranda through the corridors of power, his fighting on multiple fronts in bureaucratic warfare at which he had few equals in both attaining his aims and avoiding unduly ruffling the feathers of others. We must fully recognize his manipulative abilities and his highly creative leadership. We must wrest Attlee the politician and leader from the mythology of the 1945 government and politicized arguments about 'reform', 'consensus' and 'decline'. We must seek to understand him as a politician and not the embodiment, for good or ill, of an age.

There is something else. The whole of the period *c*.1940–79 is now genuinely a complete *historical* era. Until quite recently, at least, the 1970s have still felt contemporary, but no longer. This offers both an opportunity and a necessity to rethink the politics of that era. In the historiography of British politics, the period *c*.1880–1920 is traditionally the era that has generated extensive paradigm-changing work.[64] But the period that encompasses the Second World War to the rise of Thatcher could become conceptually the most exciting era of modern history. The book is located within this broader period and, conscious of the rapidly growing historical interest in its politics, seeks to suggest a new interpretation of the way in which that era began.

Chapter 1

Capturing the Language of Patriotism

As the heavy rain of an unusually wet summer swept across large parts of the British Isles in July 1939, the downpour found an eerie reflection in the mood of the nation's political leaders. Dispersed around the country for summer holidays, a haunting sense of foreboding united these men across hundreds of miles and in spite of their geographical isolation. War with Adolf Hitler's Germany was generally thought to be imminent, and Britain was soon to face its sternest military test for more than a century. National survival itself would be at stake, but some had other pressing concerns as well. At a house in North Wales, the leader of His Majesty's Opposition, Clement Attlee, was recuperating from surgery for a serious prostate complaint that kept him away from the political front lines from May to late September. As a result, when the Labour movement gathered for its annual 1939 conference at Southport, it was, to all intents and purposes, leaderless. Of course, considering the dissatisfaction Attlee's performance in the preceding four years generated, this may not have been such a new state of affairs in the eyes of many. Still, the weakness of Labour's political position at this time would be difficult to overstate. The party held seats only in its industrial heartlands and had little prospect of winning the next general election. Yet, despite this, the months from the summer of 1939 to the spring of 1940 were to represent the beginnings of one of the most comprehensive political turnarounds in modern British history. Out of its weakness, Labour crafted a position of great strength.

Ironically, although Attlee was to be central to this – and to his party's fortunes throughout the entire war – for the first few months, at least, he was absent. He certainly offered guidance and his hand can be discerned, if only fitfully and in outline. But it was other senior figures who took the lead in orchestrating a tactically complex balancing act in this initial period.

Most significantly, Labour's deputy leader Arthur Greenwood, a veteran Wakefield MP who achieved little in his career and has consequently been neglected by historians, plugged the gap left by Attlee and was briefly a major actor on the political stage.

What follows in this chapter is an analysis that documents the elaborate tactical arrangements required by Attlee and Labour's strategy prior to the formation of the Churchill government. Certainly, the politics of the 'phoney war' have been told and retold. Fresh analysis requires justification. The case rests on Labour's capture of the political centre. This is a story that has been badly overlooked in the previous literature and is in need of attention. Historians have tended to concentrate on the Conservatives, seen Labour as purely reactive to the worsening crisis and the outbreak of war, charged its leaders with drift and uncertainty, and viewed the party as only rescued from impotence by the political good fortune of the rise of Churchill in May.[1] 'For the Labour leaders, the first eight months of war were a non-event' is a typical view.[2] This chapter will show how, in fact, the Labour Party and its leader played a critical role in realigning British party politics, and established a secure position atop the commanding heights of Westminster. Attlee, along with Morrison, Dalton and Greenwood, was the principal architect of an effort to shore up the party's negotiating position for the creation of a cross-party coalition ministry, which, given the international crisis and the internal problems of the Conservative-dominated National government, looked an increasingly likely possibility. This generates a quite different image of the dynamics at work here. In contrast to the attitude of the earlier literature, the approach plotted for Labour in these months can only be properly understood as a concerted effort to bide time and prepare the ground for coalition. This paid dividends in May 1940.

Moreover, the events analysed here offer crucial early insights into Attlee's leadership style, particularly his blend of strategy and tactics, his party management techniques and his wider approach to politics during the war. The difficulties Attlee and his colleagues faced in 1939 and 1940 were monumental: recognition that office, achieved at the opportune moment, was the priority was balanced by Labour's strong personal antipathy for the Prime Minister, Neville Chamberlain. This, in turn, was matched by the necessity of avoiding any charge of a lack of 'patriotism' and sticking to stridently 'responsible' conduct – while still being perceived as sufficiently anti-Conservative within the Labour Party itself to retain the backing of their followers. And all this from a base of just 150-odd seats in the House of Commons. After previous cross-party alliances, during the First World War and in 1931, had torn Labour apart, coalition was an option that could only be entered into under highly restrictive conditions. With the spectre of earlier coalitions seared into the party's folk memory, and the parliamentary arithmetic of being heavily outnumbered, the only option was a strategy prosecuted through careful manoeuvre, an effort to forge a workable anti-Chamberlain bloc that would also deliver the Labour Party a powerful role in office and delicately chosen language in attempting to find purchase for Labour's ideas. The chapter also lays out the broader political context with which Attlee's subsequent decisions interacted. Though it often went unappreciated by his contemporaries, this analysis of events will indicate the real significance of Attlee's role as leader.

Creating political space

In a way that few historians have fully accepted, the Labour Party – like Churchill, Anthony Eden and other enemies of Chamberlain within the Conservatives – utilized foreign policy as a domestic political tool in the late 1930s. During the 12 months before the outbreak of war, the party had established 'anti-appeasement' as its principal political weapon. That was a wise choice, given that since 1923 Labour had been repeatedly defeated in its battle with Baldwinite Conservatism. Foreign affairs thus represented a vehicle through which to try to escape domestic failure. It was a way of showing worthiness and advertising virtue through exhortation. But that did not mean that the Labour leaders were able to articulate a coherent, alternative grand strategy of their own; the same was true of the anti-Chamberlain Conservatives. When it boiled down to it, the approach advocated by Labour, Churchill, Eden and the rest did not differ in any meaningful sense from the policies of the Prime Minister. Gesture can only obscure the cold realities of strategy so far. This problem, and the fact that dissidents within the governing party also tended to be men scalped by Chamberlain and Baldwin in the years before, has not appeared to call into question – in the eyes of historians, certainly – the legitimacy of their howls of protest.[3] A brief analysis of the essentials of the international policy the competing factions advocated is instructive. Chamberlain hoped to avoid war, restrain Hitler with alliances – the League of Nations, France and eastern European nations were all toyed with – and protect the empire while maintaining European stability in order to keep out the USSR. Churchill and other Conservative dissidents, who perceived the USSR as big an enemy as Hitler, wanted to contain Germany through alliances and defend the empire. Labour similarly sought to restrain Berlin with an alliance system and avoid war, while its leaders accepted the empire and were as suspicious of Moscow as any Conservative. These rival groups all agreed on the importance of 'collective security'. There was unanimity that many German demands were reasonable; and, in 1938, virtually everyone thought that Czechoslovakia would have to be sacrificed in the cause of peace. As Owen Hartley pointedly puts it, even for Churchill, 'quite what he wanted to do' about Hitler 'was much less clear' in the 1930s than he subsequently let on.[4] At moments of crisis, howls of protest in public or around the Cabinet table were rarely accompanied by detailed alternatives to Chamberlain's policy.

If there were differences on grand strategy here, they were in the margins. Precisely what, therefore, was at issue? The answer – naturally enough – was credibility. Fiery speeches were used to gain it and deprive others of it. And it worked, too; domestic considerations certainly compelled an isolated Chamberlain to take a harder line with Germany after Munich. While denouncing 'appeasement' as a way to recover credibility created opportunities for Labour, it also posed problems for the party once war actually came. How they navigated it was Attlee's first triumph. Before that, however, he had to contend with not one, but two, emerging threats.

A new challenge to Attlee's status as leader of the Labour Party arose in his absence in the summer of 1939; and, for once, the rival in question was not the London County Council leader and senior parliamentarian Morrison. It was – rather surprisingly – the deputy leader Greenwood, a grey man blighted by a taste for drink, but who under the leaderless circumstances of these crucial months emerged as a major figure. In the summer and autumn, this former economics lecturer at Leeds University began to lay out the trajectory that Labour would follow for the next six years. Even though Attlee provided guidance from North Wales, Greenwood became the public face of the party at this time. In addition, he performed admirably behind the scenes as well, in delicate positioning *vis-à-vis* the government and equally delicate management of the Labour movement. The most obvious man to step into the breach, Morrison, was himself taken up with his LCC duties in preparing the capital for probable attack by the *Luftwaffe*. Thus, the unlikely figure of Arthur Greenwood became the effective leader of the Labour Party for three of the most important months in national history. It was on his watch that the first glimpses of Labour's elaborate wartime strategizing to capture large tracts of political space were to appear.

Things started slowly. Greenwood began to articulate Labour's stance at the annual Labour conference at Southport in June 1939. Bringing to a close an event that had signified the general unity of the Labour movement after years of factional strife, Greenwood commented on the possibility of coalition in the event of war. In a long and aggressive speech, he told the delegates that 'I will never ... if I were called upon to do so, take office in any government that was not prepared to implement [the] Immediate Programme [Labour's 1937 flagship policy document]'.[5] He publicly poured further cold water on the idea by stating that 'those people who would sell our principles to buy the uncertain support of Liberals and Conservatives are doing this great party no good.'[6] Though this was certainly an electioneering speech – the National government had a maximum of just over a year before it had to call a general election – it must also be seen in the context of the menacing international environment. The speech had two audiences. Greenwood was signalling that Labour would demand a high price for its cooperation, something that Chamberlain would need to pursue should war erupt. In declaring this at the outset, he had given notice that the party would expect significant political concessions in return for protecting the Conservatives' flank.

Attention was focused on events in Europe over the summer. Two months later, however, with Attlee still absent and Hitler again exhibiting his bookmaker's instincts by menacing Poland in spite of the British guarantee of that country, it again fell to Greenwood to provide a lead, this time in Parliament and in negotiations with the government. Within days, the acting leader was to attain the highest stature of his entire career. Serving as the Labour liaison with Downing Street, Greenwood emerged as a key figure on the national stage and was in close touch with Chamberlain and Lord Halifax, the Foreign Secretary, as what turned out to be the final crisis gathered pace. Greenwood had a number of pressing concerns. Not only did Labour have to tread carefully, but the party – like anti-appeasement Conservatives – was desperate to strengthen Chamberlain's growing resolve at last to resist Hitler. At a meeting of the Parliamentary Labour Party (PLP) executive on 24 August, Greenwood therefore advocated a cautious strategy: in the event of war, Labour would simultaneously act 'responsibly' in the national interest while leaving Chamberlain isolated by refusing to join the government.[7] This built on the position laid down at Southport two months earlier. A strategy of professing 'responsibility' offered a means of publicly protecting Labour's flank from any charge of a lack of patriotism – the accusation that had so damaged Labour in the 1931 financial crisis – while weakening the Prime Minister. An additional benefit was that it also served to guard against any internal dissent by placing restraints on the Labour Party itself, affording its leaders a degree of freedom of action. To that end, it was decided that no MP or trade union official should enter into individual agreement with the government: any initiative must be a collective decision.[8] Independence was vital if Labour was to exert a pressure disproportionate to its parliamentary strength.

The path the leaders chose was thus beginning, fitfully, to emerge. Chamberlain had only been secure from the machinations of his enemies so long as his German policy brought peace on tolerable terms. Now he was to be kept isolated while the Labour Party wrapped itself – rhetorically – in the Union Jack. That day, Greenwood entered a robust performance in Parliament, telling a packed House of Commons that 'the war clouds are gathering. Europe and the world are in shadows. A terrible … responsibility lies on the shoulders of him [Hitler] that lets loose the hounds of war.' [9] In a measured but direct oration, the deputy leader lambasted Chamberlain's appeasement policies while emphasizing that Labour would stand four-square behind a policy of resisting the dictators.[10] What standing behind the government actually meant was left unclear, as was the foreign policy that Greenwood thought should have been pursued. Less ambiguously, the next day the National Council of Labour (NCL), linking the political wing of the Labour movement to the trade unions, backed the strategy of not cooperating with Chamberlain.[11] These were the wounds that Chamberlain's enemies had been unable to inflict while he was Europe's peacemaker. Now that had changed, they plunged the knife in with gusto. Tellingly, they decided not to publicize the decision lest it be misunderstood and Labour deemed to be acting unpatriotically.[12] Dalton, the union boss, Walter Citrine, and veteran MP, Herbert Lees-Smith, all argued that if it was announced the party would be seen as unreasonable.[13] Political calculation plainly remained paramount despite the gravity of the crisis and the plausibility of a general European war.

Although he was still absent, Attlee, for his part, was not entirely uninvolved and the Labour leader had become firm on the matter of confronting Hitler. Of course, the cynic might point out that, given the use they had made of this as a soapbox, he and Labour could now do little else. From North Wales, Attlee ensured that he retained a guiding hand over events at this crucial juncture, staying in close touch with Greenwood via telephone. He urged his deputy to pressurize Chamberlain finally to declare war, resolved that 'we've got to fight'.[14] On 29 August, as Chamberlain once more wavered towards appeasing Berlin, Greenwood delivered another highly effective Commons performance in response. He attempted to coerce the Prime Minister into adopting a tougher stance by shifting position and now publicly distancing Labour from the government, saying that 'as far as *we* are concerned aggression must stop now … *our* determination … is that these threats, menaces and open aggression will come to an end.'[15] They did not have the power to break Chamberlain, but Greenwood, Dalton and others had begun to seek more leverage than the party's numerical strength in the Commons would imply they enjoyed; as a result, Labour was slowly cutting ever more ground from beneath the Prime Minister's feet.

On 1 September, the Prime Minister responded to the opposition's new tactics by formally inviting the Labour Party to join a coalition government under him.[16] Attlee told Greenwood to refuse the offer and, displaying his customary talent for detecting the moods of his followers in advance, advised the acting leader not even to discuss it at length, so as to avoid raising suspicions in the PLP that it was being considered or that the leaders may 'betray' Labour as in 1931.[17] Unsurprisingly, the PLP executive followed Attlee's recommendation and rejected the offer unanimously.[18] This decision stemmed from two calculations: that the party was adamant it would not, and could not, serve under the loathed Chamberlain and that, for the moment, Labour's negotiating strength remained limited – as Dalton pithily confided to his diary, being given the 'Secretaryship of State for Latrines' summarized the party's prospects.[19] Labour's dilemma was that after denouncing 'appeasement' they could hardly work with the appeasers, lest their newly won credibility vanish. This was precisely the same situation that Churchill, by then Prime Minister, confronted when Hitler offered peace the following summer. But the fact that deliberations took this form makes clear that the leaders were certainly open to, and thinking of, a *future* coalition. Their subsequent actions can only properly be understood in the light of this careful decision-making and deliberate strategizing. Attlee and his colleagues could not credibly serve under Chamberlain even if they had been inclined to do so. Far from drifting aimlessly, the Labour leaders were astutely waiting upon events.

Neville Chamberlain was the man Labour claimed was responsible for the entire crisis. From the beginning, Attlee's view was that Chamberlain 'will have to go'.[20] A strong mutual antipathy had long existed between Chamberlain and the PLP, dating back to the 1920s. Chamberlain, particularly, held a low opinion of the MPs on the other side of the Commons and their 'pathetic' leaders, and was far from shy about expressing this publicly.[21] Labour consequently reviled him. Attlee, in his own words, 'detested' the Prime Minister who was 'absolutely useless' and treated Labour 'like dirt'.[22] This, more than his policy, may have determined Labour's attitude. Earlier in the year Attlee had repeatedly savaged the government for its mismanagement of foreign policy, charging Chamberlain with 'wantonly destroying' all hope of avoiding war through his 'unilateral appeasement', and said of the Prime Minister's pleas to be trusted that 'for sheer brazen effrontery it takes some beating'.[23] If the policy differences were slight, the mutual hostility was certainly not done for effect. This animosity between the two leaders would come to haunt Chamberlain during what remained of his premiership.

Labour's tactical position was further elucidated when, on 2 September – the day before Chamberlain finally bowed to the pressure and declared war – at a joint meeting of the National Executive Committee (NEC) and PLP executive, Morrison introduced, and vigorously argued for, a motion that Labour should not join the current government.[24] The resolution was then passed. It amounted to another symbolic blow to Chamberlain's position, while still leaving the party free to serve in a *different* regime in the future. Labour was sending smoke signals. The two bodies also decided that Greenwood should stress immediately to the Prime Minister, and then in the Commons, the necessity of honouring the guarantee to Poland.[25] After prevaricating for years on what to do about Hitler, Labour was advocating war. The domestic political incentives were – and are – obvious.

From there events proceeded rapidly: that day, when Chamberlain's meek response to Nazi aggression brought no retreat from Hitler, the House of Commons was in ferment. As Greenwood got up to follow

Chamberlain in the debate, the Conservative anti-appeaser, Leo Amery, famously shouted across to him 'Speak for England, Arthur!' Greenwood entered a performance that Richard Whiting has described as the high-point of his career.[26] Announcing that the Prime Minister 'perturbed' him, he used the speech to leave Chamberlain's final bid to avoid war in ruins and Cowling suggested that Greenwood could have 'destroyed' Chamberlain if he had gone further.[27] The acting leader distanced Labour from the government more fiercely this time, demanding that Britain 'must march with the French ... the die is cast', and refused to afford the Prime Minister any room for compromise.[28] With this rebuff, Chamberlain finally relented and declared war on Germany the following day; uncertainty on his own backbenches and Hitler himself had combined with Labour in forcing his hand. It is entirely possible that if not for Chamberlain's desperate bid to protect himself politically from Labour, Churchill, Eden, the Foreign Office and even Halifax during 1939, the guarantee to Poland would never have been given and war avoided. Either way, domestic political opponents had bounced Chamberlain into declaring a war that any glance at a map of the empire would indicate was likely to prove devastating for Britain's standing as a world power. But whatever the political machinations, Greenwood, for his part, conducted his duties with great effectiveness in Attlee's absence, and his personal standing – non-existent three months previously – was at its apex. Embodying the mood of the political nation, he was labelled by *The Times* as 'the authentic voice of Britain'.[29] In Greenwood's capacity as acting leader, Dalton wrote that he was 'seeing the PM and Halifax frequently, taking notes [and] reporting fully to his colleagues'.[30] Moreover, in Dalton's not entirely unbiased opinion, he was doing the job 'better than poor little Rabbit [Attlee] ever did'. Greenwood performed a difficult task, at once striking at the detested Chamberlain while still defining Labour's position as being one of support for military action and setting out a stall for whatever the future brought.

Before long, this was to translate into a full-blown threat to Attlee's leadership. For the moment, however, Greenwood was left to articulate Labour's stance *vis-à-vis* the government now that war was underway. He again took up a position of 'patriotic detachment'. Greenwood immediately announced that Labour's methods of opposition would be 'constructive',[31] a stance that, like his earlier linguistic stress on 'responsibility', at once underlined the party's patriotism while still implicitly emphasizing to Chamberlain the damage that might be inflicted on the government if Labour were provoked into a more active opposition. [32] In other words, it was rhetoric – no more and no less. Before British forces had even fired a shot, then, Labour's political leverage over the ministry was extensive – particularly given that, as we have seen, Chamberlain wanted Labour to join a coalition to protect him from the revolt brewing on his own benches. Far from crafting a position of 'tedious impotence', as asserted by Smart, Labour in fact occupied advantageous ground.[33] The longer the party held out, the stronger its hand for conducting negotiations became. Despite all the historical ink spilled on these iconic eight months, the true dynamic of politics during the first part of the Second World War has still not been fully appreciated. What becomes clear when an analysis is conducted from the perspective of the Labour leaders is their orchestration of what was essentially a game of musical chairs.

There was always the risk, of course, that Labour could miss the bus, but given that Hitler had certainly caught his own bus and was intent on making full use of it, that seemed somewhat unlikely. It is therefore necessary to place the Labour leadership's cautious positioning in the context of what was simultaneously occurring within the Conservative Party. There was nothing inevitable about Chamberlain's fall eight months later. At the outbreak of war, with Attlee and Greenwood's rejection of his coalition offer and in a bid to protect his flank, the Prime Minister 'decapitated' the leading dissidents in his own party by bringing Churchill and Eden into the government at the Admiralty and Dominions respectively.[34] Duff Cooper felt that when war was declared Churchill had the 'power to go to the House and break [Chamberlain] and take his place'.[35] That was hyperbole; but Labour's refusal to be co-opted forced the Prime Minister's hand and he responded with boldness. Yet, while the muzzling of Churchill and Eden, and the absence of serious military engagements, underpinned the resilience of Chamberlain's position, he was still perceived as vulnerable from the outset. It has been pointed out that among 'informed people' the lifespan of the government was widely expected to be short – in other words, the fall of Chamberlain was always considered a distinct possibility.[36] The diaries of politicians are replete with predictions of Chamberlain's demise. 'Discontent with the government … is growing rapidly. The atmosphere of the House of Commons is impregnated with gloom and criticism.'[37] This was the political space in which the Labour parliamentary leaders should be seen as operating. Within the Conservatives, Lord Salisbury's 'Watching Committee' alone was almost half the size of the entire PLP; Eden's supporters – now led by Leo Amery – and the group of Churchillians were smaller, but nonetheless there were already a significant number of Conservative rebels organized against Chamberlain.[38] The chronic instability of government politics bolstered Labour's position.

In this environment, the imperative for the Prime Minister to avoid Labour coming out against him energetically was self-evident. Accordingly, liaison arrangements were immediately established between Labour and Whitehall departments.[39] That might have been a way of trying to smother the party, but it was becoming clear what the policy of 'constructive opposition' meant in practice. Greenwood had exploited Chamberlain's problems to lever Labour into a position in which it would have significant influence over the future shape of politics. The party used 'constructive opposition' to manufacture a legitimate political voice where it lacked one before; it was also something that could find purchase among a public dissatisfied with Chamberlain's leadership. It enabled the Labour leaders to establish themselves as 'patriotic' while still standing apart from a Prime Minister they detested – and also prepare to enter office themselves if an acceptable opportunity arose. The second key element of the party's reading of the political situation was the immediate negotiation by Greenwood and the government of an electoral 'truce', so as to prevent partisan politics damaging national unity.[40] In the event of by-elections, the party that previously held the seat would be unopposed by the other.[41] Therefore, in addition to boxing in the Conservative government, the Labour leaders began to place their own party in a virtual straitjacket as well.

The perception of Greenwood as Labour's principal politician at this time is again striking. Despite some dissension, he won the NEC's backing for the policy.[42] Although it was contentious, by agreeing to a 'truce' and consenting not to contest any Conservative seats, the leadership had further consolidated its bargaining position – as implied by Attlee's threat that the truce could be terminated at any time.[43] It was another means of blackmailing the Conservative Party. The measure provoked long-running and considerable unrest within the Labour movement. Aneurin Bevan denounced it as 'voluntary totalitarianism' in *Tribune*[44] and in an interview Attlee asserted to the rank-and-file that the truce had been 'forced upon us' by the war, intimating that he had not wanted it.[45] While this may have been true, in reality the agreement also constituted a new and valuable bargaining chip. Coupled with Labour's critiques of the government and the visible planning for the future undertaken by senior figures, this series of developments should be interpreted as evidence of a consciously pursued plan consistent with the positions adopted in the days and weeks before the war began. It is insulting to the political skill of men such as Attlee, Greenwood, Morrison and Dalton to contend – as most of the preceding literature seems to – that they developed no plan for the situation in which they found themselves. It borders on naïveté when the fact that they had articulated no alternative to Chamberlain's international policy is borne in mind. 'Drift' it was not.

In opposition, heavily outnumbered in the Commons and operating under severe restrictions, the Labour leaders established virtually overnight a nuanced posture that offered the possibility of real political benefits in the future. Considering the scale of discontent within the movement during this period – and the rank-and-file certainly felt themselves to be drifting[46] – their ability to maintain it was itself a significant achievement. The strategy orchestrated by the leaders can be illustrated by quoting from some of the language they employed. In an anonymous *Political Quarterly* article, a senior figure advised Labour to bide its time until the war situation exposed the government's failures to its own backbenchers, advocating a policy of standing aside while the Conservatives 'committed suicide'.[47] The anonymous author, 'Politicus', said that Labour's leaders were playing a deliberate waiting game: the party's 'chief objective' should be 'the achievement of a position which can be exploited when hard facts compel the resignation of Mr Chamberlain', while 'a frontal attack ... would be ... politically foolish'.[48] From their language and behaviour, it seems apparent that the party's senior figures had carefully hedged their bets, adopting a position that enabled them to strike different poses to each of their three audiences – the Labour Party, the parliamentary Conservatives and the public. Their approach was based on a 'studied moderation of language'.[49] Thus, even before May 1940, the party wielded a degree of influence much greater than its parliamentary representation would imply. The *New Statesman* described Labour as coming to wield 'power without responsibility' during the phoney war.[50] This was applied in a negative sense but, in fact, precisely the opposite was true: Labour publicly behaved 'responsibly' while distancing itself from the government, maximizing its strength and preparing to exact a heavy price if an opportunity to enter a different ministry arose. These tactics underline the manner in which the party and its leaders exploited the opportunities of war to effect a realignment of the political environment. For good or ill, Labour did indeed exercise 'power without responsibility'.

Yet, bizarrely, the party's entire approach in this period has come in for heavy criticism or, at best, neglect from historians. Brooke, for instance, derided the policy of pulling Labour's punches as a 'stasis';[51] but where was the value of plunging straight in? Vocal complaints from those who wanted an all-out offensive should not prevent recognition of the party's intangible gain in position. Much of the Labour movement would doubtless have preferred rhetorically more vigorous opposition, but the time for that had passed; the course its leaders plotted reflected a pragmatic reading of political realities, the danger facing the country and a calculation of future advantage. If senior figures permitted Labour to attack the administration's every initiative, they would have appeared unpatriotic. In Attlee's absence, Greenwood and his colleagues had implemented a consistent, creative and tactically coherent strategy.

The return of Attlee

Attlee finally returned from his Welsh fastness in late September.[52] Doubts persisted about his health and, more importantly, some now wanted a new leader. Attlee thus faced a situation quite different from the one he had left in May. Moreover, even before his illness a challenge to his leadership seemed a strong possibility. Morrison was apparently preparing a move against Attlee throughout 1939. One newspaper labelled it 'an immense and far-tentacled intrigue' and, earlier in the year, the *Sunday Express* observed that Morrison's 'closest friends scurry around the lobbies at Westminster, there and here, to and fro, staking out his claim [for the leadership] … their propaganda is meeting with some success'.[53] His principal allies in the venture were Dalton and his old friend Ellen Wilkinson, who made her name on the Jarrow march. Attlee's position remained fragile not only because of the actions of his rivals but also because he had made so little public impression. At the 1939 conference, the TGWU boss Ernest Bevin complained to Dalton about 'the weakness of [Attlee's] leadership', and Dalton recorded hearing that both Bevin and the TUC general secretary Walter Citrine felt that a change of leader 'must be made'.[54] These signs of discontent indicate that the leader's standing remained tenuous. For all his hard work in managing Labour since 1931, it is obvious that, by 1939, Attlee's party was tiring of him.

Following the conference – and with Attlee ill – Dalton began politicking to get rid of the leader, telling the influential Francis Williams, editor of the *Daily Herald* and another Morrison supporter, that 'I am prepared to go to all lengths to get the right sort of change.'[55] Dalton also said uncomplimentary things about the only possible contender besides Morrison, Greenwood, whom Dalton felt was the head of a secretive Masonic cabal inside the PLP.[56] Williams then sent up a public 'kite' for Morrison's claim to the top job. In an article in the *Daily Herald*, he wrote that political leadership 'is at this moment shown pre-eminently in the commanding position in public respect which has been achieved by Herbert Morrison through the great qualities of courageous and imaginative leadership he has brought to the control of London'.[57] No mention was even made of Attlee.[58] Shortly afterwards, the plot emerged into the open when Wilkinson published her own newspaper piece expressing a lack of confidence in Attlee.[59] Wilkinson advocated that Morrison should replace Attlee, with Dalton, Greenwood and Sir Stafford Cripps serving as his chief 'lieutenants'.[60]

Attlee was probably saved by the fact that attempting to knife him in his absence was not well received, particularly by the mining MPs, who were Attlee's closest allies. Greenwood and his supporters also suspected that the articles were a preliminary to a strike by Morrison. But the intrigue then veered into farce. The deputy leader's name was canvassed as an alternative to Morrison and, in Dalton's words, the Masons feigned 'indignation at this attempt to stab a sick man [Attlee] in the back' – while perhaps hoping that Greenwood would wind up with the job should Attlee retire.[61] Greenwood – apparently inebriated at the time – told Wilkinson that he intended to see her censured,[62] which she only narrowly avoided. With the PLP visibly hostile to intriguing while Attlee was seriously ill, Morrison swiftly abandoned his promise to engineer 'an open discussion on the leadership' and retreated to fight another day.[63] He reaffirmed his loyalty to Attlee and claimed to have had no knowledge of the articles beforehand.[64]

This drew a line under the issue, and the fact that no formal challenge was made indicates the depth of Attlee's support among the union MPs alongside whom he had worked in the tiny PLP of the 1931 Parliament, the same men who voted him leader. Yet, the bungled end to the episode does not obscure the fact that Attlee's position was under serious threat. He was isolated, most other senior figures wanted rid of him – even if they could not agree on who should replace him – and he had failed to stamp his seal on the party in four years as leader.

None of this augured well for when Attlee returned to duty. Having a poor leader in peacetime was one thing; a poor leader in wartime was quite another. Moreover, Greenwood had made a major impression, and may have even leapfrogged the obvious heir apparent, Morrison, in the eyes of the party. Greenwood performed what Brooke describes as an 'exemplary' job, and had been a more commanding parliamentary presence than Attlee.[65] Consequently, in September, Dalton abruptly shifted his support away from Morrison and began agitating for Greenwood to assume the leadership instead, in doing so instigating a disruptive campaign that continued until November. Dalton informed Greenwood that 'as things are, I am in favour of [you] being leader' and that Attlee was not 'big enough or strong enough'.[66] He also told Greenwood that he would no longer back Morrison.[67] The only explanation Dalton offered was that Morrison had 'sacrificed major things to minor things', presumably a reference to the latter's concentration on the LCC.[68] That Dalton was so fickle in transferring his support is evidence that his motivation was simply desperation to get rid of Attlee. Greenwood made no recorded comment on Dalton's proposal. Despite his new prominence, though, it seems unlikely that he could really have defeated Attlee, who retained the allegiance of the union MPs who had backed him four years earlier and protected him in June. Morrison would surely have been more likely to challenge the incumbent successfully.

Still, there is no doubt that Attlee's leadership was facing a crisis. Moreover, upon his return he had to deal with the first outbreak of discontent against the policy of biding time from those in the party who either did not understand its subtleties or chose to ignore them for their own ends. At the NEC on 15 September, London School of Economics Professor Harold Laski – immensely popular with the rank-and-file and one of the most famous intellectuals in the Western world at this time – circulated a memorandum entitled 'Labour's Peace Aims'. It advocated that the party publish a formal statement of what it hoped to achieve from the war.[69] This was the first indication of the mixed success of the leaders' strategy in terms of its resonance with party members. Greenwood argued against it, and Dalton similarly sought to restrain Laski by moving a motion that the executive publish a pamphlet containing various existing statements, and that Laski's suggestion to be submitted to the International Subcommittee to consider – an adept usage of Labour's institutional apparatus to bury the suggestion and a tactic that was to be employed frequently.[70] Attlee, the other parliamentary leaders and the TUC were all reluctant to give any explicit statements, themselves undecided on the matter. Nonetheless, the memorandum represented the beginning of a long bid by Laski to nail down an official declaration of the party's objectives – which, as time passed, it became evident he meant only as a means to 'nail' the leaders – precipitating constant difficulties in the coming years. The effort to control Laski did not stifle the dissent that rapidly accumulated over the issue, as the subject of 'peace aims' became highly symbolic to a party left frustrated in its political restraints.

In the Commons on 3 October, Attlee sidestepped the controversy, saying vaguely that 'we shall require deeds, and not merely words, before we get any substantial basis for peace.'[71] The following week, during a debate about the government's recent refusal of German peace feelers, the leader finally acted to quell the dissension and adopted a position entailing rejection of a peace that allowed Hitler to keep his gains, while still refraining from any discussion of domestic policy specifics.[72] Attlee took a firm stance, telling the Commons that 'we must with resolution pursue this struggle' and that Hitler's word was 'utterly worthless'.[73] Albeit as vague as everything else that Labour had said for months, it was an efficient performance in Attlee's bid to suppress the issue and assert his disputed authority. On the same day, the unions decided they were now opposed to *any* elucidation of aims at all.[74] This was backed by the NEC and PLP executive.[75] The upper echelons of the Labour movement had resolved to close down internal debate on the subject altogether.

Yet, within days, it became evident that the clamour would not subside, for almost forty local parties requested a statement of peace aims.[76] The NEC looked to Attlee and decided that he should make a public speech on the matter, finally consenting to set out Labour's position but agreeing that he should do so in as broad a sense as possible.[77] The speech was made on 8 November and it concentrated on the kind of Europe that the party would like to see emerge, but remained suitably vague.[78] Attlee cleverly threw a sop to anti-militarist sentiment in giving no indication that a war may actually have to be fought.[79] Attlee turned it into a pamphlet and published it in December as *Labour's Peace Aims*.[80] The leadership also adroitly utilized Laski's popularity in the party – he had topped the poll in the election to the NEC constituencies section at the annual conference – to help bring their followers into line, tasking him with writing a separate pamphlet emphasizing, in emotive language, Labour's commitment to removing the conditions that facilitated the rise of Nazism.[81] They were more willing to be explicit about their intentions when they used the pamphlet again to publicly rule out joining the Chamberlain government.[82] Other than this, though, Laski's pamphlet remained unspecific about 'peace aims'. As his biographers have observed, it was essentially a balloon sent up by the leadership group, exploiting his popularity but committing them to no particular course of action.[83] Attlee, Dalton and Morrison tasked themselves with the vetting of all documents worked on by Laski, thus keeping him on a short leash.[84] Not for the last time, Laski's name was associated with their policies. These events underline once again the rationale for the party leaders' careful signalling. Like their campaign against the Prime Minister, the entire 'peace aims' episode – from the initial attempts to restrain Laski, Attlee's speeches and the eventual recognition that they would have to say *something* – was marked by the intention to appease a restless party while preserving the freedom of action of Attlee and his colleagues.

Attlee had been central in containing the controversy over peace aims. It was a combustible issue that was deftly defused. Moreover, for the first time there were hints of Attlee's own leadership abilities, which would become clearer in subsequent months. But although Labour's senior figures cooperated in ensuring the continued success of their shared strategy, with the military war still characterized by inactivity, events now swiftly reverted to the power struggles between them. The persistent uncertainty over the leadership was destabilizing, and hence needed to be resolved one way or another. Building for months, this challenge amounted to the crucial test of Attlee's position. The weakened leader had either to see off his enemies or face defeat.

Overcoming this obstacle thus represented the first step in the rise of Attlee. Given the destruction of the PLP minutes, our main source of evidence for this episode is Dalton's diary, though much of it is corroborated in other memoirs. There was speculation in the press at the time that Greenwood could win a leadership contest if one were held.[85] It seems at least plausible that circumstances might have converged in late 1939 to push Morrison into third place in a ballot. Greenwood was more popular than ever before, while Morrison had not been particularly visible. Yet, even Dalton admitted that internal support for replacing Attlee had evaporated following his return, despite the fact that he remained 'much below even his own … par'.[86] Greenwood had, however, certainly attained a new level of respect, and Dalton opted to press ahead. He tried to persuade Greenwood to challenge Attlee openly, telling him that he was 'the only possible change', as well as expressing this opinion to numerous MPs in a bid to generate momentum for a contest.[87] Whether Dalton's apparent defection from Morrison was entirely sincere, however, is questionable. He admitted that he was amenable to a further change of leader once Attlee was removed and, moreover, both Dalton and Morrison knew that the PLP as it was presently constituted – dominated by the MPs that Attlee had won over when both those men were out of Parliament following the 1931 rout – simply would not elect Morrison.[88] This was what had held back Morrison since 1935. It would likely require a significant change in the PLP's personnel – such as that facilitated by a general election – before the LCC boss could ascend to the top.[89] Greenwood was, 'as usual, dilatory in decision', but that he did not dismiss the idea suggests he may have been open to the possibility.[90] He was perhaps weighing his options, but his prospects were scotched in that no other prominent figure came out in support, and days passed with rumour and speculation spreading throughout the party, but no action taken.[91] And though Dalton attempted to start a petition requesting Greenwood to run, this too quickly 'petered out' – indicating once again a lack of enthusiasm for replacing Attlee.[92]

Yet, just as it appeared that Dalton's intriguing would come to naught, Alfred Edwards, a backbench MP, wrote to Dalton, Greenwood and Morrison asking them to permit their names to go forward in a contest against Attlee.[93] Morrison was receptive, for while he blandly suggested that he did not feel 'that there is a general or substantial desire [in the PLP] to reconsider the matter at this juncture', he gave away his real object twice in his reply, telling Edwards that 'I should have to reconsider this if a contest were forced from another quarter,' and then reiterated that he reserved the right 'to accept nomination at any time'.[94]

At the PLP meeting on 15 November, it became apparent that somebody, probably Edwards, had nominated all three potential challengers against Attlee.[95] But then, in the discussion that ensued, amid many 'expressions of gentlemanly good will' – an indication that no one was prepared to make the first strike – Attlee took the initiative and moved decisively to outmanoeuvre his opponents.[96] In a display that knocked them off balance, the leader got to his feet and stated that he did not regard an alternative nomination for his job as 'disloyal'.[97] Of course, once he said this, any challenge would appear precisely that! It was a beautifully simple response. Attlee had acted effectively, if belatedly, to preserve his position; there was little sense in forcing a contest if Attlee could not be defeated, which, once he had called his opponents' bluff, seemed likely. Greenwood was surely aware that his internal strength was less than it seemed. More importantly, given Morrison's assumed status as the heir apparent, some MPs who actually favoured Greenwood might have switched to Attlee to stop Morrison, as they had four years earlier. Accordingly, Greenwood told the assembled MPs that he would withdraw his candidacy.[98] With his retreat, there was no possibility of the other two men forcing a contest without provoking accusations of putting ambition before party and country. Even Dalton knew better than to close in on Attlee, and he and Morrison were left with little choice but to withdraw their names as well.[99]

Attlee, then, had played a political masterstroke in seeing off his adversaries in such a fashion. His military background instilled a business-like approach to politics, which doubled handily as ruthlessness when necessary. Dalton's dismissive references to him being a 'rabbit' betray a failure to recognize Attlee's proficiency as a political operator – a proficiency he skilfully employed to isolate and embarrass both Dalton and Morrison. Attlee aborted the challenge to him even before a vote was taken; the statement that he would not consider alternative candidates disloyal put irresistible pressure on the three nominees to emphasize their loyalty. Moreover, having been absent for four months perhaps helped him to deflect the challenge; that he had not been at the centre of events meant that the onus was on his enemies to force a contest. With their target not present, Dalton and others lacked a publicly acceptable reason to trigger an election that would not be viewed as a simple power grab. Through a combination of quiet skill and the misjudgements of his opponents, Attlee ensured the security of his position once more.

Morrison, by contrast, had once again failed to become leader. The next week he suffered another blow to his standing when, having angered MPs by intriguing, he polled poorly in the elections to the PLP executive.[100] The strain on his relations with Dalton also did not assist his continuing ambition to replace Attlee. If he was to do so, he needed the allegiance of as many senior figures as possible. Morrison had struggled to achieve this and, within a year, his task would be made still more difficult by Bevin's entry into Parliament and the formation of the formidable (and essentially anti-Morrison) Attlee–Bevin alliance.[101] In backing away from an overt challenge, Morrison had not possessed the courage – or was too astute – to cross his personal Rubicon.

Attlee was therefore now free to direct the party's strategy of 'constructive opposition'. His efforts over the next six months were to be focused on the work of appeasing disaffection while preparing to enter government if more favourable circumstances should arise, and bolstering Labour's strength in the interim. It required crab-like movement. On 16 November, the day after the aborted contest, Attlee again imposed himself on his party, entering one of his best performances in Parliament in a debate on the war and acting to assuage Labour's discontent by calling for the beginning of planning for the eventual peace.[102] This new decisiveness represented something of a departure from his previous years as leader; with the whiff of office in the air, Attlee was now more than willing to take the Labour Party by the scruff of the neck and force it in a direction of his choosing. The effectiveness of the party's strategy throughout the 'phoney war' – culminating in a complete turnaround of Labour's fortunes in the space of a few months – was in fact to be attributable more to Attlee than to anyone else.

Taking the lead against Chamberlain

Over the next three months, Attlee and his colleagues began to undertake a concerted increase in the pressure they brought to bear on the government. Their attacks became more frequent and aggressive, eventually precipitating an overt trial of strength once the façade of cooperation with Chamberlain became impossible to sustain. This marked something of a departure from the approach adopted during the first months of war; while their overall strategy remained intact, the change signified not only a means to defuse disillusionment within the Labour Party but also their growing confidence. The shift in tactics was given impetus by the fact that 'things were turning increasingly against Chamberlain' in his own party, with the Watching Committee the 'prime agent' in creating disaffection.[103] However, this was still balanced by awareness on the part of Attlee that they could not move until an opportune moment presented itself. The leaders thus continued to bide their time, unashamedly exerting their leverage over Chamberlain while accumulating political capital to be expended if circumstances changed. In the interim, they continued to harangue Chamberlain by presenting fresh policy initiatives to harass the government along the lines of Attlee's 'peace aims' declaration.

The House of Commons thus became the central political battleground where the Labour leaders advertised their stance. On 5 December, Greenwood introduced an amendment in the Commons, assailing the ministry for the 'absence of any proposals for organizing to the full our human and material resources … [for the] effective prosecution of the war … and for the solution on the basis of social justice of the problems which will arise on the return to peace'.[104] Greenwood charged the Prime Minister with having dismissed reconstruction planning 'cursorily', and of being 'contemptuous' towards the issue.[105] Such language was useful for emphasizing Labour's independence and striking at Chamberlain while actually committing its leaders to no specific courses of action. Greenwood's speech was targeted at his own party as much as the Prime Minister, opting to clash with the government over high-profile symbolic issues and calling for the new, expanded role of the state to be made permanent, saying that 'there can be no going back.'[106] The Prime Minister confided to his sister that Labour 'find it hard to keep the truce', and their 'nagging and fault-finding' was more 'difficult' after 'Attlee's return'; they 'sneered' and 'every complaint' was 'exploited to the uppermost'.[107] Chamberlain even wanted to suspend the House before the chief whip convinced him that such a move was impossible.[108] His wife said that 'Labour don't seem to understand that a war is going on.' [109] The leaders had also threatened to oppose Chamberlain's attempt to prolong the life of the current Parliament as well as making clear that as soon as peace was achieved Labour would insist on an immediate election.[110] Simultaneously, Morrison worked to increase the intensity of Labour's public critique, becoming a weekly contributor to the *Daily Mirror*. His tone was the most partisan of any senior politician since the declaration of war, repeatedly mounting bellicose attacks on Chamberlain and his ministry.[111]

But, oddly, it was Attlee – now reinvigorated by the task before him and with the advantages that his style of leadership lent to its realization – who took on the most central role in harassing the government both in Parliament and outside. He became a frequent public speaker and harried the Chamberlain ministry relentlessly in the Commons, at rallies, in broadcasts and in newspapers. Yet, he also displayed caution in how far he pursued his attacks and was careful to stray no further, ensuring that the party as a whole observed these same limitations. Attlee thus embarked on a campaign of aggressive critiques interspersed with conciliation. Though badly outnumbered and with little freedom of action, this underlines how fully, and deliberately, the Labour Party was engaged in the parliamentary struggle; these were not impotent attacks, but part of the ongoing realignment at Westminster.

That the goal of the leaders was not only an effective war effort but a strengthened political position for the Labour Party as well suggests once more the problems in how historians have neglected Labour's role. Patriotism was a lethal instrument. In January 1940 Attlee made another well-received BBC broadcast in which he assiduously pushed both sides of his agenda. He justifed his position in terms of the need to destroy Nazism and advance socialism while – ominously for the Prime Minister – suggesting that heavy criticism of the government was the only route to victory.[112] Attlee also increased the pressure at Westminster and frequently targeted the ministry in the Commons, attacking it for its decision to declare war on behalf of India without consulting that country, for failures in social provision, for inefficiencies in conscription, taxation and economic organization, and for the continued heavy unemployment – all good Labour causes.[113] He declared that Labour 'have no illusions. We are convinced that to win the war and win the peace there must be a great advance along the socialist road.'[114] The leader also affirmed that the electoral truce was not a 'political truce', and that the Labour Party 'disagree[d] profoundly with the government'.[115]

One of Attlee's frequent targets for attack was the composition of the government. He lambasted the Prime Minister on literally dozens of occasions for having War Cabinet members who ran individual government departments rather than focusing on overall strategy, as well as the failure to include in the inner circle someone tasked with organizing the domestic front for all-out war.[116] Attlee stated that 'it does not seem to me that the government are taking nearly seriously enough the organization of the home front,' and declared that 'I do not understand ... on what principles the War Cabinet has been founded. ... I gather that it was mainly on the score of personality.'[117] He called for Chamberlain to act like a 'statesman', stressed that Labour was the party of 'practical' expertise in organization, described the Prime Minister as 'Utopian' in hoping that Hitler could be defeated without full-scale mobilization of the country, and wanted the government run on military lines.[118] He demanded that Chamberlain be 'ruthless' and warned that 'if the ministers cannot get on with their jobs then we must get other ministers.'[119] Despite ducking the issue himself, Attlee again displayed little embarrassment in assaulting the government for failing to set out peace aims as 'this is not a matter that can be set aside'.[120]

But he also led the way in anchoring Labour's most cherished intellectual concept of the late 1930s – 'planning' of the economy and industry by the state as a means to achieve the party's political objectives – to the cause of the war effort. Efficiency in managing the war had been the key theme in Attlee's critiques of the government – carefully remaining within the boundaries of 'acceptable', rather than party-political, questioning – and he used that to stress the applicability of planning as a concept.[121] This served the additional purpose, of course, of pushing Labour's values to the centre ground of political discourse and presenting them as simple common sense. In February 1940, Attlee declared that 'in this war we need the planning of our resources … and for that purpose we want ministers who grasp the function of planning.'[122] He therefore used the months following his return to lead his party with decisiveness for the first time; furthermore, in doing so, Attlee made planning more than just a nebulous, abstract concept into one with immediate, real-world political relevance. This sent the message that Labour had the answers to mobilizing the country and the Conservatives did not. Attlee also assailed the Conservatives for their lapses into personal scheming – conveniently ignoring the overlapping power struggles in which he was engaged – and claimed that Labour had 'one point of view only … the interests of the country', contrasting this with the 'personal squabbles and personal rivalries' that hindered the government.[123]

Under Attlee's direction, in these crucial months Labour built on its earlier success in the first weeks of war and captured the language and spirit of patriotism. The Conservative Party had lost that with the failure of Chamberlain's German policy. Attlee, by contrast, made Labour appear upright, sober and steadfast. Considering Labour's poor performance before the outbreak of war, and the political dangers unique in a situation of national emergency – where a word out of place, or being either too hesitant or too aggressive, can lead to charges of inaction or even disloyalty – this turnaround was a significant achievement. It is attributable only to the position that the Labour leaders had chosen to establish. Hesitation would have yielded nothing; aggressive criticism would have left Labour appearing to be just as partisan as the Conservatives. Attlee had helped Labour stand 'above' politics. It was a remarkable feat of leadership. That the party evidently had little choice but to bide its time and hope for the best tells us little. Knowing precisely where to draw the line, like so much else in politics, may seem clear in hindsight, but was far from clear in 1939 and 1940. Under Attlee, the Labour Party got it exactly right. This rich tapestry of tactical positioning and cautious language suggests that conventional views of Labour as drifting and a failure in this period fail to appreciate both the difficulties of their situation and what the party's senior figures were actually doing.

In February, Bevin joined the fray for the first time by issuing a warning to the government that if Chamberlain imposed control of labour and wages, 'I will lead the movement to resist this government'. [124] Later that month, the leadership demonstrated its ability to hinder the Prime Minister by flexing its muscles and forcing 30 divisions in a two-week period over the Old Age and Widows' Pensions Bill.[125] The strategy also entailed emphasis on official political literature and publications as a tactical device, usually to appease the Labour Party. For instance, another pamphlet on the subject of 'peace aims', this time drafted by Dalton and published early in the new year, provided an explicit signal of the ascendancy of the senior figures over their followers.[126] In contrast to the earlier statements, which avoided answering whether or not a war would actually have to be fought or if a diplomatic settlement was feasible, *Labour, the War and the Peace* now made clear that the military struggle would have to be conducted. It was more detailed than *Labour's Peace Aims*, while still working to appease uncertainty by suggesting that the conflict would lead to the spread of socialism.[127] The leaders buttressed this with the organization of almost forty conferences across the country on 'Peace Aims' over the period between Attlee's speech the previous November and the annual conference in May.[128] For several months the senior figures were to encounter less opposition once this document was issued. The peace aims controversy had already lasted for months and needed to be resolved; it was prudent to placate the party with a clearer statement of some sort. This emphasis on using policy declarations and other party management tools to cultivate the necessary political space within both Parliament and the Labour Party itself is also interesting in other ways. It was at the heart of the strategy Attlee and his colleagues adopted; it required patience and incremental movement, but was central to the parliamentary struggle. Contrary to appearances, their careful positioning during the preceding months was not a set of disjointed statements and activities but represented a bid to shape the environment for when – and if – circumstances altered. Attlee and his colleagues had been neither as inattentive, nor purely reactive, as previous accounts would imply.

Continuing to recognize the utility of policy declarations, in March Attlee ordered an NEC draft on the domestic arena to be rewritten, feeling it did not sufficiently stress the line that the war had accelerated the advance towards socialism.[129] He redrafted it himself and it was published as the pamphlet *Labour's Home Policy*, which the executive intended as a 'comprehensive' statement of domestic policy.[130] The document became the basis for all the party's wartime policy initiatives, and the leader once again employed heady socialist rhetoric in affirming that 'there can be no return to the old order ... the occasion should be seized to lay the foundations of a planned economy.'[131] Attlee explicitly fought within the NEC, and overruled his subordinates, for language that would resonate with party members in presenting the war as a unique opportunity.[132] Similarly, Greenwood produced a pamphlet entitled *Why We Fight: Labour's Case*, declaring the need once again for the implementation of 'planning' if Britain's resources were to be utilized efficiently.[133] A book by Dalton, *Hitler's War,* amounted to the most forceful statement of support for the conflict made by a member of the leadership group since the previous September.[134] Senior figures also published a series of articles in the *Daily Herald* heavily critical of the government and suggesting that war would spread 'socialist values'.[135] Meanwhile, Laski was again deployed, unwittingly, to guard his leaders' flank. He was tasked with writing another pamphlet, *Is This an Imperialist War?*, his ability to argue in Marxist terms making him ideally suited to a propagandist role.[136] The pamphlet attacked the Communist Party line and supported the war. In a collection of essays edited by Attlee, Laski contributed a piece championing the link between conflict and social reform.[137] Aggressive attacks on the government in the Commons, particularly by Morrison, kept up the parliamentary party's morale in late 1939 and early 1940.[138] The overall shift in Labour's tactics is clear. Far from being the routine stuff of politics, that this combination of literature, declarations and orations was itself thought of by Attlee and his colleagues as the centrepiece of their strategy becomes clear from the explicit emphasis afforded to these activities in their report to the 1940 annual conference.[139] Devoting two appendices to the subject and identifying these measures as the things they had spent the phoney war doing, this underlines precisely how the leaders conceived of their role and strategy: to bide their time and prepare the ground.[140] Far from an excuse for inactivity, from the outset Attlee and the others had intended these measures to establish political landmarks.

The finale

Attlee's assaults were extensive and placed further pressure on the government, while also acting to counter the discontent in the Labour Party that his strategy inevitably entailed. Gradually chipping away at Chamberlain, Attlee and his colleagues slowly manufactured a strengthened position for Labour. Having consolidated their grip, they were well positioned for what transpired to be the final phase of the phoney war. In March 1940, it briefly seemed that the leaders may depart from their course when the possibility arose of the party entering the Chamberlain ministry after all, as rumours began to circulate that the Prime Minister had offered Labour three seats in a reconstructed War Cabinet.[141] On 9 April, the PLP executive discussed the notion of joining a Chamberlain-led coalition. Morrison and Greenwood were apparently in favour, but Attlee, by contrast, still urged caution.[142] Dalton's diary records that the mood of the meeting was that, though the party *should* join a different government, to serve under Chamberlain would legitimize him.[143] It was decided that, if Chamberlain was removed, the matter would immediately be reconsidered.[144]

This again strengthens the contention that one should reinterpret the parliamentary leaders' actions over the preceding months as at least in part an active bid for office. Moreover, the architect of Labour's course as it gradually manoeuvred to take part in a government was once again not the domineering Morrison or Dalton, but Attlee. The question also remained as to whether it would be necessary to call a special conference in the event of a decision to enter government. Greenwood advocated that the upcoming annual conference at Bournemouth be asked to empower them to make such a choice themselves, but Attlee bluntly argued that they should simply accept office on their own authority and then present their followers with a *fait accompli*.[145] His stance demonstrates both a greater awareness of the location of power within Labour and the extent to which the parliamentary leaders could simply act and then carry the party with them. It also reinforces the notion of Attlee's new decisiveness. The meeting agreed to his suggestion.[146] For his part Morrison was aggrieved at the decision not to go in immediately, telling Charles Peake, a Foreign Office official, that most of the Labour frontbenchers were 'frightened of power' and would be unable to add drive to the government.[147] Morrison also apparently said that there was no 'better man' for the premiership than Chamberlain.[148] Harris has suggested that Morrison favoured joining the government immediately because Chamberlain might regard him, rather than Attlee, as Labour's leading parliamentarian, presumably awarding him a more powerful position than his old enemy.[149]

Yet, shortly thereafter the war situation altered irrevocably, as the phoney war came to a halt with the German invasion of Norway in April 1940. It was now clear that the period of biding time was finally over. This prompted Labour's senior figures to increase the tempo of their attacks – already straining at the limits of 'constructive opposition' – even further. Within the Conservatives, the Watching Committee and the Amery group began to move against Chamberlain and, as Dutton and Witherell have demonstrated, this shift of support away from the Prime Minister did much to create the atmosphere that brought him down. With Conservative opposition to Chamberlain crystallizing, the determination with which Attlee and his colleagues had sought to retain their freedom of action began to bear fruit.[150] Thus, the Labour leaders likewise began to close in on the government, the *Daily Herald* running a series of articles by senior figures attacking the prosecution of the war.[151]

At the beginning of May, as the British expedition to fight the Germans in Norway foundered, Attlee told Dalton that the moment for action had arrived.[152] However, despite his plotting with Churchill and intermediaries from Salisbury, Attlee still rebuffed the efforts of rebel Conservatives to persuade Labour to openly challenge the Prime Minister.[153] He had long been fiercely critical of the 'docile' Conservative backbenchers: 'again and again they will vote against what I believe in their hearts they desire.'[154] The leader was resolved to resist their efforts to get Labour to make the first move.[155] Attlee's stance was that if Chamberlain was to be displaced, Labour could play a role, but the main challenge would have to come from the Prime Minister's own party.[156] He thus marshalled Labour's strength and instead effectively forced the Conservative dissidents to expose themselves as the 'advance guard' for an attack on Chamberlain.[157]

Attlee evidently intended that Labour should refrain from getting into close proximity to them until they did. More limited collusion, however, was actively occurring.

For example, at Churchill's behest, Morrison urged the government to attack German shipping wherever possible, bolstering the arguments that Churchill was advancing in the Cabinet and bringing further pressure to bear on Chamberlain's prosecution of the war.[158] Attlee thus read the situation effectively. He had in fact established himself as the key parliamentary power broker at this crucial juncture – a product of months of skilled and deliberate leadership in restrictive conditions – and his strategy of constructing a position where he could, if not blackmail the Conservatives, then at least effectively dictate terms to the rebels if they wanted anything done, had worked. Attlee refused to blink first, a risky and far from inevitable decision in the circumstances of 1940. That he and his colleagues were sensed to have completely seized the political initiative *prior* to the fall of Chamberlain in a way that has not been appreciated is clear in the complaints of Cuthbert Headlam, the Conservative backbencher, that 'the sooner some of these damned Labour people are made to join the Cabinet the better' – while recognizing the insurmountable problem that 'the Socialists won't serve under Chamberlain'.[159]

As the British forces were evacuated from Norway, however, the Prime Minister finally became vulnerable enough to provoke his opponents to seek to remove him. This was the decisive moment. Morrison called for Chamberlain's resignation in the press in what he called 'the most bitter indictment' he had ever made,[160] and, on 7 May, Attlee led the attack in the famous two-day Commons debate on the war.[161] In a strong critique, Attlee set the tone for what was to come in assailing Chamberlain for being 'over-optimistic', 'over-complacent', and leading a 'blind and deaf' government: 'the Prime Minister talked of [Hitler] missing buses. What about all the buses which he and his associates have missed?'[162] Though it was Amery and Lloyd George who landed the most damaging blows, with a Conservative revolt brewing Attlee now openly called for government MPs to withdraw support from the Prime Minister, affording Conservative rebels a critical opening to act:

> They [Conservative MPs] have seen failure after failure ... they have been content, week after week, with ministers whom they knew were failures. They have allowed their loyalty to the Chief

Whip to overcome their loyalty to the real needs of the country. I say that this House of Commons must take its full responsibility … to win the war we want different people at the helm.[163]

Morrison's speech, meanwhile, so 'staggered' Chamberlain that the Prime Minister immediately made an appeal for the support of his 'friends' – a personalizing of the debate that proved a serious error given the national emergency.[164]

It is clear that the Labour leadership was determined to see Chamberlain fall; yet, from the outset, they wisely displayed caution and refused to rush in. Given the willingness of Morrison and Greenwood to go into government in March, this is further testimony to the patience of the leader himself. Attlee had ensured that the party properly prepared the ground for the achievement of its objectives, rather than prematurely going into either coalition or alliance with the rebel Conservatives at the first opportunity.

Many accounts of Churchill's rise to the premiership have been supplied elsewhere, and this book is not the place to reiterate the final fluctuations in the Conservative Party. Yet, Attlee's deft leadership, guiding Labour through a fluid situation, certainly undermines the resilient belief that he was unsuited to being leader as well as again calling into question the view of Labour as a secondary force in the struggle. At the PLP executive on 8 May there was disagreement over whether to force a division on the government's motion for adjournment of the Commons, essentially amounting to a vote of censure on Chamberlain.[165] As Addison has recognized, Attlee saw the opportunity to now consolidate with the Conservative dissidents and achieve a large anti-Chamberlain vote.[166] This offered the best prospect of breaking the Prime Minister and forcing his resignation, as well as a boost to Labour's potential strength in office if it now suddenly placed itself at the centre of events. He and Morrison argued in favour of a division, and were supported by the majority.[167] The full PLP backed their strategy.[168] It is unclear whether the decision to divide the House belonged primarily to Attlee or Morrison. Morrison later wrote that it was he who persuaded his colleagues to do so, suggesting that they were 'bemused' by the 'shock of the idea'.[169] Attlee, however, also claimed credit, asserting that his rival had in fact been reluctant.[170]

Regardless, deprived of many of his backbenchers' support in the division lobby, with Labour having finally struck at him, and a large reduction in his Commons majority signifying a collapse in confidence, Chamberlain's position was at last untenable. [171] While the withdrawal of substantial Conservative support sealed his fate, the point is that the position Attlee constructed for Labour was a strong one. Lloyd George even told Attlee that the king might invite the Labour leader to form a ministry if Chamberlain resigned, which Attlee rightly thought ridiculous.[172] Rather than plunging into an alliance with the Conservative rebels, the leadership group ensured that Labour stood back and let others make the first move.

From the outset, the Labour leaders refrained from expending their hard won political capital. They may have had little choice in 1939 but to adopt a strategy based on 'wait and see', but this did not mean that they would play a weak hand so adeptly. Thus, the powerful position that Labour gained in May 1940 did not simply drop into its lap. This course could easily have come to grief, not least because of the resentment their caution engendered within the party, because of Labour's hostility to an alliance with others, or because of the temptation from the beginning to attack the government more aggressively. On 9 May, Attlee and Greenwood met the Prime Minister and were 'very rude' in yet again rejecting his overtures to join the government, the former telling Chamberlain that 'our party will not serve under you, nor does the country want you.'[173] Attlee was 'evasive' about what would happen next,[174] but, considering how obdurate he had been, Smart's charge that Attlee 'had to be prodded into displaying any killer instinct' during the period seems difficult to accept.[175] He and Greenwood did agree, however, to go to the annual conference, then in session in Bournemouth, and ascertain whether Labour would serve under someone *other* than Chamberlain.[176] Things were now out in the open. 'Until that moment he thought he could hang on,' Attlee recalled.[177]

Had the phoney war not ended, the 1940 conference would likely have witnessed a clash over the policy of 'constructive opposition'. The disaffection within the party had been contained but had not dissipated, and would no doubt have erupted. The rank-and-file members, keen to go on the attack, remained hostile to the 'truce'. Significantly, one-quarter of all resolutions submitted to the conference opposed the policy.[178] For the leaders, then, the change in the political situation was timely. In the event, the NEC followed Attlee's recommendation and decided that Labour would join a coalition, but only under someone other than Chamberlain.[179] As Smart has acknowledged, it was thus the 'tedium' of NEC procedure that sealed the Prime Minister's fate.[180] This was the final blow to Chamberlain. The NEC also agreed that the conference should be informed of the parliamentary leadership's *decision* to enter the government, rather than a *recommendation* to do so, hence presenting the action simply for symbolic endorsement, not authorization.[181] This was the *fait accompli* that Attlee had advocated the previous month. The once hesitant leader clearly now had few qualms about imposing his authority in such a manner.

Attlee and Greenwood quickly returned to London to inform the Prime Minister of the decision.[182] Chamberlain immediately resigned. Attlee then had a meeting with his successor, Churchill – now embarked on his own moment of 'destiny' – and agreed to take Labour into a coalition under his leadership, along with the Liberals under Sir Archibald Sinclair.[183] The two men also agreed on the division of spoils in the new ministry. With both Attlee and Greenwood in the five-member War Cabinet, the extent of the former's success in engineering a strong position for Labour in the Churchill coalition is evident.[184] Under his direction, the Labour Party secured a powerful platform. While giving an impression of inactivity at times, Attlee's guidance of the Labour Party – with its emphasis on caution, patriotism, 'responsibility' and being 'constructive' – in fact created the basis for a very favourable deal from the Conservatives. The other members of the leadership group played only a peripheral role in the formation of the government. Bevin was not present at the conference – though he told Attlee he concurred with his decision – and Dalton and Morrison remained in Bournemouth.[185] Instead, the crucial decisions were taken by Attlee himself.

Some members of the NEC were briefly reticent over entry, chiefly due to the fact that Chamberlain was to remain in the War Cabinet.[186] Churchill's weak position in the Conservative Party precluded any exclusion of the man who remained party leader. Morrison, particularly, was unsure, stating that he was disinclined to join the administration after all.[187] He told the meeting that 'this didn't sound like a government that would stand up any better than the last one.'[188] However, Morrison toying with staying out most likely stemmed from the fact that he was not in the War Cabinet, having been offered only the Ministry of Supply.[189] Upon hearing that Attlee and Greenwood were to be in the War Cabinet whereas he was not, Morrison bitterly complained that 'these aren't the right people to represent the party.'[190] As his biographers observed, Morrison had wished for a different coalition.[191] He hoped to be in the War Cabinet without a department, and later admitted that 'Supply was hardly a post to run after.'[192] Stung at being excluded from Churchill's inner circle, in a fit of pique he considered staying outside the government altogether.

Morrison was also anxious that his old enemy, Bevin, was to become Minister of Labour, a major challenge to his position as Labour's dominant politician.[193] Had Morrison made good on his threat he would have been the party's sole senior figure not in office, a course that would afford him the opportunity to construct a formidable personal power base relative to the rest – creating an even more discernible division between the Labour ministers and the party than was ultimately to occur. Staying out of office in 1940 perhaps offered Morrison the best opportunity he was ever to have to weaken Attlee, by being able to exploit disaffection with the coalition and to ensconce himself as the most effective representative of Labour interests – something he was to attempt to do anyway. In the end, his instinctive desire to exercise power compelled him to disregard his reservations and accept Supply. If he had not, the history of the period, and indeed the shape of postwar politics, could have been quite different.

The NEC again quickly offered its support to the outcome of Attlee's negotiations with Churchill, and the following day the conference endorsed the decision to enter government by a majority of more than twenty-five to two.[194] Attlee made an oration described as the 'speech of his life' in support of the proposal.[195] He framed the coalition as a means not only to serve the country but to advance socialism in Britain. However, that Attlee had – in reality – already taken the decision was noted by *The Times*, the newspaper observing the next day that the Labour leaders had officially joined the government before requesting the conference's support.[196] It was a triumphant culmination to a year of skilful leadership and the emergence of Attlee for the first time.

Conclusion

Upon the formation of the coalition, Addison has argued that the Conservatives were still much more powerful within the government, holding 52 posts to Labour's 16.[197] Yet, though Labour was indeed heavily outnumbered at the lower ranks of the administration, at the top they faced the Conservatives on almost equal terms. As Lord Privy Seal, Attlee was soon to exercise extensive influence over the domestic front and come to dominate the machinery of Whitehall in a way that historians of the war have overlooked in favour of more publicly prominent men like Churchill, Bevin and Morrison. For his part, Greenwood became Minister Without Portfolio. The latter's remarkable rise to War Cabinet member was thus complete. Dalton was given the Ministry of Economic Warfare, Bevin went to the Ministry of Labour and Morrison got Supply. Moreover, in office the party's senior figures cooperated far more effectively than did the Conservatives, who were now fractured between eccentric Churchillians and discredited Chamberlainites. In this respect, the Labour ministers constituted the strongest single faction inside the new government. That was a position out of all proportion to Labour's unimpressive parliamentary representation. Most of the party's key politicians got jobs, and its War Cabinet representatives, Attlee and Greenwood, wielded considerable domestic authority.

Tactical analyses of leadership sometimes obscure the larger picture; yet here it is illuminated by such an approach. What this shows is that Labour was far more proactive in attempting to cultivate political space than has previously been understood. Realization of this alters our perception of the dynamics of politics here in crucial ways. In the light of the foregoing examination, one should reassess the role of the Labour Party as one of the competing groups in this struggle. Attlee, Greenwood and others pursued a careful and consistent strategy, which enabled them to act as key players over the course of the period. They established signposts and landmarks. That they had few ideas that differed from those of Chamberlain was irrelevant. Viewed in the context of Labour's tumultuous 1930s, from reduction to a parliamentary rump to a series of internal clashes, the eight months from the outbreak of war until the entry into government represented a triumphant climax for the party's senior figures. The gamble of concentrating on international affairs after 1935 had paid off. Furthermore, Labour's shattering experience over the formation of previous coalitions was not repeated. This was partly because of the viciousness of Nazi Germany, but partly also as a result of the efforts of Attlee and his colleagues to guide the party and their skill in awaiting an opportunity to enter office. That Labour retained its unity under such conditions is striking. Just as the fall of Chamberlain was not inevitable, so we might also qualify the sense of inevitability in Addison's suggestion that the political parties would 'in the end have to work together'.[198] The notion of coalition was inimical to the Labour Party, and it required not only events, but also skilful management, to achieve it.

In addition, events suggest that it was actually Attlee who was the key figure in getting Labour from an effective political wasteland to the inner citadel of power. Contingency, of course, played a major role; military events and Conservative politics were bound to be unpredictable. But the crucial point is that the actions of the party leader in the interim were consistent and central to the course of events. As Swift observed, 'Labour's entry into the government on its own terms was a vindication of Attlee's leadership'.[199] He forced Labour to stand fast on his chosen political ground even as this appeared to some to resemble inaction, just as, between 1936 and 1939, he had resisted all attempts to steer the party towards a 'Popular Front' with other 'progressive' forces. Attlee knew that the real opportunities were to be found at the centre of the body politic and not on its fringes. Never in its history in opposition had Labour wielded such political leverage as it did here. Hence, Jefferys's bizarre suggestion that Labour found itself with the 'worst of all worlds' ought to be reconsidered.[200] That a renewed outbreak of internal conflict was avoided, far from being inevitable in the circumstances of war, was – as the splits in 1914 had shown – a significant achievement. The documentary material shows quite clearly that this is what Labour's leaders were thinking about between 1939 and 1940 – forcing the Conservatives into a corner, extracting an agreement from them on favourable terms, and all the while keeping their followers quiescent. Attlee and his colleagues consciously and consistently awaited this opportunity; they did not simply drift in a political limbo for eight months.

Despite the success of the course it had chosen, however, the party's decision to join the coalition remained a supreme gamble. Labour had been in office in a minority before, and the prospect of again being buffeted by stronger opponents, or divided by a coalition, would not have been attractive. It was obvious that it would necessitate some degree of distance between those in the government and those outside it. This distance could easily provoke a crisis, either of authority – over who controlled the party – or priority – what its leaders should perceive their role to be. From our contemporary perspective, we tend to view parties as enduring entities, in which internal divisions may occur but do not threaten their existence. From the vantage point of May 1940, however, matters appeared rather different. For the previous 60 years, politics had been marked by fluidity in the party system, with innumerable realignments and defections. In 1940, then, political parties did not appear to be enduring; quite the opposite. Yet, Labour displayed remarkably little reluctance in entering the coalition, despite the danger of being over-powered by the Conservatives or the leaders being repudiated by their followers. At the root of this, of course, might well have been patriotism: political cooperation was vital if the war effort was to be a success. But the formation of the Churchill ministry also offered a major opportunity for Labour and its leaders. It remained to be seen what they would make of it.

Chapter 2

Capturing the Home Front

The previous chapter showed how Attlee fought and won two separate battles – to outmanoeuvre Morrison to retain the Labour leadership, and to take his party with him along a political path of his own choosing. In doing so, he established his personal authority over the Labour Party for the first time since becoming leader four years before. The formation of the Churchill coalition in May 1940 was to prove a milestone for the party, and the Labour ministers' first year in high office was marked, for the most part, by the continued success of the strategy they had adopted. Though in government, their priorities and behaviour changed little. Acclimatizing to office and with the war at its most critical stage, the new ministers were, despite these distractions, able to retain their ascendancy to a remarkable degree. Moreover, it was only here that the true scale of the success engineered by Attlee and his colleagues became apparent.

This chapter considers the period from mid-1940 to 1941 and the realignment of politics that took place. Most significant was the way in which the Labour ministers were to continue extending their power even beyond what they secured in May 1940, across the entire apparatus of government, and completing the transformation in their political fortunes they had engineered in the shadow of national crisis. In addition, Attlee took the lead in beginning a major reordering of British government and an overhaul of the state. Within a year, he was on the way to being one of the most powerful men in the machinery of Whitehall. His leadership style was to have a major and long-lasting impact on British politics. This chapter begins to document that. Inside the Labour Party itself, meanwhile, Attlee – virtually on his own authority – reconstructed the parliamentary party to entrench his new order by imposing pliant – and deeply uncharismatic – veteran MPs onto his followers as their 'acting leaders'. The result was that Parliament lacked anything in the way of an opposition for some time.

Previous analyses of this period, 1940–41, have dealt almost entirely with the readjustments of the Conservative Party and the consolidation of Churchill's authority. Both the standard texts on the war, Addison and Jefferys, follow this pattern. This chapter shifts attention to Labour's role, and the methods employed by Attlee and his colleagues to further their own aims. It locates the Labour ministers in their new environments and considers their early impact on the state. It also assesses the challenges they faced in managing the Labour Party once they entered office, as well as their protracted struggles with their new Conservative allies. It shows them continuing to face in several directions, taking decisions aimed at multiple audiences and with various purposes, and implementing an assertive strategy within the new regime. In contrast, the Conservative Party was fatally fractured by the overthrow of Chamberlain. The inmates – Churchill, Eden, Brendan Bracken and Lord Beaverbrook – were running the asylum. After a long period in the political wilderness, then, the seizure of power by the Labour leaders described in the previous chapter was confirmed. With Attlee's new ascendancy, a war effort to run, the existential threat to Britain, and new jobs to be mastered, politics after the fall of Chamberlain was no longer about sheer calculation. But reaping the rewards of their efforts during the phoney war and with new challenges before them, Attlee and the other Labour ministers worked to continue along much the same trajectory as they had pursued since 1939. As Chamberlain's most fervent devotee perceptively moaned that spring, 'it will be years before a really Conservative government comes in again.'[1] If only 'Chips' Channon had known that such a momentous reordering of the political world was to take place because of Labour's entry into the coalition that 'a really Conservative government' of the sort he meant would take almost *forty years* to come about – and, perhaps, not even then.

Revising the rules of political engagement

Over the weeks following the founding of the government, the Labour leaders again assumed the major role in redefining political practice in Britain, this time altering the rules of engagement between the parties to reflect the new circumstances. This involved reworking how the Labour Party was to operate in its position straddling government and opposition. The immediate problem Attlee faced upon the assumption of office was the question of who to leave in charge of the PLP. There was an obvious imperative for him to entrust the parliamentary party to people he could rely on to maintain loyalty to the new administration. If those given the task were prominent in their own right – if Morrison had made good on his threat to stay out of office, for example – Attlee and the Labour ministers could have found their authority challenged once again, or even rejected. The prospect of a repudiation of the leaders, and a consequent split, had always been a possibility during the phoney war, and would surely increase now that the Labour ministers were separated from the day-to-day running of the party.

As it was though, Attlee initiated another restructuring of the environment that, like the measures taken over late 1939 and early 1940, reiterated his new ascendancy in the political world. The dependable Herbert Lees-Smith and Frederick William Pethick-Lawrence, two veteran MPs highly respected in the PLP who had proven instrumental in keeping the parliamentary business ticking over while Attlee and his colleagues plotted to bring down Chamberlain, represented the ideal candidates to be entrusted with this role.[2] Likely to be compliant to the Labour ministers' decisions, they were to prove useful proxies. Thus, their exclusion from the government was not a slight; the two were tasked with more critical work instead. Though Attlee expressed to Dalton the view that Lees-Smith and Pethick-Lawrence were both too old for ministerial work,[3] nonetheless it seems very unlikely in the light of subsequent events that the leader undertook negotiations for government offices without a plan for who would be left to run and manage the PLP.

The week after the formation of the coalition, Attlee – yet again acting unilaterally – took the decision that Lees-Smith was to become 'acting chairman' of the PLP and formal Leader of the Opposition in Parliament, with Pethick-Lawrence his deputy. He made this choice prior to approval by the PLP and apparently even without discussions with senior colleagues.[4] Once more, then, in taking a significant leadership decision simply on his own authority and then imposing it on the party, Attlee displayed his new authoritarianism as well as a penchant for forcing choices on people with a minimum of fuss once he had formed an opinion. This was how the party leader had operated since September 1939 and how he was to continue to operate until 1945. It was this style and manner, often disguised as collegiate and conciliatory, that represents the key to understanding Attlee's fundamental realignment of the rules of the political, and governmental, 'game' during these six years. The decision was accepted as a *fait accompli* by both the PLP executive and the full PLP, as clear an indication as conceivable that Attlee had recovered from the nadir of his fortunes a year earlier and of his now commanding position.[5]

There was a second component to Attlee's plan to maintain the Labour ministers' authority. This became clear a few days later when the PLP executive – the Shadow Cabinet – voted to dissolve itself for the duration of the war and recommended setting up an 'Administrative Committee' in its place.[6] Characteristically, this was deliberately structured to preserve the internal ascendancy of the main leaders. With Lees-Smith at its head, it consisted mainly of Labour ministers, who were to be ex-officio members, and loyalist MPs. Jim Griffiths, a young MP and considered a potential star of the future, described its main function as to sustain the leadership in the government, protect their flank from internal attack, and to preserve party unity –a sound analysis of the manner in which the leadership had constructed the committee.[7] Attlee was to remain leader of the party as a whole, with Lees-Smith and Pethick-Lawrence simply put in charge of directing the MPs.[8] The new settlement represented in many respects a reversion to the original practice of a PLP chairman who directed Commons duties but lacked real personal power. Brooke criticized Lees-Smith and Pethick-Lawrence for displaying a lack of 'rigour', arguing that there was no 'effective' parliamentary leadership during the war.[9] But surely, this was precisely the point.

The Administrative Committee was apparently at first unelected, though the destruction by enemy bombing of the PLP minutes for 1938 to 1941 makes this impossible to ascertain. Its twenty-three members were to include nine Labour ministers and six members of the old executive who were not members of the government.[10] Besides Lees-Smith, Pethick-Lawrence and the ministers, key figures included notorious rebel Emanuel Shinwell, Griffiths, the elderly party icon J. R. Clynes, Philip Noel-Baker and Wedgwood Benn.[11] The Administrative Committee became the central institutional arena within the PLP, Labour MPs looking to it for authority and direction. At the beginning of the next parliamentary session, annual elections were held, acting as an important gauge of party feeling.[12] Attlee felt that 'the party generally knows what it is doing on these occasions.'[13] The decision to weaken the PLP so systematically did provoke some opposition, yet this tended to centre on the frustration of personal ambitions.

Shinwell, who had emerged as a very vocal parliamentary figure during the phoney war and was at this time Labour's coming man – a hero for scalping MacDonald at Seaham – was fuming at his exclusion from his coveted Ministry of Shipping and resolved to cause trouble. 'Shinbad', according to Dalton, was 'in a state of nervous and egocentric volubility' as the decision to leave Lees-Smith in charge was announced. [14] He was particularly energetic in arguing against the idea that Lees-Smith should become Leader of the Opposition.[15] The choice, Attlee later conceded, was a 'practical illogicality', but the emphasis was certainly far more on the 'practical' side of the ledger in informing the decision.[16] While Dalton's loathing of Shinwell doubtless engendered bias, his view was that Shinwell 'regards himself as the only possible leader', and was angling to get the job himself.[17] Shinwell advocated a more vigorous form of opposition, with the Labour ministers excluded from the ruling body of the PLP.[18] This would have turned the Administrative Committee into precisely what Attlee intended it would *not* be – an alternative leadership group. Although Shinwell was to be an instigator of dissent for the rest of the war, for the moment his protestations had no effect. Still, as this incident makes apparent, neither the formation of the coalition nor the crisis on the continent – the *Wehrmacht* had reached the Channel coast and cut off the British and French forces three days before – produced a discernible shift in the nature of political behaviour, any more than had the declaration of war the previous autumn. As Leo Amery commented around this time, 'However desperate the national crisis, men cannot help thinking of themselves.'[19]

Attlee had clearly forged the ability to have his own way with the Labour Party. Personal disappointments aside, the non-confrontational tone of the political situation following his revision of the PLP became clear at once, as Commons debates quickly turned into an occasion for mutual appreciation between the front benches. The day after the formation of the committee, Attlee introduced an Emergency Powers Bill, and was faced at the dispatch box by Lees-Smith, who struck a note of conciliatory politics:

> I thank the Lord Privy Seal [Attlee] for his speech … this is not the time for a lengthy discussion. It is a time for action and for show-ing that the House of Commons can be a completely efficient instrument in the conduct of the war. I have only to say that [the Opposition] will give the Bill all facilities.[20]

And so it continued. Lees-Smith and Pethick-Lawrence's speeches were deliberately emollient, often offering no questioning or criticism whatever.[21] But though the fact that Lees-Smith and Pethick-Lawrence frequently seemed to act as government spokesmen would become deeply antagonistic as time passed, given the international situation for the moment it aroused little animosity. The next day, Pethick-Lawrence made a long speech on the limitations of the Dividends Bill. He discussed several parts of the bill that were unclear and then set out to the House of Commons how it in fact already dealt with them satisfactorily![22] Ensconced atop the PLP and tasked with a critical job by Attlee, neither 'that poor little creature'[23] Lees-Smith nor Pethick-Lawrence were to press the coalition with any degree of frequency.

Yet, Attlee's new arrangements contained the seeds of future problems as well. These were to encourage overt challenges to his leadership from 1941 onwards. Though the ministers worked diligently to control the PLP, their differing perspectives from others on the Administrative Committee were eventually to pose acute difficulties of party management. Despite their close links, their jobs, concerns and physical location in the House of Commons separated the Labour ministers from the rest of the Administrative Committee. This diffusion of power was to prove a regular feature of the fluctuating nature of Labour politics. For now, though, any difficulties lay in the future. Its weakness in the seniority of its membership emphasized that the committee was a purely administrative body. Only five of its 23 members had NEC seats and, of these, three (Attlee, Dalton and Morrison) were ministers. The others were Noel-Baker and Shinwell. The statistics make apparent that while the committee played a key role at Westminster, it did not constitute a power base in the party more broadly. It would have been a simple matter to give the new head of the PLP and his deputy ex-officio membership of the NEC; that this was not done is suggestive of the priorities of Attlee and the ministers. As so often since his engagement with the 'peace aims' controversy in late 1939, Attlee moved the pieces around the political chessboard in such a way as to preclude the emergence of a viable challenge. If his political style was to be a success, it was dependent on keeping alternatives – and rivals – weak. This was what he had done so diligently since the outbreak of war, and what he continued to do during the coalition. Restructuring the PLP in this way was to prove a masterstroke. Even considering the fact that Attlee and the other ministers were now cut off from day-to-day affairs in the party, it was almost half a year before discontent became a renewed problem; even when it did, the neutering of the PLP over May and June 1940 was to prove important in preserving their balancing act through the subsequent years of bitter conflict. In imposing Lees-Smith and Pethick-Lawrence rather than more charismatic figures like Shinwell or Griffiths – both of whom were touted as possible 'acting leaders' – and ensuring that power remained in the hands of the main leadership group, Attlee established powerful structural impediments to any overthrow of the Labour ministers.

Attlee and Labour in office

While he had reordered the Labour Party, Attlee offered little indication of wanting to give up the political dual existence he enjoyed through his followers straddling government and opposition. The first few months of the Churchill coalition were marked by a major extension of the influence held by the Labour Party's representatives held in government, and their role in running the country. It was here that the full extent of the success they had manufactured during the preceding period became apparent. And at times it was a dirty business as well. Labour's leader had cut an impressive figure during the eight-month 'phoney war'. He became the key power broker in party politics, controlled his own party, and displayed perceptiveness in knowing when to deal with the Conservatives and when to rebuff them. In his negotiation of government places, Attlee secured strong Labour representation in key posts. He was, moreover, to continue extending this over the next few months, being 'very firm' with Churchill and describing the task as 'a labour of love'.[24]

Escaping the isolation and weakness that seemed certain to kill off his leadership little more than eight months earlier, Attlee's adeptness as a political operator was at its apex in 1940. Once in government he faced a new test, for he had to cope with huge and ever-increasing ministerial burdens while retaining Labour support for his decisions. As a minister, Attlee quickly became a formidable figure, not through a domineering personality, but a quiet yet critical influence over the machinery of government. This has previously been systematically overlooked by scholars – and most contemporaries – a failure that needs to be redressed if both the secret – and success – of Attlee's leadership is to be comprehended and the extent of Labour's audacious turnaround grasped.

From the beginning of the coalition Attlee largely dropped from public view, particularly compared with men like Churchill, Bevin and Morrison, who became politicians of great national prominence. Hence, complaints about the leader's elusiveness, or that Attlee had a poor war, should be seen in this context.[25] Yet this is to underestimate Attlee and neglect his strengths. For the rest of the conflict, he was the critical figure in holding the coalition together, reconciling Conservative and Labour opinion, and directing a bold reconstruction of the state – both administratively and doctrinally – that guided it in the direction of Labour policy, all the while simultaneously balancing 'the national interest' and the imperative for his party to remain 'responsible'. He lived at, and worked from, Downing Street, visiting his family when possible at weekends. Adopting a strict regime, Attlee rose early and worked until midnight, taking committee meetings in the mornings and afternoons – typically with intermissions for breakfast and dinner at the Oxford and Cambridge Club in Pall Mall, and lunch at the Commons.[26]

A founding member of the War Cabinet, Attlee's natural efficiency at committee work meant that he played a central role in that body, particularly in ensuring its tasks were carried out effectively and meetings did not last for hours due to Churchill's tendency to talk for too long. He was unofficially Deputy Prime Minister from May 1940 (and became so formally later), and was, crucially, the only man to serve (as deputy chairman) on all three of the key committees that directed the war: the War Cabinet,[27] the Defence Committee[28] and the Lord President's Committee,[29] the last of which Attlee himself pushed for the creation of, and from the start was led by Chamberlain in name alone. Moreover, though he did not assume the title, from May 1940 Attlee also informally acted as Leader of the Commons. He organized its business, answered questions on behalf of Churchill, and reported on the progress of the war.[30] By the summer of 1940, the Labour leader began clustering together an ever-increasing range of powers and became a central figure in the direction of the home front.[31] Far from not being a 'heavyweight', like Addison and others judged him,[32] as a Churchill aide put it, it was widely recognized in Whitehall that in cross-party conflicts 'if C. R. A. [Attlee] digs his heels in, he will win.'[33]

From 1940 Attlee turned the Lord President's Committee, created to save the Cabinet's time, into 'the engine of government' on the home front.[34] Initially, besides himself, its members were Chamberlain, Greenwood, the ostensibly non-party civil servant Sir John Anderson

(Home Secretary and in charge of civil defence), and Sir Kingsley Wood (Chancellor of the Exchequer). From the moment he entered office, Attlee campaigned for the establishment of this committee to direct and coordinate the work of those individuals, and within a month Churchill agreed.[35] The Lord President's Committee was the principal body covering domestic affairs. It has been described as 'a Home Cabinet'.[36] Its function was to ensure coordination of the Production Council and of the Economic Policy, Food Policy, Home Policy and Civil Defence Committees. To all intents and purposes, Attlee directed it himself from the outset, making it his personal fiefdom at the centre of Whitehall; Chamberlain's fatal illness that would kill him before the year was out meant that he only chaired it for a brief period and allowed Attlee quickly to circumvent him, while Anderson, who succeeded Chamberlain in the autumn of 1940 and was one of Attlee's few peers as an administrator, always had little political standing.[37] Churchill was never a member. In October, when Chamberlain resigned, Attlee had the Lord President's Committee restructured with a new membership – as well as himself and Anderson, it now consisted of Bevin, Morrison (Home Secretary by this point), Greenwood, Wood, and Sir Andrew Duncan (Morrison's successor at Supply) – and officially designated as a 'steering committee' with a wider-ranging brief to oversee economic organization and the general workings of Whitehall.[38] As a result of its new membership, Labour utterly dominated the committee. Its revised terms of reference were:

- to keep continuous watch on behalf of the War Cabinet over the general trend of economic development;
- to concert the work of the economic committees and to deal with any differences not requiring reference to the War Cabinet; and
- to deal with any residual matters and special questions, which arise from time to time.[39]

The range of subjects overseen by the Lord President's Committee was vast. From the beginning, it was responsibile for dealing with financial policies, prices, home consumption, foreign trade and export surpluses. It also soon had at its disposal the government-employed economists who previously worked for the Central Economic Information Service.[40] By early 1941, it had become the War Cabinet's leading body for coordinating all social and economic policy on the home front. This made it a perfect vehicle for the injection of Labour doctrines into the political nation. Furthermore, its responsibilities continually expanded as other committees were gradually wound up. It was a congenial body in which to work, filled with people minded towards both Labour's ideological orientations and yearning for efficiency. Attlee had constructed a position of influence that was unmatched in the British polity.

He chaired the Food and Home Policy Committees, and sat on Greenwood's Production and Economic Policy Committee.[41] Freed from departmental responsibilities, Attlee could roam across the entire field of governance. This wide-ranging brief facilitated not only a major expansion of Attlee's political reach, but, in time, laid the foundations for a Labour-orchestrated reform of government. Most significantly, this encompassed the idea of central planning. Immediate moves were made to improve controls over capital, industry, consumption and rationing, and elaborate regional planning schemes were drawn up. 'Planning' did not quickly translate into military good fortune, or, for that matter, into rapid improvement in the efficiency of war production. A sense of crisis remained on that front until 1942. But how quickly the change brought results is less important than the fact that it occurred in the first place and the role of not only Attlee but Labour as a whole in carrying it out. Labour's much-criticized leader, then, held a uniquely powerful position; it may have been very much a behind-the-scenes role, but no one was more influential in Whitehall with the exception of Churchill himself. The extension in the power, role and duties of the state will be examined more fully in the subsequent chapters. For now it is sufficient to state that, as Beckett has observed, while the Prime Minister focused on the military conflict, it was Attlee who 'looked after the shop', effectively running the home front from the inception of the new ministry.[42] Beckett noted how the political 'iron' in Attlee's 'soul' became apparent once he guided Labour into office, and described him as 'the greaser of wheels ... at the heart of the government'.[43] It has been suggested by Peter Clarke that Attlee's 'hero' was Lord Salisbury, for his understated but 'well on top of his job' style of leadership.[44]

Immediately on entering office, Attlee, working alongside Greenwood, began an overhaul of the machinery of government.[45] They dissolved dozens of committees, centralized decision-making, reduced the ability of ministers to 'pass the buck' to others and produced a considerable improvement in administrative efficiency. As Attlee rather succinctly put it later on, 'we proceeded to scrap most of the committees.'[46] Given Churchill's lack of patience with such matters and Greenwood's deficiencies, Beckett judged that the achievement in providing the drive and expertise was Attlee's.[47] Even Dalton said that Attlee was in 'very good form' in his ministerial responsibilities.[48] Attlee, then, was a well-respected figure in the coalition. Already Addison's harsh assessment that Attlee played only a peripheral role in wartime government and party politics seems difficult to sustain. Despite his enigmatic manner and air of a 'bank manager', the 'pipe smoking', and 'remote' man who led Labour had given a further persuasive demonstration of his abilities.[49] Morgan, the historian of the 1945 government, has recognized that Attlee was capable of 'extreme decisiveness' in the postwar era.[50] But what these developments suggest is that is was in fact during the war when Attlee first constructed a position of influence and, in eventually creating after 1945 'an interlocking system of permanent committees' that 'magnified the authority of the deceptively modest' Attlee and 'remodelled the Cabinet structure', he was only continuing where he left off after 1940.[51] It is therefore to the war where we can best trace the impact of Attlee and observe him as a politician.

A new picture of Attlee's centrality in wartime politics thus begins to emerge, as well as – no less crucially – the real extent of Labour's influence in the new regime. His leadership style as demonstrated here suggests much about how to address 'the Attlee problem' as a whole and how we can start to understand his political practice in a more sophisticated fashion. This interpretation of Attlee as slowly ensconcing himself at the heart of government, like a spider in a web, is reinforced by the fact that he was quick to get rid of a potential rival when Sir Horace Wilson, Chamberlain's adviser and a powerful figure within the machinery of state – Rab Butler called him 'the most powerful man in England'[52] – was eased aside during the review. Wilson 'infected' the government machine.[53] Attlee recalled that 'he had a hand in everything, ran everything. We got rid of him at once.'[54] This was ostensibly because of Wilson's links with Chamberlain, but, in abolishing his influence so quickly, the Labour leader displayed little reluctance in dispatching the competition.

Yet, Attlee and his colleagues continued to play the dirty side of politics as well. This was where their double life as members of the coalition, but with the Labour Party remaining on the opposition benches, was the most effective. Even though they were now in office, the Labour ministers stuck to their tried and tested techniques. They continued to ensure that Labour still appeared as unerringly 'responsible' to the public – Lees-Smith immediately lined the party up behind the government's decision to reject Hitler's peace feelers in the aftermath of Dunkirk, for instance[55] – but, as before, this was just one part of their strategy. From the outset, the Labour ministers were also aggressive inside the government in pushing their own agenda, both political and personal. As soon as the new ministry was formed, Attlee and Greenwood confronted Churchill and 'expostulated strongly' against the inclusion of Chamberlain.[56] Though the Prime Minister's weak standing among Conservatives meant that any move to get rid of his predecessor was impossible, Churchill was nevertheless left 'shaken ... considerably'.[57]

Around the same time, in an episode that suggests much about the centrality of political gain even in a situation of dire emergency like May 1940, Attlee and his colleagues brazenly expanded this into – or, at the very least, tacitly encouraged – a full-scale attack on the credibility of the Conservative Party, playing a role in a vicious campaign begun following Dunkirk in which virtually the entire spectrum of the Labour movement – including the leaders themselves – repeatedly and publicly assailed the Chamberlain ministry in the press for 'betraying' the country through its foreign policy, placing the responsibility for the crisis squarely on the shoulders of the former government.[58] They were easy scapegoats and, striking a chord with national opinion, the Labour leaders made much of the opportunity. That Attlee now enjoyed 'quite friendly' personal relations with Chamberlain was no impediment.[59] In July, Attlee openly attacked his government colleague Lord Halifax, the Foreign Secretary, in *The Times*.[60] The Labour ministers thus continued to pursue their vendetta against the former Prime Minister; in doing so, they both exacerbated the ruination of the Conservatives as the party that failed to stop Hitler and stood firm on a cause – the hated appeasers – certain to win them public credit.[61] Attlee and his colleagues had the freedom to make political capital in this respect in a way that Conservatives, even those who opposed appeasement, never enjoyed. By mid-1940, the credibility of the Conservative Party was shot. The Labour ministers exploited this to full, marking out valuable political space with a brazen – and wounding – barrage against their partners in office.

In encouraging such attacks and defining a distinctive Labour position, these tactics unsurprisingly reignited cross-party tensions just weeks into the life of the new administration. Conservative MPs were infuriated by their coalition partners openly blaming them, Cuthbert Headlam observing that the electoral truce 'is only observed by one side ... every speech made by the Labour people ... is a party speech and is propaganda.'[62] The Conservatives' sense of defeat was evident when the chairman of the 1922 Committee of backbench Tories gave off an air of desperation in warning that his party 'was by far the strongest in the country' and 'have no alternative but to defend ourselves'.[63] This assault by the Labour Party, and especially its leaders, on the record of the Conservatives is even more revealing for its timing. That the Labour ministers had the time to observe, and indeed in the first place whip up, these party attacks for several weeks amid the blackest national emergency for centuries suggests much. Not only did politicking continue as usual, then, despite the confines of wartime and of the coalition, but it represented an effort to conduct a hatchet job on their new allies. It was quite evident to Conservatives what was going on, with Channon seeing the whole coalition as a 'racket'.[64] Fear and anxiety were to be the constant companions of the Conservatives for many years: Headlam, worried about the risk that 'the Socialists will have it all their own way',[65] despaired that without Labour membership of the government the working-classes 'could not [be] count[ed] upon' for a 'whole-hearted effort' in the war,[66] and of a debate in Parliament, complained that 'it was mainly conducted (as all debates now are) by the Labour Party' and went on to say that 'it is odd how the Conservatives ... have passed out of the picture'.[67] Conservatives were acutely conscious – perhaps without foundation, but perhaps with very good reason – of a sense of having been overrun, and that Labour was now politically dominant.

The nature of this change in the political situation, like others after 1939, has not been properly appreciated. Churchill, once again badly shaken, was forced to insist that the Labour ministers cease their attacks.[68] He asked Attlee to 'call off the *Daily Herald*', to 'stop this campaign', and, after Cabinet on 6 June, kept the Labour ministers back to 'exhort' them over the 'heresy hunt'.[69] Though the plea did have an immediate effect on his colleagues in the coalition, assaults from the Labour movement continued unabated as *Tribune* published its famous *Guilty Men* book in July.[70] Only now did senior figures make an effort to muzzle the criticism. Union boss Walter Citrine denounced the campaign as a thinly veiled attempt to go back on Labour's entry into the government.[71] Attacks emanating from the Labour Party against Chamberlain persisted, but, as 1940 wore, the effort to suppress them did at least reduce their intensity from fever pitch. For the Conservative Party, though, the damage to its reputation was already done. What this opportunism suggests about the priorities of the Labour leaders, whose objectives seem to have still been primarily 'political' rather than 'national', is another matter. The image conjured up is of Attlee and company gleefully dancing on the Conservative Party's grave amid the collapse at Dunkirk, the bombing of cities, the RAF fighting desperately in the skies above and the *Wehrmacht* massing on the other side of the Channel. It is, of course, the nature of politics. However, one should at least recognize it and the consistency of the methods and tactics that the Labour leaders under Attlee, facing multiple directions simultaneously, had used since the outbreak of war.

The Labour ministers' collective position on the possibility of peace with Germany following the defeat of France is worth briefly pondering for its implications about the wider dynamics of politics in this period. With the French collapse, Hitler extended renewed peace feelers to the British government. The thrust was that Germany would keep her gains, and the British Empire left alone. John Charmley has argued that it was not in the national interest to prolong a fight that Hitler apparently did not want. [72] Owen Hartley contends that 'it was and still is questioned whether fighting Hitler was worth any sacrifice.'[73] Parley might have been a sensible policy. But the matter was virtually dismissed out of hand by Churchill and his colleagues in the coalition. Attlee and the rest did nothing to restrain the Prime Minister from treating the fate of the British Empire as a *Boy's Own* adventure. Perhaps Hitler would have demanded 'unacceptable' terms anyway; but there is no doubt that, politically speaking, those who had broken the Chamberlain regime now found themselves with little choice but to carry on the war.

The new Prime Minister was not the only one who had nailed his flag to the mast of resisting Hitler. Labour and other Conservatives did too. Such exhortations had reaped dividends in the promotion struggle; but that now restricted freedom of action in the diplomatic and military realms.[74] Churchill, the modern-day 'Pericles',[75] or, less commendably, 'the greatest adventurer of modern political history',[76] would have quickly found himself at the mercy of his Chamberlainite enemies if he sought a settlement; remember that Chamberlain remained leader of the

Conservative Party. Having established a parallel if rather less grandiose self-image, Attlee and the other Labour ministers would certainly be forced to walk away from the government if a peace policy was pursued. Politically, then, the careers of Britain's new rulers were so associated with this course of action that the war simply had to be continued. Such considerations had a long tradition of influencing decision-making in foreign affairs.[77] There is no reason, other than blind romanticism about our national myths, to assume that 1940 was any different. Even if rejecting Hitler's gesture *was* the most sensible option – a debatable proposition – it is worth bearing in mind that it was the only one that these men could realistically choose.

Meanwhile, Attlee and his colleagues sought to assuage discontent among their followers in another, more important, fashion. This time they held out the promise of legislative achievements, a tactic they were to persist in – often successfully – until the break up of the coalition five years later. The issue of precisely what Labour wanted to achieve from the war had been a potent topic throughout 1939 and precipitated a challenge to Attlee's leadership; 'to achieve high office' would not have sufficed as an answer and 'national survival' also seemingly made little impression. Now Attlee, angling for something of substance from the coalition to give to his party, sought to head off fresh criticism by pushing within the government in mid-June 1940 that the ministry

> should put before the country a definite pronouncement on gov-
> ernment policy for the future. The Germans are fighting a
> revolutionary war for very definite objectives. We are fighting a
> conservative war and our objects are purely negative. We must put
> forward a positive and revolutionary [statement of aims] admitting
> that the old order has collapsed and asking people to fight for the
> new order.[78]

This was 'war' in a democracy. 'The independence of these islands', the old rallying cry, was no longer enough. But Attlee had already diagnosed the problem – and Labour's opportunity. He persisted in his arguments over the subsequent weeks, and on 23 August the War Cabinet relented and agreed formally to set up a War Aims Committee, with Attlee as its chairman.[79] Bevin was also to be a member.[80] This met for the first time on 4 October.[81] Though it failed to make much headway in 1940 –

Churchill feeling reconstruction planning to be premature – that Attlee's agitation was again successful reiterates the extent of his influence, as well as enabling the Labour ministers to make reassuring noises on reconstruction and reform to their party. Viewed in the context of very public calls within the Labour Party from Bevan and Laski for nationalization and socialism,[82] Churchill's agreement to the establishment of the War Aims Committee was an important victory.

This was an early example of Attlee's tactics in manipulating his role in government. His desire to placate his followers while beginning to push for future social reform by extracting from the coalition a declaration of postwar policy continued to be central to his calculations over the summer of 1940. It enabled him to address two audiences at once. From August, at the behest of Pethick-Lawrence, Attlee worked to persuade Churchill to abolish the hated household means test as another inducement for loyalty;[83] in the autumn it was dually announced that the household test was to be scrapped and replaced by an individual test.[84] These methods were to be a great success and a milestone on his, and Labour's way, to capturing the British state between 1940 and 1945. It was yet further confirmation of the effective start the Labour leaders had made in integrating themselves within the apparatus of government – an arena, incidentally, in which even the most senior of them had very little prior experience. One Conservative told Attlee that 'what strikes one about your chaps is that they know their jobs.'[85] Though major, new social legislation was not likely to be implemented at the height of the military crisis, nonetheless, Attlee – as ever concerned with being the first to shape the environment – was beginning to put down the markers that he would use to great effect over the coming years.

Despite the Prime Minister's resistance, no one could accuse the Labour ministers of, as feared, having 'abandoned' Labour. Instead, Attlee was quietly waging war for Labour doctrine at the heart of government. Over five years, the party representatives' obduracy, manoeuvres and outright bullying were crucial in yielding legislative harvests. Attlee displayed an adroit ability in manipulation, knowing when to exact a concession from the government, when to take a firm line with the Labour Party and when to strike several poses simultaneously. In doing so, he stumbled remarkably infrequently. Moreover, that he was able to do this up to 1945 without precipitating a schism in the government demonstrates his skill in managing people and guiding them in the direction he wished them to go – often without their knowledge that he was doing so. Despite the criticisms directed at him by contemporaries for his style, when Attlee's wartime role is examined afresh, it is here, early in the war, that we can discern the true extent of his quiet ability in the political arts.

After persuading Churchill to establish the War Aims Committee, Attlee's pressure was no doubt significant in the Prime Minister's acquiescence in December to the formation of a new, dedicated Reconstruction Committee.[86] Moreover, the previous month Bevin joined the fray by making a speech in Bristol that emphasized the need for reform after the war.[87] His tone was sufficiently partisan to provoke Lord Londonderry to complain that 'I am frankly disturbed by Bevin's rise to power … he is more than useful, but as a director of … policy I see nothing but disaster.'[88] Attlee and the Labour ministers displayed an astute awareness of their leverage over both their followers and the Conservatives, as well as the fact that Churchill could not do without them. The leadership group held office, but the Labour Party occupied an ambiguous position. As demonstrated, the Labour ministers could comfortably afford to be relatively partisan in their behaviour, making speeches on the need for reform and advancing a Labour policy line within the coalition, all the while knowing that as long as they were cautious the alliance with the Conservatives would hold. As during the phoney war, it may have been readily apparent to Labour's partners what they were doing, but Churchill needed them. He had no one else, after all.

The Prime Minister's own party never liked him and for a time in 1940 engaged in bitter 'guerrilla warfare' against him.[89] The contrast with the sleek vehicle into which Attlee had transformed Labour could not be sharper. Until 1945, the Labour ministers repeatedly utilized a particular method of securing concessions. They would agitate within the coalition on a specific issue and push to set up an investigation to consider it, thus laying the groundwork within Whitehall; the NEC would produce a policy document that Attlee could then present to the government as a Labour 'demand', attempting to force Churchill's agreement. This tactic bore fruit with the War Aims Committee in August 1940 and the Reconstruction Committee in December, and was to yield similar success in the future. Moreover, Attlee and the rest of the ministers could easily protect their flank within the coalition by drawing a distinction between their own understanding of political realities and the irresponsible demands of their followers. Once again, then, the Labour ministers proved themselves willing and able to persist in the same kinds of tactics used during the phoney war. The harsh assessments made by Addison and others therefore seem difficult to bear out. On the contrary, the foregoing analysis suggests the validity of a quite different perspective: Attlee and his colleagues were willing to exploit their position for all it was worth. It would be an exaggeration to state that they still enjoyed 'power without responsibility', but they undoubtedly had the best of both worlds.

Attlee was not the only important Labour minister we need to consider. On becoming a member of the Churchill regime and being parachuted into Parliament, union boss Ernest Bevin, the Labour movement's most powerful individual, entered the world of conventional politics for the first time. He had never been an MP, or even sat on the NEC, but as head of the TGWU he had dominated union politics across the country for years and possessed expertise in most of the areas he now had to oversee. Under Bevin, the Ministry of Labour became one of the great offices of state. There, and after the war at the Foreign Office, he proved to be Labour's 'one man of greatness'.[90] His secret was that he was 'a classic working-class authoritarian', a species the middle-class intelligentsia has never grasped (or perhaps even encountered) but that others will happily recognize.[91] Bevin read huge amounts very quickly, remembered it and mastered a brief as few others could do. Never short of confidence in his own abilities, he enjoyed making decisions that would have intimidated others. In 1940, he faced major shortages of men and materials, and while his bullying manner caused friction, he immediately gave the department a new sense of drive. Before the end of May the press was hailing Bevin and declaring 'mobilization at last!'[92]

He began shifting the government away from mobilizing 'fiscal' resources to mobilizing 'physical' ones instead. Bevin ensured that his powers to direct any individual to any workplace were used sparingly and that a mood of cooperation was sustained with the unions: he met the government–TUC Joint Consultative Committee several times a month. The power of the trade unions increased hugely throughout the war, now that the unemployment of the 1930s had disappeared. Under Bevin, the coalition stuck to existing rules governing collective bargaining, increased industrial consultation and ruled out strict wage controls. The government brought the TUC and Employers' Confederation into formalized contact, set up thousands of local joint production committees between unions and owners across the country and, for the most part, avoided direct intervention in industry.[93] The coalition, under Bevin's direction, instead exercised *de facto* control by formulating production programmes, directing labour and material, and controlling contract prices. Such was the power that Bevin enjoyed that, within five months of the formation of the coalition, he was elevated to the War Cabinet. Bevin, like everyone else, was concerned with national survival rather than long-term planning in his first year in office. Yet, the new way of doing things inaugurated on his watch led to fundamental changes (for better or worse) in the relationship between the state and industry and played a key role in the transition to the post-1945 'mixed economy'. Whether or not it was 'consensual' is surely less significant than the importance of the change itself.[94]

In office, Bevin and Attlee quickly cemented an alliance grounded in mutual respect, shared priorities and wariness towards Morrison. It was to be unlike any other in modern political history. Bevin's biographer records that when Attlee became leader, Bevin held his usual suspicions of him as 'middle class'.[95] Once Bevin entered the government, however, he felt bound to Attlee. As Bullock writes, 'Attlee had the sovereign virtue, in Bevin's eyes, of being straight: you could rely on what he said.'[96] The two came to enjoy a genuine friendship and entrenched a formidable axis that was to last until Bevin's death 11 years later. Attlee told Francis Williams that 'we understood each other very well.'[97] With shared perceptions of what mattered in politics and ambitions that did not conflict – Bevin never had the slightest interest in being leader of a motley band of MPs – jealousy and rivalry between the two never seems to have developed. The backdrop to this axis, of course, was their mutual feud with Morrison. The Minister of Supply, and soon to be Home Secretary, was Attlee's greatest rival; Bevin also despised him and had done so for a decade. This antipathy underpinned the Attlee–Bevin alliance, acting as a bulwark against Morrison. It did not prevent either of them working alongside him – Bevin and Morrison retained a 'façade of amiability',[98] while, as we have seen, Attlee and Morrison could cooperate on many issues, but it was a source of recurrent conflict. By the formation of the coalition, Bevin held an 'immovable prejudice' towards Morrison, viewing him as 'the politician personified', and telling colleagues 'don't you believe a word the little bastard says.'[99]

Lacking sympathy for the political wing of the Labour movement, Bevin was even more determined than Attlee to keep the party in its place. He did not have the slightest interest in an arena – party politics – he regarded as little more than a game. Bevin expected the PLP to fall meekly in line, an attitude that was to provoke poor relations with Labour MPs. Hence, as we shall see, Bevin's authority over the union movement – and within the machinery of government – was not matched within the PLP. His bullying style failed to attract support; his colleagues feared and respected, but never loved, the newest member of the PLP. Attlee was regularly compelled to play the role of fire fighter after spats between Bevin and the party. With Bevin perceiving himself as a representative of the trade unions, the Minister of Labour saw Attlee as someone who would keep the PLP, with its annoying socialists and Fabians, out of his way. Bevin never even sought membership of the Administrative Committee. Nonetheless, their partnership worked, Attlee later remembering that his relationship with Bevin 'was the deepest of my political life. I was very fond of him and I understand that he was very fond of me.'[100] Power, whether in government or in a union, the ability to make decisions, was what interested Bevin. That was the only 'pole' that the single-minded Bevin was interested in ascending, but it was not trade union parochialism; Bevin instinctively understood what really mattered. Many years later Attlee said of him that:

> Because of his own genius for organization and his confidence in his own strength he did not fear – he embraced – power. Lord Acton's famous dictum in power probably never occurred to him. And if he agreed that power corrupts he would have said that it corrupted only the men who were not big enough to use it.[101]

The Attlee–Bevin axis swung into action for the first time within days of the new government's formation in May 1940. One of the greatest threats to the unity of the Labour movement – and something that could provoke a revolt against Attlee's whole strategy – was the task faced by the Labour ministers in reconciling the trade unions to the new emergency powers of compulsion and direction held by the state. The laws systematically challenged the freedoms and prerogatives of individual workers across the country.[102] In giving the government the authority to direct any person to services required for the war effort, and to take over any industrial establishment, the Emergency Powers Bill of May 1940, which Attlee himself introduced, could easily be perceived as a major attack on union freedoms.[103] Doubtless, Attlee's stewardship of the measure through the Commons was significant in securing its passage unmolested from the Labour side of the House, and it seems certain that Bevin applied similar pressure on the TUC.[104] He called for 'a little less democracy and a little more trust'.[105]

On 24 May, the Minister of Labour addressed a crowd of 2000 union executives and made an appeal for national unity, emphasizing the need for the unions to place themselves at the disposal of the state, identifying this as a 'test of our socialism'.[106] He was to utilize such language frequently. Bevin constantly pushed the unions to make concessions and act 'responsibly'. The wrangle over the new powers continued for the rest of 1940. In October, Attlee addressed the TUC himself, making similar appeals to those used by Bevin and with the terminology of 'national unity' and 'responsibility' again the major linguistic devices employed.[107] Precisely as in the past, this posture afforded Attlee, and Bevin, a means to secure compliance while defining themselves to several different audiences as statesmen and not sectional politicians. Tellingly, Harris has recognized that by the time Attlee made his speech, he and Bevin would certainly have been aware that the government might well need to introduce full-scale industrial conscription; yet, in his address, Attlee actually gave the TUC the impression that workers' freedoms would be preserved.[108] This was the Attlee–Bevin 'axis' in action: Labour's leader and the most powerful union figure in the country contriving to avoid a public conflict with the unions – a demonstration of their sometimes ruthless response to political necessity in wartime.

The last of Labour's 'big three', Morrison, however, was a very different story. That Attlee and Bevin lined up on one side, and Morrison on the other, was to be of central importance in shaping the course of wartime politics when the struggle for the Labour leadership eventually resumed. By 1943, it dominated relations between these men and had a major effect on party and government more widely; eventually, even the question of continuing the coalition after the war became a battleground in the conflict. The wartime struggle for the leadership between Attlee and Morrison has neither been analysed nor treated as central. This is a mistake. As this book will demonstrate in, it was in fact to prove one of the central issues in British politics between 1940 and 1945.

On assuming government office, Morrison largely dropped from sight within Labour, although this was only temporary. Although he had not wanted the Ministry of Supply, Morrison worked to master the post and, like Bevin, was a more visible public figure than Attlee. [109] He was a major success, a master at both politics and administration. By July, Churchill wanted to bring him into the War Cabinet, but retreated under pressure from the 'Tory machine', as the appointment would 'disturb the balance of the parties'. [110] Morrison addressed serious administrative problems in his ministry with characteristic flair. Facing major shortages of machine tools and armaments, and the abandonment of military equipment at Dunkirk, Morrison set up a new committee structure to streamline the planning of army needs, address the shortfalls in the supply of machine tools and steel, salvage suitable waste materials and counteract bottlenecks. [111] Using a new Emergency Powers Act, Morrison had the ability to take control of factories and direct production. [112] As with Bevin and Attlee, this did not have an overnight impact on the national war machine, but Morrison played a crucial role in establishing the structures that would make war production a success.

Consumed with the demands of office and with no suitable opportunities on the horizon, Morrison was, for the moment, compelled to forego his campaign to displace Attlee. His temporary neglect of the Labour Party – as in the autumn of 1939 – annoyed some and had Citrine complaining that Morrison was 'much too entangled with his officials … he is disinclined to see people without them'. [113] Nonetheless, he remained highly influential on the NEC after the founding of the coalition, attending most of its meetings as well as those of the Emergency, Policy, Elections and International subcommittees. [114] In the election to the PLP Administrative Committee in December, he polled an impressive third in the ballot with 74 votes. [115] Harold Macmillan, Morrison's under-secretary, said that while he worked with him, Morrison 'thought more about publicity than armaments'. [116] In October, after just five months in the post, Churchill moved Morrison to the Home Office because of the stress the Blitz placed on the country and the perception that Anderson's personality was too bland to inspire the necessary resistance. [117] For the heir apparent it represented a career milestone; though he was not a member of the War Cabinet until 1942, Morrison quickly became one of the most powerful and prominent politicians on the home front – a prominence that stood in stark contrast to the obscurity in which his rival Attlee toiled. Morrison was to make a great success of this job as well, elevating him to a public stature greater than that enjoyed by any other Labour minister with the possible exception of Bevin.

Hence, the best strategy open to Morrison, and the one he pursued, was to work to strengthen his credibility while awaiting a suitable moment to strike at the incumbent leader. That provided the platform for a remarkable war and a protracted campaign to replace Attlee. The model of leadership Morrison symbolized was very different from the one Attlee offered. The struggle between them was a clash between two distinctive styles. Though both skilled administrators and politicians, closely matched in all respects, the two men were polar opposites: Attlee was grey and difficult to penetrate, while Morrison was domineering, a compelling speaker and deeply charismatic. Moreover – and, once again, quite unlike Attlee – Morrison was an 'ideas man', the only senior Labour figure to have actually devised a blueprint for nationalization with his 1933 work on transport.[118] Though circumstances necessitated patience, Morrison quite deliberately laid the groundwork for the future from early on in the lifetime of the coalition. As will be seen later in the chapter, he was to begin to push this line more forcefully during early 1941, humiliating Attlee amid the most contentious political struggle since the fall of Chamberlain and reigniting their feud.

Besides the 'big three', Dalton was a moderate success at the Ministry of Economic Warfare. Attlee's political ascendancy meant that even Dalton, the man who usually likened the leader to a rabbit or mouse, ceased plotting against him for a time. Dalton was to rely heavily on Attlee to shield him over the next five years from the machinations of bitter Conservative enemies like Bracken, who loathed him. The only major Labour minister who turned out to be a political failure was Greenwood. Within weeks of the formation of the coalition he was struggling to cope with his ministerial work, displaying a 'visible lack of drive'.[119] Attlee was soon 'dissatisfied' with his 'slowness and inertia'.[120] This was an unfavourable contrast to his earlier conduct. After having been the party's key politician in the period of Attlee's ill health from June to September 1939, becoming 'the authentic voice of Britain', the deputy leader's ministerial career had stalled.[121] Much of this may have been due to his taste for drink, but, regardless, Attlee's unhappiness was probably fatal for Greenwood's prospects, for, without his leader to protect him, he was to prove an easy target for those who wished to see him demoted. By December Greenwood was being mooted as ambassador in Washington,[122] but the idea was quickly dismissed, probably because Churchill wanted someone sober in the post. Halifax went instead, which also dealt neatly with a Conservative rival to Churchill. Then, just two weeks later, Greenwood was the main victim in a reshuffle of the War Cabinet. He lost the chair of the Production and Economic Policy Committee and gained, clearly as a sop to Labour opinion, the new Reconstruction Committee, where he was to oversee a study of postwar problems.[123] Though he was to remain a member of the War Cabinet, Greenwood's meteoric rise came to an ignominious end.[124]

That Churchill – increasingly secure after becoming Conservative leader on Chamberlain's death – did not take reconstruction seriously at this point is evident. The Reconstruction Committee did not even begin to meet until March 1941.[125] Greenwood was simply too lacklustre for such an important job as supervision of the industrial field, and the committee over which he presided instead became a Production Executive, directed by the altogether more formidable Bevin.[126] The combined influence of the Attlee–Bevin axis within the government was now even higher, with both men holding multiple key posts, but Greenwood entered into a steep decline from which he was never to recover. Though his position as deputy leader shielded him for a while, by late 1940 Greenwood's inefficiency had effectively called time on his ministerial career.

Overall, then, it is clear the Labour ministers' efforts were meeting with considerable success and – particularly through the work of Attlee, Bevin and Morrison – they established themselves as the most powerful group in the new ministry. In addition, they had reconfigured the structures of the Labour Party to work in their favour. Tactically and strategically, their role was both more significant and consistent than historians have previously recognized. This bolsters the case for rethinking what was important in British politics before 1945 and emphasizing new issues. As we have seen, these men also aggressively pursued a Labour agenda as well. Within months of joining the coalition, not only had state intervention and production 'planning' become more extensive than ever before, but the ministers – especially Attlee – had almost surreptitiously acquired a unique level of influence within the machinery of Whitehall. This was the situation during the last six months of 1940. Moreover – if beyond the scope of this book – at a local level the role of the Labour movement was similarly significant, with thousands of joint production committees. The trade unions wielded more power over the economy than ever before. Labour-sympathizing civil servants were playing roles in formulating policy within the government apparatus.[127] The system under creation may have been incomplete, but the direction of the tides was clear enough.

Addison's doubts about the position of the party's representatives are therefore difficult to uphold and in need of revision. Similarly, so is Jefferys's argument that the Labour leaders only 'gradually' measured up to the demands of high office, and 'in the short term, Labour ministers were … in no real position to begin influencing important areas of government policymaking. Attlee … like Morrison and Bevin … struggled to impress for many months.'[128] This has repercussions for understanding the course, and outcome, of British politics as a whole in the years prior to 1945. Partly, of course, Labour's advantage was due to the breaking of the Conservative Party – in which they themselves, along with Chamberlain, Churchill and Hitler, had played such a central role. Yet none of this, nor for that matter, the new political orientations – both 'consensual' and otherwise – which would make the coming years so historically important simply *emerged*; they were the result of hard political graft at the heart of the system. The individual quality of the Labour leaders was, for the most part, greater than that of their Conservatives counterparts. Their success – and the relevance of a new interpretation that stresses the possibility of Labour coming to a position of near political dominance – is clear from the fact that, despite now being in office, Attlee and his colleagues persisted in virtually the same tactics as they had employed in opposition – preaching a doctrine that demanded acquiescence from the Labour Party while ruthlessly imposing themselves on the Conservatives, securing major economic reforms, and *still* exploiting any opportunity to undermine further the credibility of the party that Churchill now led. Under Attlee's guidance, the Labour ministers occupied vast tracts of political land. His leadership style, reserved yet at the same time decisive and deliberate, was becoming clear. Given Labour's position prior to 1939, it was already one of the most audacious, and complete, turnarounds of the twentieth-century. As subsequent chapters will show, the position they carved out was to represent a powerful springboard for Attlee and the others to dominate, and shape, British politics for the rest of the war.

A restless party

Attlee's careful attempts to position Labour had paid off. Yet, despite this, the period of stability for the Labour Party did not last very long. A sea change was to occur in Labour politics from early 1941. The disillusion-ment with the continued inaction of the party, which we saw in the previous chapter, had been restrained since the formation of the coalition but now finally erupted again. General disaffection was exacerbated by the the activities of rebels like Shinwell, Aneurin Bevan of *Tribune*, and particularly LSE professor Harold Laski, who played a role in wartime party politics that has not always been appreciated. The prominence of such men expanded as they made a name for themselves. Bevan and Laski were probably the two most controversial individuals in wartime public life. With the risk of a German invasion seemingly low as the war reached stalemate in the period prior to the Nazi attack on Russia, the political nation turned in on itself again. The party gradually became less willing to accept its leaders' diktats, and, in consequence, for the next four years Labour was gripped by bouts of internecine strife as Attlee and his colleagues struggled – often in vain – to assert their authority.

This, at root, was a reaction from the Labour Party to the parallel demands for loyalty and inaction on which the Attlee strategy depended – with a resultant tendency to fasten on any prominent issues and turn them into a crisis about what Labour was 'getting' from the government. In the minds of many, the party was getting very little indeed. Attlee's leadership had been inventive and often commanding. But it nonetheless had the effect of leaving opinion across the Labour movement exasperated. Attlee still failed to make much public impression. While this may suggest an inability to discern that, though the government refrained from making socialist *noises*, it was in reality implementing much of Labour's policy agenda, it did not render the problems the leaders faced any less acute.

Shinwell, fuming at Lees-Smith's appointment, became a venomous critic from the front bench despite his membership of the Administrative Committee. His constant sniping at party meetings and in the Commons led to bitter personal feuds with Bevin and Dalton that did much to advertise a new lack of unity.[129] Bevan, meanwhile, set about establishing himself as a leading manufacturer of dissent and the most prominent opponent of the government in the House of Commons. In doing so, he began to cultivate a reputation that would elevate him to being a major figure later in the war. Although still an inexperienced mining MP with little standing and who had actually been formally expelled from the Labour Party in January 1939, Bevan's formidable oratorical abilities meant that after the formation of the coalition he was by far the best parliamentary speaker not in the government, and, unsurprisingly, its sternest critic in the Commons.[130] Combined with his dominance of the influential *Tribune* socialist newspaper, an important force within the Labour movement, Bevan, like Shinwell, came into frequent conflict with Attlee and the other ministers.[131] Soon after the founding of the coalition, Bevan declared of Attlee and the rest that 'in the realms of higher policy they have conspicuously failed', and, a few months later, charged that 'blind men are leading us.'[132] The effect of these spats on the standing of the two PLP rebels was very different. Shinwell's poisonous manner and evidently frustrated ambition dented his image, while Bevan's stock rose the more he became 'a national bogeyman' and perceived as a 'malicious, frustrated ... demagogue'.[133] Both, however, represented the first breaches in the façade of unity that the leadership group had carefully constructed. In 1941, this helped to swell a tide of discontent against Attlee's line.

Of most significance, however, were the activities of Laski. The influential and popular academic was a very unusual sort of political outsider. He was not even a politician *per se*, but an intellectual. Professor of Political Science at the LSE, Laski produced thousands of essays and was one of the best-known intellectuals in the world. Long active in the Labour movement, Laski was a member of the NEC continually from 1937 until months before his death in 1950. His importance in wartime politics has not been detected by historians who tend to concentrate on the decisions taken within government rather than the interplay between events within and outside the regime.[134] His collapse into illness early in the 1945 Attlee regime and premature death are doubtless significant in explaining why he has received so little emphasis. By convention, intellectuals tend to attract limited attention from political historians. But in fact the historian cannot help but notice the importance of his role.

Professor Laski constructed a powerful institutional platform within the party on the NEC, taking a leading role in its activities and, for a time, to all intents and purposes driving it single-handed. Laski, like others, personally loathed Attlee, whom he believed was as a weak figure, and consequently from late 1940 set about establishing the only coherent alternative to the party leader's strategy articulated between 1939 and 1945.[135] Further, this was more than just talk. Far from being an isolated figure, in the very unusual conditions of war and the straitjacket of coalition Laski was to be central to many of the key political dramas played out within the Labour Party over the course of the next few years.

He was popular with the Labour constituency activists and consistently topped the poll in the annual election to the constituencies section of the NEC, a symbol of his stature.[136] Laski was no unrepresentative intellectual. He was a creator of discontent and even a major 'high political' protagonist of Attlee. In a real sense, almost all of the calculations about Labour Party management that Attlee made were to be directed against one of either Morrison or Laski. The LSE professor entered into a vicious conflict with Attlee over Labour's approach to the war, a conflict fought out both privately – in the institutional arenas of the Labour Party – and publicly – via the press. Laski was a troublesome opponent precisely because he was not a politician; Attlee had few sanctions available to bring Laski into line. Disciplinary measures, even formal censure by the NEC, quietened him for a few weeks and nothing more. His challenge was consequently to prove difficult to snuff out. Quite uncharacteristically for the normally unflappable Attlee, Laski – determined to engineer a wholesale repudiation of the ministers and the overthrow of Attlee personally – truly got under the leader's skin. Even Morrison did not do that. The two men, party leader and intellectual maverick, engaged in a vituperative personal duel that lasted until the eve of Labour's general election triumph in 1945.

Immediately upon the formation of the new government, Laski began to agitate against Attlee's precarious balancing act. Taking advantage of his influence on the NEC, he sought to bring rapid pressure to bear on the Labour ministers. Attlee had not neutered the NEC as he had the PLP. Indeed, the people who sat on it were not the sort of individuals tamely to vote themselves out of existence as the PLP executive had. In June 1940 Laski produced a new pamphlet, *The Road to Power*, which the executive refused to publish because it was too inflammatory.[137] In it Laski called for the complete nationalization of all the nation's resources.[138] This was, needless to say, somewhat different from the line that Attlee stressed to his party and inside the government. Laski then exacerbated the Labour ministers' awkward position by demanding, at the NEC, that the government enact 'at least a number of definitely socialist measures'.[139] While this may seem unexceptional – the Labour Party was a socialist party, after all – the point is simply that nobody else was arguing for these things at this time. The Labour ministers utilized a quite different political language and their followers were mostly quiescent. The aura of unity and responsibility that Attlee had imposed was so enveloping that barely a murmur of discontent escaped from it, let alone talk of alternatives. What Laski had begun to do at the heart of the Labour movement was to argue the case for a different approach. By August 1940, precisely what that alternative was became clear. Professor Laski wanted to exploit Labour's leverage and bargaining power over the Conservatives even more than Attlee, Bevin and Morrison were already doing by demanding a full rethinking of the coalition government and blanket acceptance of Labour nostrums by Churchill.[140] His efforts to badger the Labour ministers and constant calls for extensive nationalization prompted a rapid response from the leaders and Laski received a severe verbal drubbing at the NEC Policy Committee on 16 August.[141] Some 11 days later, Attlee successfully got a Laski resolution that the coalition had to achieve a 'revolution by consent' dropped on the grounds of government unity.[142] But nevertheless this barrage of requests, interventions and Laski's pushing of a line quite different from that of Attlee meant that, just three months into the lifetime of the new government, dissension against the Labour ministers was already being heard.

In October – in an assault given context by Churchill's stonewalling on Attlee's request for a statement of peace aims – Laski shifted the fight from the privacy of the NEC to the public arena and launched an overt, and blistering, attack on the Labour ministers in the *Daily Herald*, under the headline 'An Open Letter to the Labour Movement'.[143] Asking readers to 'Demand War Aims' and calling again for Labour to extract concessions from the coalition, Laski now publicly demanded 'renegotiation' of the terms on which Labour had entered the government, calling for the leadership to press for a publication of war aims as the 'title-deeds' to the Labour–Conservative alliance.[144] Considering the Labour ministers had extracted from Churchill the Cabinet War Aims Committee, the abolition of the means test, and were restructuring many of Whitehall's most important bodies to dominate the home front, this was perhaps a little unfair. Yet, Laski actually accused the party's representatives of 'betraying' the working class in failing to lead a 'great rebellion' against capitalism and secure 'socialist measures' from the government.[145] Given that Laski had described such rhetoric as 'the raving of a lunatic' when the communist John Strachey espoused it in 1939, it is possible that his new posture was simply an angry response to the snubs that his NEC efforts since the outbreak of war had received.

Regardless of his motives, this public criticism of the Labour ministers' supposed 'failures' was the most open attack on them so far. In making it, Laski defined his own position – to great benefit – as being an authentic representative of the party against a leadership that had betrayed it. The NEC immediately called a special meeting of the Emergency Sub-committee to discipline him on 5 November, which Dalton described as putting Laski 'on the mat'.[146] Laski was censured outright for his conduct.[147] The meeting also saw the igniting of the feud between him and Attlee that was to dominate NEC politics until the end of the war. The two men engaged in a vicious row about the Labour ministers' record.[148] Laski had worked alongside Attlee as a policy adviser in early 1940, but this proximity encouraged a belief that such an uncharismatic man, lacking 'an ounce of leadership', was unfit to hold Labour's top job.[149] Overt personal clashes were hardly characteristic of Attlee, yet no one matched Laski's ability to antagonize him. Laski had been disciplined, but the truce secured by his censure held for just five weeks. He returned to the attack in December with another public denunciation, this time in the *New Statesman*, in which he heavily criticized the government, and the Labour ministers specifically, for the lack of sweeping social reform.[150] These events, if containable for the moment, signified an important change in tone.

Stinging as it was, though, this was as bad as disaffection got in 1940. Certainly in the cases of Laski and Shinwell it was, moreover, attributable largely to personal vendettas. But the party's unhappiness with Attlee's authoritarian attitude and stifling of Labour was to explode in 1941. Early into the new year, a series of party crises occurred in quick succession and made the period from January until the annual conference in May one of constant conflict. The episode that marked a real shift in the disposition of the Labour Party came in January and impacted upon the standing of Attlee's chief rival, Morrison. As Home Secretary, Morrison took the contentious decision that month to ban the Communist newspaper, the *Daily Worker*, in response to its 'seditious' activities in opposing the war.[151] Favouring peace with Hitler and advocating 'revolutionary defeatism', the paper had been warned by the government in the summer of 1940 and, by December, Morrison was in favour of banning it.[152] Though the *Daily Worker* was widely loathed the ban provoked a civil liberties storm and Morrison was subjected to attack on the issue for much of 1941.

Revealingly, the Home Secretary briefly attempted to deceive his party over the ban; he decided in favour of suppression some days before actually announcing it, but brazenly gave the impression to the NEC in the interregnum that he would not suppress the newspaper.[153] Dalton said Morrison 'did not trust some members … and therefore felt he could not say much in front of them, except to try and put them off the scent'.[154] Yet, this only protected him for a while: when the ban was announced Labour opinion reacted with fury, and Morrison was confronted by vocal opponents, particularly Bevan, at an inflammatory PLP meeting on 22 January.[155] The Home Secretary made a robust defence and adopted an unapologetic posture emphasizing the need to suppress seditious publications, but that only antagonized his critics still further. The following week, Lees-Smith and Pethick-Lawrence defended the Home Secretary's flank in the Commons by acting yet again as virtual government spokesmen, formally lining Labour up behind Morrison and backing the need for 'measures [to] be taken against the habitual and persistent publication of material which is calculated to impede the national war effort'.[156]

But this did nothing to calm the storm now brewing. Bevan, determined to confront the Home Secretary, put down a Commons motion opposing the decision, cleverly framing his argument not only as a defence of freedom – 'the government are winning the war against us' – but questioning why Morrison had not utilized legislation against sedition already available to him, instead employing powers meant to apply in the rather more dangerous circumstances of actual invasion.[157] Combining oratorical flair with a grasp of detail, Bevan's speech was the most commanding parliamentary performance of his career to date. Evidence of his new stature as a troublemaker is apparent in Morrison's equally hostile response:

> If I wanted to find one distinguished member of the [Labour] party, who more than any other, has set aside the democratic decisions of the majority of his colleagues, I think I should choose him [Bevan]. Therefore his democracy is skin deep. He speaks of democracy for himself and not so much for the other fellow.[158]

Bevan led half a dozen Labour MPs into the division lobby.[159] Though this registered only a small revolt, and the NEC backed Morrison's decision in early February, there had nonetheless been widespread disapproval of the Home Secretary's manner.[160] Moreover, the controversy inaugurated a pattern that was to recur until 1945, whereby Morrison's attempts to strengthen his credibility, and establish an identity for himself quite different from that of Attlee, were to be consistently undermined by his decisions as Home Secretary and natural unwillingness to be conciliatory when challenged. Morrison's resistance to all forms of criticism damaged the standing he was otherwise so concerned with cultivating. Bevan was giving vent to these feelings of disquiet when he bemoaned the direction of the party and declared in *Tribune* that 'It's Time Labour Kicked', openly charging that the Labour ministers had 'brought about no change of importance on the economic front'.[161] The next week the Ebbw Vale MP was agitating for the wholesale ending of the electoral truce and asserting that Labour MPs should not be bound by the government whip.[162] Attlee was warned that the term 'MacDonaldism' was being used in reference to the Labour ministers,[163] and Bevan publicly stated that 'the present policy of the Labour Party gives the party no work to do except to take poison.'[164] In April, Bevan declared that the only explanation for the 'failure' of the coalition was 'lack of political guts on the part of the leaders of Labour'.[165]

All this was compounded by the second, and more destructive, round in the Attlee–Laski conflict between February and May. It was, just as before, instigated by a major new effort by Laski and this time inflicted considerable damage to the personal authority of Attlee. Unlike the earlier controversies, this was not a public row but one fought at the heart of the party's institutional machinery itself, on the leadership's supposedly secure power base of the NEC. Yet, it was just as threatening in that it raised the prospect of a repudiation of the doctrine of coexistence with the Conservatives that they had promoted, dragging Attlee into a fierce dogfight in defence of his own strategy. It first began in January when Laski provoked a struggle with the Labour ministers by marshalling opposition to the efforts of Jim Middleton, the general secretary, to cancel the annual conference on the grounds of a possible Nazi invasion in mid-1941.[166] Laski suspected that this was an effort to avoid giving a public platform to growing internal disaffection – certainly something the leaders were to attempt later in the war – and said as much at the NEC.[167] Expostulating strongly, he won the support of a majority of the executive, and also wanted the NEC to compel the Labour ministers to give reports of their work in government to the conference for consideration.[168] In addition, Laski gained assent for his proposal that the NEC should submit policy resolutions to the delegates for decision.[169] This was something that Attlee and company – conscious of the dangers of being boxed in – were hoping to avoid, preferring an event without any policy formulation at all.[170] The party's position between government and opposition meant that any commitments could neither be implemented nor campaigned on; Laski's proposal was patently intended to stir up trouble. The episode constituted a clear warning of Laski's ability to play the leadership group's own game of bureaucratic politics against them.

Emboldened by this success, just days later Laski instigated the most sustained political battle of the war thus far – and one that also became a contest for personal ascendancy between himself and Attlee. He resurrected the 'peace aims' row by folding it into a wider indictment of the Labour ministers and outlining a full-scale alternative strategy. Submitting a new memorandum to the NEC, simply entitled 'The Labour Party', Laski asserted that Britain was approaching a 'turning-point' in the war, predicting that Germany would soon fail in its bid to bring the conflict to a quick end.[171] As a result, it was 'imperative' to consider the 'approach to victory and the use to be made of victory'.[172] Building on his earlier appeal for 'title-deeds' to the coalition, Laski pushed for an open confrontation with the Conservatives on the subject of the future. Calling for a 'basic agreement upon fundamentals between parties in this country', his proposal represented the most powerful challenge to Attlee's policy – and for that matter the policy of coalition as a whole – since the fall of Chamberlain.[173] Few of Laski's 'fundamentals' were likely to prove acceptable to the Conservatives.

Laski explicitly charged 'the Labour leaders' with having 'secured nothing' from the Conservatives 'that industrial and political pressure could not have secured by what has been termed "constructive opposition"'.[174] Pouring scorn on Attlee's personal record, he wrote that 'so far as I know, our representatives in the government have not asked for [assurances that the failure to implement social reform following the First World War] will not be repeated.'[175] Laski had not only sought to provoke a repudiation of the Labour ministers' course, but also seemed to have reversed his support for the coalition. But the matter of these 'fundamentals' was where Laski concentrated his most devastating fire, demanding urgent action on 'reconstruction' and, in doing so, entrenching a new concept at the centre of the political lexicon for the next four years.[176] In a transparent attempt to protect himself after his censure the previous autumn, he concluded with the ridiculous suggestion that 'nothing in this argument is in any way a reflection of the work of our leaders.'[177] The rebellious academic proposed that a joint committee of the NEC, PLP and TUC be set up to coordinate action with the Labour ministers, who would then bring pressure to bear on Churchill.[178] He wanted this committee to formulate policy and pass it on to the ministers, so as to make them 'fully aware of the principles by which we expect them to be guided' – in other words, an attempt to curtail the autonomy of the Labour ministers and bring them under the yoke of the NEC.[179]

Attlee was seething. Laski had come out belligerently against everything he had spent a year and a half building, provoking the Lord Privy Seal into a furious response. Before the NEC had even considered the document, Attlee wrote to Laski privately, criticizing his proposals and implying that Laski – a non-politician – failed to understand the reality of political manoeuvre.[180] Using a military metaphor, the leader bluntly explained that 'the frontal attack with trumpets … is not the best way to capture a position,' and that pursuing a consensual approach with Labour's partners was more effective than making demands.[181] Then, in an epic example of the Labour bureaucracy in action, in early February the NEC resolved to pass Laski's document to the Policy Committee for consideration.[182] Thereafter, the leaders manipulated the NEC's committees to stall it for two months. They simply shunted the proposals back and forth from subcommittee to subcommittee until April.[183] Laski's conduct so antagonized Attlee that the latter again wrote to him on 1 April and actually told him that he wanted no further contact, official or otherwise, with him.[184] To openly cut off a colleague is poor tactics for any politician, but for one as astute as Attlee it was doubly surprising. That Attlee's air of unflappability – which, after all, was so impenetrable that it had produced many complaints over the years – was disrupted in this fashion underlines the intensity of the feud that now existed between the two men.

Yet, just when it seemed that Attlee would come out on top through his delaying tactics, Laski took the step of appealing directly to the leader's rival, Morrison.[185] The outcome was Morrison's re-entry into party politics and the reigniting of his struggle with Attlee. The Home Secretary constituted a formidable political shield for Laski. As already suggested, Morrison was keen to establish a certain image of himself to bolster his claim to the leadership. The heir apparent also perhaps sensed in the Laski–Attlee exchange the opportunity to gain some badly needed political capital after the *Daily Worker* incident and manufacture an embarrassing blow to his opponent. The Home Secretary thus energetically joined in with Laski's efforts. On 21 April, he wrote to Middleton that 'I am a little uncertain as to how far consideration of ... economic and financial problems after the war' was being undertaken by the NEC, arguing the case for a 'special subcommittee' to study reconstruction – Laski's proposal in disguise.[186]

Given that Morrison was quite aware that Greenwood was already engaged in this within the government, one can only read this as an effort to assist Laski in isolating Attlee. In late 1939, Morrison had also experienced first hand the internal dissidence that could result if Labour went down this route, not to mention his demonstrated temperamental unwillingness to tolerate criticism. Middleton tried to block the Home Secretary, replying that work was already being carried out, but Morrison's unfriendly response was insistent, following Laski's assertions in arguing that 'I hardly think that the matters dealt with in your letter [about Greenwood's study] ... meet the point raised in my letter to you,' and complained that 'in these circumstances, I should have expected that you would have placed the matter on the agenda' of the next meeting of the executive (Middleton, probably deliberately, had not). 'I shall therefore be glad if you will include the item.'[187]

Two weeks later, Morrison reiterated to the NEC that Labour needed actively to develop its policies.[188] In declaring his own views as being in favour of a push for extensive reconstruction planning, the Home Secretary was deploying his influence to ensure that he was seen as championing a populist line in the face of Attlee's public resistance. Suddenly intervening in a conflict in which Attlee had made his own prejudices very clear, Morrison employed for the first time the tactic that was to become his favourite weapon throughout the war. He opened a *rhetorical* divergence between his position and Attlee's where, in reality, no such division usually existed. It was an attempt to exploit the fact that Attlee had taken a stand and place himself directly between the Labour Party and its leader. Morrison, of course, did not want to bring the coalition down, or see a rejection of the ministers. What he did try to do consistently until 1945 was to advertise his own credentials as a Labour stalwart, define his position as speaking for the party's soul, and, by extension, imply that Attlee did not.

After Morrison's intervention, the NEC referred the matter once more to the Policy Committee, a damaging blow to Attlee's authority.[189] In May, the Policy Committee, which Morrison had long dominated, agreed to recommend to the NEC that a special subcommittee be set up, with Laski as secretary, to consider postwar problems and make recommendations.[190] This proposed body, the Economic and Social Reconstruction Subcommittee, was then accepted by the NEC.[191] After a four-month struggle, it was a major, if unlikely, victory for Laski and – visibly outmanoeuvred and isolated – an embarrassment for Attlee. The leader had publicly made a stand against Laski's challenge and been overruled for the first time since 1939. The decision was to provide Laski and others with the scope to cause trouble over the coming years. The affair also demonstrates that the contest between Attlee and Morrison remained very much a live, if temporarily latent, issue. The Home Secretary has been described as 'not so much disloyal, as watching for a favourable opportunity to be disloyal'.[192] Attlee had suffered an embarrassing defeat in his own area of expertise – bureaucratic politics – and made by Morrison to look unsympathetic to his followers' concerns. Over an issue of great symbolic importance, it was the biggest reversal Attlee had sustained since the outbreak of war. After being roundly outmanoeuvred the previous year, the episode also provides a demonstration of Morrison's ability to get the better of Attlee after all.

Conclusion

The political strategy of which Attlee and his colleagues were the architects, orchestrated and implemented so effectively during the phoney war, was prosecuted with a similar degree of efficiency during the first year of the Churchill coalition. The convergence of three key factors – the skill of the party's leaders, recognition by a majority of their followers of the need to remain in office, and the less than favourable progress of the war with Germany – ensured that their high-wire balancing act was not fatally upset. As prior to their entry into government, they had sought to buy the support of their party with measures – both legislative and rhetorical – that would permit them to continue down their chosen path. They had sought to establish signposts and landmarks. This is not to suggest that the Labour ministers did not believe in these measures, or the things they said about planning and reconstruction. But, as actors concerned with avoiding a challenge to their authority, such appeasement was a crucial element of leadership in the circumstances of cross-party alliance.

Moreover, this was also a continuation of the tactics they had used between September 1939 and May 1940 to keep the party quiescent, and which they were to persist in employing as a means to ward off dissent until the break-up of the coalition in 1945.

Little was changed as a result of their entry into office. But, in addition, the Labour ministers had exerted their influence across the whole of the governmental machine as well. Jefferys's suggestion that, by early 1941, 'there were still few signs that Labour had broken out of its bridgehead', is debatable to say the least.[193] Bevin was the key figure in organizing the domestic war effort, Morrison held similar prominence and the party's other representatives – with the obvious exception of Greenwood – were mostly well ensconced in office. As so often, it was Attlee who represented the key to Labour's exploitation of their situation. The leader possessed a unique degree of power within Whitehall, having entrenched himself at the centre of government. Further, in constructing the Administrative Committee and entrusting the party to Lees-Smith and Pethick-Lawrence, Attlee demonstrated his intention to keep Labour on a short leash. By engineering a situation where there were two relatively separate spheres within the Labour Party – the NEC and the PLP – the leadership group ensured that they remained the only figures with sufficient authority in either to exercise decisive influence in both.

However, as we have seen, storm clouds were beginning to gather. Conflicts over the highly charged matter of the competence of the coalition were becoming apparent. Though isolated and largely unrepresentative up to now, Shinwell, Bevan and Laski were all significant manufacturers – and exploiters – of discontent. Yet, to some extent, the three were ahead of the tide; it was dissatisfaction among the ordinary rank and file towards alliance with the Conservatives and a government that was not overtly socialist that was to pose the greatest threat. This resided at the root of the sea change that occurred later in 1941. As a result, despite their balancing of competing tensions, the leadership group's newly-acquired executive power was wielded against a backdrop of deteriorating relations with the Labour Party itself. Over time, this was to facilitate a state of affairs in which several combustible elements constantly threatened to provoke an open revolt. Even Attlee could do little but attempt to manage these crises. Hence, while during the first months of the coalition the party had largely supported its leaders, over the following period the situation was to change dramatically. The genie was now out of the bottle and subsequent chapters will show how this worsened, particularly when Attlee sought to buttress the electoral arrangements that underpinned the coalition shortly afterwards. The outcome was a party racked by dissent for the rest of the war, continually kicking against the straitjacket of coalition, and a gradual weakening of the leadership group's ability to impose their authority. A new, and vicious, attack by Bevan in *Tribune* set the tone for what was to come:

> It is now clear to all ... that the Labour Party under its existing leadership is ossified and may soon cease to be an effective political force. We deceive ourselves if we imagine that by a continuation of the present leadership ... can [Labour] ever be a vehicle by which socialism can be achieved ... [in the] leadership, pygmies have taken the place of giants.[194]

More dangerous times lay ahead.

Chapter 3

Remoulding the State and Defending the Alliance

Never easy to discern at the best of times, as the war entered its third year the future remained as difficult to peer into as the thickest Channel fog. The fortunes of the British Empire were uncertain. Britain was surviving, but enjoyed little prospect of taking the offensive. Even after London gained an ally in the USSR when the two giants of world socialism, Joseph Stalin and Adolf Hitler, went to war in June 1941, the idea of victory remained as distant as ever.[1] And the country suffered a series of shattering imperial blows at the hands of Japan. Although Churchill supposedly celebrated on hearing of the attack on Pearl Harbor six months later, the entry of the United States into the conflict promised no immediate turn of the tide. Yet, no such difficulties impede our view of the positions, and progress, of the Labour Party and its ministers at the heart of the coalition regime. The remoulding of the British state reached its peak in 1941 and 1942. Events in this period strengthen the case for recognizing a major shift towards the Labour Party in the political tectonic plates, orchestrated by its leaders. The state itself, and the doctrines by which Britain was governed, were being remodelled at an alarming pace.

However, while they continued to meet with tangible success, Attlee and his colleagues also began to encounter resistance as the Conservatives rediscovered their equilibrium. Having captured power in 1940, reshaped political discourse and then fundamentally reconstructed the framework in which they operated, from 1941 the Labour ministers settled down to the nitty-gritty – and often highly mundane – process of slugging it out for legislation with their coalition partners. As successful as this would turn out to be, it lacked glamour. There was less talk of a socialist Utopia. Political life became a nastier, scrappier affair. The protestation that 'Labour in the government has fully justified itself ... Labour ministers hold key offices, and are taking a full share in the direction of the war effort,' was not in itself sufficiently persuasive to offset the corrosive discontent.[2] As a result, parts of Attlee's strategy began to crumble.

This chapter therefore documents how the challenges confronting Attlee's leadership mounted up. It has several elements and its focus remains unashamedly 'high political'. As before, this perspective facilitates study of the period with a greater degree of nuance and the identification of new themes. It continues to trace the issues explored in the preceding sections and, treating the political world as a single organism, locates the Labour ministers in the broader context of public life. Persistent advancement for Labour causes – the manner of industrial mobilization, the creep in state power and the consolidation of Labour's grip on the domestic front – all indicated that political and doctrinal momentum still resided in the hands of ministers like Attlee, Bevin and Morrison. Labour remained prosperous. The chapter thus adds clarity to previous, unclear, judgements about the development of government policy. It also examines how decision-making interacted with what is now commonly termed political 'culture', particularly the presentation of leadership activity.

Despite this, the idea of coming out of the coalition – stemming from the view that Attlee had somehow failed his party – gathered force. It will be shown how the priority of defending the coalition became just as significant in the eyes of Attlee as advancing Labour's interests. His creative leadership began to take on the characteristics of a rearguard defensive action. The chapter also considers the way in which this brought about deep-seated changes in Attlee personally. This time the Lord Privy Seal sought to shore up the very structures of the cross-party alliance. For the next four years, it was he who took the lead in driving all attempts to protect the government against those who would bring it down. This was his major preoccupation. Oddly, that defence of the coalition has been almost entirely overlooked by historians keen to rush on to debates about social policy and, as before, neglecting the importance of leadership in reshaping political realities. Previous interpretations suffer from being suffused with 'Lib–Lab' certainties; but, as we have already seen, nothing was inevitable and everything was contingent. In neglecting the defence of the alliance, we overlook the trend that hints more than any other as to what wartime politics really 'meant' to its practitioners.

Looking for traction

Brooke fitted the mounting discord in the Labour Party into 'the long-running dialogue between loyalists and dissenters' in the party[3] – in other words, a 'left-wing versus right-wing' ideological struggle. Reality was more complex. The events of the war, no more than for any period, can be made to conform to a 'left–right' paradigm of recurrent ideological struggle. Quite the reverse, the pressures were new and unique. What had occurred since late 1940, with Bevan running attacks on the leadership and then Laski's undermining Attlee, was not the latest manifestation of a conflict between moderates and extremists but, like the activities of the leaders from 1939, a series of power-political struggles that cut various ways. Despite ideological language, it was about the maintenance and exercise of hard power by different individuals operating in multiple contexts and facing diverse horizons.

With tempers fraying all around him, in the first half of 1941 Attlee reverted to more sensitive methods of political management. This section draws out the interaction between political communication and leadership during that period. Trying to engender stability across both the government and Labour Party, the Deputy Prime Minister resumed his earlier practice of flying 'kites' with the now customary emphasis on policy statements, official literature and partisan declarations. In February and March 1941, Attlee gave two major public speeches on the theme of 'reconstruction'. In Tonypandy on 16 February, he once more used the heady rhetoric of socialist advance when he asserted that 'there can be no return to the prewar world' and declared that the government was engaged in a major restructuring of the country.[4] The following month at Glasgow, Attlee stressed that 'unity in the face of the enemy demands the suspension of party political strife, but this does not mean that people should give up considering political, social and economic questions, or that people should not publicly discuss such questions and state various points of view.'[5] As before, Attlee was attempting to mould political landmarks. It remains difficult to uphold the view that he still refused to give a lead. He was asserting a vigorous and consistent line at a time of Conservative exhaustion.

These methods had worked in the past, and were again utilized energetically at the top of the Labour movement over the subsequent months. In March the NEC published a new flagship policy document, *The Labour Party, the War and the Peace*.[6] Consisting of memoranda intended for submission to the annual conference, it reflected at length on the strengths of quasi-scientific economic 'planning' of the kind the coalition was adopting. It also made detailed proposals for social and economic reform, most of which – naturally – paralleled remarkably closely what the government was already doing, simply under the alternate terminology of 'socialism'.[7] The Labour ministers

> have been concerned to make their maximum contribution to the great task of winning the war as speedily and decisively as possible. At the same time they have done their utmost to lessen the heavy burden which war inevitably casts upon the workers and to preserve, and even enlarge, their rights. ... The area of the social services has been increased ... the standard of life has been well safeguarded ... in every sphere [Labour's] activities have done much to improve the provision for the safety and comfort of citizens. ... Finance is the servant, not the master, of political policy in wartime; it must continue in that relation when peace comes. ... Our great national resources are ... assets to be efficiently administered for victory; they must be similarly administered as we turn from war to peace.[8]

That was the sternest defence yet of the bridgehead occupied by Attlee and his colleagues. Attlee was to remind his followers of it repeatedly over the next four years. Just weeks later, in May 1941, the NEC published a second document, *Labour in the Government: A Record of Social Legislation in War Time*, which is worth dwelling on at some length.[9] This document was quite different in appearance from most other political publications of the era: rather than having a relatively plain front cover, it was unusually professional and featured nine photographs of prominent Labour ministers, a presentational device obviously intended to convey a sense of the status that these men enjoyed.[10] The document gives the impression that Attlee and his colleagues fully recognized that they now faced a much more challenging environment. Alongside the usual denunciations of the 1930s' National governments, it stressed the leading role the Labour ministers played in Britain's resistance to Hitler, asserting that this resistance represented 'a triumph of government' in which the party's representatives had taken an 'outstanding' part.[11] 'The government has transformed the war effort' in 'a great move forward'.[12] It went on to declare that 'there is general recognition, for the first time, of the vital power of the workers in the state. ... Persuasion is giving way to planning.'[13] Eight-and-a-half of the pamphlet's fourteen pages were devoted to detailed descriptions of legislation and reform extracted by the Labour ministers from the Conservatives – protection of workers' rights, compensation, increases in unemployment insurance and pensions, payments to servicemen's dependants and a minimum wage for agricultural workers were held up as examples. Continually underlining the ministers' role in all this, the document acknowledged that while the coalition, because it was an alliance, 'does not always do what any one party would like', nonetheless

> Labour in the government has fully justified itself. Labour ministers hold key offices, and are taking a full share in the direction of the war effort. Clem Attlee, leader of the party, shares with the Prime Minister the great responsibility of leading the country to victory and a successful peace.[14]

Thus, the coalition was to be properly understood as a 'triumph'. Then, at the party's annual conference at Westminster, the Labour ministers were still able to use their record in the coalition as their platform, and, backed by trade union bloc votes, deprived the recent dissension of a voice. Attlee gave a measured performance introducing a document on *The War*, and both it and its counterpart, *The Peace*, were passed by overwhelming majorities.[15]

The methods of appeal utilized in these examples point to the tactical consistency of the Labour ministers in adhering to an established script, but the second pamphlet, particularly, reinforced something else of note as well – the sense that the utility of such methods of communication was now being fully grasped at Transport House and by senior parliamentarians in a way they had never been before. Labour literature was becoming more overtly propagandist and less sober. Socialists, of course, have long adored writing; but the purposes of such communication seem to have evolved. There was less emphasis on persuasion. Addison may have been right to warn of the 'danger of exaggerating the significance of pamphlets and radio talks' in the realignment of broader public opinion;[16] the traumas of war provided ample justification for that. But such things suggest a great deal about the political world itself. What the connections were between advances in *government* communication for propaganda purposes, and parallel shifts in methods for *party* politics, is deserving of study in its own right. It seems difficult to believe that politicians failed to see the innovations in official communication across a range of media after 1939 and wonder about their applicability for other purposes.

The analytical narrative of preceding chapters has already established that Attlee was, contrary to myth, a central figure. It is worth pausing briefly to conduct a different kind of analysis – an investigation of his speech. The evolving character of his political appeals is in need of exploration, as is the changing nature of his vocabulary. This had significant 'real world' implications. As the situation before him worsened in 1941, the Lord Privy Seal returned to constantly emphasizing the theme of 'unity', just like earlier in the war. But in doing so his language began to change as well: in a short space of time it became not that of an exponent of partisan politics, but an articulation of moral, and even spiritual, values. This book is principally about political *action* rather than public statement. The former sphere is where we detect Attlee best. Moreover, Attlee was never a particularly skilled orator. We must be careful not to mistake him for something he was not, but 1941 is still interesting in respect of his public declarations. The sorts of values that Attlee was seeking to propound during the war were on show in his conference address, and that makes it worth examining at length. They tie into his later activities. Indeed, 'values', not 'ideology', is the right concept to explain the signals that Attlee had been trying to give off since 1939. Formal speeches and other orations are poorly utilized as a form of evidence;[17] to appreciate them – like appreciating the purposes of *all* political language – requires properly contextualized study. Certainly, parts of the Deputy Prime Minister's conference address employed a vocabulary that was, by now, the norm:

> We stand unbeaten, we stand stronger than ever before, we stand united as never before ... I do not suppose there was anyone who seriously imagined [when the coalition was formed] that in this last year we should see a great turning of the tide, that by some miracle ... we should overturn the enormous military machine brought against us. It is almost a miracle that we have not been overrun.[18]

Attlee's speech used the rhetoric of patriotism that had become the lingua franca of politics. But, critically, it also strayed into something else, something new:

> Spiritual forces are rising against Hitler ... there is a realization that Britain ... is the spearhead of democracy and civilization against barbarism. ... Let me say it is not very easy to mobilise a country organized for peace and turn it into a war machine, particularly when ... we wanted to avoid the evils of totalitarianism and keep the freedom of our people, when we know that our strength lies in the free spirit of our people. ... I say to you that looking back over the past twelve months, Britain has done a miracle. ...
>
> I think there is a realization now that this is a fight for spiritual values ... it is this that has brought us unity today in this country. ... That kind of unity is not something negative, it is positive; it is the acceptance by ordinary decent people of certain standards of value ... it is in this spiritual unity that we must build this new world, a new world whose watchword must be freedom and social justice. ... We are determined that in the future we shall not have poverty in the midst of plenty, we shall not have unemployment, we shall not have progress in a world full of potential wealth held up through lack of organization.[19]

The Deputy Prime Minister's language, calm and measured in contrast to Churchill's high-flown oratory, was no longer the characteristic, knock-about stuff of politics. It signified something else: it was deeper in tone, and almost visibly reverential about unity. In concentrating on the moral worthiness of pulling together, it was not the rhetoric of politics that Attlee was using, much less the flourish of partisanship; instead, it was the quiet language of common cause and hope for the future. The speech was largely depoliticized. This is what stands out the most. It was an attempt to make 'unity' carry a solemn appeal. Attlee was neither speaking in abstract theory nor sounding like a 'thinker', but calling instead on a richer imagery of distinctly British culture and values. More: these were the prevailing social values of pre-1945 Britain.[20] The ethos of hard work, respect and decency lurks within his address, not 'socialism'. This was an important development. Attlee had begun to take this new line earlier in 1941, as soon as the conditions facing politicians started to change.[21] Speaking at a Fabian Society luncheon in January, he declared that:

> Our victory in the war and in the peace … must not only be on a physical but on a spiritual plane … This [is] not a fight between forces contending for a larger share of the same thing … It [is] a fight between people … wanting different things which [are] inimical to each other.[22]

Likewise, *The Peace* had replicated this new tone to official declarations, talking of a 'national restoration' and 'equity' as being 'the central principle underlying the nation's war effort'. The document also affirmed that:

> Socialism asserts, as the Nazi faith denies, the intrinsic worth of man. By our determination to defeat the Nazi effort, we are making the human values for which socialism stands more clear and more compelling to millions of our fellow citizens … victory and reconstruction are indivisible, the spirit and the idea of the one are the spirit and idea of the other. … History has given us the opportunity to consecrate the sufferings of the world by fulfilling its hopes. That is the vision to which we must dedicate our lives.[23]

Though the effort to emphasize the moral value of 'unity' failed in its object of encouraging stability –Attlee was, in the end, just not that type of leader, neither a Churchill nor a Baldwin – analysis of the structure of his speeches at this point is still instructive of what he was trying to accomplish, and the sensibilities in which he wanted a political action to be framed. Moreover, despite its stress on non-party, national virtue, and its *depoliticized* texture, it was pre-eminently *political* in purpose: in a climate of instability, Attlee was utilizing a resonant vocabulary in a bid to restore calm. He was claiming these aspirations for the Labour Party as well.

It was also prescient given how things were to unravel. That Attlee deemed this line of discourse sufficiently powerful to anchor himself to it, is suggestive of something else that historians have consistently failed to appreciate. Wartime political 'culture' was about two things – the language and spirit of 'fair shares', and the language and spirit of patriotism. The first has received ample attention and been tied to the social-democratic reforms of the 1940s by historians keen to emphasize such things. The second, by contrast, has been largely overlooked yet was consistently crucial to public discourse.[24] That Attlee's whole political approach was grounded upon it should imply something significant. All measures, proposals and innovations had to be wrapped in the vocabulary of patriotism in order to get a hearing. It seems necessary to appreciate this to grasp the wider paradigm of political thought and assumption within which the events described here occurred.

Attlee's exertions were warmly welcomed by *The Times*, an editorial describing the conference address as 'a speech of real leadership' and displaying an understanding of national unity that was 'vigorous and indeed vital':[25]

> So much of the speech could have been made by any convinced and stalwart believer in the cause of freedom against Nazism. The leadership was rather in those passages where Mr Attlee, party leader notwithstanding, discerned, as an outcome of national unity in waging the war, an increasing national unity of resolution and purpose to win ... security ... at home. In these interlocked enterprises national unity should continue to be a great power. This line of argument led to an exposition of the meaning of national unity far removed from, and loftier than, the narrow ... view contained in *The Peace* ... [which] seems another way of saying that socialists will only consort with socialists. ... Not so Mr Attlee. The leader of the Labour Party has another conception and sees a [different kind of] national unity.[26]

But, in a brief sequel to his spat with Laski, Attlee still found traction in other – more conventional – ways too. After Morrison engineered his defeat at the hands of Laski – and confirmed the latter as not just an intellectual strutting the public stage but a high political protagonist of the Deputy Prime Minister in his own right – Attlee worked to recover the position on the NEC as much as he could. To this end, he set about trying to restrict the scope of Laski's officially sanctioned Reconstruction Committee to provoke trouble. That committee launched what was one of the most ambitious projects ever undertaken by a British party,[27] but in late June the Lord Privy Seal oversaw last minute changes to the membership of Laski's new body when it was decided that all members of the main NEC Policy Committee should be appointed members of the

Reconstruction scheme as well.[28] That placed Morrison in the awkward position of either having to endorse policies with which he did not really agree, or rebut proposals he had affected to support to undermine the leader. This was some reward for his labours. It was thus Attlee's turn to manoeuvre. At that same meeting, Morrison abruptly resigned his membership of the Policy Committee.[29] Why did he do this? The Home Secretary's explanation was that he no longer wished to be a member and would rather sit on the Elections Committee.[30] Yet, given that the Policy Committee was the key arena for developing and advertising new ideas – so central to Morrison's plans – this seems a slim justification; the obvious answer is that Morison recognized that Attlee had outmanoeuvred not only Laski but him as well. Managing both to tie Laski up in new knots and to turn Morrison's scheming against him, Attlee had the last word. With the worrying portents of just a few months earlier temporarily quietened, Attlee and his colleagues could reflect on what had been a prosperous phase in office. For the moment, the defence of the alliance was proceeding smoothly.

Exploring the limits of political action

But there was soon a new problem; by the middle of 1941 the impact of these methods turned out to be decidedly limited. With it, the scope for a 'positive' conception of leadership began to contract. Attlee and the rest of the Labour ministers were not miracle workers. They had performed exceedingly strongly in a number of respects over the preceding two years, but in 1941, they began to come up against real boundaries for the first time. As in the first two chapters, this section draws out the wider political context in which events occurred. The Conservatives began to get their act together, and Churchill discovered means of obstructing the Labour ministers, principally through Anderson, Kingsley Wood and his friend, the notorious press magnate, Lord Beaverbrook.

The situation facing Britain remained perilous. There was no socialist commonwealth; measures now had to be fought for. The slow progress on devising detailed plans for reform left the Labour ministers in something of a holding pattern, as far as the public face of politics went. And, as a result, the dissatisfaction of the Labour Party – ever present for a decade – returned with a vengeance. Historians have had difficulty finding clarity in their accounts of this particular period: neither Addison nor Jefferys managed to convey a clear direction to politics from 1941, shifting from exploring the radicalization of the intelligentsia to war mobilization to Labour and Conservative politics.[31] A definite texture remains elusive. This section steps back from the business of politics and maps instead the broader state of political tectonics. Yet two themes should be underlined at the outset: that for several reasons – Conservative recovery, the continued crises of war production – in some areas the Labour ministers now found it tougher to advance social democracy; but also that the direction of events remained very much in Labour's favour and the Conservative Party still woefully demoralized.

Making speeches was one thing, but Attlee needed to win something. In the approach to the conference, he tried to extract from the Prime Minister a pledge to repeal the Trade Disputes Act – universally loathed by Britain's trade unions – as a symbol of the coalition's credentials. Comparing the act with a 'Brest–Litovsk Peace', Attlee sent Churchill a long letter in which he argued for repeal on the grounds of conciliating the unions.[32] Yet Churchill resolutely refused to budge. The Conservatives would have been up in arms if the Prime Minister acquiesced; but still, the refusal constituted his first significant rebuff to Attlee. Then, in July 1941, growing pressure from the Labour Party to take Britain's railways formally into state ownership began to damage Attlee's authority. He and the Labour ministers had been fighting stubbornly within the Cabinet for nationalization of the disorganized and unprofitable industry, Attlee personally pushing a recommendation for public ownership through the Lord President's Committee twice that month.[33] In another memorandum, 'The Railways and the War', Attlee linked the need for an efficient rail network to the management of war production.[34] He said that the current system was 'fundamentally unsound', and connected public ownership to future reform: 'all forms of transport must be used as an instrument of reconstruction schemes after the war.'[35] Anderson drew up a summary of Attlee's arguments, the Deputy Prime Minister trying his familiar trick of appealing for a policy in the spirit of 'statesmanship': 'The Lord Privy Seal also urges that railway nationalization has been for many years put forward by the Labour Party, and that it is not unreasonable that Labour, as a partner in the Government, should desire that some part of its programme should be implemented.'[36] Despite his best efforts, the War Cabinet took its cue from Anderson's contrary recommendation and Attlee was overruled .[37] After a second rebuff over an issue of symbolic value, Attlee found himself exposed on the front – control of the means of production – where his strategy was most vulnerable.

Consequently, in the autumn, for the first time the Labour Party registered a formal criticism of the government, the NEC expressing its 'profound dissatisfaction' with the decision not to nationalize.[38] Pethick-Lawrence broke with the coalition on the floor of Parliament by putting down a PLP motion advocating outright public ownership of the railways and attacking the current policy of informal state influence as a 'half-way house' and the 'worst of both worlds'.[39] He called for other industries to be brought under 'the full control and ownership of the nation' as well.[40]

That language constituted a significant shift from that to which politics had become accustomed. It signified growing discontent with the public presentation of government policy. To be sure, Whitehall had been remodelled and innumerable schemes and investigations set up about reform; but this was not enough to satiate a Labour movement impatient for more emphatic public measures. Once again, walking the line between remoulding the state and the bitterness of party politics was proving Attlee's greatest challenge.

The Labour ministers encountered obstruction elsewhere as well. Greenwood's much vaunted Cabinet Reconstruction Committee swiftly turned out to lack real power, and was tasked only with coordinating the work of different ministries. Unsurprisingly, a 'grandiose'[41] memorandum drawn up by Greenwood back in February – proposing to examine subjects as diverse as foreign trade, employment, educational reform and town and country planning – came to nothing.[42] And the Conservatives gradually began to dispel the impression of a disorganized mob. As Chancellor, Wood proved a significant opponent to many of Labour's schemes. Though he quickly became heavily influenced by the economist John Maynard Keynes – for who the war was the first opportunity systematically to test his theories – Wood held fast to many orthodox ideas; he was unpopular among the Labour ministers for attempting, throughout 1941, to introduce statutory wage restraints to combat inflation.[43] Richard Whiting was correct in noting that the Labour members of the coalition were not central to the making of financial policy; Keynes was far more significant in that respect.[44] It was Keynes and Wood then, after Wood's death in 1943, Keynes and Anderson who were the principal actors in shaping finance.[45]

Another playing this anti-Labour 'spoiler role' was Anderson. As Lord

President, following Chamberlain's death, Anderson was an administrator *par excellence* – as well as effectively being a Conservative despite his non-party 'National' label. With his experiences in India and Ireland having familiarized him with the business-like exercise of power, by 1941 Anderson was establishing his own grip on the machinery of state.[46] He performed another key task alongside Bevin in manpower planning. A conscious effort was now being mounted by the Conservative leadership to recover the position it had ceded. In early 1941, Churchill told Anderson that it was 'essential that the larger issues of economic policy should be dealt with by [the Lord President's Committee] *and primarily by you*'.[47] The Prime Minister ordered Anderson 'not to hesitate to take the initiative over the whole field. You should summon economists like Keynes to give their views to you personally. … *I wish you to take the lead prominently and vigorously in this committee.*'[48] This can only be read as a desire for much greater influence over those 'larger issues' to be exercised by non-Labour individuals. It was not unreasonable to take the view – as most Conservatives did – that Attlee and his colleagues had hitherto largely been permitted a free run.

The idea that Labour ran into the sand in 1941 is a key part of the image propagated by Addison and others that the Labour ministers were overawed in their first years in office, did not perform well, and it took a long while for them to make an impact. Of course, the other component woven into that narrative is that it was not until the increasing radicalization of the electorate and intelligentsia – as well as the ascendancy of Liberal intellectuals like Keynes and William Beveridge – reshaped the environment *for* them, that the party's representatives came to exercise real influence. Think, for instance, of Keynes: occupying a room at the Treasury, he was central to the reform of government budgets, as well as the need to control the allocation of materials; he also produced his famous tract, *How to Pay for the War*.[49] Meanwhile, much to Churchill's bemusement, it was a Conservative, Rab Butler, who got to work on educational reform in 1941.[50] That individuals from all ends of the spectrum were now partaking in 'reform' and planning for 'the future' is where much of the force behind the 'consensus' thesis originates. According to this narrative, Attlee and his colleagues – the beneficiaries of the reconfiguration – often appear as passive observers. The bureaucratic slog and confrontations of 1941 and 1942 might be taken, implicitly, to confirm that. But it is a mistake. Political opinion is dependent on grand gestures, but historians should not be. We must not overlook the real movements in underlying tectonics or the changes in the content of political discourse.

Precisely *because* it no longer had to take the form of public gestures, the idea of a triumph for Labour doctrines is all the more convincing in this period. As the issue was in many cases now principally about the practical implementation of these measures, the great leap forward that Labour had made since 1939 should scarcely need stressing. A better guide to the state of affairs might be offered by contemporary Conservative observation. In May 1940 Butler complained that Chamberlain and Halifax 'weakly surrendered to a half-breed American' and his 'rabble'; this was 'a disaster' – 'the pass had been sold'.[51] Things did not improve thereafter. Indeed, Conservative disillusionment grew markedly over the remainder of 1941. For instance, the chairman of the 1922 Committee of backbenchers told Amery that 'the feeling of restlessness in our party is getting very acute' because the rank and file 'did not feel that there was anyone inside the Cabinet who stood for the Conservative point of view at all'.[52] An attempt to call a party conference was blocked.[53] For his part, Headlam recorded that the Conservatives were 'quite futile and useless' and 'never do anything or act together in any way with the result that the party is ceasing to exist'.[54] The private communications and thought-world of Conservatives reveal a mood of profound despondency; the country was being refashioned before their eyes and they could do little about it. The Conservative ministers might have been getting their act together, to some extent at least. But their party remained, as Headlam put it, 'an inert mass'.[55] Meanwhile, over the five years of coalition, Attlee himself acted as Prime Minister for at least six months while Churchill was abroad. He took to the role with élan. For instance, while he was deputizing for Churchill in August 1941, John Colville recorded that Attlee 'kept ringing up to know whether there are any papers for him to sign, like a child with a new toy it is longing to use'.[56]

There is more. State interference in industry and the economy continued to grow rapidly throughout 1941; the powers of government were expanding. Licensing for manufacturing and building, as well as control of the workforce, confirmed it. The British state found a hitherto unused gear. It was, moreover, now being accepted across the spectrum. 'The possibility of controlling the economy, which was at the heart of Labour's thinking, had been strikingly confirmed by wartime government.'[57] Wood's 1941 Budget, the 'critical one of the war', heavily reflected Keynes's influence in devising new means of paying for the conflict far removed from the Conservative tradition.[58] That the economic views of Labour's own senior figures evolved from seeing nationalization as a cure-all to a preference for more limited public ownership, or the growing recognition of the advantages of supplementing planning with Keynesian demand management, does not alter this. It is true that some of the great changes in Labour's favour documented in the previous year were not matched in this period. But that is only true of the *public* face of politics. In the *private* dimension of that world, there continued to be enacted a large number of reforms that, in truth, had far greater substance than the sometimes rhetorical innovations made in 1940. If anything, all that changed was the tone in which they were presented: there was less talk of new Jerusalems. The measures won now actually had to be carried out; mobilization and production needed to be overseen and improved day by day. Bottlenecks and shortages still hindered efficiency.[59] It was a time for governance, not further linguistic innovation. But administrative innovation was constant as 'planning' became entrenched at the heart of the state. Labour's doctrines were being translated into real-world activity.

The role played by Bevin was central. For instance, he was successful in opposing direct control of wages despite fierce opposition from the Conservatives and Whitehall, which feared industrial anarchy and, particularly, runaway inflation.[60] Leaving the way clear for unions and employers to work out their own agreements was a major victory for the Labour ministers – if one that could not be publicly claimed. March 1941 saw the introduction of the Essential Work Order to keep people in a job.[61] 'Working in the dark',[62] Bevin and his department had seen a growth of three-quarters of a million new workers in munitions and one million new personnel in the armed forces since May 1940.[63] Bevin's sole concern, as he put it, was 'the winning of the war'.[64] His department and the Lord President's Committee were discovering ever more sophisticated tools for 'planning' an economy, its industry and workforce. The allocation of manpower and resources was now being directed for the next 12 months rather than stop-gap measures targeted at the threat of German invasion. Bevin, particularly, was in his element when grappling with a mass of detail; no government minister matched his ability in this regard. He wielded 'powers undreamed of in the philosophy of any previous British minister',[65] was one of the few individuals who knew his department as well as the permanent officials did,[66] and, in Attlee's words, he became 'a national leader'.[67] In their battles over production, Bevin proved more than a match for Beaverbrook, who was Minister of Aircraft Production up to April 1941 and then, from June, Minister of Supply.[68] His department 'achieved ... greatness' during 1941, becoming 'the keystone of the war effort' in Britain.[69] An Oxford economist, one Harold Wilson, acted as secretary of the Manpower Requirements Committee.

These developments represented the most important series of innovations on the domestic front between 1940 and 1945. As such, the shape of politics here is beginning to come into focus. It confirmed the decisive political swing to Labour; yet it continued to resemble plain common sense as well, the most practical means of achieving mobilization. That this has not previously been absorbed seems attributable to a failure by historians to see past public presentation and peer beneath the surface. It represented the sort of 'planning' the Labour leaders had been aiming at for years. Headlam believed that the party 'are trying ... to utilize the war as a means of introducing socialism'.[70] And in the intellectual context of the time, the concept of the 'plan' meant only one thing – socialism. 'You are not firms, you are merely a branch of the national effort,' Bevin told an audience of businessmen;[71] 'individualism is bound to give place to social action.'[72] As Bullock noted, 'it was a mark of the changes which were ... taking place in Britain that a member of the War Cabinet could talk like this.'[73] Headlam complained of 'our overlords – the TUC people', whom he feared were aiming to be 'as powerful as Parliament'.[74] Hyperbole aside, even a sober view of these developments confirms the validity of Conservative anxiety. Despite Churchill's attempt to harness Anderson, Wood, Beaverbrook and even Keynes to fence Labour off from key policy areas, the balance of political advantage showed no signs of altering. Anderson, for instance, was judged by Eden to be 'a good committee man, but zero in Cabinet'.[75] Formidable difficulties in managing the war effort remained – not least because Bevin still tried to exercise his powers with moderation until the end of 1941 – but this did not alter the reality of the situation.

Thus, for all the challenges of this period, the second phase of Labour's advance already resembled another success. Events here underline the value of the position constructed under Attlee's direction in the preceding two years. The Labour ministers enjoyed real credibility, had undiminished power to instigate policy and lead reform, and also displayed that most important of political attributes, resilience. If there is a lesson to learn, it is that serious politics was now occurring privately, behind closed doors, not publicly. The Labour ministers no longer talked; they governed. Their influence in the areas on which they focused – which were largely those that interested them in the first place – far outstripped that of the Conservatives. This extended from industry to social policy, where Labour's suzerainty was just as marked. For instance, in May 1941 the Ministry of Health set up a wide-ranging investigation to explore how social insurance could be improved in the future.[76] Bevin, eager to get the antagonizing Beveridge out of the Ministry of Labour, persuaded Greenwood to make Beveridge the head of this new body.[77] Greenwood 'at once saw the opportunity which had come his way. He inspired Fleet Street to write up the committee as the harbinger of social security for all.'[78] By the end of the year, Beveridge had drawn up the first outline of his famous report that would change Britain forever.[79] Though Attlee and his colleagues were not intricately involved in finance, their influence was firmly consolidated over social, industrial and mobilization issues. By the end of 1941, the Ministry of Labour had passed the National Service Act through Parliament, which did much to resolve the remaining impediments to mobilization and set Britain on the path to a greatly improved war effort in 1942.[80] As the authors of an official history commented of Bevin's National Service Bill, with its passage

> the system was in all its essentials complete. It was a system which demanded for the state the services of men and women on a scale that Britain's totalitarian enemies never dared ask of their own people. Nevertheless, it was founded upon a rock; for it had carried with it the consent of the nation.[81]

Around the same time, with many of the new factories completed and production ready for expansion, Bevin began using his powers to move the workforce around the country more readily.[82] Compelling everybody aged between 18 and 60 to engage in national service and, particularly, finding older men to carry out non-combatant duties in the military so that younger women could be utilized in industry, proved the key.[83] Anyway, any individual areas of policy aside, the Labour ministers' general political ascendancy was unmistakeable. Attlee got Churchill to agree to create new Labour peers (thus enhancing the party's limited representation in the House of Lords) as 'an act of state'.[84] The Lord President's Committee behaved increasingly as if it were the Cabinet for domestic politics and, in Bullock's view, through it 'Britain came nearer than at any other time in its history to having an effective instrument for planning.'[85]

Brooke, by contrast, has written of the leadership's failure to obtain serious change on the economic front between 1940 and 1943, of 'barren achievements', and of 'the difference between rhetoric and reality'.[86] If anything, 'the difference between rhetoric and reality' was the *reverse* of what he meant: the rhetoric was not socialist, and framed in terms not of a grand cause but a targeted legislative response to conditions, but the reality was a triumph for Labour's priorities. It was *they* who had created the political paradigm in the first place in which these and subsequent events occurred. This has not always been appreciated. In capturing the home front so effectively in 1940, and acquiring many of Whitehall's levers, the Labour ministers fashioned a new framework in which government policy, and even *thinking* about policy, had to be conducted.

The adverse shift in the political weather hints once more at the centrality of language in public life. If Attlee and his colleagues had been free to dress up the things they were doing – which, after all, already represented the biggest series of reforms for a generation – as 'socialism', their party would most likely have been in raptures; only the most impatient could have quibbled. Yet, because they avoided doctrinal terminology and passed it off as incremental 'common sense', it stimulated disillusionment. Moreover, public support for vigorous state intervention was well consolidated.[87] Labour's position was now transformed from its sorry state before the war. Jefferys correctly observed that, contrary to appearances, 'the Conservative Party had been pushed more and more on the defensive.'[88] That, for instance, Keynes and Beveridge were Liberals should not mask the Labour ministers' success. The differences between Liberal and Labour instincts on social policy were minimal. Anyway, much of the legend of Keynes and Beveridge can be attributed to their talent for self-promotion. But even men like Keynes and Beveridge were playing in what had become Labour's sandpit. These developments in government thinking allowed Labour policy for the remainder of the war, and then in the Attlee regime, to pursue an integrative approach rather than a sectional one; think of Attlee's conference speech examined earlier. To understand it properly, it must be recognized that it was not the product of an ethereal 'consensus' but of a wider political realignment in which Attlee and his colleagues had played the leading role.

Still, while the importance of these developments might be evident at a distance of six decades, in 1941 not everyone agreed. Frustration continued to articulate itself. Soon this was believed to pose serious risks. Bevan openly attacked Attlee and Bevin for not delivering formal measures of nationalization and charged them with failing 'a test of will and courage' over the railways.[89] He accused the Labour ministers of 'working against the public interest' and declared that the leaders 'have allowed themselves to be manoeuvred into a weak position'; the party should consider whether to 'regain its independence'.[90] Bevan also called for the government to be 'wholly reconstructed'.[91] The ambitious Welshman's customary splenetic tone aside, Bevan was expressing disillusionment felt by many. For his part, Laski – via his NEC project – constantly assailed Attlee and the rest of the ministers both privately and in the press ('Don't Keep Us Waiting, Clem') with yet more calls for nationalizations, the implementation of reconstruction schemes *during* the war, and a confrontation with the Conservatives on the issue of immediate socialist reform.[92] That the activities of men like Laski and Bevan represented the continuation of vendettas and self-advertisement did not alter their destabilizing impact. James Chuter Ede, a Labour minister at Education, noted that the entire party was 'restless' with the direction of its leadership.[93] Ede had already identified parallels between the ministers' current exposure and the regicide of 1931.[94]

The ill temper was sufficiently widespread that even Attlee came under fire at the TUC conference in October over the old issue of 'peace aims'.[95] Confronted by a hostile audience, while he boasted of the Labour ministers' effectiveness in office that 'the principles for which the trade unions have fought throughout their history have now been recognized as … fundamental to civilization', more significantly Attlee was also decidedly unapologetic in tone, stressing that while the Cabinet did take reconstruction seriously, nonetheless the government was 'engaged in seeing that the ship weathers the storm'.[96] With the scars on his back from a year in high office, Attlee was now increasingly unbending in response to criticism. This was significant. The previous month, he had implied that the notion of an assault on the continent to relieve the Russians was 'stupid' and nothing more than a 'futile' gesture: 'we will give all we can to

Russia, but remember, it has to come out of our own production, which is not yet adequate for our own needs.'[97]

The complaints might betray an element of wishful thinking about precisely what Labour *should* be achieving, but whatever the advances made in the coalition, Attlee's leadership was unquestionably having less of an effect in the sphere of party politics. Stability was proving elusive as the tone of public life altered drastically. These were worrying harbingers. The attempt to create fresh political breathing space had failed, and, in increasingly fraught conditions, all the elements were present for an explosion of some sort. There was a parallel – and deep-seated – change occurring in Attlee himself. There were already clear indications of this. The previous chapters showed how the reticent leader of the 1930s gave way to a decisive figure capable of having a major impact on the political world. Now another layer to Attlee's leadership evolved – a tougher, more intransigent side. He would need it.

Defending the alliance

Attlee plainly thought that all this presented certain imperatives. As a result, in the autumn of 1941 he led an attempt to renavigate the political waterways. In doing so, he added the political 'stick' to his existing proficiency with the 'carrot'. Attlee's reaction was not another bout of preaching the virtues of national unity, but a quite different initiative: it was a bid to strengthen the very structures of the cross-party alliance. The Deputy Prime Minister's object was to tie his party inextricably to the coalition and render it impossible for Labour to deviate from his assigned course. It is worth stressing that it was Attlee himself who instigated this departure from previous norms, and he who took the lead in implementing it. He began to move his party beyond the boundaries of the electoral truce established in 1939 and the coalition agreements of 1940. Moreover, it sowed the seeds of something bigger. Attlee's activities here were to prove the first of numerous, similar, measures over the next four years that would eventually set him against the Labour movement in advocating maintaining the coalition when the war was over.

There is another problem. The importance of this sequence of events – much less Attlee's centrality in it – has never been properly analysed. It is possible, however, to link them together into a new narrative of political decision-making from 1941 to 1945 that reveals a great deal. Attlee's decision to revise the electoral agreements that provided the basis for the government was given impetus by a trend of mounting opposition from the Labour movement to the by-election truce. Many saw no reason why the parties could not compete against one another when parliamentary seats fell vacant. In particular, rank-and-file hostility to the truce remained visceral.[98] In this situation, rather than retreating Attlee actually tried to *extend* the arrangement even further. In September 1941, he approached Churchill and suggested that the by-election truce ought to be buttressed by a more emphatic statement of the alliance between the main parties than had been the case hitherto.[99] Attlee proposed the introduction of a joint 'statement of support' for all coalition candidates at by-elections signed by the Prime Minister, Attlee, and the Liberal leader Sinclair.[100] This would be issued to anyone backed by the government, regardless of their individual party affiliation.[101] The suggestion was ambiguous, yet clear in its implications. In effect, the idea amounted to a political 'coupon' – although everyone studiously avoided that phrase– to lock the truce into place. 'Coupon' politics were widely thought to have had a pernicious influence on public life in 1918, and Labour also suffered from lacking the 'National' ticket in 1931; as such, this new measure had to be framed in a different, more neutral, terminology.

Despite the bland language, we ought not to overlook the significance of Attlee's proposition. It marked an important tactical shift. It hints at the fluidity of a politics that at first sight appeared quite static for five years. If nothing else, it demonstrated Attlee's willingness to bind the two main parties ever closer together as a means of controlling them. The appearance of disloyalty could provoke even the tolerant Churchill into a snap general election, and it remained difficult to see where the Labour Party stood independently in public opinion right up until July 1945. That was the larger, strategic question beneath the surface. Establishing a standardized, formal appeal as the practice for by-elections would create something that Labour could only break with at its peril. As such, the significance of the measure – and those that followed – should be properly absorbed. Warnings of what might happen if Labour was foolish enough to precipitate the collapse of the coalition were to prove Attlee's primary means of enforcing his authority over the next four years. Just as he had at the outbreak of war, Attlee was threatening his party with the fatal spectre of appearing 'irresponsible' unless it followed him.

Unsurprisingly, Churchill agreed to the idea immediately and Attlee put it to the NEC the same day.[102] Historians may have missed its symbolic significance, but the inner councils of the Labour movement grasped it fully. There it met heavy resistance – including from many on the executive who generally supported Attlee but were now sceptical about revising the existing arrangements.[103] It conflicted with assumptions about political identity derived from the experience of the 1930s. Despite this, though, after a row Attlee's proposition was accepted – albeit only by thirteen votes to ten.[104]

What had happened? Attlee's by-election 'coupon' laid deeper foundations for the coalition than had existed previously. Through his earlier stress on the virtues of national unity, and now this fresh electoral measure, Attlee was attempting to define a new political centre ground and to anchor his party in it. This consisted of the values of hard work, decency and 'unity', with the coalition government as its political expression. It was a means for Attlee to conceptualize and defend the political experience in which he and his colleagues were engaged. It made sense as well. Cross-party fluidity had marked the previous 25 years; it was the norm, no matter how much the 'losers' in a particular instance derided it. We must remember this if we are to understand how Attlee and other leaders sought to reframe politics over the next few years. What we need to realize, then, is that this was not about *public* persuasion or communicating with 'the people', but about the *private* persuasion of – and attempts to control – the smaller world of Westminster and the political parties. Recognition of that further reinforces the value of thinking about 'leadership' as an explanatory instrument. The by-election proposal is another instance where Attlee's somewhat languid style, and characteristically light touch – leaving few fingerprints – engenders misinterpretation.

Far from being static, then, politics after 1939 required constant maintenance; in addition to his other roles, Attlee acted as head groundsman. This development also suggests much about Attlee's changing leadership: forcing Labour still deeper into its alliance with the Conservative Party hardly alleviated the mood of the disaffected. As he became more experienced in government, the Deputy Prime Minister displayed a growing willingness simply to ignore the wishes of the Labour movement if he deemed it appropriate. The by-election proposal was an elastic one: over the next few years, Attlee sought to stretch it again and again. It thus marked the beginning of a new era of political possibilities. In late 1941, Attlee's authoritarian tendencies – only intermittently visible before – were much clearer.

Let us return to events. This latest measure was all very statesmanlike, but new pressures crowded in. The government was still in danger of looking miserly. As things turned out, the defining moment in the rupture between the now distinct spheres of government and party came in early December 1941, when Labour MPs erupted in an outcry after Bevin's National Service Bill failed to include the public ownership of key industries. On 2 December, Bevin was confronted at a PLP meeting by a resolution from the Administrative Committee declaring that the nationalization of railways, coal and munitions ought to be an 'essential' part of government policy.[105] Attlee was unable to square this particular circle. Though he and Bevin had, once again, fought their Cabinet colleagues for public ownership,[106] when faced with this revolt they now gave a characteristic display of solidarity with the Conservatives.[107] Bevin even told the PLP that he was 'unconvinced' that nationalization would have any benefit.[108] Attlee, meanwhile, argued that public ownership could not become government policy without a general election mandate,[109] as well as stressing that while the coalition would take 'all necessary steps' in the prosecution of the war, 'ideological considerations were ruled out'.[110] It was another stern rejection of the Labour Party's complaints, but Ede deemed it 'ineffective': many MPs had evidently determined to oppose the bill come what may.[111] The next day, Attlee made one last attempt to avoid a public split, threatening that he and his colleagues would not go on in government unless the PLP backed them, but this desperate plea was seen through as the bluff it was.[112]

Parliament met on 4 December. More than a third of the PLP abstained in the House of Commons and 36 Labour MPs – a fifth of the total – rebelled, voting outright against the National Service Bill.[113] It had been building all year as overtly 'socialist' measures were rejected time and again. Ede feared that the government might collapse and that the withdrawal of Labour's support from the coalition was likely.[114] An authoritarian rant from Morrison against the rebellion, meanwhile, indicated the contrast between his efforts to aid Laski against Attlee earlier in the year and his true position now that the coalition was actually in danger, with some MPs openly 'light-hearted' at the prospect of 'bringing the government down'.[115]

'I do not think we are entitled to go on with Mr Churchill'

As 1942 dawned, then, all was changed. Labour was in disarray. To that, add the likelihood of more big revolts in the future. It is worth reiterating that similar problems were still being encountered within the Conservative Party. Amery noted that 'there [is] considerable regret … that Winston had been made leader of the party for it deprived the party of someone who could speak on its behalf to Winston and stand up to him.' [116] Channon recorded his view that Churchill had 'lost the House', and thought that democracy was 'slowly committing suicide'.[117] The parallels are striking and indicate that the real problem was that both sets of MPs were bored. They had been called upon to do very little for two whole years.

Difficulties continued to lurk. First, in December, Lees-Smith suddenly passed away,[118] and Attlee – again occupied with running the country for several weeks while Churchill went to Washington after Japan's attack on Pearl Harbor – put Pethick-Lawrence in his place.[119] Yet, his stint only lasted a matter of weeks. In early February, Churchill, back in the country, caused a crisis of the first order when he undertook a Cabinet reshuffle and sacked the ineffectual Greenwood from the government altogether. The decision, politically, was tone deaf; with many taking it as confirmation of another failure to respect Labour's interests, it was a turning point on the wider political scene. Frustration turned into outright hysteria. Within months, an enraged Labour Party almost voted to discontinue the electoral truce. While the fact that Attlee did not move to save Greenwood might be thought telling, the latter's dismal performance since May 1940 did little to mollify MPs.[120] At the next PLP meeting Attlee simply took the chair himself, shunted Pethick-Lawrence aside and appointed Greenwood as the new acting chairman.[121] Once again democracy was notable only in its absence.

The Cabinet reshuffle hardly weakened Labour: in fact, it produced a further extension of Labour's influence, with Attlee now formally confirmed as Deputy Prime Minister and made the Secretary of State for the Dominions, though this carried few departmental responsibilities and he continued to act as a roving administrator. He also retained his seat on the Lord President's Committee.[122] Stafford Cripps – having served as ambassador to Moscow, receiving plaudits for crafting the Anglo–Russian alliance that really should have gone to Hitler – replaced Attlee as Lord Privy Seal, a boost despite his officially remaining outside the party. Dalton, meanwhile, became President of the Board of Trade, and there were few signs elsewhere of Conservative reassertion. In early 1942, Attlee was largely responsible for fresh progress on the Indian issue as the new chairman of the Cabinet India Committee,[123] while he and Bevin also vetoed Churchill's plan to make Beaverbrook – the new Minister of Production – overlord of the entire economic front. Attlee – not about to concede primacy over home policy to the Conservatives – warned Churchill in no uncertain terms that Bevin would resign if Beaverbrook was granted such an important post; the matter was promptly dropped, and Beaverbrook himself quit the government in protest.[124] Although Anderson remained powerful and the Conservatives successfully excluded Labour from finance, this was Churchill's last attempt to recapture lost domestic territory.

Any reasonable observer might thus be expected to concede that, at the beginning of 1942, the Labour ministers stood at the apex of their influence. But not everyone agreed. As we have seen, Harold Laski was far from being reasonable when it came to Attlee. He had already told his wife that Labour would make no progress 'until we blow Attlee up'.[125] Greenwood's dismissal created the opportunity Laski had been looking for to initiate a second major confrontation with the Deputy Prime Minister. This, even more than the PLP revolt, was the most significant row of the period. In March, on the pretence of protesting about Greenwood's sacking, Laski wrote to senior parliamentarians and openly questioned Attlee's suitability for the top job, urging the necessity of finally resolving the 'leadership issue'.[126] He desperately badgered Morrison, Dalton ('the only viable alternative'),[127] and even Bevin (telling the Minister of Labour that he was 'easily the most outstanding figure in the Labour Party', and 'a fighting leader' who should become 'the first man')[128] in trying, unsuccessfully, to pressurize them to move against Attlee. Laski contended that Labour's stature in the coalition had been fatally compromised, suggested that the party would be excluded from reconstruction planning, and asked why this had been allowed to occur – a barb unmistakeably directed at Attlee.[129] The underlying plot was the same as a year earlier. The maverick confessed that he aimed to exploit the furore over Greenwood to precipitate the wider collapse of Attlee's strategy, which would then 'give me a chance of fighting [at the annual 1942 conference] for our exit from the government'.[130]

Laski's priorities seem to suggest that sheer personal antagonism motivated his actions. The feud with Attlee had now come to dominate his career, but Laski managed to find a more profitable angle of attack just a fortnight later when, in late March, he decided to target Attlee publicly as a failure in the *New Statesman*.[131] Then, in a keynote speech to the Society of Labour candidates, he told an audience of prospective MPs that 'the net result of Mr Attlee's leadership was to keep Labour united with its historic enemy ... it was a betrayal of democracy.'[132] This was an overt public attack and, in a private letter to the leader, he accused Attlee of 'surrender'.[133] In early April, Laski followed this up by submitting a bitter indictment of Attlee's entire political approach in the form of a ten-point memorandum ahead of a meeting that had been called between the NEC and the leader.[134] It was not unusual for Attlee to meet the NEC; but what made this particular session unusual was that disillusionment was so widespread that Laski was able to lever it into an inquiry into Attlee's leadership.

Though Laski asserted in the memorandum that 'no personal consider-ations [*vis-à-vis*] Mr Attlee' had informed his actions,[135] coming mere days after his attack on Attlee to the parliamentary candidates, this was an obvious untruth. Nevertheless, it was a wounding assault and the clearest articulation yet made of an alternative to Attlee's position. In a bitter critique of everything that Attlee had done in the preceding two and a half years, Laski declared that the rank and file were 'gravely perturbed' by the 'drift' and 'inaction' that was favoured by ministers and charged that Labour was 'being dragged along at the tail of the Conservative Party'.[136] Alleging a 'failure' by the ministers to secure adequate reformist legislation, Laski wrote that 'in return for a handful of social reforms, none of them fundamental in character, we are assisting the vested interests of this country ... not a single measure has been taken by this government which offsets this belief.'[137] 'The immense support the movement has brought to Mr Churchill has not resulted in any measures for the future of the workers. ... Mr Churchill has conceded very little to us that he would not have been compelled to concede had we remained in Opposition.'[138] Directly challenging Attlee's public strategy of accommodation, Laski asserted that 'I do not think it is an answer to ... say that coalition government is a process of give and take. I suggest that on all the fundamental matters we do all the giving and the Tories do all the taking.'[139] He went on to demand that 'steps must be taken [to implement socialism] *before* the cessation of hostilities.'[140]

The core of the argument, then, was that Attlee had led the party into deep trouble. Laski might have failed to distinguish between the public and private worlds of politics, but he was clearly now willing, and able, to go much further than in the past and confront Attlee directly. His NEC berth and the reconstruction investigation bestowed on him a powerful credibility in the years prior to 1945. In its conclusion, Laski's memorandum proposed the end of the electoral truce as well, unambiguously declaring that 'I do not think we are entitled to go on with Mr Churchill' and calling for the NEC to formulate a 'minimum programme' of reform that should be demanded from the Prime Minister: it was a 'solemn duty ... to then stick to that programme at all costs. If it be said that this risks the breakup of the government we must take that risk.'[141]

Laski had proclaimed that Attlee's stewardship had failed; the implication of this, which his private communications confirm, was that Labour needed a new leader. Greenwood's sacking was no more than a vehicle to proclaim this. Yet, when the NEC convened on 9 April, Attlee's answer signified the development of his own political style. Despite Laski's perfunctory disclaimer, it was perfectly clear who the attack was directed against, and the minutes of the session begin simply with the statement that 'the chairman suggested that Mr Attlee should give his views regarding Mr Laski's Memorandum.'[142] Attlee – as always unable to keep his cool when grappling with his *bête noire* – launched a counter barrage of his own. In a powerful riposte, Attlee accused Laski of political naivety and ignoring the 'fundamental facts' of the situation, in that Labour was vastly outnumbered by the Conservatives, and hence outright 'socialism' was unfeasible.[143] The Deputy Prime Minister also again made clear that there was no public majority for a 'socialist policy' and pointed out that a wartime general election was impracticable anyway.[144]

Pouring scorn on Laski's proposition that the Conservatives should be confronted with a choice between submitting to blackmail or the collapse of the coalition, Attlee again raised the spectre of electoral rout in threatening that, if Labour pulled out of the government 'when things looked black', the party would be perceived as having run away from its duty with 'disastrous' consequences in an election – 'we should be out of it.'[145] He warned that 'the effect of the continual decrying of the Cabinet had already been extremely damaging.'[146] It was an uncompromising stance. Characteristically defiant, Attlee yet again rejected the notion that the formal nationalization of industry was necessary and declared that 'it [is] not true to say ... that Labour was doing all the "giving" and the Tories all the "taking". The Tories [hold] the other point of view.'[147]

It was a bruising encounter, the most open political street fight since May 1940. Attlee's pursuit of retribution underlines how far Labour's leader had come in three years, the meek figure of the 1930s emphatically banished to the past. As well as his personal loathing for Laski, we should also see his defiance in the context of his earlier work on the government's foundations. This, alongside the remoulding of the state and Attlee's own concern with 'unity', signified the birth of a very different national politics. Moreover, 'the people' had not brought it about, and the Conservatives were prostrate. That conclusion is admittedly reflective of studying politics in terms of the impact of individual actors instead of 'policies', 'processes', or 'ideas'. But when analysed in this way, Attlee's importance becomes still clearer the further we proceed.

After Attlee's speech, the 'general feeling' of a divided NEC was that, while there was much dissatisfaction with the government's measures, the breakup of the coalition would be 'disastrous'.[148] Attlee had won. Yet he had not settled the underlying issues. As over the unpopular by-election 'coupon', the Deputy Prime Minister – lacking any more positive means of persuasion – was only able to get his way by an open appeal to self-preservation. Laski impotently fumed that 'if you don't want to give a lead, get out and give way to someone who will,'[149] but, regardless of the failure to destroy Attlee's position, the episode had come to exemplify the new disunity of national politics.

Conclusion

It seems worthwhile to attempt an interim assessment of Attlee's stewardship of his party and its political position. One can detect two parallel themes: first, the significance of Attlee's role in the government – his roving mandate, influence over Churchill and powerful position on the Lord President's Committee – and second the fact that he had been the central figure in each major reshaping of the political landscape. He was creative in responding to problems before others and, since 1939, willing to use his prerogatives aggressively. Far from being a minor actor, a more important – and politically skilled – figure should now be emerging. When the layers of opaqueness are stripped away, for all the importance of other men, it was the plans, methods and initiatives of Attlee that had the most impact. It was the Deputy Prime Minister – not Bevin, Churchill, Morrison, Anderson or anyone else – who remained the vital power broker in British politics. He exerted a unique influence over both government itself and high political strategy and tactics. The by-election ticket looked like all things to all men. It was a clever response. Yet again, then, the weaknesses of the interpretative tradition surrounding Attlee struggle to get beyond bemusement as to who the 'real' Attlee was. Drawing it out requires questions to be sensitively addressed, but the continuities are clear. Moreover, the manner of his leadership was beginning to evolve as well. Threatening the party with electoral annihilation, brazenly ignoring its complaints and taking his followers still deeper into their alliance with the Conservatives all signified the emergence of a very different figure. Leaders often change when they have been in office for a time, and Attlee was no exception.

The first three chapters have used different kinds of examples to show how, in various ways, Attlee and the other Labour leaders conducted a series of campaigns against the Conservative Party – to acquire office, construct a major role in Whitehall and, finally, to remodel the doctrines of the state. They used collaboration with the Conservative Party to secure concession after concession and advanced the interests, goals and priorities of their own party. That a great deal remained to be done before Britain could be called 'socialist' should not deflect recognition from either this change or where its origins lay. Despite yielding so many conflicting interpretations, this is the inescapable reality of British politics after 1939. It seems worthwhile to observe after the first three chapters that everything we have seen so far was ultimately all about power, pure and simple. Electoral politics and the features of British democracy determined that politicians would have these priorities; legislation was a by-product of a struggle for credibility and, ultimately, the keys to office. British foreign policy in the 1930s had reflected this; it was even truer of domestic politics during the war. And, apparently, few understood this better than the Deputy Prime Minister.

Despite the party showing signs of fracture on key fault lines, then, an assessment of the advancement of Labour doctrines would be even more favourable. By mid-1942, Labour was the dominant partner in the coalition. The platform established in the first two years of war served as a launch pad for a realignment of key areas of state thinking. The sole area of domestic policy in which Labour's representatives were not the major players was financial policy, but in terms of industry, mobilization, social policy development and relations between the government and populace, the Labour ministers exercised greater influence than their Conservative counterparts did. They were playing the principal role in the establishment of an economic, welfare and social system far more egalitarian by the end of the war than it had been in 1939. Moreover, the Conservative Party remained morose, a 'rotten lot',[150] before what it recognized as the washing away of 'their' Britain. Just as significantly, Labour's credibility – so weak in the 1930s – had been renewed. It was a vindication of the strategy chosen by the party's leader. As such, the entire paradigm within which enquiry into British politics between 1939 and 1945 has been conducted needs to be rethought.

Emphasizing 'Lib–Labism' might be a key part of writing the history of the war as the brokering of a new agreement midway between socialism and conservatism, but it fails to reflect the underlying *political* balance of forces that had now emerged. Sam Beer wrote that the new contours created by the war were stimulated not by changes in 'the electoral balance of power', but in 'the balance of economic power'.[151] That is true, so far as it goes, but Beer's argument also misses something just as important. This shift in economic power was only possible in the first place because of an even larger shift in *political* power. It was the product of the actions, decisions and purposes of a small group of ministers. In essence, perhaps the tide flowed *from* Labour, rather than Labour drifting *with* the tide.

Attlee's moves to strengthen the coalition would have a major impact on the course of national politics for the duration of the conflict. They also reinforce what had become the closed nature of the political world since 1940. However much public opinion might have developed, politics was still principally determined by politicians. The by-election measure is indicative of how far these men had come to see their interests as residing with each other rather than their parties. The coalition was more than a marriage of convenience: senior politicians now viewed conventional party politics with scepticism and impatience. The preoccupation of leading actors was soon to become maintaining that alliance into the postwar era. Some months earlier, Greenwood had declared that all members of the government wanted 'not merely to avoid the mistakes made after the last war, *but to cooperate to the fullest measure in working together* to restore the shattered fabric of our civilization'.[152] In March 1941, at a Conservative event, Churchill said that 'the ties of friendships which are being formed between members of the administration … will not be very easy to tear asunder.'[153] The basis for something approaching a 'consensus' in the sphere of *politics* – not necessarily in the better-studied *policy* sphere – can be detected. It was arguably rooted more in personal relationships than in policy. Attlee's endless talk of 'unity' reflected not only social but also political preferences. Harold Macmillan offered the most perceptive expression of the change when he noted that 'all the symptoms are developing which marked the end of the Asquith coalition (a coalition of parties) and the formation of the Lloyd George coalition (a coalition of personalities)'.[154] He was right.

Chapter 4

'Parliament is Given over to Intrigue': The Political System under Siege

By the middle of 1942, and for the next year at least, there developed a pervasive sense that politics was in a state of deep crisis. Party strife had returned. There was no turn in the military tide just yet. The sense of emergency was genuine, particularly in the context of military disasters like Tobruk, but it was also political. The language of emergency, crisis and the need for immediate action was an accepted part of politicians' vocabulary: 'almost every year produced a "political crisis".' [1] Legitimate problems were 'deliberately used to heighten tensions, with the purpose of defending, or more often criticizing and attempting to force changes in, existing policy or personnel'.[2] That was 'a well-understood public language in which "crisis", "principle" and "novelty" were conventional instruments for establishing positions in the monastic, or Rotarian, world we are discussing'.[3] It was employed equally by the critics of the government – most often 'outsiders' who were now sworn adversaries of those in charge of the system – and the 'insiders' who sought to employ it to entrench their own power and demand obedience.

It is impossible to know how vigorously the positions taken up were 'believed' in individual cases. Certainly, Laski was a socialist, but he also displayed egotism and hatred for Attlee. The same could be said for Bevan or, from within the government, any of the leading figures. The question of belief is unrevealing anyway; it is better to look at observable activity instead. For instance, the Labour ministers had exploited the dangers raised by war to alter the landscape of politics. It was used to recover respectability for a party that had lost it a decade before, and had done little to recover it by 1939. Labour doctrine did not yet straddle the entirety of political opinion; but linkages had been established across the system, and that process was very much underway. Moreover, for the first

125

time Labour had shed all talk of the class war, and found another device instead – the virtues of the British nation and people. That was more useful and recognized as such long into the postwar era. Attlee's Labour Party had effectively reversed the position of Baldwinite 'national' conservatism.

This chapter turns away from government, and returns to the politics of party. The political system as a whole came under siege in 1942. Events began to slip beyond the control of leading figures, as crisis after crisis broke over Westminster. And, connected to that, the political world began to reorder itself yet again. The party system constructed in 1940 faced a new challenge. That came from two, opposing forces. The first consisted of efforts emanating from both parties – but most energetically the Labour Party – to bring about the collapse of the coalition and a reversion to a two-party system. This stemmed from complementary beliefs that the government was a failure and that the Labour and Conservative leaders needed replacing. Men like Bevan and Laski were its most energetic exponents, but it took in increasing numbers of people from both parties, such as Jim Griffiths, John Wardlaw-Milne and Sir Roger Keyes, and even included ministers like Beaverbrook and Cripps. Issues like the Beveridge Report fanned the flames. Open clamouring to end the coalition or, in some cases, rejuvenate it with different personnel began to pose serious problems. The second force exerting pressure on the system was the quite different objective some held to entrench the cross-party alliance even more deeply. That was chiefly an outcome of Attlee's policies as he extended his efforts to consolidate the electoral alliance. It involved an attempt to remodel the structures of the parties and tie them together. Over the next three years, it was to evolve into an important obstacle to a return to independent parties in the near future. In time, virtually all the nation's leaders came to share this same view. The chapter shows how these competing visions of both the present and the future became the central battleground in national politics. It juxtaposes Attlee's central strategic commitment to the coalition alliance – electoral policy remained where his leadership was most evident – with the serious challenges to its maintenance that he now faced. All this required focus on party-based problems for the first time since 1939.

Going beyond the 'truce' and searching for 'witches'

By now, then, instability was rife and discipline in the Labour Party especially was in tatters. In April 1942, Attlee launched his second significant effort to buttress the cross-party alliance. To that end, he tried to cultivate a new kind of political space. His impeding of Laski provided him with an opportunity to retake the initiative. Moreover, for several months some had been hankering after a return to party politics. Though unrepresentative for the moment, men like Laski and Bevan were well suited to the politics of harassment. The existence of a diffuse threat to Attlee's strategy was thus becoming apparent.

The other background against which we should locate Attlee's newest measures was that, through early 1942, the government sustained a wave of by-election defeats to candidates designating themselves as 'Independents'.[4] Grantham fell in March and Rugby, Wallasey and Maldon swiftly followed. In itself that was purely symptomatic of the austerity of wartime. What made it into a serious problem was that some constituency-level Labour Parties chose to defy both the electoral truce and Attlee's new 'joint statement of support' by assisting Independents against Conservative opponents. By late April, the coalition had lost two contests – at Grantham and Rugby – where party activists brazenly violated the truce.[5] By-elections were a major issue as a gauge of political feeling; there had been around eighty since the outbreak of war.[6] The government was therefore subjected to constant, and dangerous, political tests. Defeat carried great symbolic importance, and questions were now being asked about the structure of politics at both the upper and lower levels of the parties. Only with this in mind can we understand the capital that Attlee invested in the issue. His was principally a strategy of preclusion. In January, Attlee had submitted a memorandum to the NEC, 'Platform Propaganda', in which he emphasized the need for caution in public speaking and the avoidance of 'party aggrandizement'.[7] That was one of his more revealing proposals. In the immediate aftermath of the first defeat at Grantham – and the expectation of more widespread violation to come – an anxious Attlee went even further.[8] In early April 1942 the Deputy Prime Minister proposed to both the NEC and Churchill that representatives from the Labour Party should now be able to appear on the hustings for Conservatives at by-elections – and vice versa – to speak in support of individual 'government' candidates.[9] The idea represented a further bid to cement the coalition into the political landscape; indeed, it was the polar opposite of 'party aggrandizement'. We should see it as having continuity with Attlee's decisions of the previous autumn and the others that were to follow.

True to form, the measure was heavily assailed in the Labour-sympathizing press.[10] Then, equally predictably, when put to the NEC, Attlee's proposal provoked yet another fierce row.[11] But the increasingly uncompromising leader did, once again, somehow manage to generate the support of a majority for his policy.[12] Dalton's view, as expressed in his diary, was blunt:

> Are we in favour of the government or not? Are we in favour of the war or not? If the answer to both questions is yes … how can we refuse to support a member of the government, who happens to be either a Tory or a Liberal, against an opponent of the war?[13]

Attlee immediately dispatched Labour speakers to help the Conservative Secretary of State for War, Sir James Grigg, against the ILP's Fenner Brockway at East Cardiff, and soon thereafter started sending a personal message of support to all government candidates.[14] *The Times* labelled the endeavour 'Mr Attlee's Action'.[15] Within a month he had sent five such messages to Wallasey, Glasgow, Rugby, Putney and Chichester.[16] Innocuous enough on the surface perhaps, this second revision of the electoral agreements that underpinned the cross-party alliance in fact constituted an important reinforcement of the government and confirmed how Attlee, and other leaders, now wanted political action to be framed.

Yet, this new practice turned out *still* not to be enough: Attlee wanted to go even further. Ignoring the steady stream of rank-and-file protests,[17] in May the Deputy Prime Minister argued for even greater and – crucially – standardized, as opposed to case by case, intervention by all parties on behalf of the candidates of the others.[18] Attlee's efforts on by-election policy were underpinned by the fact that the NEC Elections Sub-committee – through which the arrangements were directed – consisted, besides Attlee himself, of George Shepherd, the national agent, Jim Middleton, the general secretary, and the miners' James Walker, all of whom backed the leader's latest idea.[19] Attlee was able to turn this committee into his personal instrument. On 13 May, it recommended that the executive should adopt a policy of giving the party's automatic, and public, backing to *any* 'government' candidate.[20] It was a daring bid to give permanence to Attlee's new direction. From a cautious start the previous autumn, Attlee had now gone the whole way. In a new threat environment he was taking the Labour Party ever deeper into the cross-party alliance as a means of preventing its escape. Attempting to bounce the NEC into accepting the plan before it had even been debated, that same day the proposition was openly trailed in *The Times* as the new official policy.[21] Who was behind that leak is unclear. But the policy itself was another instance of the more forceful management of the party that Attlee instituted. It constituted a significant extension of his October 1941 'coupon' policy and even his efforts of the previous month where he had wanted to establish the *option* of backing the candidates of other parties; now he aimed to enshrine a firm *obligation* to do so. The differences may appear slight, but they amounted to a discernible 'creep'. Moreover, it was Attlee's Elections Committee, rather than the main executive, that would determine the precise form intervention in each case would take.[22] Under this plan, the Elections Committee would be granted additional powers to compel local parties to campaign actively in support of non-Labour candidates.[23]

The nub of it was a new election system. No wonder the idea generated such rancour. As we have seen, the opposing goals that some held for a return to the old party system were already exerting a significant pull. In addition, by early 1942 a largely unrepresentative band of Labour, Conservative and Liberal rebels were deemed to be plotting to just that end,[24] and there was a serious row over the opposition front bench in Parliament when members of the Conservative 1922 Committee requested to sit there, provoking fierce resistance from the Labour Party.[25] Conservatives also complained about their representation in the War Cabinet.[26] Bevan was engaged in constant public and private activism against the Labour ministers.[27] He attacked Attlee for placing 'the sole obligation of maintaining the unity of the government' on the Labour Party: 'Labour must make no demand as that may split the government. ... Labour is the victim of permanent blackmail.'[28] Bevan claimed this left the party with the 'dilemma of either having to repudiate [its leaders] or sink with them'.[29] He, from within Parliament, and Laski from outside it,[30] were doing their utmost to bring the government down. A few in the PLP wanted the party to become an opposition and remove ministers from the Administrative Committee.[31] That was, in effect, the decapitation of Attlee and the rest. A split was deemed possible and often discussed.[32] 'Parliament is given over to intrigue', as Ede put it.[33] Political debate had thus already come to centre on the survival of the government or, alternatively, the extension of the alliance. The realignment of the party system had already occurred; it was what to do *next* that was now the battleground. That situation was recognized in Greenwood's appropriately titled memorandum 'The Labour Party and the Future', in which he warned that 'Labour's future will be gravely imperilled if the PLP were to form an "Opposition".'[34] The knowledge that, in the end, the new system did not last beyond 1945 should not minimize our focus on its implications for politics in 1942. Politics was in flux and there to be remade. Attlee, more than anyone else, was alive to the possibilities.

The unpopularity of this proposition therefore set the stage for a fight to the finish over the wider issues of the electoral truce in the approach to the 1942 party conference. For many in the party, it was a step too far: speaking in support of candidates from other parties on an occasional basis was bad enough, but a blanket backing for all Conservatives and Liberals was insufferable. When the NEC considered the latest measure on 22 May – just three days before the opening of the annual conference at Westminster – it was firmly rejected.[35]

Attlee, however, refused to accept this latest setback. Characteristically, he resorted to manoeuvre to get his way. With the annual gathering of the Labour movement imminent, and the electoral truce due to be voted upon, the Deputy Prime Minister had the advantage that a formal position, of *some* sort, had to be crafted, and quickly. As a result, the NEC tasked his Elections Committee with going back to revise its policy.[36] Days later – with the conference now actually underway – it submitted a virtually identical proposal in its place, which was only different in that it carried the caveat that the 'views' of local parties would be taken into account.[37] What that meant was unclear. With apparently little choice, the executive accepted it.[38]

Attlee had – once again – won through. But the margin of victory was becoming slighter each time. He had now revised the electoral arrangements three times in eight months, moving incrementally and then pausing. Despite tactical departures, his decisions remained consistent with his purposes since 1939. Every bit as much as his careful positioning between 1939 and 1941, an examination of Attlee's activities over 1941 to 1945 reveals a set of decisions and methods consistently, and rigorously, followed. He wanted to bind the Labour Party into its alliance with the Conservatives. Moreover, historians should draw clear lines of continuity, in a way they have not yet done, between these initial efforts to protect the coalition and the under studied bid to preserve it. Previously, scholars have noted the establishment of the by-election 'coupon' and the commitment actively to back all government candidates only in passing, investing them with little significance compared with, say, the radicalization of the intelligentsia or the war-weariness of the populace. The possibility of the continuation of the coalition has never been taken seriously. Opponents of 'consensus' doubtless ascribe this to the persistent tensions and differences between the parties; proponents have an air of inevitability to the separation, despite the cross-party agreement, after a virtuous alliance. Thorpe offered a more realistic, and testable, conclusion in putting it down to the strength of the party system.[39] From the perspective of 'high politics', these latest innovations tell us a great deal.

That Attlee's continued direction of high political tactics and strategy remained broadly a success was confirmed at the conference. The annual gathering also, however, affirmed how unstable the ground on which Attlee toiled had become. The debate on whether to maintain the electoral truce – which, after all the recent crises, had become seen as a referendum on the record of the coalition to date – was a major rebuff.[40] With disaffection towards the government given free rein on an issue that Laski had earlier identified as the occasion to overthrow Attlee, Bevan made a fiery denunciation of Attlee's cooperation with the other parties and constituency delegates joined with several major unions – the MFGB, NUDAW, NUR and AEU – in opposing retention of the truce and advocating a return to open party conflict.[41] For its part, the *Daily Herald* called for 'a renewed and bolder demand by the Labour Party for the recognition of its claims upon the National Government'.[42] Morrison – as always unwilling to countenance real concessions – made a stern defence of the official line,[43] but the extent of the hostility was unmistakeable. The delegates only opted to maintain the truce by the humiliating margin of 66,000 votes.[44] As a judgement on the leadership group's strategy over the preceding three years, it was hardly a ringing endorsement. The Labour Party was now divided between those who wanted to shake the coalition – if not end it – and those who wanted to entrench it. Bevan aligned himself with the former view by announcing that Attlee's policy was leading the party to 'the graveyard' and that if it continued, 'we shall have a complete fusion of the Conservative and Labour parties.'[45] Moreover, many of those who still backed the leaders were themselves profoundly disillusioned.[46] The defection of several unions with large bloc votes was doubly worrying. After 15 months of the gradual disintegration of its equilibrium, the party had come very close to the effective repudiation of the coalition – which would, it hardly seems necessary to say, have prompted a very awkward test of loyalty for the Labour ministers.

In addition to that crisis, Morrison came into bitter conflict with the delegates when he amazingly launched an open assault on them over the complaints against the coalition. This posed separate problems for his personal leadership ambitions. In the first of several notable wartime conference performances, an obdurate Home Secretary quite brazenly poured scorn on the mood of the auditorium:

> The main point that is worrying delegates is that Labour ministers … are not getting all their own way. Anybody who says we are not getting any of it is really talking nonsense. … The fact is that this party is never happy when it is in government. It is not happy with Labour in this government, because the party has got too much the mind of perpetual opposition, because it has too much of the perpetual minority complex, and because some of you have too much of the perpetual inferiority complex as well.[47]

It was astonishing stuff, an open attack on the party by the man who styled himself its leader-in-waiting. Morrison was still smarting from being viciously assailed by much of the movement some months earlier over his decision to suppress the mainstream *Daily Mirror* newspaper for sedition,[48] a move that earned great opprobrium in the press.[49] A mass protest by a civil liberties group had been held in London,[50] while Bevan eagerly entered the fray and actually garnered support from a full third of the PLP for a Commons censure motion against Morrison.[51] In March, in an epic clash in Parliament – itself engineered by the Welshman, and which marked his maturation on the political scene – Bevan labelled the Home Secretary a 'witch-finder':[52]

> I [am] suggesting that the right hon. Gentleman in his writings in the *Daily Mirror* [prior to May 1940] did many things which he is now accusing the *Daily Mirror* of doing. … He is the wrong man to be Home Secretary. He has been for many years the witch-finder of the Labour Party. He has been the smeller-out of evil spirits in the Labour Party for years. He built up his reputation by selecting people in the Labour Party for expulsion and suppression. He is not the man to be entrusted with these powers because, however

suave his utterance, his spirit is really intolerant. ... The right hon. Gentleman exorcised with bell, book and candle from the Labour Party a gentleman who has now been taken into the War Cabinet [Cripps]. ... It is a shameful record.[53]

Even Attlee was forced to come to his defence at a party meeting.[54] Despite the damage inflicted, Morrison refused to back down – lest it be thought that he had 'surrendered to the Bolshies'[55] – and so was still aggrieved when the conference came around. The personalized nature of his attack on the delegates did little to dispel this 'witch-finder' image. Rather than attempting to bridge the gap between the Labour ministers and the party, the Home Secretary revelled in it, displaying his combative instincts to the full. Privately, however, he purported to be displeased at being put in that position, complaining to a journalist that 'I have to do all the dirty work [of defending the official line] on these occasions. Really it's Attlee's job, not mine, but they put it to me ... when there's a really nasty job like this I have to do it.'[56] He ascribed the party's instability to Attlee personally, blaming him for 'too much soft leadership in the past'.[57]

The contrast between the approaches of the party's two most senior figures was clear from the speech that Attlee had made just prior to Morrison's attack:

We have had two years of working in this government, and there may be some who think that we have now turned the corner in this war and can afford to return to party strife. ... They make a great mistake. In partaking in this government we necessarily had to work with those who do not share our views. ... We cannot dictate to others the acceptance of our socialist programme ... in the give-and-take of government ... you have to work by agreement.[58]

The tone was very different. There might have been some truth to Morrison's protest that a forceful personality like him was deliberately left to assume the unpopular, disciplinarian role; certainly, Attlee often used Morrison as a troubleshooter and it would be naïve to think there was not an element of calculation in that. Regardless, the episode was deeply wounding to Morrison's prestige. After his attack, the same day the conference delegates only decided not to censure him for his interference with the press by the utterly humiliating margin of 13,000 votes.[59] Twice the Home Secretary had narrowly escaped censure by the party he intended to lead. In the election to the NEC, Morrison then fell to second from bottom of those elected.[60] For all his earlier efforts to mark out his credentials as leader, this reinforced both the contradictory nature of Morrison's tactics in pursuit of Attlee's job – his determination to win the support of the Labour Party, but caring little for what it thought – and the fact that, while he enjoyed a more public role than his rival, this was in an office that rarely produces popular decisions. That was the challenge he faced. We shall later see how Morrison began to respond to it.

First, though, there was a coda to the saga of election policy. Within mere days of the conference finishing, Attlee *yet again* returned to the problem of the truce, and sought to capitalize on his most recent victories. This time he wanted to consolidate comprehensive control of the policy in his own hands, and remove the influence of the party machinery from decision-making altogether. Having given no intimation of his thinking to either the executive or the delegates when the issue was being debated just days earlier, Attlee suddenly asserted that the NEC's method of administering the by-election policy – whereby the executive still formally authorized him to issue the joint statement of support in each individual case – would lead to 'undesirable conclusions [being] drawn' if candidates did not receive endorsement in a timely fashion.[61] The Elections Subcommittee, which Attlee dominated, then suggested that the leader ought to be assigned the authority to act as he deemed fit.[62] Attlee's criticisms of cumbersome procedures were a convenient smokescreen to gain personal control over the policy. Having already clustered oversight into the hands of the Elections Committee, this latest measure – identical to the others in being proposed out of the blue – enabled the party leader further to circumvent critics and deprive them of the means to challenge his authority. When this proposal, too, was accepted by the NEC, Attlee secured the freedom to plough on with his adherence to coalitionism unfettered by the need constantly to secure the acquiescence of his followers.[63]

Attlee was doing his best to ensure that future arrangements would be dependent, at least in the Labour Party, on his judgements alone. The Deputy Prime Minister was moving gradually towards a position where, by establishing certain norms of non-opposition for the other parties, an environment would be created in which political cooperation would be consolidated. He had certainly reduced the possibility of the Labour Party being able to break with the truce while the war continued. In adhering to the non-party language of 'unity', in suppressing manifestations of 'party politics' at every turn, and in remoulding the foundations of the cross-party government, Attlee and the others engaged in this effort – the other leaders of the Labour and Conservative parties – were only reverting to a style familiar to that which prevailed between 1930 and 1931.[64] Whether the Deputy Prime Minister had already come to favour extending the lifetime of the coalition cannot be ascertained; but the mental direction in which he was travelling, at least, was starting to come into focus.

Storm warnings

The second half of 1942 saw the pattern of the past few months repeated. Politics slipped deeper into crisis and the Churchill regime faced constant challenge. Part of this sprang from a lack of effective guidance: Greenwood lacked robustness in directing the PLP, being unable to impose discipline or push it in the direction the Labour ministers preferred. His continued dependency on drink was evident when he turned up at a dinner one evening 'half-squiffed'.[65] Dalton recalled that 'it used to be said in Whitehall … that "the poor old chap couldn't even sign his name after midday".'[66] With Attlee an increasingly remote figure, Greenwood's limitations left a leadership vacuum. Sure enough, when Dalton's white paper on the coal industry stopped short of outright nationalization, a revolt ensued: Bevan declared it a 'test case' of the government's credentials,[67] at the conference the NEC and the delegates forced through a call for public ownership,[68] and a resolution had been put forward explicitly to demand nationalization even if that resulted in the collapse of the alliance.[69] Greenwood's attempts to sell the measure as a major advance for socialism came to naught,[70] and the Labour ministers' determination to 'give something to the [miners]' on 'psychological grounds' – in itself a further important indication of how the leaders saw themselves operating – generated nothing from the Conservatives.[71] A massive rebellion was only averted when trade union pragmatism – content with the creation of a National Coal Board – prompted the NCL to back the white paper.[72] The PLP could hardly rebel in those circumstances.[73]

But there were further revolts. A potentially huge cross-party rebellion in June following the fall of Tobruk saw Labour and Conservative dissidents unite for the first time, but fortunately for the government fell into farce.[74] That preceded another serious outbreak of instability within the

Labour Party over pensions, in the largest rebellion since the forging of the alliance.[75] Only 57 Labour MPs backed the government in the Commons on the latter issue – 20 of whom were ministers anyhow.[76] It all prompted characteristically robust stances from Attlee and Bevin – the Deputy Prime Minister giving 'the most forceful speech' Ede had ever heard him make over Tobruk[77] – but even the Minister of Labour was beginning to have grave doubts that the government could survive.[78] Ede wrote that:

> The Conservative Party [is] at sixes and sevens. Its members had no contact with ministers but spent their time in the smoke room consuming expensive drinks and intriguing ... some members of the Labour Party spent their time in other parts of the House consuming less expensive drinks but also intriguing.[79]

The coalition's response to this fragmentation was to keep Parliament in recess as much as possible and the Commons met only 15 times between August and November 1942. The party's response was another flurry of publicity and communications activity: most notably, a propaganda film with a budget of £1000 was to be produced,[80] a deal was struck with Penguin publishers to print longer texts[81] and it was decided that the editor of the *Daily Herald*, Percy Cudlip, would attend meetings of the NEC Campaigns Committee after he signalled that he was 'serviceable' to guiding public opinion away from demands for 'immediate' reform and kicking the issue into touch until after the war.[82] Cudlip suggested that the *Daily Herald* 'was not being used to its maximum potential' as an organ for the official line.[83] Similar arrangements were established with *Reynold's News* and other pro-Labour outlets.[84] And a standing committee of Cudlip, Greenwood and Citrine was set up to determine in advance the 'publicity' treatment of key issues.[85] Back in June, Greenwood had called for 'the immediate issue' of 'directives on policy' for the 'guidance of the movement'.[86] Like those episodes before it, all of this might be taken as offering quite striking insights into the true arts of political management, showing how leading figures suddenly hit on the idea they had better churn something out to keep their party happy. It had little substance. That also raises questions about how important policymaking – when divorced from *politics* – is; given the (understandable) perception of parties as essentially machines for policy creation, this point is significant.

In the midst of all of this, Attlee's high political wrangling with Laski very nearly came to a head when he almost got his enemy booted out of the Labour Party altogether. That in the event Laski was not expelled only signalled the re-emergence of another, more significant problem – Morrison's desire to acquire the leadership. As in the previous clashes, the episode was precipitated by a vicious attack on Attlee by the LSE professor. Between July and September 1942, Laski published a set of scathing articles in *Reynold's News* on the Labour ministers, employing highly provocative language and hurling public accusations of betrayal. He declared that they were doing 'less than their elementary duty' in not implementing socialist reforms, and took aim at the party leader directly in suggesting that 'no one … can point to any serious effort by Mr Attlee to make the idea of a partnership with the people a conscious part of the Prime Minister's policy.'[87] Meanwhile, under the headline 'Leaders are Paralysed', Laski absolved Greenwood and the PLP of responsibility for the current difficulties, charging instead that 'paralysis' had 'settled down like a blight' on the Labour ministers.[88] They had secured 'no single measure' that was worthwhile.[89]

Laski, as already demonstrated, would have liked the government to fall. Furthermore, while noisy, he was more than that – his popularity and standing made him a big player. Rather than being merely a troublesome *internal* nuisance, Laski was in fact the ministers' principal *public* protagonist as well, as evidenced by the frequently public nature of his assaults on Attlee, the audience he reached as a political columnist and his consistent topping of the polls in the NEC elections. Maurice Cowling's assessment of Laski bears reiteration. 'That Laski had fantasies about his own importance is well understood. But Kramnick and Sheerman have shown how real some of those fantasies were.' [90] Moreover, he 'made a claim to public leadership', was a 'symbol' and provided 'a mental struc-ture for the reading classes'.[91] What Cowling also observed about Laski's career as an intellectual was equally true of his political career: he had a 'desire' to be 'thought an insider in an influential establishment'.[92] Recall too that Laski had taught a large number of Labour MPs and future ministers at the LSE.[93] To act out his role as an important figure, he needed an 'issue' upon which to fasten himself. With these latest articles, he expanded that beyond Attlee to encompass the supposed failures of the ministers as a group.

It precipitated a furious response: the NEC Organization Committee unanimously declared that the articles were 'reprehensible and deserving of censure'.[94] Before action could be taken against him, Laski made his situation worse by publishing another piece, in which he once again argued in favour of demanding reform from Churchill via the explicit threat of ending the coalition.[95] His language seemed intended to antagonize his adversaries – and it succeeded. When the NEC met on 23 September, the leadership was incredulous.[96] There was a desire to see Laski publicly demolished.[97] The executive agreed to hold a special meeting on 12 October to 'consider the powers [of the NEC]' – an obvious allusion to the possibility of expulsion.[98] Certainly, Dalton felt that the union boss Sam Watson wanted Laski out of the party altogether.[99]

That Bevin, not a member of the NEC, was invited to attend the meeting reinforces the notion that the Labour ministers had resolved to carpet Laski once and for all.[100] Described by Dalton as the 'inquest into the misdemeanours of Laski', this and another meeting on 28 October were the major confrontations between the leadership group and their accuser.[101] They were 'the stuff of high drama' and witnessed a protracted demolition of the rebel figure.[102] Attlee and Bevin personally led the counter-attack themselves, provoking Laski foolishly to reveal his earlier efforts to persuade the Minister of Labour to challenge Attlee for the leadership.[103] He also denied the principle of collective responsibility and claimed that he had a 'right' to appeal to the wider Labour movement, making clear that he had 'completely lost confidence' in Attlee.[104] Laski made reference to there being 'only two possible alternatives' as leader, neither of whom he named.[105] That proved to be a mistake and saw his loyalty called into question.[106] Watson and other union figures now definitely favoured expulsion.[107]

However, just when it appeared that Attlee would finally inflict a decisive bludgeoning to Laski, Morrison abruptly terminated the bid to do so at the last moment.[108] He had protected Laski in early 1941 and, once again, the heir apparent now suddenly intervened and restrained Attlee, Bevin and Watson. The Home Secretary outlined a conciliatory middle course, emphasizing that while Laski's criticisms were 'more public than was desirable' he did not want to 'muzzle' him.[109] Furthermore, he took it upon himself to affirm that 'no one questioned' Laski's loyalty – which was precisely what Attlee and the rest *were* questioning.[110] It was an intriguing intervention. Morrison simply requested Attlee's *bête noire* to give an undertaking not to use the press to attack the leaders.[111] Laski agreed, pledging only to make personal critiques within the confines of the NEC, and he escaped the bid to expel him by thirteen votes to four.[112] It seems probable that Attlee, Bevin and Watson were three of those who resisted Morrison's solution.[113] The Minister of Labour was incandescent, continuing to berate Laski even after the issue was sealed.[114]

Yet again, one has to place this episode in the broader context of fresh tremors within the political tectonic plates. Some soon sensed movement underfoot. Why did Morrison, a natural opponent of dissent, once more impede the effort to squash Laski? One answer might be that it was of benefit to Morrison if Attlee failed to expel his most recalcitrant critic and re-establish his authority. Thus, while he remained unwilling to brook challenges to Labour's position in the government, suddenly to step in here on Laski's behalf was consistent with both Morrison's past and future conduct in certain contexts. Certainly, he and Laski enjoyed a reasonably good personal rapport; but, as we have seen, the Home Secretary was ruthless when others tried to alter Labour's course. Although he was taking a gamble in donning the masks of both 'authority' and 'liberation', it was politically astute in the context of his longer-term ambitions. He had used Laski as a Trojan Horse against Attlee 18 months earlier. As Brooke has observed, it was no coincidence that Laski was an energetic supporter of Morrison's July 1945 leadership challenge.[115]

We can only understand the intervention if we bear in mind that the Home Secretary was already in the process of restarting his campaign for the leadership. That very day, Ellen Wilkinson relayed to Dalton the news that her patron, having been consumed with the demands of office since 1940, was now once again in 'running order' and 'taking much interest in wider questions', particularly the future of the Labour Party.[116] This 'interest' was plainly intended in the context of the leadership, Wilkinson proposing an arrangement with Morrison as leader and Dalton as his deputy as the basis for an alliance.[117] It is almost certain that the Home Secretary was thinking along these lines when he blocked the move to expel Laski. The fulfilment of his ambitions would require the destruction of the leader's position, and it cannot have escaped Morrison's attention that Laski was well placed to assist in that.

Within months of narrowly escaping censure himself, then, the Home Secretary reverted to cultivating his party in the role of its champion – the hat of which he was fondest. Soon thereafter, standing for free expression seemed to pay off when Morrison polled strongly in the elections to the Administrative Committee – a powerful symbol of intra-party legitimacy.[118] He could not have attained that amid his unpopularity earlier in the year. Most significant of all, the Home Secretary saw a further major advance in his general public prestige the following month, when he was made a member of the War Cabinet in November 1942. He thus entered the government's inner sanctum at last. Morrison was now on a par with Attlee and Bevin, and, as his biographers have noted, his 'star was shining'.[119] Alongside the Minister of Labour, Morrison far surpassed Attlee as a national figure, and he was probably the most recognizable Labour politician in Britain. The press warmly welcomed his promotion,[120] and the Labour Party published a pamphlet of his recent speeches entitled *The Spearhead of Humanity*.[121]

Whatever else was going on in national politics – most notably the wrangles over electoral policy and the remoulding of the state – the Home Secretary had now returned his attention to winning the leadership from his great rival. This time he was doing so from a much stronger position than the one he had enjoyed while trying to dislodge Attlee in the 1930s. The theme of Morrison's rise will be at the heart of the next chapter, but he began to come into focus as a real challenge to Attlee here. Morrison was increasingly seen as one of the giants of the political world. In all respects – his renewed scheming, his efforts to reinforce his prestige and as a ruthless troubleshooter for the government – his actions were to bear that out. This was to have a major impact on the course of events over the remainder of the war. Before long, he was even spoken of as leader of a future, postwar 'centre' coalition.[122] It is not an exaggeration to suggest that the evolution of politics until July 1945 cannot be fully appreciated without bearing the Attlee–Morrison rivalry in mind. Holding one of the country's key offices, matched only by Bevin and Churchill as a public figure and perceived as a man of dynamism, Morrison occupied a strong platform for the campaign to replace Attlee that would dominate the rest of his war. Given the near collapse of his position earlier in the year, this turnaround was remarkable. Not for the first – or the last – time Morrison rebounded with a vengeance, and the question of the leadership was to bubble beneath the surface of British politics for the next two and a half years.

The storm breaks

The scale of the challenge confronting those who favoured the status quo of cross-party alliance became abundantly clear soon afterwards, when the biggest single instance of party strife during the entire Second World War struck. The resultant storm lasted three months and threatened to destroy both the government and the Labour ministers. Unsurprisingly, perhaps, the crisis occurred over the government-commissioned study on reconstruction and social policy, the so-called Beveridge Report. Contrary to myth, what William Beveridge did was not so much offer a coherent blueprint for a Utopia as engage in a series of wild gestures of the kind usually seen in radical students' unions. He was, after all, largely a failure as a civil servant and behaved in a 'despotic' manner as director of the LSE.[123] Exceeding his limited brief by an order of magnitude, this frustrated man used the study as a soapbox. Declaring as being self-evident that 'the object of government' was nothing less than 'the happiness of the common man' (something that was far from being self-evident) the final product outlined a comprehensive overhaul and expansion of the British welfare state.[124]

Unsurprisingly, this opened up major political fissures. The resultant schism is perhaps the best-known aspect of all wartime politics, but the crisis is still worth tracing in some detail. From the beginning, the Labour movement's view on the report was one of demand – demand that the government would agree to implement it in full.[125] Yet, that was coupled with continued scepticism that the coalition would show much interest in the matter. When the Beveridge Report was published in November 1942, the entire spectrum of 'progressive' opinion in the country seized on it as a blueprint: although Beveridge was a Liberal, the report lit a fire under the Labour Party and became nothing less than a national phenomenon, tapping into a mood of hope for the future after the privations of war.[126] Polling suggested that 88 per cent of the country backed the report.[127] In early December, Greenwood and Pethick-Lawrence both called for prompt action. They bizarrely stated that intense division over the issue would not harm the coalition, and that it 'must not hide behind the smoke-screen of non-controversy',[128] whereas a few weeks earlier Laski had suggested to his wife that Attlee's leadership was in danger over the issue of reconstruction policy.[129]

Meanwhile, in the columns of his *Tribune* mouthpiece, Bevan again took the opportunity to attack the coalition and his leaders when he demanded that the government accept the report in full and placed the onus on the Labour ministers to ensure it did.[130] 'We hope ... that the Labour Party and the trade unions will go all out for adoption [of the report] ... it is now in Labour's hands.'[131] The following week, Bevan's private preferences were finally given free rein. Exploiting the mood of optimism that accompanied both the turn of the military tide at El Alamein and the excitement that greeted the report, the Welshman advocated the outright breakup of the coalition and a return to conventional party politics, arguing that the coalition had served its purpose and Labour would now be in a better position free from its harness.[132] Bevan was similar to Laski; he hoped the government would fall, and discerned in Beveridge a suitable problem upon which to adopt a 'position'. Over the subsequent months, he led the attack and carved out that position effectively.

What turned all this into a much larger crisis was that the coalition refused to give firm commitments to implement the Beveridge reforms. This decision was taken on the grounds of the great cost. Sympathy for the aspirations of the report was affirmed, but financial realities – and a purported need for an electoral mandate – precluded formal acceptance.[133] There was another problem that provided ammunition to the likes of Bevan: around 90 per cent of the Conservative Party was apparently hostile to the report.[134] Placing the government at odds with the popular mood of the nation played into the hands of those within both parties who wanted to destroy the coalition. One Labour MP demanded that Attlee tell Churchill to 'go to Hell'.[135] Even a minister like Ede felt that 'the Tories mean to dish the Labour Party'.[136] But the Labour ministers generally adhered to the Whitehall line, at least at first. There is no evidence in the government papers from late 1942 of opposition on their part to the policy of caution.[137] That support for the government stance left Attlee and the rest implicated in a decision easily cast as proof of 'betrayal' by those who had shown their desire to realign the party system. On 15 December the NEC and Administrative Committee welcomed the report as 'a great advance in the social services', identifying it as the basis for postwar reform.[138] The NCL expressed a similar view.[139] The objections made by Attlee and other Labour ministers about the sheer impossibility of implementing it during the war were overruled.[140] On the contrary, a motion was passed that the party 'accepts the emphasis of [the report] upon the importance of giving effect to the general policy ... *before the end of the war*'.[141] Plans were quickly made for almost seventy official Labour 'conferences and demonstrations' on the report to be held across the country.[142] The party, the TUC and the Co-operative established committees to study the report.[143] The PLP was tasked with 'improving' the report when it was debated in the Commons, in effect granting MPs official licence to harass the government.[144]

Left formally rebuffed on a highly symbolic issue with major strategic connotations, this was a stinging slap across the face for the Labour ministers. The reticent stance the coalition adopted thus placed the leadership at odds with *every* institutional arm of their movement – the NEC, PLP, TUC and the Co-operative. Things rapidly got even worse. Isolated and vulnerable, the clamour persisted remorselessly into 1943 as the government tried for many weeks to find traction. Argument after argument wracked public life. With the Labour ministers now greeted with such derision by their followers, a resolution to cut their representation on the PLP's ruling body was suddenly put forward, and accepted, in January.[145] Laski declared the report to be another test of the influence of the Labour ministers over policy, called for withdrawal from the government if Beveridge was not accepted,[146] and drew up a 22-page memorandum in which he set out the case for leaving the coalition.[147] He derided ministers who 'ask for congratulation' for their work and implied that Attlee and Bevin were not real socialists.[148] Then a large Conservative revolt occurred, 116 MPs from that party rebelling over Bevin's innocuous Catering Wages Bill in a rebuff to the 'socialist' drift of the regime.[149] Too Tory for some and not Tory enough for others, the coalition was caught. In early February, as it became inevitable that the approaching Commons debate on Beveridge was to witness a major confrontation between the Labour Party and the government, the Administrative Committee promptly moved even further away from its own ministers. It agreed to put down a motion in Parliament expressing Labour's wholehearted support for the report and demanded its immediate implementation.[150] Greenwood stressed his anxiety at the prospect of rebelling against the government, but was voted down.[151]

With the Labour ministers trapped helplessly between the Conservatives' reluctance, the PLP's fury, and the desire of their leading enemies to see them overthrown, the threat of an outright withdrawal of Labour's support for the entire coalition project loomed for the first time in February 1943. It was feasible that if Labour moved against him *en masse*, Churchill could be provoked into dissolving the alliance and fighting a general election. The result would be inevitable victory for the Prime Minister. Attempting to head off this nightmare scenario, the Labour ministers desperately intensified their efforts to secure a more enthusiastic response for the report. Morrison, particularly, was vigorous, agitating ceaselessly within the government on the issue.[152] As Addison has observed, the Home Secretary quickly emerged as the government's leading champion of Beveridge, pressurizing the coalition for a public pledge to adopt the scheme.[153] After Kingsley Wood effectively tried to bury the report,[154] in late January 1943 Morrison circulated a Cabinet paper on Beveridge in which he articulated a more optimistic view of the feasibility of accepting the proposals. He asserted that 'finance is within very wide limits a handmaid of policy', and argued that the report

> represents a financial burden which we should be able to bear, except on a number of very gloomy assumptions. ... I can see no need to make or act upon such assumptions. I should certainly not like to have to expound or defend them to a nation bearing the full burden of total war.[155]

For Morrison to agitate on Beveridge was, for the moment at least, a win-win situation. Just like others, then, he took the opportunity to establish a clear 'position'. Whether this was also linked to his resumed campaign to position himself as Labour's most committed partisan, as part of his leadership ambitions, is open to interpretation. It was certainly a powerful contrast to Morrison's usual highly reactionary attitudes towards dissent. Nonetheless, there was undoubtedly major political capital to be made in establishing himself as the report's most ardent supporter. From the outset, he positioned himself in the PLP as the report's ministerial champion, telling a party meeting in November that 'we must advocate measures of reconstruction not because they [are] socialistic but because they [are] good for the country.'[156] He was hardly trying to damp down the issue. With his ever-growing visibility and renewed interest in the leadership, it meant that Morrison was firmly on the march once again.

Morrison was not the only figure to recognize the strategic problem. Attlee too put pressure on the Prime Minister. With the Commons debate imminent, Attlee went on the offensive against Conservative resistance and, in a bid to secure last-minute concessions, submitted to Churchill a lengthy memorandum often cited by historians:

> I doubt whether in your inevitable and proper preoccupation with military problems you are fully cognizant of the extent to which

decisions must be taken and implemented in the field of post-war reconstruction *before* the end of the war. It is not that persons of particular political views are seeking to make vast changes. These changes have already taken place. ... I am certain that unless the Government is prepared to be as courageous in planning for peace as it has been in carrying on the war, there is extreme danger of disaster. ... My contention is that if ... it is not possible ... to have a general election ... the Government and the House of Commons must be prepared to take responsibility not only for winning the war but for taking the legislative and administrative action which is thought necessary for the post-war situation.[157]

Both Attlee and Morrison were pressing for the implementation of the report *during* the war. The Deputy Prime Minister called for the parties to cooperate in agreeing to 'carry through measures which the course of events and public opinion [demand]'. He buttressed the position by telling Churchill that this 'was certainly my understanding when I joined the government'.[158] That was one of his oldest, most familiar tricks. Reflective once again of Attlee's ability to sway Churchill, this pressure had an important effect: the Prime Minister largely relented, and gave a pledge to implement what he called 'Beveridge-type' reforms *after* the war.[159] Considering that Churchill knew he was running the risk of a major Conservative revolt, with 90 per cent of backbenchers apparently opposed to expansion of social security,[160] his virtual capitulation was instructive.

Kicking reform into touch in this way was still insufficient. On 16 February, the first day of the critical Commons debate, the government's primary speakers, Anderson and Wood, gave 'inept' performances in which they, amazingly, failed to emphasize the important shift in the government's position that the Labour ministers had extracted.[161] That anti-Labour forces within the administration were resolved to taking a stand was clear when Bracken told the press that 'the government is going to get tough with its critics.'[162] A new appeal for loyalty by Attlee to the PLP was reinforced by another from Morrison – the Home Secretary once again turning aggressively against discontent as the coalition came under threat – but had no impact.[163] At the instigation of Jim Griffiths, the PLP opted 'overwhelmingly' to force a division.[164] Bevin launched into a bitter tirade against his own party that 'this is not the way they do things in the unions',[165] while that night Morrison went to see the Prime Minister and tried to secure new concessions, and Attlee again 'fought like a tiger' against Churchill in the War Cabinet.[166] As the Cabinet secretary recorded it in his notebook, Attlee declared that 'the mandate of this government is not limited to "blood, tears and sweat". This government must either govern, or get through a general election a government that will.'[167] The Prime Minister resisted implementation, and the exchange continued:

CHURCHILL: Peril to financial security – irresponsible commitments.
ATTLEE: Labour Party are not irresponsible about this.
CHURCHILL: Everyone wants it, but can you pay for it? You can't pass the bill until you know where you are.[168]

For his part, Morrison contended that 'if we said "no legislation until after the war", the House of Commons won't have it. Political crisis … We shall be treacherous to the country.'[169] But it was all to no avail. The Labour ministers were in no-man's land. Fighting for their political lives, their own rhetoric of 'unity' was turned against them, as Griffiths demanded:

I say … to this House, today, by our decision, let us send a message to the British people and say to them that together we will go on until victory is won, and when victory is won we will go on to another victory which will guarantee to all the social security which our people deserve.[170]

The Labour Party and its leaders were headed in opposite political directions. Already compelled to undermine his most recent efforts to prepare for a challenge to Attlee by showing solidarity with the Cabinet, it fell to Morrison – who was widely perceived as the government's troubleshooter – to wind up the Commons debate on behalf of the coalition, mounting a last-ditch defence of the Churchill ministry's policy.[171] Though he himself remained 'profoundly dissatisfied' with the Conservatives' resistance – and doubtless at having again publicly to cross swords with the same MPs he was so keen to cultivate – Morrison had made clear in Cabinet that '[I] am prepared to defend the decision', and came out fighting on behalf of the coalition in what Ede described as the best speech he had heard ever the Home Secretary make.[172] Even Attlee admitted that 'Morrison was first class.'[173] In a tremendous performance,

Morrison spoke for over an hour,[174] covering the details of the report at length, and making plain that the coalition had broadly accepted the plan; it was simply a matter of timing.[175] The Home Secretary reiterated the official line that such extensive postwar financial commitments were impossible to enter into, and warned the Labour Party that its amendment would 'raise constitutional and parliamentary issues of a serious order', a clear and unsubtle reference to the potential breakup of the coalition.[176] Morrison also emphasized that of the report's twenty-three recommendations, sixteen had already been accepted and six more with reservations: the government's position, as Ede summarized it, was merely 'not promising … more than you can pay for'.[177] Dalton wrote admiringly that if Morrison's speech had been made on the first day of the debate 'I am quite sure … there would have been no crisis at all.'[178] This episode offered a glimpse of Morrison's formidable skills as a political fighter. The question remains as to why the Conservatives did their best to avoid making clear Churchill's last minute shift. The answer might be thought obvious.

In the end, even the dynamism of Morrison was unable to shore up support from the Labour benches. In the division, 97 Labour MPs revolted against the government, joining with other rebels in registering a vote of 119 against the coalition's 335.[179] Only a meagre two backbenchers voted with the government.[180] With typical understatement, Attlee described it as 'not a good show'.[181] In truth, it constituted by far the largest rebellion of the war. Moreover, since the PLP had *formally* resolved to do this, the ministers were the ones who technically violated the party line. Attlee bemoaned to his brother that 'I fear our people cannot ever understand when they've won.'[182] Those who wanted to precipitate a break with the leaders spotted the ideal opportunity. The Labour Party viewed the report not only as a route to 'Eldorado', as Churchill described it, but an indication of the influence of the Labour ministers within the government.[183] Despite Attlee and Morrison dragging Churchill into *de facto* acceptance, they had failed on all counts.

With partisan feeling at its height amid the worst crisis since May 1940, many felt the collapse of the coalition to be imminent.[184] It was a difficult moment for Attlee's leadership. He, Bevin and Morrison were all indignant.[185] At a private meeting of the Labour ministers, an 'incandescent' Bevin wanted to demand that the party either publicly acquit or expel him.[186] This threat was leaked to the press, which entrenched the divides.[187] The

Home Secretary, meanwhile, denounced the party as a 'suicide club' that would rather have a romantic defeat than victory, and counselled that it 'could not play the fool' with the nation's finances.[188] Once again the tensions with which Morrison, more than anyone else, had to grapple were clear. Dalton predicted that 'if the electoral truce was broken up ... the Labour Party would be "scrubbed out" worse than in 1931.'[189] Some of the lesser ministers, meanwhile, wanted to appeal for a special conference to be asked to 'protect' them.[190] Earlier, Bevan had spoken of witch-hunts; now the Labour ministers were the ones cast as heretics.

The following day, Attlee warned the party that it had placed the ministers 'in a very difficult position', while Morrison gave the assembled MPs a stern rebuke, reiterating his view that Labour was akin to a 'suicide club'.[191] Greenwood, however, seemed 'paralysed' and unable to control the PLP as dissension raged unchecked.[192] Ede complained of their 'completely irresponsible' party.[193] Shinwell openly advocated that Labour should now 'go on without its ministers' – in other words, leave the coalition and overthrow the leaders.[194] Bevan, for his part, threatened to make the crisis 'endemic' and to come together with disaffected rebels to run their own parliamentary candidates at by-elections against Conservatives standing for the coalition.[195] What this entire crisis underlines is not merely the incendiary nature of the Beveridge Report, but – in a way that historians have not picked up – how the party system itself was now the key political battleground.

This rebellion was part of a much longer running argument and the future of the government was always top of the agenda. Bevan, Laski and others had folded the Beveridge schism within their broader critique of the ministers and used it to worsen the impact greatly. The pressures to revert to independence were powerful; the coalition had come to generate hatred in some quarters. The issues were to stay in the coalition or leave it; as we have seen earlier, to Attlee, and other leaders, the issue was also how to strengthen that alliance. This was an especially fluid period. Transport House was adopting dozens of candidates across the Labour movement for the next general election.[196] Discussions were being held about Communist Party affiliation and even some figures on the NEC like Griffiths were wavering.[197] Plans were being drawn up for an emergency wartime election;[198] and there was heavy pressure regarding the redistribution of constituency boundaries.[199] Then, the crisis was compounded. At the NEC, the Labour ministers suffered an even bigger humiliation when the executive reaffirmed its position in support of immediate implementation.[200] Attlee made another lengthy speech in protest, emphasizing that the position of the ministers had been 'very adversely affected'.[201] The Deputy Prime Minister called for it to be recalled that Labour was in a 'national', not party, government and hence 'it could not be expected that the full Labour policy would be acceptable in its entirety to the other … parties.'[202] Moreover, 'there were very real reasons' why the government had reservations about the report.[203] Dalton backed him, and called if necessary for a special conference to decide the issue.[204] But most humiliating of all, an attempt by two remaining loyalists, James Walker and George Ridley, to propose a motion that despite the row the NEC still 'records its confidence in the Labour members of the government' was defeated by the overwhelming margin of thirteen votes to a desultory four.[205]

This was a third hammer blow in the space of six days. With support for the leaders rejected by a majority of more than three to one, Attlee and his colleagues seemed on the verge of formal repudiation. An apoplectic Bevin – who always believed that the compulsory contributions required under Beveridge would make the scheme unpopular with the working classes[206] – even briefly tried to have the TGWU disaffiliate itself.[207] But, at the same time as the NEC was rejecting them, the ministers at last received a boost when the TUC unanimously passed a resolution expressing its full confidence in them.[208] In addition, the general council was only with difficulty persuaded from passing another resolution *condemning* the PLP for its behaviour.[209] Union representatives at the NCL made similar speeches and that body also offered its support.[210] As over the coal crisis the previous year, the schism saw the trade unions ride to the rescue against the political wing. Exploiting this upturn in their fortunes, and with the unions' backing, the Labour ministers eagerly took the offensive. Attlee was tasked with conveying to Middleton that if anyone were to make public the NEC's refusal to support them, they would call a special meeting of the executive and demand an equally public vote of confidence in response.[211] It was now the leaders who were delivering threats, with the prospect of electoral annihilation, and Labour being perceived as having 'run away' as in 1931, again heavily implied. That posture afforded Attlee and the rest their best chance of facing down the challenge.

Bevin called for a special conference to crush the rebellion and proposed that such a conference be asked to vote on a motion of no confidence in the NEC itself, launching into another diatribe about the 'political side'.[212] He ascribed the whole crisis to a strategy to 'change the leadership', end the truce and break up the government.[213] With perhaps more questionable judgement, Bevin also believed that the whole episode was a 'double conspiracy' aimed at not only bringing down the government but removing Attlee personally.[214] Presumably, he suspected Morrison was behind it all – Dalton, for one, thought this was what Bevin was suggesting[215] – but that was hardly a fair assertion given how vigorously Morrison had fought. In the end, the Home Secretary again played peacemaker and weighed in to damp down the splits, finding approval for his proposition that, unless reports of the NEC's decision appeared in the press, the Labour ministers should take no further action.[216] It having earlier seemed likely that the government would fall, in the end politics moved on and the conflict lay unresolved.[217] The Labour ministers, by hook and by crook, had survived.

Planning for 'the future'

The Beveridge Report made apparent the vulnerability of Attlee's strategy. It also highlighted that, contrary to appearances, arguing over the shape of politics, not an ideological agenda, was the chief preoccupation in British political life. In this context, the other side of the debate over the political system soon reasserted itself. Moreover, with military victory increasingly likely – if still a long way off – the issue of 'the future' now began to take on a new, and potent, significance.

A string of fresh by-elections in early 1943 informed this development.[218] Reconstruction featured heavily in these contests. Independents pledged allegiance to Beveridge and the Common Wealth Party – a pseudo Labour Party formed the previous year – began to make headway.[219] Addison is right to identify this spate of electoral contests as amounting to a return to the cut and thrust of partisan politics.[220] The shape of postwar politics thus moved to the top of the agenda from the spring of 1943, not least in the minds of Attlee and other Labour leaders. The crisis over the report had, on the most obvious level, intimated the need for a return to traditional party politics; yet, it also leant itself to another interpretation, that the issues facing government were now so important that it would be both dangerous and potentially impossible to pass legislation to deal with them without all-party agreement. If the recent storms were the shape of things to come, that could hardly have been enticing. Like reconstruction, then, the future of the coalition and

Labour's postwar independence – or lack thereof – became central to political calculation. It was another manifestation of how the chief area of contention was now the political system itself.

In late March, Churchill broadcast to the nation on postwar policy and put down markers for maintaining the alliance by floating the possibility of prolonging the coalition even after the cessation of hostilities.[221] He spoke of a four-year plan for reconstruction.[222] His 'kite', which was published as a *Times* pamphlet and sold well,[223] aroused much excitement of various kinds. For instance, Morrison and Dalton met privately on 22 March to discuss the issue and agreed that it would be prudent for the coalition to continue into the postwar era – for an unspecified period – and to hold a general election with candidates from all three parties designated as 'Government' candidates.[224] That was self-evidently both a 'coupon' election and a programme for a prolonged arrangement. Under the plan the two favoured, the parties would run candidates against each other but would still stand on one common manifesto, simply varying their policy emphases.[225] Whether the strategy was principally Morrison's or Dalton's is unclear.[226] Dalton thought that 'this might be the only way out' of electoral annihilation.[227] He confided to his diary that 'now and till after victory, the PM personally dominates the scene, so that any attempt to fight him … would mean that [the party] would be blown away like feathers in a tempest.'[228]

More publicly, at a political luncheon on 26 March, Morrison affirmed that if the Labour Party 'insisted on committing suicide', he would join it; nonetheless, he would 'do his best' to prevent that from happening.[229] His repeated usage of the 'suicide' metaphor is indicative. He acknowledged that Churchill's broadcast had set 'all the politicians chattering', and that 'it was difficult to foresee the political set up immediately after the war.'[230] Soon thereafter the Home Secretary affirmed at a public meeting that 'the general interest must be put before the sectional' and complained of Labour's 'reluctance to accept responsibilities'.[231] 'Chips' Channon recorded 'a growing report' that Morrison was angling to 'follow Churchill and lead a coalition government' himself.[232] *The Times* plainly approved of 'supers[eding] the party system'.[233] Attlee, likewise, wasted little time in turning back to the matter of political alignments. He gave an effective speech about Churchill's broadcast at a PLP meeting, where there was apparently 'very little violent feeling or speaking against it'.[234] This is highly significant. The planning and discussion underline not only the fluidity of a situation in which no one could see the outcome, but also that the notion of a long-term alliance was far from outrageous. It was treated seriously. As the rest of this book will show, even though it has rarely featured in historical analysis it was in fact central. In more ways than one, then, the political system, the structures that underpinned it, its future development, and who ran it had become the issue by early 1943.

As already witnessed in Attlee's electoral policy over the previous year and a half, and then in Morrison and Dalton's discussions, senior figures were strongly attached to the coalition and determined to preserve it while ever the war continued. The *entire* core leadership group – Attlee, Morrison, Bevin and Dalton – also quickly came to favour maintenance of the coalition after the war, for a significant period of time at least. Bevin remained bound to Churchill: a year earlier, he announced that 'I have never served with any body of men ... who have done more to work as a team than the Churchill Cabinet. ... This wicked filthy business of trying to play Winston Churchill off against his colleagues ... is the most diabolical thing I have ever known'.[235] The issue aroused not only calculations of advantage but also passion. As we have seen, personal and cooperative relations between leaders had become central to politics. The men on the other side of the table were the sort with whom deals could be struck. That was significant. Moreover, as made apparent above, at least some of the ministers *already* wanted to maintain the government into the postwar period, and there is no sign that any of them were actually against that notion.

It is unknown if Attlee, for his part, had reached that view by this stage. Precisely when, and why, he did is unclear. The lack of documentary evidence on the timeline of his decision-making remains frustrating. He might have been alive to the continuation of the coalition all along; that was hardly unwise given the amiability of cross-party cooperation, as well as the unknown strength of the Labour Party and the seeming invincibility of Churchill. Alternatively, that view might not have formed by 1942; at this point, he could just have been attempting to meet all possibilities and keep his options open. He might initially have favoured political independence. But prolonging the alliance he had crafted and maintained was certainly to become his preference, and he was to fight for it until the day the government collapsed in May 1945. Though these conflicts will be more critical later in the book, it is worth introducing here the calculations, and available policy options, that came so to dominate the remainder of the war. As Dalton had described, it was widely feared – especially among the

Labour ministers – that a return to political independence would only permit Churchill, as a victorious war leader, to smash the party in a 'khaki' election. The prospect of heavy defeat and a return to opposition cannot have been attractive. Some were inclined to remain in harness with the Conservatives regardless, both 'in order for the peace to be worthwhile', and because of the genuine affinity that had developed between Labour and Conservative colleagues.[236] Coalitionism and loyalty to their partners were powerful influences. Simple preference for power over opposition was also significant. Other concerns included that Churchill may spring a 'coupon' election, a fear that Attlee's own by-election 'coupon' made plausible, with the result of either annihilating the party or – the best case scenario – rending it in two, between those who wielded the 'coupon' as members of the government and those who did not. What senior figures most consistently seem to have favoured – and this would become clearer later – was an 'understanding' between the parties rather than a full-scale 'fusion'. The duration of that understanding, for now, remained uncertain. A belief in the near invulnerability of the Prime Minister was to be important in the calculations of the Labour leaders up to – and beyond – the eventual collapse of the coalition. There was some discussion about remaining in alliance for.a fixed period to allow Churchill's victory aura to dissipate, while some even seemed amenable to carrying on indefinitely.

When the matter of Churchill's speech was raised at the NEC on 24 March, the leaders attained a minor success when, 'quite amazingly', there was broad agreement that to announce anything publicly at such an early stage was unwise.[237] Greenwood, at the PLP, refused to accept a motion that Labour explicitly rejected a future 'coupon' election.[238] Two weeks later, on 7 April, Attlee addressed the PLP at length on the postwar election and Labour's status as an independent party.[239] In an adept performance, which remained as vague and inoffensive as was now customary for the Deputy Prime Minister, Attlee avoided declarations that might inflame things. Nonetheless, he began, unmistakeably, cautiously to lead Labour down the path to postwar alliance. First, he argued that it was sensible to be 'entirely uncommitted and [remain] free' to take a decision on coalition or independence when the right time arose.[240] Then Attlee also claimed that the Labour ministers had no preference for the 'political composition' of any future government.[241] The leader was striking a more conciliatory pose than those he had adopted during the crises of recent months, the issue offering the ministers a profitable, symbolic, means of emphasizing their loyalty to Labour and tethering themselves to the party once again. Yet, it also made the possibility of continuing the coalition an acknowledged option. Attlee argued that no one could know what circumstances might prevail at the end of the war, and hence commitments were foolhardy – a line to which the leader could thus return in the future as a reason for staying in office.[242] His route was circuitous and incremental, keeping all his options open while being clearly sympathetic to the coalition. The PLP accepted his position and Dalton recorded that there had been a visible improvement in the mood of MPs.[243] Moreover, Attlee publicly released a statement to the press about the option of extending the coalition, something that strongly reinforces the notion of an attempt to prepare for a bid to continue the government.[244] The appearance of legitimacy was everything. Gesture, positioning and instrumentally employed rhetoric remained Attlee's most valuable assets.

Attlee's activities were a sensible exploration of the new possibilities that both the war and his own strategy had thrown up. Conventional party politics was unlikely to yield the same sort of preponderance he had achieved. Not just fear of Churchill, but opportunity, drove the support of men like Attlee, Bevin, Dalton and Morrison for prolonged coalition. The problem was that it rested on a misapprehension: both main parties were uninterested in coexistence. This was the major political legacy of the 1930s, just as much as economic crisis and a game of chicken over international policy. Regardless of the agreement to avoid commitment, the Labour Party at large was fiercely opposed to any retention of the cross-party alliance; since 1941 Attlee had only courted support by appealing to its survival instincts. The Conservative Party as a whole was similarly hostile. Despite these qualifications, however, the formal agreement to rule nothing out still constituted an important step, building on Attlee's efforts since late 1941 to consolidate the government. Giving an impression of fealty, loyalty and non-commitment, and imploring the party not to afford the Conservatives the means to wreck Labour's credibility, the leadership group, long ago seduced by the coalition's promise of office, were once again ingratiating themselves with their followers while being fully prepared to strike out in their own direction.

A full range of tactical possibilities therefore existed in political discussion. The problem of 'the future' moved beyond 'reconstruction' as the central area of dispute in political life for the remainder of the war. The question even eventually came to provide the public substance of the final struggle for the leadership between Attlee and Morrison in 1944–45. Coalitionism as a force in its own right may have been airbrushed out of historical perceptions of the Second World War, stemming from a romanticism about the parties virtuously coming together to meet a national emergency and then separating amicably, but in reality this is a caricature.[245] These anxieties and calculations featured heavily in all of what we can discern of the decision-making and mindset of not only the Labour leaders but also the nation's senior politicians more broadly. What united them all was both survival and exploitation of the opportunities that their status as major members of the government threw up.

Events in 1942–43 had begun to make clear how dynamic wartime politics really were. The system was highly fluid and in the process of a remaking. No one knew where it was going. The outcome could have been the supersession of the party system altogether for a while. It could have been another halfway house, as in the 1930s. Alternatively, it could have been the triumph of 'party' itself. 'It was the tension between existing and possible party alignments' that gave individuals – most notably Attlee – 'the chance to identify their futures with unexplored possibilities'.[246] Likewise, it afforded even those who were not really established senior figures – men like Laski and Bevan within the Labour Party – 'the opportunity to exercise power'.[247] (The absence of Conservative 'outsiders' from this analysis is not because of a desire to focus disproportionately on the Labour Party, but because of the paucity of talent outside the ministry following the breaking of that party in 1940.) The formation of the coalition had torn the fabric of politics. The position not only of parties but also of every politician in the system had altered. The old ruling circle was broken; a new one was imposed; 'outsiders' as diverse as Macmillan and Bevan grasped the chance to make a serious name for themselves. It required dexterity but was ripe with potential.

All these people needed 'issues' to which to attach themselves; we have already seen what sorts of themes the most vocal, Laski and Bevan, selected, but there were many others. More than a year earlier, even before Tobruk, an 'alternative government' had been named in Parliament. [248] It included the powerful backbench Conservative, Sir John Wardlaw-Milne (chairman of the prominent all-party Finance Committee, which had so much to say on waste and inefficiency), Admiral of the Fleet Sir Roger Keyes, Shinwell, Griffiths, Clem Davies and Earl Winterton. [249] That was not taken seriously, and Wardlaw-Milne and Keyes wrecked their growing credibility three months later when their attempt to censure Churchill over Tobruk collapsed with the patently ridiculous suggestion that the Duke of Gloucester should be made Commander-in-Chief.[250] Their status as the main Conservative 'outsiders' never recovered.

Bevin certainly took seriously Beaverbrook's observation around this time that Churchill might be on the way out and a new regime would have to be formed with the two men as its leading figures.[251] Beaverbrook was apparently whispering in the ears of both Labour and Conservative rebels.[252] Churchill also took seriously Cripps's soundings about seizing the premiership for himself.[253] Headlam tried to persuade Oliver Stanley to pursue the Conservative leadership, but he showed little interest before Churchill absorbed him into the government.[254] Given the destruction of their pre-eminence, there was plenty of discussion of who would be the next Conservative leader.[255] In early 1943, Ede was recording speculation about the Prime Minister forming a 'centre party' to fight the next election. He claimed that the busy jockeying of Morrison, and possibly Eden, was part of their preparing a bid for the premiership of a postwar coalition.[256]

That Morrison was thought to have a claim to the premiership was a mark of how successful his stewardship of the Home Office was perceived to be. Channon felt Morrison's defence of the government over Beveridge 'revealed his increasing Conservatism – was it a bid for the future leadership of a coalition government?'[257] That might be just gossip, but it does show the curiously Janus-like appeal of Morrison. The key battleground was no longer ideology, social pressure or reconstruction. It was theorizing and arguing abour the world of party and government, its future development and what 'politics' should add up to in the context of a mature democracy. Some of it was gossip, some of it was flying kites, and just enough of it had substance. It is only possible to understand the prospects of the party system if one appreciates the interconnectivity of the attempts to dislodge and safeguard the coalition. All this was occurring on the same political stage. Feuding about war 'efficiency', 'social policy' and 'reconstruction' had far greater resonance than simply the issues at hand. As we have seen, the guises of 'crusader', 'safe pair of hands', 'patriot' and 'philosopher' were just some of those that had been adopted, and even if they were believed they served instrumental purposes. However, all of this, in turn, was linked to an argument over the long-term direction of public life. The future of the party system was the keystone of that debate.

Conclusion

After experiencing his most trying moments of the war in recent months, and being in serious danger of abandonment altogether in February 1943, Attlee, as so often before, not only survived but turned things to his advantage. The discontent had proven manageable because conflict remained within the framework that Attlee, more than anyone, had marked out. As described, from early 1942 the Deputy Prime Minister was shifting away from a mere 'truce' with the Conservatives and coming to place much more onus on the cross-party alliance. His revisions of electoral policy amounted to strengthening the foundations of the coalition. Throwing in his lot with the government in this way, the extent of Attlee's commitment to the alliance he had crafted could not be clearer. What that meant in the long term remained hazy, but a shape was slowly emerging. His was a strategy of patience. Meanwhile, the priorities of others, most significantly the Home Secretary, were also moving in this direction. The future of the alignment was now a key issue. We shall see the rise of Morrison through this lens in the next chapter. Although the period had witnessed a reversion to focus on party politics, there were few indications of the Conservatives regaining the political momentum. High political strategy remained chiefly in the hands of Attlee: and that was an asset. The Conservatives had constructed an economic policy that politically excluded Labour. That tactical victory hardly translated into a strategic success, even in the area of finance, let alone anything else. Their blocking of Beveridge was another, more important signal. But equally significant was the spectacle of Attlee and Morrison grinding Churchill down to an accommodation to 'Beveridge-type' reforms – about as far as he could go without a Conservative revolt. Though his U-turn was not in time to prevent a party crisis, it did signify the political ascendancy of the Labour ministers. Too often historians have focused on the surface and not on what was happening underneath. The notion that Labour ministers got bogged down in inaction in the mid stages of the war is a misapprehension; it is to be diverted by party complaints rather than realities. 'I fail to understand why all and sundry should be ready to accept … all the silly gospel of the socialists … today the most old-fashioned Tories and Liberals keep assuring one that practically everything they have hitherto stood for is no longer either right or feasible,' Headlam lamented.[258] Politically, at least, he was spot-on.

Moreover, the party system itself was now coming under serious scrutiny. From different perspectives, everyone recognized that this had become the crucial problem in British politics. That is not to suggest that Attlee and his colleagues spent all their time plotting about the future rather than focusing on their ministerial responsibilities. We must place these political manoeuvres within the broader story of the war itself. Nevertheless, at the same time it is patently obvious that there are important facets to the political events of this era that we need to appreciate properly. The pressures to reverse the political alignments of 1940 or, alternatively, to press them even further were exerting a powerful influence. It was in that environment of competing tensions and anxieties that Morrison now began to clamber upwards.

Chapter 5

Future Uncertain

With the military-industrial might of the Allies at last beginning to tell against the Axis states, Herbert Morrison launched his own, not all that dissimilar, campaign to grind his way towards victory. Rather than the occupation of capital cities, though, the Home Secretary's priority was to wrest the party leadership from his old rival Attlee. Over the following year, this was to evolve into a persistent campaign to thrust himself forward and seek out a suitable platform to do just that. These next two chapters make Morrison as central as Attlee. The focus of this one is the politics of *leadership* itself: it explores, through Attlee, its practical influence in multiple spheres; but, more than that, through Morrison, it considers the length to which others will go to attain it.

What it seeks to do is integrate the fortunes of Morrison with the evolution of national politics. Thereby both are illuminated. In a very real sense, the Home Secretary was at the heart of most key developments in public life through until the summer of 1945. As such, the chapter proceeds to examine Morrison's political impact; it establishes him as a challenger to Attlee; shows his strengths and weaknesses; and it will highlight how the Home Secretary presented one face to his party – for a partisan depiction of socialism and for independence – and another in private. Moreover, only by examining Morrison's role from 1943 to 1945 does it become feasible to grasp quite how formidable an operator he was. The chapter also shows the challenges that confronted him, as his feuding with Bevin, and difficult decisions at the Home Office, threatened to undermine his plans. Over the next two years Morrison tried to smash his way through the walls that restricted his career. Addison, Brooke and Jefferys have bestowed as little importance on Morrison as they have on Attlee. Indeed, it is in the latter stages of the war that earlier accounts have tended to lose their way. There is little visible recognition in the literature of what senior politicians were aiming at. Still less is it made central to the analysis woven.

At this juncture it seems appropriate to reflect briefly on the character of the politics I have considered. What events hitherto have confirmed was that, rather than being an instance of the triumph of the ineluctable forces of 'public opinion' or 'the people', it is equally plausible that the Second World War was an instance of the primacy of elite action. Crucially, the personal and party struggles that marked it had done much more to determine the shape of public life than the war itself, which, despite its human dimension, was always principally a formidable administrative problem. The Whiggery surrounding the era – consult Calder's magnificent *The People's War* for a flavour – has emphasized the role of sociological developments and intersected them with politics. The result is a distortion. To be sure, it was not just – or even primarily – skewered by historians, but by many of the journalists and intellectuals of the 1940s – men not of fighting age and so with abundant opportunity to daydream from their armchairs. But the events of this period have had, as stressed at the very beginning of this book, a major impact on how public life in the whole period *c.*1940 to 1980 is conceived. The present account makes no claims to exhaustiveness: for purposes of exploring the leadership of Clement Attlee, it abstracts one story out of a much larger context. Yet, it seems difficult not to hold that the politics and government of the Second World War ought to be reassessed with urgency.

There is something else. The period described here, 1943–44, represented the zenith of the Labour ministers' collective influence, as the Conservatives were forced into headlong retreat. Both the gradually emerging struggle between Morrison and Attlee over the leadership, and the conflict within government over policy, fed into the problem which had, in the minds of politicians, already been established as the principal consideration in national politics – the future of the Churchill coalition. The previous chapter integrated cases like the Beveridge crisis within a broader debate about the shape of politics. That had been the main conflict – and conversation – in public life for some time. It was from 1943 that Britain's political leaders came definitely to favour extending their cross-party alliance into the postwar world. What remained to be thrashed out was the precise formula that it would require. Unlike in the preceding two years, there was no longer any serious danger of the coalition being brought to a premature end. Now the problem was how to proceed *after* the war.

Morrison's Midlothian moment

Deep games of more than one kind were now being played. And, as so often, the Labour ministers proved better players than their Conservative counterparts. As we shall see later in the chapter, from 1943 Churchill was to cede the policy initiative to his partners to a degree that confirmed the ultimate success of Attlee's bid to establish Labour as the 'hub' connecting the 'spokes' of government. In contrast to the disarray of the Conservatives, however, Herbert Morrison was in the ascendant. This section tracks his efforts to ring-fence his status as Labour's most committed advocate, and steal a march on the Attlee–Bevin axis. It shows how he supplemented that with a brilliant campaign to centre public attention on himself in contrast to the staid, dull Attlee. Morrison's strategy was complex and carried contradictory intimations. But there is an explanation. He saw linkages that escaped others. And he, as much as Attlee, had to walk on a tightrope of his own.

Already coveting Attlee's place atop the Labour movement, the Beveridge schism catalysed Morrison into action. He seized the opportunity it presented to seal his growing status in the public eye. We have seen how he championed the report inside the government. Outside Whitehall, the Home Secretary's campaign was even more energetic. From November 1942, he spent three months travelling the country and making a series of major speeches to packed meetings as far afield as London, Newcastle, Swindon and Nottingham.[1] Centring on reconstruction, his addresses were aggressive and highly partisan, encompassing subjects like social security and economic and industrial reorganization. They stressed the need for socialist solutions to the nation's challenges. In one typical speech, at Swindon, Morrison performed his self-appointed role as the champion of reform by announcing that there could now be 'no doubt' that government had to ensure 'a minimum standard of life':

> Once a community had reached a point of enlightenment and education ... there [is] an imperative moral obligation. ... We must rise above domination by our economic machine. ... After the war ... we should have to approach all our economic problems on the basis that the interests of the community come first. We should have an annual economic budget as we now had an annual financial budget. We should, in fact, have to estimate the size, not

merely as we did now, of the state budget, but the national income as a whole, and relate it to the demands we wanted to make of it.[2]

He suggested that government would need access to statistical information 'much more extensive ... than anything we possess today' in order comprehensively to plan the national economy.[3] Morrison was a man who needed power like other human beings need oxygen. His speeches were a watershed in national politics. On one level, they hinted at how the instincts of the Labour ministers had been confirmed by the experience of war; but on another, Morrison's speaking campaign should be seen as calculated to establish a position of individual pre-eminence. No one had done anything like it for several years. Since 1939, political actors had been cautious not to utter a syllable, or write a word, without care. And Morrison was alternating between different guises at some speed: in December 1942, he had tried that of the 'planner';[4] in January 1943, it was the minister warning colleagues of the imperative to give way;[5] and in February 1943, it was that of the moralizer.[6] Jefferys has drawn parallels between the speeches and Gladstone's Midlothian campaign.[7] And we know well enough what that was about – to unify the Liberal Party behind the leadership of the GOM.

Morrison thus carved out a distinctive identity as the loudest proponent of the principles contained in the report. The Home Secretary even used a speechwriter to help him.[8] No one associated with the government was so vigorous in stressing that the goal of a postwar new Jerusalem was feasible. *The Times* attributed Morrison's campaign to a bid by the government to win public backing.[9] But that was a misinterpretation. His biographers concluded that Morrison 'undoubtedly' saw the benefits of the campaign for his prospects of capturing the leadership.[10] It was a strategy every bit as complex, and reliant on signalling, as Attlee's. The Home Secretary was utilizing a resonant vocabulary for political purposes, just as Attlee had done. In contrast to the depoliticized vocabulary favoured by Attlee, the speeches were all heavily imbued with the language of socialism. The Home Secretary used 'reconstruction' to find a political voice, and – as he had in the past – positioned himself politically, rhetorically and stylistically in the space directly between his rival Attlee and the Labour movement.

In sum, the speaking campaign was an important advance. Morrison was to persist in these tactics for the rest of the war, and later described his approach to W. P. Crozier, editor of the *Manchester Guardian* and occasional confidante, as being 'to stir things up a bit'.[11] He was now rising fast in political estimations. After a year of these methods, Beaverbrook conveyed to Morrison the view that 'Churchill apart, you are today by far the biggest figure in the country.'[12] That was testimony to his success, and reinforces the view of Morrison that was now in circulation and hinted at by Channon, Headlam and others in the previous chapter. It also vividly underlines the two, quite contrary, identities the Home Secretary enjoyed.

It is perhaps worth pausing to reflect on the fact that Morrison was a very different kind of politician from Attlee. He possessed the leader's flair for manoeuvre and for governance, but he also had the dynamic style that Attlee lacked, and that political parties always covet. Furthermore, his public standing was much greater, for the visibility of the Home Office pushed Morrison to the fore of the national consciousness. He was a constant presence in newspapers and on newsreels. Not only was he the most prominent domestic politician, but, of the core leadership group, he was also certainly the most popular figure in the eyes of the Labour Party. His speeches, whether at open public meetings, party gatherings or in Parliament, were often the best. Morrison, then, was far more than just a Tammany Hall boss. He was waging a public campaign to broaden and deepen his standing, while, as we saw in the previous chapter, being privately hopeful of avoiding a return to the party politics that he so relied on in his language. Morrison's energy went unmatched by anyone of that generation; indeed, he was one of the few genuine all-rounders of the twentieth century. That rendered him a formidable threat to Attlee's ascendancy.

At the beginning of the year, Morrison decided to seek the post of Labour Party treasurer following the death of George Latham – a position that would yield ex-officio status on every one of the executive's subcommittees. MacDonald and Henderson had used it to great effect in the past; 11 years into the future, Gaitskell wanted it for that same reason. Morrison was already attending NEC meetings with increased regularity, and his old alignment with Dalton was renewed.[13] Morrison's loyal base of support, the London Labour Party, nominated him for the job in January 1943.[14] Donoughue and Jones are most likely correct in thinking it improbable that the Home Secretary did not know of the nomination beforehand;[15] the job would reaffirm his credibility, particularly profitable at a time when Attlee's approach was markedly unpopular.

Indeed, Morrison's prospects of adding the post to his portfolio were initially promising. They were enhanced by his persistence in saying the right things. In March 1943, he pushed the NEC for a debate on reconstruction at the annual conference to be 'lifted to the highest possible level' – hardly an indication of hoping to avoid disagreement – while he was simultaneously closely involved over several months in drafting the keynote policy statement for that event, *The Labour Party and the Future*.[16] Then, in June, the Home Secretary was central to a new initiative by the Labour ministers to produce a forceful Cabinet paper on postwar policy, in a fresh bid to bring the Conservatives around to a more favourable view.[17] Attlee and Bevin – keen to secure fresh concessions if possible – strongly backed it,[18] but the Home Secretary's influence was the strongest in both its tone and contents, pushing the government for an explicit commitment to take specific reconstruction decisions as a matter of priority:

> The most urgent need in the immediate postwar period will be to find a home and employment for all those who have served the country. ... All this involves taking definite decisions of policy. But no real progress can be made in shaping government policy for the postwar period so long as we adhere to the principle that decisions involving financial commitments cannot be made until our postwar financial position is definitely known. Without a firm decision by the War Cabinet ... our plans must remain uncertain and nothing can be brought to the point of legislative enactment.
>
> The principle of refusing to make piecemeal decisions is sound, but the moral cannot possibly be to make no decisions at all. ... Only one course remains and it is a reasonable one. It is for the government to make now the best forecast it can of the financial and economic position of the country after the war and on that basis to take a major decision as to the items which it is prepared to carry through into law before the end of the war.[19]

'The best forecast' was the clearest statement yet of the Labour ministers' way of conducting government. The Home Secretary was running separate efforts along parallel tracks. But the object – in public, party and government – was the same, to dominate debate. Though it was a further instance of contesting policy with the Conservatives, again we ought not to lose sight of the wider context of Morrison's priorities. In all manner of ways, he was centring attention on himself and occupying large tracts of political ground.

This phenomenon of Morrison's rise and its impact on the political world has been sorely understudied by historians. Rab Butler, head of the Conservative's postwar problems committee, and with an ear to the ground on such matters, said that 'Herbert Morrison is bidding for the Treasuryship and, some say, the Leadership.'[20] Butler went on that, 'his technique is to make speeches on other people's subjects, and to please the very gullible *Times* by being so intensely reasonable.'[21] Reasonable or not, Morrison's work to establish himself as a more authentic representative of the Labour Party than Attlee, was, in many respects, just smoke and mirrors. That is not to suggest that he was acting in bad faith, merely that no one was more explicit in his amenability to a prolonged curtailment of independent party politics after the war. He had, after all, earlier advocated what amounted to a 'coupon' general election. The 'Janus' analogy made in the previous chapter is not an inappropriate one. Now, in May 1943, Morrison let his guard down on his true views during an interview with Crozier, in which he revealed that 'I hope there won't be an election immediately at the end of the war. I don't want an election for twelve months at least after the end of the war.'[22] As if that was not clear enough, the Home Secretary said that the coalition could continue even *after* an election – the parties might stand on a joint 'Government' manifesto, but with each campaigning from a particular angle.[23] This exchange is important because, when coupled with the preceding analysis of his behaviour, it offers clarity about Morrison's train of thought. He set out to Crozier the details of an arrangement that was not dissimilar to the scheme he had discussed some months earlier with Dalton. Morrison suggested that Labour's recent revolts were 'stupid', that the party was 'much better' in opposition and it needed to be 'educated for governing' – hardly the words of someone eager for a reversion to traditional party politics.[24]

Morrison, then, had two broad strategies. The gap between the Home Secretary's ambition to be leader, and the reality of his position on party politics, is quite evident. Indeed, the true direction of Morrison's priorities was made plain when he attributed the ongoing difficulties in the party to a perpetual 'crisis of leadership', an unsubtle barb at Attlee; he suggested that his rival was not up to the job in charging that there was a 'lack of leadership'.[25] In yet another, and startling, insight into his concerns, Morrison tried to get Crozier to stress when he wrote up the interview the damage that would be inflicted to 'the fortunes of the party' if he were removed from the NEC – which would happen if he lost the treasurership election.[26] In a further conversation with Crozier soon afterwards, he asserted that 'the bulk' of the Labour Party 'don't in the least understand the political position', believing that they would sweep to victory in a general election, when, in fact, the Conservatives held all the cards.[27] Morrison's preference for prolonging the lifespan of the alliance is clear. His posturing in his speeches, as well as his carefully selected sabotage of Attlee's leadership since 1941, was merely point scoring. Like Attlee, the Home Secretary was keeping his options open – building up his position in the bid to become leader but with no inclination to give the party what it wanted, in the form of independence, when he did.

Despite his success over recent months making him one of the few politicians not to be in the doldrums, Morrison's plotting to shove himself forward reawakened dormant rivalries. The deal brokering surrounding the treasurership dominated the conference at Westminster between 14 and 18 June – and everyone involved knew what was really at stake. As such, an election that Morrison had calculated he would win handsomely turned out to be far tougher. Greenwood also put up for the post, as did W. Glenvil Hall, of the mineworkers' union.[28] Morrison deeply resented Greenwood's decision to stand.[29] If he lost, he would be deprived of his current seat on the executive – which he was abdicating to stand in the contest. With ferocious private politicking underway before the event opened, Morrison quickly found himself embroiled in a desperate fight. Fulfilment of the goals he had identified depended, in large part, on stimulating an aura of legitimacy; defeat would constitute a blow to that. Dalton – as so often in the past – put himself to work as Morrison's agitator, working tirelessly to secure union bloc votes as well as ensuring that the Home Secretary's winding up speech in the debate on *The Labour Party and the Future* was timed to occur just when it might give him a boost in the poll.[30]

But things immediately looked black for Morrison. While each candidate was to be backed by unions of various sizes, it was reckoned that Greenwood might attract a majority.[31] What had been intended as a virtual coronation was turning into a humiliation. Central to the reversal, unsurprisingly, was Bevin. Though refusing to attend the conference in protest against the party's treachery over Beveridge, Bevin ranged the huge vote of the TGWU behind Greenwood – in truth, no more than a 'cardboard member' of his union – in an attempt to block Morrison.[32] Bevin despised Morrison to begin with, of course; but, as we saw in the preceding chapter, he took the view that Morrison was fortifying a position he could use to seek the leadership itself.[33] With the constituency parties factored in, Dalton calculated that Greenwood would poll 1,074,000 votes compared with Morrison's 791,000 and Hall's 470,000.[34] Hall's candidacy was important because, if the contest went to a second ballot – which remained unclear as the rules had still not been finalized even as the conference opened – it seemed likely that, if he were eliminated, the miners would switch to the Home Secretary.[35] Certainly, their leaders, Watson and Lawther – compelled to support Hall due to internal union politics – were in reality only too eager to throw their weight behind Morrison.[36]

The Labour movement thus descended into the old-fashioned intriguing and vote counting so reminiscent of bygone years. Dalton and Lawther engineered an emergency session of the NEC to discuss the rules.[37] Laski, too, worked to assist Morrison by introducing a motion in favour of a second ballot.[38] Alerted to what Morrison's supporters were up to, Greenwood and his union allies on the executive – James Walker, W. A. Robinson and George Dallas – were 'in full force and in full cry', trying to shout down everyone else and arguing vigorously against the motion.[39] When a vote was taken, the executive was tied, 11 votes to 11, but the chairman, A. J. Dobbs, crushed Morrison's hopes when he used his casting vote against Laski's resolution, defeating the proposal for a second ballot.[40]

That same day, Morrison gave one of his now common virtuoso speeches in the debate on *The Labour Party and the Future*. Attlee opened with a competent disquisition, but Morrison wound up with a brilliant display of his platform abilities.[41] In contrast to Attlee, he was – again – much more aggressive than the leader. Morrison's language was combative and distinctly socialist: promising a 'planned economy', he declared that 'we *must* have the public ownership of the natural monopolies; we *must* have the socialization … of those restrictive monopolies of capitalism … we *are* going to be triumphant at the expense of our enemies in the field.'[42] The speech received a thunderous ovation,[43] while his biographers have described it as 'a moment of triumph', Morrison resembling 'an authentic national leader'.[44] To be sure, few people ever said that about Attlee. Delivering one of the great conference performances – a symbolic culmination of months of work – the Home Secretary strikingly reemphasized the fundamental differences between himself and his rival.

But, it was all to no avail. The day after, with the bid to procure a second ballot rejected, Greenwood captured the treasurership in decisive fashion by attracting 1,253,000 votes to Morrison's 926,000 and Hall's 519,000.[45] Morrison had done better than the 791,000 that Dalton predicted and swept the board with the local parties – evidence of his effectiveness in attracting the rank and file over the preceding months.[46] For all his popularity, however, Bevin and the trade unions proved too much. Morrison complained to Crozier that he had only been defeated because of Bevin,[47] a view endorsed at the time by Ede.[48] Headlam thought that sections of the party opposed him because he was 'too clever by far'.[49] A furious Morrison raged to Dalton that this was the third time 'they' had engineered his defeat – the other two cases being the 1935 leadership election and in 1936 when Middleton bested him for the post of general secretary.[50] 'They' was plainly a reference to the trade unions. Even so, Morrison was wise enough not to appear bitter; he did not follow through on his initial instinct to provoke a public row 'if it can still be arranged' by asking the delegates personally for a second ballot.[51]

Thus, the defeat highlighted something profound. That was the very real challenge that Morrison would have to overcome if he was to succeed in dislodging Attlee. It might be accurate to suggest that Morrison was principally unlucky in the timing of many of his major initiatives. His abilities in governance, or, alternatively, his rivalries in the Labour movement, always seemed to lead him into conflict with his own ambitions. The question that will immediately spring to mind for the reader is this: what on earth did the Home Secretary need to do in order to win? His assiduous work since late 1942 had secured him a public and political stature higher than ever before. He was doing things that no other member of the body politic, with the exception of Churchill, was able to do. Yet, he had been bested by a failed minister like Greenwood. This theme will be returned to later in the chapter, but for now it seems sufficient to observe that while Morrison was admired by many, he was loathed by others. His future deeply uncertain, one historian observed that Bevin had 'cooked [Morrison's] goose'.[52]

Retaking the initiative
These events occurred against the backdrop of a fresh reminder of Attlee's own abilities. Moreover, while Morrison's fortunes were suddenly in flux, Attlee and the other ministers underwent a significant recovery in 1943. The conference saw a surprising upturn in the party's disposition

and an attack on the ministers for their stance on Beveridge was defeated by a majority of two to one.[53] An affirmation that Labour 'welcomes and applauds' the Beveridge Report was buttressed by the qualification that the legislation ought to be readied for implementation '*after the war*'.[54] All this might well have been connected to new signals emanating from the leadership implying that politics would revert to independent party conflict once the war was finally over. As the conference opened, the NEC agreed that Attlee might 'intimate' to delegates that a special event would be called at the end of the war to decide Labour's future.[55] But that was, in reality, only a continuation of Attlee's approach in recent months. Alerted by the recent troubles, it was very clearly intended to reassure the movement that decision-making power would be vested in its members. It was accepted by the delegates without challenge.[56] In reality, the signal was largely meaningless and, when taken together with Attlee's guidance of electoral strategy in the preceding eighteen months, one wonders whether it should be seen as a double blind. It certainly did not preclude efforts by Attlee and the rest to take the initiative as they saw fit. In fact, the conference only finalized Attlee's bid to entrench the cross-party alliance: *The Labour Party and the Future* affirmed the need to maintain the electoral truce, stressing that the public would look with hostility towards any party opting for 'the short-term satisfaction of partisan politics'.[57] Attlee himself told the delegates that they could not naively end the truce while remaining in the coalition, it being impossible to conduct by-elections 'on a kind of limited liability'.[58] The Deputy Prime Minister was unusually robust in defending the Labour ministers' role in office, telling the delegates flatly that he 'would not accept' the ending of the truce: 'The government must act collectively. Every member must take responsibility for all its actions or get out ... the fact remains that a vote for the ending of the electoral truce is a vote for ending this government.'[59] That was the new, intransigent Attlee once again. After deploying the usual tactic of alluding to the electoral consequences of a break with his strategy, continued support was granted for the truce by an overwhelming margin of 2,243,000 votes to 374,000.[60] Given how narrow the vote on that same issue had been just 12 months previously, it was a crushing rebuff to alternative strategies.

Attlee's management of the party, and particularly his political approach, was thus publicly re-endorsed. He secured mandates in the areas he had been preoccupied with since 1941.[61] Though the desire of men like Bevan and Laski to dive headlong into the abyss remained as strong as ever, most of the party backed away: the prospect of a serious schism had become real and, anyway, Attlee had intimated that ministers would not try to prejudge the shape of postwar politics. With a reorganization of the NEC shortly thereafter, which reduced the number of committees on which individuals could sit, the scope for troublemakers like Laski was restricted and the executive became more serviceable to Attlee once again.[62] Attlee had already bluntly warned the TUC that the party 'entered the government on the basis of fighting the war, with the approval of the whole movement; they never expected to be able to carry through [Labour's] party programme'.[63] Finally, in July, the Labour ministers played a masterstroke by bringing the oversight of party policy on reconstruction into their own hands. They abruptly announced that, as the matter was clearly so important, responsibility for planning it should be left to them personally.[64] Laski's Reconstruction Committee was consequently dissolved.[65] Dalton recorded that policy was now in the hands of 'not a bad bunch of chaps'.[66] It was a bold reassertion of their authority by Attlee and the rest.

Sure enough, policy planning for the future got underway.[67] *Full Employment and Financial Policy* – the definitive statement of the party's wartime thinking – announced an intention to retain existing economic controls, as well as for the state to stimulate purchasing power to maintain full employment.[68] It signified a blending of socialism with Keynesianism; and it displayed a savvy ability to absorb the innovations of war. Thus, for the first time since 1939, policy preparation in the party became more than mere rhetoric. But that was because Attlee and his colleagues – none more so than the Home Secretary – had come to recognize the power of 'reconstruction'. Even more significant than the issue *per se* was its language. The Labour ministers had skilfully shifted their position and used it to regain the initiative. Like any seasoned politician, Attlee and the leaders said whatever they thought it sensible to say.[69] In late July, Attlee's Organization Committee submitted a memorandum, 'Policy Campaign', calling for an intensive scheme of 'party activity' – particularly public rallies – to revitalize Labour.[70] But all of this work should not give the impression that the bid to prolong the cross-party alliance was not alive and well – far from it. The ministers' intention to control carefully what was said was made plain by the fact that, under the plan, speakers were to be 'assisted' by 'notes prepared in the office'.[71] It was an obvious bid to manage debate and restrict it to carefully predetermined areas. It is difficult to escape the belief that 'activity' and 'policymaking' were another instance of smoke signalling. Attlee, for one, had utilized reassurance to jostle the party into compliance on too many occasions since 1939. We saw in the previous chapter how, in April, he prevented the party from ruling *out* the idea of continuing the alliance. As always with the Deputy Prime Minister, separate actions were linked by an underlying vision. It was the choreographed politics of theatre.[72] That was Attlee's genius – an ability to shape an environment by narrowing the range of options.

Attlee thus continued to keep the balls in the air. And political leaders tacked more openly in the direction of postwar alliance. Evidence in the Dalton papers conveys information about the preferences of several key figures. By September 1943 Dalton was discussing with Attlee how to remain in harness with the other parties after the war. According to Dalton's account, he suggested to Attlee that the best strategy would be to postpone a general election for as long as possible and continue the alliance in the interim, as well as to ask Churchill to address the PLP on the imperative of unity.[73] He was terrified of Churchill winning a khaki election. Dalton also gleaned from Halifax that it was common knowledge, even in Conservative circles, that both Morrison and Bevin were similarly thinking along the lines of maintaining the coalition for some time into the peace: Morrison, as we have seen, with his ideas of a 'common manifesto', and Bevin reckoning that he could persuade the TUC to back continuation if Churchill agreed to repeal the Trade Disputes Act.[74] Halifax himself reportedly favoured Morrison's approach, and relayed his belief that Churchill wanted 'to go on into the peace with a National government, if we would play'.[75] That certainly conformed to Churchill's romantic tendencies. While Dalton expressed anxiety about the feasibility of achieving the goal – Labour 'are great experts … at suicide'[76] – Attlee, *yet again*, does not appear to have given Dalton any intimation of his own plans. No doubt he had little inclination to be hoisted by his own petard. But the direction in which events were drifting is clear.

This record of the perspectives of leading government figures is additional, and quite striking, evidence of the breadth of opinion favourably disposed to prolonging the alliance. Far from being the goal of a minority – which might explain its neglect – it garnered near universal endorsement from senior politicians. This underlines afresh the point that

171

the self-conception of the British body politic in the years prior to 1945 must be comprehensively reassessed. Yet, even so, that is not to suggest that the enduring hostility emanating from both of the main parties – particularly backbenchers and the rank-and-file – on the matter did not stack the odds against the whole initiative.[77] As Thorpe has shown, alliance had *always* been a hard sell. In October 1943, for instance, Bevan exploited the fact that military victory was seemingly assured to argue again that the coalition had done its job and should be disbanded.[78] For their part, the Conservatives complained even more bitterly, no doubt compounded by the fact that they were patently coming off worse in government: Headlam bemoaned that 'young Conservatives' were so 'afraid of being considered unprogressive that they adopt socialist ideas without due consideration and surrender the fort without fighting'.[79] Earlier in the year, 36 MPs had established the Conservative Reform Committee to reconcile the party to new economic and social dogmas.[80] And there was 'serious unrest' towards Conservative ministers. Anderson was a 'dreary dog',[81] Churchill's *faux pas* of making Beaverbrook – the 'Minister of Midnight'[82] – Lord Privy Seal upset 'a large and powerful section of the party',[83] and the cabal of the press magnate, Bracken and Viscount Cherwell was thoroughly loathed – Channon called them a 'triumvirate' who 'run the country when the PM is away'.[84] Churchill did not have a firm hold because he 'ignore[d] the party as a whole'.[85] These examples capture the flavour of the debate. They did not bode well for any bid to keep the main parties welded together. Indeed, that all of these discussions on 'the future' were conducted in secret is indicative that ministers were fully cognizant of the difficulties. So too is the fact that even by-election policy had been developed by Attlee under a cloak of secrecy. In consequence, Attlee, and to a lesser extent his colleagues – Labour and Conservative alike – were to obfuscate about their stance until the very end of the war.

On the other hand, however, Attlee was undoubtedly in the ascendant once more from 1943. His general influence in public life stood at its zenith. Running parallel to the reassertion of his authority was his replacing Anderson as Lord President in September, a consolidation of Labour's power in the government.[86] Anderson was shifted to take over at the Treasury upon the death of Wood.[87] That was a big blow to the Conservatives: the most effective resistance to the Labour ministers had come through the duopoly of Wood at the Exchequer and Anderson on the Lord President's Committee. They impeded the two key transit points of finance and policy creation. Anderson's move thus provided the Labour representatives with more freedom in Whitehall than ever. Having informally been perhaps the leading figure on the domestic front for the previous three years, Attlee now became so officially and was placed in charge of the 'engine of government'. It is worth taking the opportunity to stress that Attlee thus occupied the roles of Deputy Prime Minister, Lord President of the Council and member of the War Cabinet, and sat on virtually every Whitehall committee – concerned with either domestic affairs or the war itself – that mattered. He also remained backed on the Lord President's Committee by Bevin and Morrison. The ability of the Labour ministers to straddle the bridge between office and party was therefore bolstered considerably as their influence over reconstruction planning grew. All three men redoubled their efforts to contest Conservative influence and pilot through their pet policy projects. Within a month of assuming the leadership of the 'domestic War Cabinet', for instance, Attlee argued forcefully that the government should make postwar plans based on what he deemed a 'reasonable' judgement of the country's finances at the termination of hostilities – like Morrison's 'best forecast' a somewhat different stance to that which prevailed hitherto in either the Lord President's Committee or the War Cabinet.[88] The tougher style of leadership he had practised since 1941 was increasingly pronounced as Attlee flatly warned Churchill that he would make his case for action on these issues when he pleased, and was not concerned with the reaction of the Conservative Party.[89] According to the official record, Attlee told the War Cabinet that:

We [are] nearing, if we [have] not already reached a point at which the formulation of postwar policy would be held up [if decisions were delayed any longer]. ... Decisions could and ought to be taken on the basis of the best assumptions we could make about conditions at the end of the war.[90]

Perhaps indicative of his belief in coalitionism, he went on that:

It had sometimes been argued that it would be inexpedient to try to go too far in the formulation of postwar policy for fear of raising political controversy on party lines. [I believe] however that

173

on many of these questions there would be a large measure of agreement between ministers. ... The discussions in Cabinet committees had so far disclosed relatively little difference of view on party lines, and the government could now, without risk of serious party controversy, proceed to make certain assumptions on which decisions ... could be based.[91]

Churchill, as usual, resisted by pointing to the sheer uncertainty of the situation. But he also raised the objection that the Labour ministers had pledged at the conference that they would 'resign office' at the end of the war if the party called upon them to do so – which, as we have seen, was actually not quite what they had promised.[92] Having 'no assurance of the continued cooperation of the Labour ministers' was a hindrance, Churchill claimed.[93]

The minutes of this Cabinet meeting in October make for fascinating reading. Despite the strains on the party system, Attlee had plainly not forgotten about the old struggle with the Conservatives. Although Churchill began the meeting by vocally stressing his resistance to further reforms, by the end his ability – or willingness – to block them had wilted under sustained pressure from first Attlee, then Bevin and, finally, Morrison.[94] Each man made a long disquisition bullying the Prime Minister; and by the end of the meeting he had capitulated spectacularly. In closing, Churchill asked Attlee for a list of 'four or five major projects' on which action was required.[95] It was a startling case of political browbeating. Anderson's effort to stress that much had already been done on reconstruction made little impact.[96] A bruised Churchill complained that he had been 'jostled and beaten up by the Deputy Prime Minister'.[97]

In October 1943, the efforts of Attlee, Bevin and Morrison had, in one shove, forced Churchill to give as much ground – perhaps more – as he had ever given before. It was a remarkable relinquishment of political authority. Churchill was arguably not paying adequate attention to the political balance of forces. It is difficult not to conclude that he was as bad a party leader as Attlee was a good one.[98] Perhaps he was doing what he deemed necessary to ensure the government's survival. After all, 'the provisional character of his political philosophy' was one of Churchill's few constants, but the point remains valid.[99] In response to Churchill's request, Attlee pointed to exports, increased unemployment insurance, and the transitioning of industry and the armed forces from a war footing as areas in need of attention.[100] Five days later, outflanked and exhausted, the Prime Minister circulated a memorandum to the Cabinet that underlined exactly who was doing the running in the government: it by-passed inevitable Conservative protests by explicitly stating that, on these problems, action 'must be taken now, whether or not they involved legislation and whether or not they are controversial'.[101]

To a considerable degree, then, through his new position as Lord President, Attlee – with Bevin and Morrison by his side – was able to set the domestic agenda. That confirmed how far he had come as a leader since 1939, and particularly in his marked change of temperament in the previous two years. In contrast, the largest party in the House of Commons was in meltdown – still failing to bounce back from the destruction of Chamberlain three years earlier, led by a man who was a shambolic political operator and his team of cranks, and consistently unable to withstand the carefully formulated assaults of its own allies. Such was, and is, the nature of coalitions, but that was no comfort to the Conservatives. Just weeks later, the Prime Minister tried again: he decreed that a Minister of Reconstruction should be appointed with a seat in the War Cabinet, and the work of the Reconstruction Committee given top priority.[102] But even worse for Conservative influence, Attlee, Bevin, Dalton and Morrison were all members of this increasingly powerful coordinating body. Anderson and Butler were the only significant Conservatives. These shifts, with their ramifications for government priorities, confirmed the realignment of the British state and its governing assumptions since May 1940. Policy is inevitably an arbitrary and imperfect mixture of ideas, filtered through too many individuals to facilitate easy analysis;[103] what might be considered more important, as argued in earlier chapters, was the underlying balance of forces and possession of the initiative. These events demonstrate how effectively the Labour ministers had captured the political centre ground. Moreover, through dominating the language of 'national community' and the state itself, they had actually reconstructed that ground.

In many respects, then, the latter stage of the war was the time of the Labour ministers' greatest influence. Churchill initially wanted Beaverbrook to do the job of 'postwar Controller',[104] as his 'hatchet man', as Attlee put it.[105] But Attlee warned him that Bevin would be furious if Beaverbrook was appointed to Reconstruction, and the Minister of Labour himself told Churchill that 'I wouldn't stand it'.[106] Churchill tried to hold fast and meekly pledged that 'he won't interfere with _you_,' but, in the end, gave way yet again and the less objectionable – and less combative – Lord Woolton got the role instead.[107] Woolton was not remotely sympathetic to socialism but was easily overpowered by men like Bevin. Attlee was keen to break up the influence over the Prime Minister of what Dalton called 'the two Bs' – Beaverbrook and Bracken – and went so far as to tell Churchill that they gave him 'false inform-ation'.[108] Weakening their power was, of course, a blow to their efforts to contain Labour's influence in the regime. With the Anderson–Wood duopoly broken, they were the last major bastions of Conservative resistance. By contrast, Attlee deftly brushed aside Churchill's weak bid to play the same game: when Churchill told the Deputy Prime Minister that backbench Conservatives disliked him, Attlee paid little attention.[109] It seems appropriate to reflect briefly on Attlee's opposite as a party leader. Addison rightly observed that Churchill 'failed to lead in any consistent direction'.[110] And Conservative ministers were already up in arms about his benign view of the United States.[111] By December, when Churchill came down with pneumonia in Algiers, political minds at Westminster quickly focused on the succession should he die, and Channon reckoned that Anderson and Eden would be the 'rival claimants'.[112] The vacuum occasioned by Churchill's neglect was filled principally by Attlee's decisive style. Ian Harris has written that 'political conflict … produces a signal result. It creates roles of authority.'[113] Attlee, once an individual who possessed very little 'authority', had reworked the landscape to generate a situation in which he wielded extensive personal authority in multiple contexts. The story of the war was the rise of Attlee to this level of influence.

All of this was another victory for Labour's agenda and further affirm-ation, if any were needed, of the success that accrued via Attlee's quiet commandeering of the mechanisms of Whitehall. Earlier in the Second World War, the Labour ministers had won concessions, but they were still repeatedly frustrated; now, from 1943, it was they who set the agenda, and it was all Churchill and the Conservatives could do to act as a brake. Attlee still sat atop the intersection between government and high political strategy; moreover, he was directing the traffic along it with aplomb. In a note to Attlee, which he decided not to send, an anxious Churchill complained that there was 'a solid mass of four socialist politicians of the highest quality and authority', dominating the government by their 'force and power'[114] – a statement that confirms the degree to which Attlee had manoeuvred the Prime Minister into a corner from which he could not escape. All in all, judged Attlee, things were now 'quite satisfactory'.[115]

The isolation of Morrison

For all the Labour ministers' strategic success, with his own failure to defeat Greenwood the Home Secretary's advance had, to some extent, been checked. It highlighted his – for now – limited ability to forge the coalition needed to oust Attlee. Even his old alliance with Dalton withered as the latter moved into the orbit of Attlee and Bevin.[116] Yet, Morrison possessed an uncanny ability to recover from setbacks. As such, the defeat would quickly prove to be a far from cataclysmic blow. He was as defiant as ever in informing Crozier just days after the defeat that he intended to step up the intensity of his public statements and speeches regardless. 'The lines of policy should be clearly laid down, and no one else [is] doing it.'[117]

In a series of fresh public speeches, the Home Secretary began arguing more aggressively than ever before in favour of extensive reconstruction planning.[118] He followed precisely the same path as the previous winter, and it was suggestive of the Home Secretary's profile that, in November, Headlam began a diary entry by writing that 'Morrison as usual has made a speech this weekend.'[119] The tone of Morrison's public addresses in the six months following the conference was so partisan that Churchill eventually became angry with him for destabilizing the government.[120]

Since late 1942 Morrison had begun to link together the numerous, contentious issues about the postwar world that were animating public life – Beveridge, reconstruction, the economy, industry and party politics – into a distinctive sectarian rhetoric quite at odds with the ethos of the coalitionism espoused by Attlee. He established himself as a public and political champion of each. It is worth stressing again that this was principally a matter of *presentation*; it is striking how little he actually differed from Attlee – firm adherence to the government, resolute intolerance of any complaint and an unwillingness to take hasty decisions about the future. But by November the results of this dual approach were plain to see: that month Morrison topped the ballot for the Administrative Committee.[121] The Beaverbrook press (which offered consistent support to Morrison, most likely because Bevin was the nemesis of both men) gave him perhaps as much coverage as pro-Labour outlets.[122] The Home Secretary's controversial speeches and his status as unquestionably the most 'party-political' of the nation's governors, further elevated him in the public eye. He continued to act as the government's principal trouble-shooter in parliamentary debates on sensitive issues[123] and still possessed his various anchors in the government, the LLP and the PLP. With good reason, Ede observed privately that Churchill and Morrison were very alike, displaying 'no real grounding principles' besides ambition.[124] Both were adventurers and bookies. But it was a spirit that paid off: by October 1943, the *Daily Express* was declaring Morrison's seemingly inexorable rise 'the outstanding political event of the last three years'.[125] Perhaps Bevin had not 'cooked his goose' after all.

The juxtaposition between Morrison's great successes and enduring difficulties is a powerful one. It was confirmed in November 1943 when the Home Secretary found himself at the heart of the worst crisis since Beveridge. The touchpaper was lit when Morrison decided, with reluctance, to authorize the release from prison of the ailing British Union of Fascists leader, Sir Oswald Mosley. He was persuaded by doctors that Mosley might die of ill health and chose to free him and place him under house arrest instead.[126] The decision to release Britain's most notorious prisoner, a quisling in the eyes of the public, quickly generated an unprecedented uproar. Bevin, for one, was incredulous, making his opposition known publicly.[127] His biographer even contended that this incident crystallized his enduring hatred of Morrison,[128] but that was merely the beginning of what Donoughue and Jones termed the 'biggest storm of Morrison's wartime career'.[129] The crisis rapidly accelerated out of control – Bevan denounced 'collaborationist Labour leaders'; mass protests were held across the country; and sacks of letters attacking Morrison were received at the Home Office. Worse, while he was giving a speech in the House of Commons, there were violent clashes outside Parliament between police and 2000 protesters.[130] Though assembled MPs, mostly Conservatives, gave Morrison an ovation, and sections of the press labelled his performance 'a great political triumph',[131] nevertheless, an even more serious problem than the fury of the British people was the deep and visceral odium felt by the Labour movement.

Bevin's union, the TGWU, immediately passed a resolution deriding the release as 'an insult to the people in the fighting services', while other unions –the railwaymen, engineers, miners and General and Municipal – joined in the excoriation of Morrison.[132] On 24 November, the National Council of Labour disassociated itself from the Home Secretary's decision and ordered its constituent bodies – the NEC, TUC and PLP – to consider the issue.[133] Morrison's credibility was thus under serious threat; it was immediately shot to pieces when, at the instigation of NEC chairman A. J. Dobbs – who had scotched his bid for a second ballot at conference – that same day the executive adopted a resolution denouncing the Home Secretary's decision by an overwhelming margin of thirteen votes to one.[134] Meanwhile, the TUC backed the critique of Morrison's actions, with almost every member of the General Council launching personal attacks on him.[135] To all intents and purposes, Morrison had been censured by two of the Labour movement's three primary bodies.

Not for the first time, then, the Home Office came with bearing the weight of unpopular policies. Moreover, Attlee astutely stood back and refrained from any public association with the crisis whatsoever.[136] The career of a lesser man would have been decimated already. All that remained was for the PLP to decide its stance; on 25 November, even on the Administrative Committee a motion to censure Morrison was defeated by just one vote.[137] At what had become a make-or-break party meeting, Greenwood worked to find a compromise with a resolution that expressed 'concern' at Mosley's release but stopped short of actually criticizing it, and supporting Morrison's freedom to make hard choices.[138] But a rival amendment, which called for a censure on the Home Secretary, and a motion of no confidence in him to be put down in the Commons, was also introduced.[139] Morrison, locked into an increasingly desperate struggle with the bulk of his own party, was fighting for his political life; the union-sponsored MPs, particularly, were arrayed against him.[140] For his part, Attlee still avoided engagement.[141] Given that he usually rushed in whenever the stability of the party and government was under threat, it is difficult to conclude that his restraint in this instance was not deliberate. By now the TUC, NEC and MFGB were also calling for Mosley to be reinterned.[142]

Characteristically, however, the Home Secretary went onto the offensive and brazenly told the PLP rebels that no amount of trade union pressure would alter his decision.[143] In the PLP vote that might, indirectly, decide his future, he only escaped formal censure by eight votes.[144] Greenwood's non-committal resolution was then passed by 61 votes to 15.[145] Morrison had stared into the abyss: it is doubtful that there could have been any way back after a censure by MPs. To make matters worse – if that were possible – a group of recalcitrant MPs rejected the decision

179

and put down a motion of no confidence in the House of Commons regardless. It indicted Morrison's actions as being deliberately 'calculated to retard the war effort'.[146]

As the parliamentary duel between the Home Secretary and his critics approached, the atmosphere became still more poisonous. The *Daily Express* wrote that it would be an error if Morrison's career were to derailed by the issue, as

> The Labour Party cannot in fact do without him. He stands head and shoulders above all other Labour leaders, and when in due course the party secedes from the coalition to fight its own political battles it will need his leadership and personality if it is to make any real impression on the mind of the electorate ... if the Labour Party were to demote him and put him on the shelf ... it would be making a disastrous mistake.[147]

Yet, while the Beaverbrook newspaper took great delight in backing Morrison to the hilt against Bevin – asserting the 'need' for Morrison's 'leadership' of the party, for example[148] – the Home Secretary's position nevertheless remained on a knife-edge. Dalton thought it 'quite on the cards' that he might have to resign.[149]

It was only now, with the prospect of a Labour minister suffering a vote of no confidence from a majority of his own MPs, that Attlee was finally compelled to step forward. If restless MPs discovered that they could get rid of Morrison, they might well try to do the same again. At the PLP on 1 December, Attlee became involved for the first time and warned the party that the motion, if supported, would have wider ramifications.[150] As so often when faced with a similar situation, the Deputy Prime Minister deployed calls for 'responsibility' to bring the party to heel, arguably moving not so much to protect Morrison as to preserve the position of the Labour ministers as a whole.[151] The damage to Morrison's succession prospects – if that was a calculation in Attlee's mind, we cannot know – had already been done. His timely intervention helped to turn things around: a majority of the PLP at last consented not to support the rebel motion, albeit narrowly.[152]

That might just have saved Morrison, for in a vitriolic performance in Parliament the Home Secretary openly targeted his own party and denounced those sections of the Labour movement – the NEC, TUC,

PLP and NCL – that had criticized him.[153] He even suggested they were in league with the Communists.[154] One newspaper compared Morrison's oratorical mastery of the Commons with that of Churchill himself.[155] Despite his unapologetic manner, in the crucial division the motion of no confidence went down to defeat by 327 to 62.[156] Just over half the PLP obeyed the official line, which suggests that minus Attlee's warning a majority of MPs might perhaps have abstained or voted against the government.[157] Both Morrison and Ede suspected that Bevin was behind the mass revolt by union MPs on the grounds that he could have brought his influence to bear on the rebels.[158] With the matter settled in the Commons, though, the furore soon ebbed. The Mosley crisis ended with a very empty victory for the Home Secretary. His refusal to be challenged had gravely damaged his position; and, by late 1943, the leadership looked beyond his reach.

This debacle, and, even more so, Morrison's instinctive response to it, is worth pondering. The Home Secretary spent a year vigorously intriguing to replace Attlee, only to suffer the indignity of almost suffering censure by the same MPs he would one day have to persuade to back him. The rest of the Labour movement had been even fiercer in opposing him. Animated by his natural refusal to tolerate dissent, he only inflicted further damage to the pre-eminence he had expended so much energy cultivating. Morrison was unquestionably the party's leading talent of this era, but in the labyrinthian world of the Labour movement that carried him only so far.

Tellingly, Attlee's private views were in fact supportive of Morrison; he had written to his brother that:

> We are fighting for the British idea of the supremacy of law and against the conception that an Executive can keep anyone in quod they don't like. How often have not you and I heard old Blimps talk about damned Labour agitators causing strikes and how they would like to imprison or shoot the swine. ... The real test of one's belief in the doctrine of Habeas Corpus is not when one demands its application on behalf of one's friends but of one's enemies.[159]

Moreover, Attlee explicitly backed the release in Cabinet.[160] That the Deputy Prime Minister clearly supported Morrison's decision in private, but did not enter the fray publicly until the very end, suggests the presence of political calculation in his mind. Attlee had no incentive to intervene until the crisis threatened the stability of the entire party. This chapter, like the others, has stressed that at the core of wartime politics was a series of personal conflicts and strategies – within parties and between them. The protagonists understood this better than historians have subsequently. In conclusion, then, the fiasco represented a potentially lethal blow to the fortunes of Attlee's old rival. Although, in important respects, Morrison had greater freedom than the Deputy Prime Minister – to campaign on a resonant vocabulary whereas Attlee had to assume ownership of the strategy he had created – one of the insuperable problems for him was that he carried the can for the government – suffering serious blows in the process – in a way that Attlee, buried within the warrens of Whitehall, simply never had to.

The party system eclipsed?

By early 1944, important new developments were giving clarity to the organically evolving saga of 'the future'. This section will highlight the way in which the thought processes of leading figures now came into sharper focus. In his inimitable fashion, only Attlee still kept his own counsel. But it shows how, now more than ever, he and the rest worked their way towards prolonging the Churchill regime. It will analyse how precise formulae were developed for the first time. It also stresses the challenges posed by party opposition, and, with it, the centrality of creative leadership: the Labour ministers, and their Conservative colleagues, had to proceed with great caution. The line of policy directed by Attlee and Morrison was – deliberately – capable of multiple interpretations. This section explores the various intimations and possibilities that emerged.

In February 1944, Attlee began to mould the debate on 'the future'. To that end, he issued a typically crafty personal flyer to the entire Labour movement, which, reminiscent of his 1943 conference speech, at first sight gave strong intimations of postwar independence, but, in reality, promised nothing explicit and called only for the recruitment of new members.[161] The flyer also implied Attlee's real train of thought – 'The Labour Party is playing a great part in winning the war. It must be no less active in building a peaceful world ... *to establish it demands the same self-sacrifice, self-discipline and devotion* [that it has already displayed].'[162] What is important is that Attlee resolutely *still* made no mention of postwar independence. Given the overriding importance of the issue, his persistent silence speaks volumes: it is as revealing as the professed plans emanating from Morrison, Dalton, Bevin, Churchill and Halifax. The document in fact drew on the same kind of vocabulary – of the imperative to play a major role in constructing a new order – that Attlee had made so central to his strategy since 1941, and that he would later use to advocate remaining in the coalition when the moment arrived. That it was a personal message to the party signified his determination carefully to manage events himself. The flyer bore the title 'Mr Attlee's call – I WANT THE PARTY TO BE READY!' Of course, precisely what Attlee wanted it to be ready *for* was the crux.

Days later, Attlee and Morrison both tried to take important steps forward for their strategies. It all centred on a critical special meeting between the Labour ministers and the NEC over future party alignments, held at Transport House over 26 and 27 February 1944. One problem was that, just a day prior to the session, Shinwell – perhaps wanting to predetermine the fate of electoral policy – launched a fresh criticism of the truce and introduced a motion proposing that 'the [NEC] consider the possibility of a general election taking place within the next eighteen months and take appropriate measures to determine the party position'.[163] That meant asking the mass membership what they thought – a sure way to scotch any bid to postpone independence. It was the polar opposite of Attlee's stance and, for that matter, Morrison's as well.

Fortunately, Shinwell's bid to outflank the ministers did not work; by raising the truce – a by-election issue – alongside a resolution about a general election, he committed a tactical misstep. Attlee had already entrenched the idea that it was impossible to disturb the arrangement while the conflict continued.[164] At the special two-day session, he and Morrison only solidified that position by securing agreement that any decision to amend the truce would have to be backed by the Conservatives – to which Churchill was hardly likely to acquiesce.[165] The counter argument ignored the thrust of Shinwell's motion; they had again succeeded in tying their followers in knots with a policy that cancelled itself out.

Attlee also took the – highly significant – step of having the possibility of remaining in harness with the Conservatives formally left open – rather than not *ruled out*, as in 1943.[166] The meeting concluded that 'the question of any future coalition government, its nature and terms, should be left over for further discussion.'[167] That was of fundamental importance. It did not signify a definite decision *in favour* of coalition, but it did leave the possibility open for the first time. In avoiding commitments, but moving in the general direction of alliance, it was wholly consistent with Attlee's guarded strategy over the preceding three years. The Labour ministers were establishing terms of reference within which politics might be conducted; or, to shift metaphors slightly, they were constructing a framework. Attlee, the first man by far to identify the problem when contemplating by-elections, had been exercised with it since late 1941. It required caution: but it can be glimpsed clearly in their vocabularies, their activities and the anxieties they expressed.

To be sure, the importance attached to all these schemes and arrangements will depend on whether the historian believes that what is *not* stated might be just as significant as what *is*. Moreover – and this is striking – a mistake made by the party official who took the minutes of the meeting is important. A statement in the minutes that suggested one of the conclusions was that 'there should be a general election at the earliest possible date [after the end of the war in Europe]' was crossed out after typing up.[168] Ellen Wilkinson, new chairperson of the NEC, initialled her name in the margin to signify that she had made the change.[169] Wilkinson was also, of course, the Home Secretary's leading crony and possibly his mistress; and Morrison had been more energetic than anyone against the 'suicide' of hasty independence. That correction is one of only very few such errors in the party records during the whole period analysed in this book. That such care was taken to get the formal record precisely right is surely significant for our appreciation of what Attlee, Morrison and their colleagues were doing. Further evidence might be found in the fact that Bevin refused to attend the meeting at all: according to Dalton, he did not trust the discussions not to be leaked to the press.[170] His anxiety that information may get out is similarly suggestive of what was happening.

The Labour ministers were still moving incrementally, almost imperceptibly, trying to reach their destination over many steps rather than two or three. The previous year, Attlee and the rest had fought for the party not to rule out the option of postwar coalition; now they had secured agreement that the option was formally open. The difference may seem slight, but in fact it had major implications. Morrison, Bevin and Dalton had all definitely come down in favour of delaying independence and continuing the alliance, and so had the Conservative leaders. The great romantic Churchill, of course, probably dreamed of a permanent coalition.

Addison gauged that for him the priority was to 'discover the best formula for the prolongation of his leadership after the war'.[171] It is difficult to know how much weight politicians placed on opinion polling,[172] but a seven-point gap in Labour's favour in June 1943 was a fifteen-point lead by February 1944. Probably more significant in focusing Conservative minds were two by-election defeats, at Shipley in January and West Derbyshire in February. Channon noted that a party meeting was in 'a state of panic' over the latter.[173] Of leading Conservatives, Beaverbrook was one of the few advocates of independence.[174]

At the NEC discussion, Morrison openly argued, with some vigour, that there should be a delay of 'a year' between victory and a general election.[175] That meant going on in alliance for a considerable period. It seems obvious that what they were seeking would require a fresh set of structures to replace the pact brokered in the terrible days of May 1940. Dalton, for his part, was open to a new coalition, even *after* a delayed election.[176] Only Attlee revealed none of his own thoughts; but his observable activity speaks for itself. As so often with the Deputy Prime Minister, his actions resonated louder than words.

The direction of events in February 1944 is also discernible in the fact that, while the meeting did resolve that Labour should fight a general election as an 'independent' party – and what that meant will be discussed below – it was also – and perhaps more significantly still – agreed that there should be no final decisions of any kind on 'political alignments'.[177] This again implied that Attlee and his colleagues wanted to reserve the ability to challenge the decision later, and were simply being careful not to set off a civil war in the interim. In every other respect, certainly, they had shaped the ground contrary to what that decision would imply.

It thus seems that a deeper game was being played. The reason professed for making no public declarations was to avoid presenting the Conservatives with the opportunity to win a huge majority off the Prime Minister's back.[178] That was fair enough. But, as we have already seen, independence, let alone an early election, was not the favoured option among ministers. The issue of fighting an election 'independently' was important. The previous paragraph located it as part of a party management strategy. But it had other connotations as well. Herbert Morrison was, as demonstrated previously, keen on fighting a general election on 'coupon' lines, with the parties sharing a common manifesto. That option, and the desirability of delaying an election for a full year, gives the lie to the Home Secretary's efforts in the previous 15 months to portray himself as Labour's most devoted warrior; he had sought to exploit the mood of the party for his own ends, but with no inclination whatever to accede to it. Still more evidence of Morrison's tactics were offered when he proposed, during this long session, that, given recent defeats at West Derbyshire and Skipton, at by-elections the parties might return to open conflict at *constituency level* at once – while the war was ongoing – but that ministers could stand above the fray and avoid speaking at the hustings.[179] It was agreed that the possibility could be discussed with Churchill.[180] Contrary to appearances, the Home Secretary's idea was not a blueprint for partisan politics; if anything, it would entrench norms of ministerial separation from party conflict. Even the by-election rivals would all fight as 'government' candidates under his scheme.[181] It was one more way to meet his dual purpose as coalitionist but also keeper of the party's soul.

As so often before, Morrison's strategy allowed him to reside on both sides of the fence; and, with this latest idea, he clearly remained wedded to 'coupon' politics. But, on that latter issue, the meeting saw a major blow inflicted on the Home Secretary's strategy – and one that, in the period analysed in the final chapter, would invite a drastic political leap in response. The NEC ruled during its meeting that there should be 'no question' of the party engaging in a 'coupon' general election.[182] This constituted a rejection of Morrison's entire thought process. Attlee led the opposition to his by-election proposition as well, writing a counter memorandum within days in which he summarily dismissed the idea, arguing that free elections would give succour to those who wanted Labour out of office and precipitate the collapse of the government.[183] He called for the maintenance of the status quo instead.[184] Attlee's memorandum was dismissive of the strength of party pressures, ascribing hostility to the government merely to 'the inevitable accumulation of individual irritations … which find a natural ventilation at the polls'. It went on to the effect that by-election defeats were only a protest vote, 'gratification of an impulse'.[185] In essence, he was 'explaining them away'.[186] Tellingly, Attlee's memorandum was coordinated with Bevin,[187] a sign that electoral policy was becoming bound up with the question of *who* would drive debate on the future, who would direct it, and who would exercise ascendancy within the Labour Party's inner councils. Morrison's scheme was dropped.

In early 1944, then, Attlee's leadership remained pre-eminent. Though a 'coupon' election had been rebuffed, that was Morrison's pet scheme; there is no evidence that the Deputy Prime Minister ever favoured it. Attlee had followed his strategy with typical consistency. The possibility of postwar coalition was acknowledged and left aside for future debate; there was absolutely no mention of the timing of a general election, and Wilkinson had been scrupulous in emphasizing that fact; and the electoral truce remained in place. The consummate committee man who led the Labour ministers demonstrated, not for the first time but perhaps the most important, his ability to shape bureaucratic politics from the inside and in line with his own overarching priorities. Attlee, despite himself initiating what amounted to 'coupon' politics for by-elections back in 1941, was too astute to claim too much for that incendiary political structure. But with his own version of 'coupon' policies – both for a general election and for by-elections – rejected, meanwhile, Morrison quickly began to cast around for an alternative. Soon, the issue of the future of the party system, indeed the survival of the coalition itself, would become the public battleground of the Attlee–Morrison struggle.

The meeting thus broke up with a clear victory for Attlee and the other Labour ministers; but it was no less of a defeat for Morrison personally, one of several examined in this chapter. In what can only be read an ingenious attempt to put a suspicious party off the scent, the special meeting agreed to put out a rather opaque press release, which stated only that 'a meeting of the National Executive Committee of the Labour Party was held on Saturday and Sunday and was attended by Mr C. R. Attlee and Mr Herbert Morrison. Discussion centred around the winning of the war and the problems which will arise after its conclusion.'[188] No mention was made of political arrangements.[189] Secrecy remained the hallmark of discussing 'the future'. The intent is clear – and significant in itself.

Conclusion

This chapter has explored how the political world became ever more detached from wider society in the latter stages of the struggle with Hitler. Decision-making rested with Attlee and his ilk to a degree not grasped in previous accounts. At the core of that was the singular importance of leadership, in multiple forms. It seems appropriate to absorb properly the fact that Herbert Morrison had now established himself as a serious rival to Attlee. The clamour over Beveridge gave him obvious opportunities to depict himself as an attractive, fighting leader. Morrison boasted a formid-

187

able battery of political weaponry. Moreover, his determination to take Attlee on at the first opportunity was plain to see – an opening he would at last get in the final year of the war. Morrison's positioning had already been very astute: he took up *rhetorical* positions in the space directly between Attlee and the Labour Party, while adopting *substantive* positions, the implementation of which would have resulted in a far lengthier restriction of political independence (or, in Labour parlance, 'betrayal') than anything Attlee seemed to be contemplating. He, more than anyone, had been wedded to 'coupon' politics and the possibilities of 'common manifestos'.

But the Home Secretary also faced serious questions about his ability to oust Attlee. Though the Deputy Prime Minister remained as anonymous a public figure as ever, and Morrison enjoyed a profile to which Attlee could never aspire, the Home Secretary engendered antipathy in some. The most powerful man in the Labour movement, Bevin, was his sworn enemy. That might not have been debilitating; after all, he was usually popular among both MPs and the rank-and-file. But Morrison's need to take difficult decisions at the Home Office, his inability to duck a fight, and his adversarial manner when people disagreed with him, were far bigger problems. They pitched him into conflict with an exhibitionist party he would have to persuade to support him. Morrison suffered, in his own way, from as many weaknesses as Attlee did. There is little doubt that the period considered here was defined by the rise of Morrison, an event neglected altogether by previous historians. Whether inside the political world or out on the national stage, he had been at the centre of everything. It also witnessed the great paradox of a man who had overcome the challenges of being born half blind, and suffered lasting odium as a conscientious objector in the First World War, to become lauded as Churchill's only peer in the Second. Morrison's standing in the political system rested on several pillars. Clearly, none of them was fragile: if they had been, he might already have been finished. That he was not, and was far and away Attlee's biggest threat, was remarkable testimony to his powers of survival and refusal to be beaten. Even after the Mosley fiasco, in March Channon recorded that the Home Secretary 'is high in the ascendant', and that 'if he is Prime Minister one day, we might fare much worse'.[190]

Perhaps even more importantly, however, the issue of 'the future', and the likely shape of the party system, was at last becoming clear. The main parties remained fundamentally hostile to one another. But leading politicians of all hues had made plain their desire to prolong the alliance. If there was a 'movement away from party', it was at least as pronounced at the very top as where voters supported Common Wealth and Independents. All the ideas floated in the last two chapters were routes towards a common goal. The range of possible tactical arrangements should not obscure this. Bevin, Morrison, Dalton, Churchill, Halifax and others had all nailed their flags to that mast. The prospect of a khaki defeat was not attractive from a Labour perspective. The idea of presiding over the intractable difficulties of the postwar era perhaps made independence less enticing still, for both parties. From what we can tell of the minds of political leaders, many were keenly aware that the years following the war would more likely resemble an arctic blizzard than the sunlit uplands imagined by the clerisy. That all of this is so renders the exclusion of this story from the centre of existing accounts all the more puzzling. It was clear that existing arrangements could not accommodate what would be needed after the war. Only Attlee had not spelt out – as far as we can tell anyway – a formula. Characteristically, he was the last to move. Most likely he was open to several. Yet the direction of his thoughts is discernible in the trajectory of his activity and leadership. It is no surprise that the political actors of the 1940s did not try to explain this to the public. After all, in the end they failed. But that should not bamboozle the historian.

All that now remained was for the issue of 'the future' to be played out. This posed a genuine challenge to all concerned. From mid-1944 that question additionally became the centrepiece of the struggle between Attlee and Morrison, as their rivalry at last exploded to the surface. What they were fighting for was nothing less than ascendancy in the postwar world. In a manner that highlighted the very different models of leadership they offered to the Labour Party and the country, the two engaged in a contest that finally culminated in a showdown over who would occupy the Prime Minister's office at Downing Street.

Chapter 6

Politics in the Shadow of Victory

For Attlee and the others, the prospect of victory therefore generated problems analogous to those of 1939. Indeed, the final act of the war was to demand leadership every bit as creative as the first. While the conflict with Nazi Germany neared its end as the Western and Soviet armies placed the Third Reich in a military vice, back in London the political settlement constructed in May 1940 – and which it was already clear would be inadequate to meet the pressures of peace – finally unravelled. That meant that the stakes were now as high as they could feasibly be. This chapter documents how Attlee worked to reorient his existing strategy into a new one. By the end of the war in Europe, public life had turned full circle as party politics were reanimated. The Labour ministers' advance – at its height in October 1943 – neared its end. All of this posed major problems for Attlee. Examining the political options that emerged, the chapter describes the Deputy Prime Minister's response, his bid to hold the party to his course and – most importantly – his effort to achieve a viable electoral settlement. In this situation, Attlee at last selected clear positions on the future of cross-party alliance: first, he opted to try and delay an election – and the breakup of the coalition – for six months following Hitler's defeat. Later, he decided to try and go on until the defeat of Japan, believed to require another year of war. But that was the most dangerous effort to corral the political system that even he had yet contemplated. While *The Last Days of Churchill* do not quite take on the Tacitean aura of *The Last Days of Hitler*, there was, nevertheless, a palpable sense of desperation in the air at Westminster after the Führer blew his brains out on 30 April 1945.[1]

Furthermore, the Home Secretary now capitalized on Attlee's difficulties to launch a proper challenge to his leadership. In fact, he exacerbated the issues confronting Attlee by fundamentally altering his public stance after the defeat of the 'coupon' approach in February 1944. In a series of audacious manoeuvres from the autumn, Morrison established himself as perhaps the leading political force in the country. What followed was an intense struggle between the two men over a narrow expanse of ground that held great implications for those able to occupy it. As they competed to sort through what 'the future' might look like, and differences were sharpened for instrumental purposes, it eventually culminated in Morrison bidding to destroy the coalition to oust Attlee. In shedding new light on events at the end of the war, the chapter takes a different tack from previous work. The first half shows how Attlee moved with dispatch as the nebulous issue of 'the future' at last took solid form, and considers the fate of Labour's exploration of the British state. The second half conducts a detailed analysis of a pair of critical episodes – in May and July 1945 – that have never been invested with explanatory force. Ultimately, it shows how Attlee became Prime Minister in the summer of 1945.

The dilemmas of coalition

That the ship of state was sailing into dangerous waters shone through in a speech that Attlee gave at Leeds on 1 April 1944. Buoyant after the NEC rulings, the Deputy Prime Minister reiterated in the strongest terms the need for 'unity', persisted in his adherence to an ambiguous policy on 'the future', and adopted a hard line towards dissent:

> There [is] a proposition put forward … that the government should not be concerned at defeats in the House on such matters as education or health or the social services, but should accept the verdict … and carry on. [I believe] that acceptance of this doctrine would be fatal to the working of responsible government. Members must make up their minds … what they want to get through. [I have] a clear recollection still of those who in the last days of the last Labour government took up the position of independence. Some [have] gone fascist … [I do not] wish the next Labour government to go down through the individualism of professed socialists.[2]

It was an astonishingly blunt way of putting it. In a message of support to a government candidate in the Clay Cross by-election a fortnight later, the Deputy Prime Minister included the statement that 'this year, when great operations are to take place, nothing must be done to endanger national unity.'[3]

Attlee's perspective on larger strategy thus remained clear. Yet, the problem was that the arrangements he had so painstakingly built up no longer fitted with the temper of the times. First, the coalition suffered a series of crises in March when it was defeated in Parliament over its education policy by an alliance of Labour MPs and the Tory Reform Group,[4] prompting a characteristically withering response by Morrison who declared that 'a government must achieve the general support of the House of Commons over the whole field of its policy – or die.'[5] He stated accusingly that the Labour Party might be 'afraid of power' and, while 'first-class propagandists and agitators[,] ... the question was: [can] they be first-class in the responsible exercise of power?'[6] In April and May, Bevan confirmed his new status by inflicting a series of humiliations on the Labour ministers. Over five weeks he directed a guerrilla campaign to annul Defence Regulation IAA,[7] which permitted the imprisonment of strikers who interfered with war work. Bevan instigated a party rebellion of more than one hundred MPs,[8] poured fuel on the fire by asserting that the Labour ministers were secretly plotting to stay in the coalition as part of 'a grand postwar surrender',[9] and accused Bevin of orchestrating a 'carefully-prepared campaign' of 'calumny' against British trade unionists.[10] Nor was that all. The Town and Country Planning Bill was subjected to constant harassment over the spring and summer. The challenges of providing strong leadership in these conditions were underlined when a bid by Attlee and the other leaders to expel Bevan from the PLP failed to get off the ground.[11] The Deputy Prime Minister had 'no influence one way or the other' over the party.[12] And it was all exacerbated after the successful Normandy landings on 6 June and the emergence of a widespread belief that the war could be over by the turn of the year. Attlee reckoned that Berlin might surrender as early as September.[13] It was the impact of Overlord, more than anything, that generated a new political environment; and in turn this underlined the imperative for choices to be made.

Under growing pressure, in mid-July Attlee and Dalton decided to postpone the annual conference until much later in the year.[14] Dalton's diary recounts that the Lord President was 'all for' using the new threat of German V-1 rockets as a 'pretext' for delay.[15] That intimates that the two favoured this course because Attlee did not want to run the risk that a full assembly of the Labour movement, in the current atmosphere, might force the ministers into a precipitate course of action. Indeed, after keeping his options open for so long while others schemed, Attlee now at last began to firm up his own views. He apparently believed that the ideal strategy was for the Churchill regime to be prolonged into the European peace for around six months, and then – when the time was right – to dissolve the cross-party alliance and fight an election on traditional party lines.[16]

He had revised the rules of political engagement on no less than three occasions during the war. Attlee now launched a bid to rework them for a fourth time. Waiting for Churchill's aura to dissipate before breaking up the coalition demonstrated a sensitive awareness of electoral possibilities. As usual, his grasp of the situation was keener than most of his peers. A few days earlier, at a pair of special PLP meetings on 8 and 12 July, Attlee announced for the first time that, with the end of the war on the horizon, he would enter into negotiations with Churchill on the timing of a general election.[17] Later that month, Attlee's NEC Organization Committee recommended that the Labour Party seek a majority as an independent party.[18] To be sure, both of those banal statements committed neither the Lord President nor his party to an *idée fixe*; Attlee retained his prized flexibility. That was particularly important as the most sensible course for Churchill would be to plump for a snap election.[19] Attlee offered no public indication, as far we can detect, about *when* that election might occur. The policy was thus a cautious approach to an uncertain – and dangerous – situation. Intending to lead as events demanded, it was typical of his tenacity. But when coupled with his private discussions with Dalton on the six-month option, it did signify an important political move forward by Attlee. He was now seemingly plotting a route out of the alliance. Even so, the Deputy Prime Minister remained resolute in playing his cards close to his chest.

Adjunctive evidence of how far Attlee had matured as a political figure in the previous five years is offered by the continually developing role that he was performing in government by 1944. Extending his reach into working on the future of peacetime Europe as well as domestic duties, Attlee served as chairman of the Armistice and Post-War Committee. There he began to develop his own, often trenchant, views on the future of the continent and the fate of Germany.[20] He was particularly unsympathetic on the latter. Though he remained no policy formulator, he did engage in disputes over strategy with the Foreign and War Offices. On the domestic front, in March 1944 Attlee set out a detailed plan for a new relationship between central and local government after the war, entailing a further creep in the limits of the British state.[21] That the once hesitant

Attlee now conceived of his role in this way is important not in itself, but only as a reminder of the significance assumed by a man who had dominated the private politics of Westminster for five years.

It would seem, then, that Attlee identified the need to replace the existing party framework with a different model for the peace. There is something else. It bears reiteration that, from what we can tell, Attlee's six-month plan was raised with Dalton alone. This would appear to be confirmed in the fact that a drafting team, tasked by the executive with formulating a public statement of the July decision to fight the election independently, dragged the process out for more than two months.[22] Attlee and Dalton were both members: and, by late August, the team was still in no hurry to finalize anything.[23] According to Dalton's account, on 22 August Attlee declared that 'he objects to saying publicly that we shall fight the next election as an independent party.'[24] That the Deputy Prime Minister opposed a public enunciation of his own professed policy is striking. It implies that Attlee did not desire to be committed to his private intimations, and perhaps that he also suspected the idea of staying in alliance for a not inconsiderable six months would not find traction. He protested that 'these things should be taken for granted',[25] but that is the point: they were not. And no one knew that better than Attlee.

While he supported the eventual dissolution of the alliance, then, Attlee was plainly determined to bide his time. That he chose not simply to draw a line under the rumours with an unequivocal statement might be thought proof of that. Again, what all this amounts to is evidence that previous narratives have failed to afford the problem of postwar possibilities adequate emphasis. Whatever else happened, wartime politics did not proceed from party conflict to coalition and then back to party along a linear path. There is more. Additional indications of Attlee's priorities, and his working to keep the Labour Party in the dark, were offered in a memorandum of his own that he submitted to the executive in early September.[26] He had personally drafted this document – quite separate from the principal statement that he, Dalton and the NEC team were working on – and it swiftly became the basis for information appearing in the media on general election policy a few days later. It floated for the first time allowing a 'fairly long' interval between 'the cessation of hostilities' and an election.[27] That 'the cessation of hostilities' could even be interpreted as going on until the defeat of Japan was noticed in *The Times*.[28] But it also reaffirmed the rejection of a 'coupon' election.[29] That once again highlighted how the Lord President defined, and weighed up, his audience. It was accepted 'practically unaltered', which, Attlee told his brother, was 'a wonder'.[30] In seeking personally to control the whole policy, Harris observed that Attlee moved with 'a dispatch and decisiveness'.[31] *The Times* commented that 'the electoral prophets in the party expect a considerable addition to the party's strength in a general election conducted in anything like normal circumstances, and the party desires for this reason to avert the possibility of … a 'khaki' election.'[32]

All this was true. But in early October, it became apparent that Attlee might have been concerned with utilizing the issue of electoral policy not merely to play for time, but to spike the guns of Morrison – formerly the principal advocate of the 'coupon' strategy, after all – as well. When the much-delayed official statement of future policy was finally given to the press, it was turned into a public broadside against the Home Secretary: employing unusually vehement language, and making a great show of rejecting the approach championed by Morrison, it declared that 'we do not believe that any *responsible* statement would advocate following that *evil* precedent [of the 1918 election]. Despite *malicious* whisperings to the contrary no *responsible* leader of Labour has ever toyed with the idea of a coupon election.'[33]

Whether that was meant to imply that Morrison was not 'responsible', as would appear to be the case, is a good question. The language was, however, unusually strong and certainly did not constitute a blanket denial that some had countenanced the prospect. It was a signal that only the naïve would hold not to be directed against the Home Secretary. Morrison's earlier support for 'coupon' politics now offered a useful way of discrediting him. He was, it must be recalled, no longer a member of the executive, and thus played no role in formulating the statement. It was important for something else as well: despite Laski's presence on the drafting team, nowhere in its two pages did it give precise commitments on *anything*. In fact, it made clear on no less than six occasions that the timing of an election remained deeply uncertain ('it is not possible now to foresee when conditions will be such as to enable a return to normal political life,' it was an 'obscure situation', and 'we cannot tell when that election will be held') while warning in stark terms that it should not be 'within a few weeks'.[34] This was the second intimation that a rapid election was to be avoided. It made a great show of putting that last point down to ensuring the armed services would have a chance to participate.[35] Ede remarked that it was 'purposely vague'.[36] Attlee's activity in recent months leaves open the question of precisely *what* he was trying to do. For instance, this latest statement also stressed that Labour remained 'pledged' to participate in the defeat of 'Japanese aggression'.[37] We cannot disentangle Attlee's role in the process from the contributions of the others. But we can see that the outcome fitted *exactly* with the thrust of his July conversation with Dalton, his obfuscation at the PLP, his objection to saying much publicly in August and his September memorandum. Any lingering doubts about Attlee's hold over the political situation must surely now be dispelled. Every significant sentence was a recipe for a delay of several months, at least.

That did not mean it was a popular strategy. Six days later, Alfred Edwards – the same backbencher who orchestrated the challenge to Attlee in November 1939 – tried unsuccessfully to engineer a fresh vote on his position. [38] Yet, by imposing his choices on the Labour Party in an incremental fashion, the Lord President continued to rework the political 'game' that had been underway since Hitler crossed the Polish frontier. The wrapping of a *fait accompli* in a collegiate guise continued to exemplify Attlee's leadership. The *Observer* got it right when it labelled him 'the political catalyst' and 'the brace of the Cabinet' who kept 'the caravan in line'.[39] The summer and autumn of 1944 witnessed a cunning series of decisions by Attlee to respond to the fact that military success threw up serious problems. In a very real sense, then, public life remained largely the usage of language: the words that were chosen by politicians, how their vocabulary was framed, and its texture, remained central to political calculation.

But inside the coalition, momentum was draining away from the Labour ministers at an alarming rate. To explore that, we must briefly shift perspective and ponder an alternative angle – the reawakening of the Conservative Party. Though the entrenchment of Labour doctrines on the centre ground was not reversed, further progress was difficult after mid-1944. This new situation was hinted at as early as March, in that Attlee's foreword to the heavily anticipated employment white paper was as much a fudge as the rest of the document:

> In the postwar period, the country will inevitably depend upon a mixed economy, neither wholly subject to state regulation nor wholly ruled by private enterprise; and the extent to which either one of these principles gains or loses ground to the other will

depend on the will of the postwar electorate expressed at the polls. ... The extent to which the policy here described is followed or modified in the future will depend on the political complexion of the responsible government in power.[40]

The scheme carried few detailed ideas; in short, the coalition ducked the issue.[41] It failed to resolve how to combat inflation when the state was committed to limiting unemployment.[42] It became difficult to discern how the Labour ministers' values could be linked to policy outcomes. Addison,[43] Jefferys[44] and Brooke[45] have all attributed this phenomenon, in broad terms, to the limits of cross-party agreement being reached. There is something in that. But there is another explanation besides sheer exhaustion – the emboldening of Conservative strategy and, particularly, the role played by John Anderson.

The Chancellor of the Exchequer was even more significant than Attlee in managing the deliberations on the white paper.[46] He, like the Lord President, was the sort of bureaucrat who knew how to find agreement where little existed. Furthermore, Anderson's stewardship of the white paper indicated the development of a Conservative stance capable – for the first time since 1941 – of consistently blocking the Labour ministers. The document came under assault from the PLP in Parliament, Bevan proclaiming that 'there is no longer any justification for this party existing at all.'[47] But for Conservatives, on the other hand, the Keynesian element was reined in, private enterprise remained unshackled and the budget had to be controlled.[48] As such, the Conservative Party generally supported it.[49] The principal lesson to draw was the partial recovery of Britain's largest party. The wartime Conservatives, as much as Labour, provide a rich tapestry of political fortunes. One suspects that the feeble capitulations of the previous autumn had focused minds;[50] Headlam, for instance, observed that Labour was 'intolerable' and 'playing the party game all the time'.[51] Regardless of why it happened, Anderson – in his first big test since moving to the Treasury – achieved an important success. Additional barricades to the storming of the Bastille that had been threatened in October 1943 were thrown up when leading Conservatives began recognizing the need to counter Labour by being seen to embrace reconstruction. Education policy was apparently conceived in this light, and even prior to the death of Kingsley Wood, Anderson, Churchill and the then chancellor agreed that education was a 'lesser evil' than Beveridge.[52]

Anderson's 1944 budget continued the trend: it was rooted in objection to further financial commitments on the grounds that the government had already pledged to increase spending markedly, first by around £226 million per annum and eventually by £400 million.[53] 'His stock has risen,' recorded Headlam.[54] In June, the Conservative strategy was most fully elucidated when Woolton began pressing for decisions on social insurance, citing pressure from the Labour ministers and warning that delay would prove 'most unwelcome' to Attlee and the rest.[55] Immediately, Churchill hit on the idea of sending Anderson in to bat, and the Chancellor was instructed to resist the 'rapid growth in our national burdens'.[56] In a weighty Cabinet paper drawn up that same day, Anderson highlighted the intractability of the problem and presented two rather stark options – the 'risk' of reducing taxation in a bid to generate the revenue needed to pay for postwar programmes, or a decision for postponement. [57] He warned that otherwise the tax burden might become 'intolerable'.[58] As Jefferys notes,[59] Anderson dragged the Conservative Party back to the position laid out in Churchill's March 1943 broadcast in which he stated that truly contentious measures would have to await a general election.[60] The Prime Minister leapt at the chance to conclude that nothing at all could be done.

By autumn, *The Times* was complaining that the government was 'marking time'.[61] Though Attlee was surely correct in declaring upon the release of the insurance white paper that 'these proposals [are] the most far-reaching and comprehensive ever submitted by a responsible government ... for the acceptance of the underlying conception of the scheme, the nation is mainly indebted to the Labour movement',[62] his statement was yet another fudge. The outcome of intra-governmental wrangling was now typically a score draw. By early 1945, Attlee was bemoaning Beaverbrook and Bracken's parallel efforts to delay decisions.[63] To hold, then, that some ethereal 'limits' had been reached discourages deeper investigation. It is at least as plausible to suggest that the Churchill regime ground to a halt because both party leaderships had important strategic reasons to block the others and keep their powder dry. As Bevin put it:

> The Prime Minister has taken the line that he will not agree to nationalize anything during the war. We must await a general election. Yet it looks as if Max Beaverbrook and all the forces associated with him are attempting to denationalize what we have

got ... if we cannot, as a coalition, carry any nationalization of mines, railways or electricity, surely the party must make its position clear and keep its hand free for the election.[64]

Appreciating what the Conservatives were doing would require another book, but it is not unfair to hold that even the better studies of that party usually fail to grasp the disposition that sits beneath the surface of the conservative mind. The longer unpleasant things can be put off, the better. The purpose of this detour has been to stress that, while the Conservatives never succeeded in matching Labour's appeal on reconstruction, the scope for Attlee, Bevin and Morrison to generate fresh innovations for their doctrines nevertheless receded substantially in the final year of the war. It was not a bad return on the strategy; if 1943 was the highpoint of their influence inside Whitehall, in that respect it represented the dividend from Attlee's whole approach to politics. But, even so, the Labour ministers' journey within the British state had – for the time being, at least – reached its end.

Morrison's need for a platform

While these issues were being played out, for his part the Home Secretary plainly had to find a new route forward. Though not destroyed by the Mosley crisis, he did sustain serious damage all the same. And the core of his strategy – 'coupon' politics – was decisively swept away in February. If all of that posed problems, his response – to retake the initiative – was characteristic. From autumn 1944, Morrison therefore began a second, and this time even more successful, individual campaign. In particular, he reacted to the decay of Labour's momentum in Whitehall by locating a fresh set of 'issues' to anchor himself to. Resolving the dilemmas that bedevilled him in the previous chapter, this time he opted for a platform much less risky. The contrast was palpable. On 17 October, the Home Secretary circulated a memorandum to the other Labour ministers proposing that they should press for a sustained confrontation with the Conservatives and demand concrete 'socialist' measures of reconstruction from the government.[65] Attlee and Bevin had always adamantly refused to push this issue too far; now Morrison suddenly – and vocally – situated himself in opposition to that strategy. Of course, his memorandum was linked with the struggle for party advantage described above. But it carried other, probably more important, implications as well: it amounted to the opening salvo in the contest for the Labour leadership that Morrison sparked along all fronts from late 1944.

Outlining what he labelled 'a great national plan' in the document, the Home Secretary set out a programme for the Labour ministers to put far-reaching demands before the government.[66] It would entail economic reorganization, new social policies and welfare. He pushed for an attempt to extract these from Churchill through concerted pressure – always a popular war cry in Labour circles[67] – but Attlee, Bevin and Dalton still refused to give way.[68] Yet, that only played into Morrison's hands. Indeed, the tactics he proposed were such a marked departure from existing methods that it is difficult to know if Morrison really expected Attlee to accede to them. At a meeting of the executive on 29 October, Ellen Wilkinson – his oldest ally and chair of the NEC – noticeably shaped the whole session around the contours of Morrison's memorandum.[69] From the minutes, it is clear that she took a far larger role than usual in structuring the discussion. In a long disquisition, Wilkinson explicitly brought Morrison into the debate, and she pointed to his 'great national plan' programme by pushing for ministers to pursue legislation that could 'become law before the government broke up'.[70] When framed in these terms, it was hardly the kind of thing Attlee could disavow. A majority on the executive backed the plan and ruled it 'highly desirable' that the ministers should pressurize Churchill to put as many measures onto the statute book as possible.[71] Furthermore, it was decided that the PLP 'should be recommended to take action' to facilitate it, while William Whiteley, the chief whip, was tasked with studying the parliamentary timetable.[72]

The Home Secretary had set a trap. He engineered an important evolution in the Labour Party's political approach, against the wishes of Attlee. It represented the first occasion since 1940 that Attlee had been cold-shouldered on an issue such as this. Assuming that Wilkinson backed Morrison's 'great national plan' – and it is clear she did – she helped the Home Secretary to register a significant victory. However limited the impact of his efforts in government, Morrison was now firmly re-established in the inner councils of the Labour Party in his favoured guise of a socialist crusader. There is another point though, for in its unspoken implications for policy, it amounted to a broader alteration in Morrison's whole style. Curiously, the abrupt change of garments did not appear to trouble him unduly. After all, as we have seen, such positions were instrumental, to advertise worthiness and credibility; they were revised as the need arose. It is difficult to believe that the imperative of recovering from his nadir of early 1944 did not play a role in the decision to alter the approach that Morrison, more than anyone, had sacrificed so much in holding to. After all, the NEC's thinly veiled statement – that those who toyed with a coupon election were not 'responsible' – had been passed just 12 days before Morrison suddenly unveiled his 'great national plan'.

The next month, November, the Home Secretary continued his work in this vein by drawing up a new Cabinet paper on nationalizing the electricity industry, in which he presumptuously declared that 'I feel sure my colleagues will agree with me about the crucial importance of pressing on with these matters with all the speed we can muster, for they affect the industrial and economic foundations of our national welfare.'[73] Rab Butler noted at the time that 'Morrison's cleverness increases each day.'[74] In December, at the delayed annual Labour conference at Westminster, the Home Secretary managed another advance when he was finally re-elected to the NEC. At an event otherwise marked by great hostility to the party's present trajectory, it was significant that the only real success belonged to Morrison.[75] More important, he was immediately appointed chairman of the Policy Committee, as well as a new Campaign Committee created to draft Labour's manifesto, make election preparations and direct overall campaign strategy.[76] That kind of work was Morrison's forte. This provided him with the last, and most substantial, piece of his platform.

It was a watershed moment. What followed was a series of rapid manoeuvres conducted in early 1945 through which the Home Secretary was able decisively to turn the tables on Attlee and seize the momentum. From the dawn of the year, Morrison employed his new Campaign Committee as a high-powered vehicle to map out Labour's future, and – largely on his own authority – established himself as the architect of Labour's whole programme of work for the general election.[77] This body met frequently and the Home Secretary dominated its proceedings. Moreover, perched atop both the Policy and Campaign groups, the role afforded him another, dual, task – a unique opportunity both to organize *and* present Labour policy. Indeed, the principal task to which Morrison devoted himself in the first months of 1945 was the writing of the election manifesto, *Let Us Face the Future*. This is not the place for another exploration of the gestation of postwar policies, but it is important to recognize how central Morrison was to the creation of that famous document. For instance, by the time the Campaign Committee held its first meeting on 19 February he had already composed a first draft.[78] Over the next two months, he oversaw its refinement and revision.[79] In addition, the 'pitch' of the party's campaign was fixed as being 'moderation' – which aligned precisely with the Home Secretary's predisposition. In particular, Labour's war record was contrasted with the culpability of the Conservatives in the crises of the preceding decade.[80] Morrison was resolute in eschewing the *language* of overt socialism in the document – whatever the content was – and making a pitch for the political centre instead. In its pledge to create a new and better Britain, Labour promised full employment, the control of raw materials and supervision by the state of subjects as disparate as food pricing and home building. The final result embodied how he always thought politics should be conducted. Commitments were made for enhanced social security programmes along the lines of the Beveridge Report, while nationalization of fuel, power, transport, the Bank of England, iron and steel would all go ahead. Through its ramifications for the party and the country, in many respects *Let Us Face the Future* and the accompanying campaign constituted the greatest achievement of Morrison's whole career.

Morrison's biographers have noted that 'he undoubtedly saw the opportunity to improve his political standing and above all to strengthen his claims to the leadership. ... It was a marvellous chance to shed the "municipal" image and emerge as a national figure.'[81] There is something else: Morrison was running a campaign with an important educational component too. Butler, who recognized that the Home Secretary took 'advantage of his position on the home front', recorded his envy of it.[82] As before, Morrison discerned connections that escaped others. In March, he told the party that it must capture 'workers by brain as well as by hand';[83] in April, he affirmed at a public meeting that the decision on 'socialization' of sectors of the economy would be taken not according to dogma but 'practical facts'.[84] He was a shrewd campaigner who wanted to create a 'socialism' to which party members and a sceptical 'conservative' electorate alike might respond. Throughout the war, Morrison's private antipathy towards the reflexes of his own party had been displayed regularly. Now, when allotted a midwifery role in the birth of a new era, it would have been contrary to his life's work to create a document to frighten the floating voter. To phrase it differently, *Let Us Face the Future* was quintessentially Morrisonian.

By March 1945, then, due largely to the endeavours of the Home

Secretary, the Labour Party's manifesto and campaign plans were ready for what lay ahead. In a way that might have seemed impossible when he was in the doldrums a year earlier, Morrison stamped a very individual seal on his party's future. For example, a renegade 1944 conference resolution demanding more extensive pledges of public ownership than Morrison was willing to give was simply ignored.[85] And he completely by-passed the trade unions by refusing to grant them a role in the process, much to the chagrin of Citrine.[86] But there was a larger backdrop to all this – important elements in the PLP and NEC were now actively anticipating a leadership challenge by the Home Secretary at the outbreak of peace. A pro-Morrison group of backbenchers, including Wilkinson, agitated as early as October 1944 for a ballot once the party reverted to independence.[87] Their leader, G. M. Garro Jones, reckoned that the Home Secretary would win – and that was before his recent campaign.[88] Morrison was also increasing his visibility among MPs by attending about three-quarters of the PLP meetings, whereas Attlee went to just a third.[89] And on the executive, Wilkinson, Laski and some union bosses were pressing Morrison's case there too.[90] It was obvious that the problem of the leadership was now inextricably intertwined with the question of 'the future'. The Home Secretary's work – his 'great national plan', his dominance of the NEC, and the manifesto – all flowed into this. Through late 1944 and early 1945, Morrison completely changed his political posture. As we shall see shortly, this new status afforded him the means to launch a concerted effort to instigate Attlee's downfall in the spring – even if that meant destroying the government as well.

Positions and places

Aside from the Home Secretary's reinvention, though, the winter and spring months of 1945 were politically very flat. Little of significance occurred for some time, except for fresh government defeats at three by-elections.[91] In January, Headlam recorded that Westminster 'is a lifeless place'.[92] Attention was focused abroad as the Third Reich finally crumbled. By early February, the Red Army reached the Oder, 50 miles from Berlin; in March, British and American forces crossed the Rhine. It was only a matter of time before peace was attained in Europe. And that made the decisions about postwar politics, toyed with for so long, increasingly urgent. We ought, therefore, to move our account forward slightly. What follows is a detailed analysis of two discrete periods at the end of the war – mid-May and late July 1945. The first was a struggle about the future of the Churchill coalition, the second over occupancy of Downing Street itself. Yet, neither has received the attention it warrants. It is striking that, after the war, none of those involved ever chose to speak truthfully about what occurred.

In April, the Home Secretary was presented with the opportunity to expand his influence still further, and this time at a critical moment, when Attlee was temporarily removed altogether from the London political scene. The Lord President spent much of that month, and the first half of May, with Eden at the San Francisco conference where the United Nations was to be formally established.[93] The decision to go as Eden's 'lieutenant' prompted denunciation from Bevan, who said that Attlee 'brings to the fierce struggle of politics the tepid enthusiasm of a lazy summer afternoon at a cricket match'.[94] Before he left, however, Attlee sought to limit Morrison's potential freedom of action in his absence. Given the real prospect that the war might end and electoral options have to be chosen while he was in San Francisco – as well as perhaps sensing that Morrison's position was shifting towards, or at least happily aligning with, the party's clamouring to be free of the alliance[95] – Attlee designated Bevin, rather than the Home Secretary, as officially responsible for liaising with the Prime Minister: 'I am telling the PM to look for you to guidance in my absence. It would be well for you to keep in touch with Herbert if there are any questions of elections coming up, as he is on the National Executive. CRA.'[96]

As we have seen, over the preceding year Attlee's principal concern had lain in electoral policy. Unless we are expected to believe that the Lord President had no idea of, or interest in, Morrison's growing strength (although he subsequently claimed that 'I didn't realise the poor little man was full of seething ambition'[97]), it is hard not to detect an element of calculation here. The *Daily Herald* reported that Attlee had appointed Bevin 'acting leader'.[98]

Yet, challenges arose the moment Attlee left the country. Bevin badly antagonized the Conservatives in an aggressive speech at Leeds on 8 April,[99] thus prompting Bracken to respond in kind.[100] And worse was to come the next month, when peace on the continent was finally achieved. While the public was swept up in a tide of celebration following the proclamation of VE Day on 8 May, in the Westminster village senior politicians immediately set about intriguing with an intensity unseen since

1940. The problem of victory now took on a very real form. On 10 May, Morrison and Bevin met their fellow Labour ministers and it seems to have been agreed that holding an election in October would be preferable to one in the summer of 1945.[101] In addition, the Labour movement had already vested in the hands of its ministers the freedom to take decisions about the future – 24 hours before, the NEC and TUC put out a bland statement that avoided any commitments and simply reaffirmed a 'pledge of full and effective cooperation' in seeking victory over Japan and a just peace at home.[102] That woolliness was an asset for the party's principal parliamentarians. There is some evidence that, prior to setting out for San Francisco, Attlee was already leaning towards a new policy of prolonging the coalition all the way until victory over Japan, still expected to require another year of fighting in the Pacific. This evidence is ambiguous, but Brooke held that Attlee intimated this to Churchill before he left,[103] Morrison recalled that he was 'wobbly',[104] and there were, of course, those carefully constructed public statements of the previous autumn. But Attlee certainly did seek to control events in another respect: before leaving with Eden he extracted from Churchill a pledge that Parliament would not be dissolved in his absence, thus preserving his own role in decision-making.[105]

Whatever Attlee had intimated, the idea of carrying on until victory in the Pacific was plausible. And it discovered a receptive audience in Churchill. On 12 May, the Prime Minister telegraphed Eden in San Francisco to argue that a cross-party regime was 'indispensable' for the formulation of a 'National' response to the breakdown of relations between the Allies.[106] He went on that, if pressed by Labour, 'I should on no account agree to an election in October, but simply say that we must prolong our joint venture. It is common objectives, not fixed dates, which must determine the end of such an alliance.'[107] Eden too hoped that the coalition might go on, but doubted that Labour would bite.[108] Headlam commented that 'no sane man' would want an election.[109] Precisely where Churchill's objectives fitted into this fluid situation is worth pondering. He offered signs of backing independence the previous autumn – in September, he suggested to Eden about holding an election immediately after the German defeat,[110] in October gave a public signal that this would occur unless agreement was forthcoming to carry on until the defeat of Japan,[111] and in November told his son that the showdown could take place 'two months' after the defeat of Germany.[112] However, these were exceptions. Overall, when Churchill contemplated the future, he was better disposed towards prolonging the alliance than anyone. In July 1944, Headlam heard via Eden that Churchill was apparently thinking of a longer term coalition if it could be arranged, so that 'his' 'National government' might continue, and, as such, was 'disinclined to give his own party a lead'.[113] By March 1945, Churchill was still toying with a titular 'National' government even if Labour broke with him.[114] Besides showing how wedded he was to the vocabulary of 'National' politics, it seems that Churchill, in his heart, almost certainly wanted coalition, yet was tempted by a khaki victory. But that was compounded by the factional divisions in the party. At times, he displayed sympathy for the Tory Reform Group, and at others for the 'militant party line' of Beaverbrook.[115] At a meeting of the principal Conservative ministers, the overwhelming feeling was for a June election.[116] Churchill's mistake was in not taking the plunge and going all out for an immediate contest. After all, he did not know that he would lose; it was widely anticipated he would win. The Prime Minister's romantic attachment to an alliance that common sense said that he – far more than Labour ministers – did not need seems confirmation of his woolly-headed approach. Whatever his mistakes, though, going on beyond the struggle with Hitler was avowedly Churchill's preferred option.[117]

Yet Attlee's absence from the country at what was the most critical political moment since May 1940 provided the Home Secretary with the means to take the lead himself. Seeing in Attlee's movements, and Churchill's preferences, the opportunity finally to strike after five years of false starts, Morrison accompanied Bevin to see Churchill on 11 May.[118] That heralded the beginning of a remarkable tactical perform-ance, because only when he was at Downing Street did the Home Secretary do his best to sabotage Churchill's stratagem. The Prime Min-ister suggested an agreement for either two more years of coalition or going on until victory in the Pacific.[119] Yet though this proposal was discussed, it seems that Morrison leapt on Churchill's suggestion that he was coming under intensive pressure from the Conservative Party for an immediate election – which was true enough, but given the Prime Min-ister's preferences as expressed to Eden the next day, not reflective of his own views and almost certainly a bid to frighten Labour into acquies-cence – and, to all intents and purposes, derailed the whole idea by pushing 'very strongly' for an election in October instead.[120] In addition, Morrison made it clear to Churchill that he, personally, was firmly opposed to the idea of going on until the defeat of Japan.[121]

The Home Secretary was finally beginning to take up a new position. Yet, there was a trap even here, for in his advocacy of an October election Morrison had already calculated several steps ahead. Throwing his weight behind the growing pressure from both parties, Morrison certainly appreciated that it would only encourage Churchill to opt for the alternative of an immediate election, reckoning the odds as being 'two or three to one'.[122] He told the Prime Minister that Labour 'could certainly face a June election'.[123] Bear in mind Morrison's status as one of the biggest politicians in the country; he was no mere messenger, but a power broker himself. In a sense, it was a classical case of saying one thing, but loading it with sufficient ambiguity to encourage a colleague to do something else. This was the first time Morrison had stuck his head above the parapet since February 1944. It is unclear how Bevin reacted – Morrison said Bevin 'appeared to be on Churchill's side'[124] – but, suffice to say, it was not particularly effective. The episode requires sensitive analysis: the Home Secretary had, by his own opposition, implicitly encouraged Churchill to retreat to the fallback position that was already been urged on him by the Conservative Party – even if he did not want it – of a dissolution and khaki election.

That Morrison had thrown a spanner in the works became apparent when agreement proved elusive at the meeting. Playing a careful game, Morrison had outmanoeuvred Churchill, Bevin and the absent Attlee. Considering that he had once wanted to fight an election along 'coupon' lines, it was quite a shift. But whatever his motive – which one might think is obvious – the Home Secretary kept the positions favoured by Churchill, and possibly already backed by Attlee, from coalescing. The next day, Attlee telegraphed from San Francisco to signal his agreement to pushing for an October election rather than seeing through the Pacific war.[125] He framed the decision in terms of avoiding international opprobrium due to 'absorption in party politics'.[126] Yet, with evident regret, Attlee later recalled that 'the coming general election was already casting its shadow.'[127] Morrison had stolen a march on his rivals, preventing Attlee and Churchill from aligning simply because he was in the room and the Lord President was not. It was obvious that Churchill would not accept an October election. Either he would win backing to go on until victory in the Pacific, or he would order an immediate dissolution. Morrison calculated this; therefore his impeding of Churchill was – if anything – a blueprint for the latter.

Hence, when Attlee finally returned to London a few days later, the situation confronting him was far more challenging than the one he had left behind. Both the Conservative and Labour parties were intent on a showdown, and Morrison had somehow been able to shape the landscape in his absence. Moreover, with the Home Secretary's interference, Attlee's once impregnable role in directing the political system was suddenly contested. Even without a verbatim record of the encounter it is obvious that it was a remarkable, and inscrutable, tactical performance by the Home Secretary. Dalton felt sure that, in consequence, the attempt to go on beyond October, at the very most, was finished.[128] Nor can we attribute it to opposition emanating from the parties themselves: think of the fact that this matter had not even been put to the parties in the first place, but was purely a four-way discussion between Attlee, Bevin, Churchill and Morrison. Keeping apart colleagues who were in broad agreement was indicative of the Home Secretary's own skill in these tight situations.

What is emerging is a rather different culmination to British politics during the Second World War than Addison and the rest have identified. What must be emphasized in charting the events in question was that *all* of these debates were predicated on the accepted assumption that the struggle with Japan would last for at least another year. The United States identified 15 November 1946 as the target date for the end of the war.[129] This might explain why scholars have invested the manoeuvres at the end of the war with so little significance; the conflict in the Pacific ended in August, after all. But that would be an instance of hindsight distorting what was actually happening. Compounding this, the enterprise was not recounted in the subsequent memoirs of the participants, doubtless to avoid discredit.[130] But it is what Attlee and Churchill were up to, all the same. There was no sense that the still secret atomic bomb might compel Tokyo's surrender much earlier. Calculations were rooted in very different criteria from the ones that would become relevant as a result of military realities several months later.

Morrison had thus committed his first bout of sabotage on the government. A second was soon to follow. But even so, Attlee was not defeated yet – not by a long way. His tacking towards an October election on 12 May turned out, in reality, to have been just a ruse; for, as soon as he was back in London, he reverted to Churchill's policy of the 11th. The suddenness of this shift represents further circumstantial evidence that Attlee might have been in favour of that approach for some time. On 18 May, Attlee and the Prime Minister therefore began to search afresh for a formula to attain the shared object of going on until peace in the Pacific. Yet, there was another imperative acting on them as well – the 1945 Labour Party conference at Blackpool was due to begin only three days later. That posed major problems as it was certain to be the scene of vocal appeals to leave the Churchill regime. For his part, the Prime Minister was coming under mounting pressure from Conservatives – particularly Beaverbrook and Bracken – to resolve the matter promptly.[131]

In this atmosphere of intense pressure, Churchill met with Attlee at Downing Street in the early hours of 18 May for 'a long talk'[132] to discuss how they might prolong the alliance.[133] The two party leaders resolved that Churchill would send a letter to the NEC via Attlee,[134] offering a straight choice between an immediate dissolution or waiting until the defeat of Japan.[135] Their discussion centred on the precise tone and contents of the letter and how it could be framed so as to offer Attlee the necessary inducements to persuade the executive to spurn independence and maintain the cross-party government.[136] The Deputy Prime Minister had already consulted Bevin and Dalton, with both men now 'with him' in going on for one more year.[137] If there was indeed a 'consensus', then, it was here – in amiable personal relationships at the top. There is no evidence that Attlee consulted Morrison on what to do next. The notion that staying in alliance was not taken 'seriously' is,[138] it now seems safe to judge, unsustainable. Whatever resistance there was to it in some quarters, it plainly *was* taken 'seriously' and drove the actions of Attlee, Churchill, Bevin, Morrison and many others. The two party leaders therefore displayed a considerable amount of ingenuity in seeking to stay together; for the Prime Minister it fitted his predispositions, but for Attlee it was obviously a product of careful deliberation over a long period of time. It was another glimpse into his conception of leadership that the Lord President finally took up a position on 'the future' only at the last possible moment. *Pace* Attlee's later nuanced rebuttals, Foot's charge that Labour's leading figures had to be 'hauled out of [the coalition] by the scruff of their necks' undoubtedly has a ring of truth.[139]

It was an important shift by Attlee. True, the October 1944 statement of party policy, which he had overseen, hinted indirectly at this option; and everything since was a recipe for delay of an indeterminate duration. But it does conflict with some of the, admittedly ambiguous, evidence we have of Attlee's earlier deliberations.[140] Perhaps even his previous preference for a six-month delay was as open to rethinking as all other aspects of his leadership. Indeed, it is plausible that the opaque Attlee had *never* taken a settled point of view on the problem; he was certainly an adherent of Lord Salisbury's dictum that 'there is no such thing as a fixed policy.'[141] All we can say with certainty is that Attlee was now definitely aiming to postpone an election – and hope Churchill's aura dissipated along the way – into the medium term.

Working to outfox the Conservative and Labour parties, Churchill agreed without demure to Attlee's proposition that he might include in the letter a pledge that, if the coalition was maintained, it would urgently implement the proposals for social reform placed before Parliament in the King's Speech the previous autumn.[142] That was clearly a bid to find purchase by the tried and true method of bribery. And as one of the architects of the New Liberalism project alongside Lloyd George, WSC was perfectly familiar with that style of democratic politics. It gave Attlee a valuable weapon to yield at what was likely to prove a decisive NEC meeting on 20 May. For all the hints he had dropped since the summer of 1944 about breaking up the government, the façade of that was exposed when the moment of decision actually arrived. Attlee's earlier signals, and now this activity in May 1945, conformed to his practice since the beginning of the war – keeping the Labour Party restrained while he watched and waited. Seeking to be the first to create the postwar settlement, in helping to formulate Churchill's letter to the executive Attlee at last – if with customary obliqueness – set out his own stall.

Events thus take us away from Westminster and north to Blackpool. The 1945 annual conference was the most critical since 1940, for it was there, as the event began, that Attlee's Machiavellian effort to stay in office came to a head. Yet, having had the time and space in recent weeks to prepare for what was to come, this made it Morrison's best opportunity for a decade as well. That is significant. It can be no coincidence that the Home Secretary only made his move *after* Attlee and Churchill's dual strategy became evident. Moreover, his recent work seemed to be yielding fruit. Besides his old backers, Wilkinson, Laski and Webb, Bevan also now hoped to replace Attlee – whom he claimed had been 'a humiliating representative' of the party and 'consistently underplay[ed] his position and his opportunities'[143] – with Morrison.[144] Both Bevan – a member of the NEC since 1944 – and Shinwell – also a member – were opposed to prolongation of the alliance, and conveyed that to the Home Secretary privately.[145] Laski and Wilkinson, the incoming and outgoing NEC chairpersons respectively, also began to canvass openly on his behalf, disparaging Attlee and pressing Morrison's case.[146] Wilkinson asked Dalton to put pressure on Attlee simply to stand down.[147] A sizeable group of NEC members were now aligned with Morrison's opposition to Attlee as leader *and* the direction in which he hoped to guide the Labour movement. One contingency raised by the Home Secretary's backers was that, should a general election be called and the Labour Party win it, a leadership ballot ought to take place prior to a new ministry being constructed. An anti-Attlee movement therefore coalesced at what was the most difficult, yet fertile, moment for five years – right before the Lord President was due to gamble his authority on winning support for the status quo.

The breaking of the government

At the climatic session of the executive on 20 May, Attlee, Bevin and Dalton – armed with the Prime Minister's letter of the 18th – argued in support of the Churchill plan to stay in harness until peace in the Pacific.[148] Yet the Home Secretary took the lead in opposing them, forcefully seeking rejection of the whole proposal.[149] That this also entailed ignoring Churchill's offer of major social reform – the content of his 'great national plan' – was no impediment for Morrison. In his contest with Attlee, he thus presented himself as the advocate of the party's interests against those who would delay its reversion to independence. As before – but never to such devastating effect – the Home Secretary occupied that ground directly between Attlee and the Labour movement, and used it to marshal opposition to the Deputy Prime Minister. During the discussion over how to proceed, Morrison's position was vocally supported by Shinwell – who 'let rip' against Attlee – Laski, Bevan, Wilkinson and Griffiths.[150] The opposition to Attlee's strategy was – just as nine days earlier – centred on, and driven by, the Home Secretary. Indeed, it had been partly engineered in the first place through his keeping Attlee and Churchill apart on 11 May. When the question was put to a vote, all except three members of the executive rejected outright the possibility of going on until the culmination of the Pacific war.[151] It was a decisive result.[152]

Attlee had been defeated in the struggle over electoral policy. It represented by far his biggest setback in a decade as leader.[153] The structures he laboured so diligently to set up were washed away in an instant; and many were now linking party independence to the leadership itself. The Home Secretary had not only worked to capture the party's machinery for himself, but, by wrecking Attlee's gambit, he inflicted a potentially fatal blow to his credibility as well. It represented his second act of sabotage in less than a fortnight. Since February 1944, Morrison had cast around for a new basis for public action; the one he found, somewhat ironically, was protector of the Labour movement. The Churchill coalition's staunchest defender had reinvented himself as its leading adversary.

The executive's decision yielded the disintegration of the cross-party government in barely forty-eight hours. The idea of the parties coming together to meet the needs of war, and then separating harmoniously, is a fiction. In reality, the coalition was broken by Morrison. This fact has not bee absorbed by historians, but when appreciated it underlines the strengths of treating wartime politics, on the domestic front at least, as a highly contingent episode in which all was to play for and very different trajectories were available. Just as extensively as in peacetime, politics in the shadow of war was about personal and party advantage. There is something else. Convincing evidence that Morrison's whole approach in the preceding fortnight was motivatied principally by the objective of forcing the pace and destroying Attlee's strategy, rather than a genuine change of political preferences since February 1944, is offered by the records of a meeting of the executive on 18 May – just two days prior to the decisive confrontation at which Morrison broke the government. At that session – from which Attlee was absent – the Home Secretary once again took the lead. But, this time, he *personally* introduced a motion that the conference should not be permitted to 'tie the hands' of the executive against the possibility of forging a *new* coalition *after* an election![154] This is an important piece of evidence. It was quite a contrast to his stance on 20 May. It suggests that Morrison's reinvention since February 1944 – and particularly his derailing of Attlee's own policy – could well have been a feint compelled by the necessity of locating a new 'position'. After all, no one had expressed greater, or more frequent, contempt for the Labour Party's immaturity and need to be 'educated for governing'. To reiterate, two days prior to the crucial meeting that would determine the fate of the Churchill regime, Morrison very deliberately acquired the means to reverse what he was going to do on 20 May. Then, with that official resolution in hand, he set about confronting the Deputy Prime Minister. It is hard not to interpret this as another sophisticated piece of calculation. Think of the fact that the Home Secretary had earlier backed a postwar alliance via the medium of a 'coupon' election. Bear in mind too that Morrison – like most people – judged that Churchill would probably win a general election. The Home Secretary was expected to mount a leadership challenge – and, in the aftermath of another defeat, he would surely be able to dislodge Attlee. The fact is that people did not expect an election to turn out as it did. Everyone had an opinion on the political fortunes of the parties, but it was just guesswork.[155] Attlee reckoned that 'the Tories would pull it off;'[156] opinion polling was treated with widespread scepticism. What matters is that neither the Labour nor the Conservative leaderships acted as if they expected a Labour victory. But the charade of the Home Secretary's Janus-like approach to party politics is clear. His action at the first executive meeting, and piloting of a ruling that 'circumstances cannot be adequately foreseen',[157] indicates that if he did become leader after an election defeat, Morrison might use the decision of 18 May to annul that of the 20th and reform the coalition – a far greater compromise of the party's independence than anything Attlee had contemplated.

It was a second, and this time brilliant, tactical performance by the Home Secretary. As so frequently in politics, commitments and the necessary verbiage are easily constructed and then dispensed with. And it had a major impact on British politics as a whole. Morrison managed to get *both* of the things he had sought all along – to lead Attlee into a trap that could destroy him, while retaining the option of coalition. Although we are lacking clear linearity about Morrison's constant scheming, it seems a logical interpretation of the evidence at the distance of half a century and is certainly the most plausible explanation for the Home Secretary's contradictory, and nuanced, movements in the previous fortnight.

With the Attlee–Churchill proposition rebuffed, events proceeded quickly thereafter. Replying to the Prime Minister, Attlee made a last ditch bid to stave off a khaki election by appealing for a contest in October, when they could be sure that the new electoral register would be finished.[158] Unsurprisingly, Churchill did not fall for that.[159] If an election had to be held, he quickly decided that it would occur on 5 July instead,[160] and sat down to work with Macmillan and Randolph Churchill on drafting a response that would place upon Labour 'the onus of refusing to continue' and 'preferring faction to unity'.[161] On 23 May, Churchill took it upon himself to go to Buckingham Palace to tender the resignation of his government; as head of the largest party in Parliament, he was immediately invited him to form a 'caretaker' ministry to oversee public business until the general election.[162] Colville telephoned Attlee and read him the text of Churchill's resignation letter to the king; the Labour leader then spent 40 minutes copying it down, line by line – presumably for study.[163] Finding an acceptable 'official' version of events remained important. But dissolution was a decision unwelcome in many quarters. Churchill, obviously, was 'not happy'.[164] Butler recalled that 'I was very much in favour' of carrying on – 'the coalition had not, in my view, outlived its usefulness, and I thought we should stay together at least until the Japanese had been defeated and preferably until the social reforms upon which we were in general agreement had been passed.'[165] He felt that the proposal conformed to 'the national interest' and was 'imperative' for the 'party interest'.[166] Headlam wrote that 'the more one thinks about it the less necessary an election seems to be.'[167] For his part, during the campaign Bevin told Butler that 'we ought to have kept the coalition going much longer.'[168]

So it was that the Churchill coalition – by far the most famous government of the whole century – came to an end. It had been created by the machinations of the Labour leaders; and it ended by the same route. What had it achieved? Besides the obvious – leading Britain to victory and turning a democratic country with a liberal political culture into an efficient war machine[169] – the truth is that it had principally been a triumph for its Labour members. This book has consciously avoided engagement with the stale 'consensus' debates. What it has done is illuminate the struggles for political advantage that occurred after 1939, and dwelt on the impact of the Labour ministers on the British state. There can be little doubt that Attlee, Bevin and Morrison got the better of those exchanges. It was only from early 1944 that the Conservatives offered meaningful resistance; prior to that, the Labour ministers were largely able to drive the British state, in several policy areas, in directions they chose. Moreover, they were central to a revolution in how the state operated, the roles that it assumed and the way its administrators thought. That represented a major, and permanent, expansion of the boundaries of government. True, the Conservatives excluded Labour from economic policymaking, and social reform proceeded more slowly than Attlee and his colleagues would have liked. But that did not minimize the gravity of the changes. The doctrinal innovations of socialism worked out in the 1930s had, in many respects – none more so than intellectually – been enshrined at the heart of the state. Planning, the core of those developments, was now the lodestar of government.

215

Perhaps it would have happened whatever the Labour leaders did; a new kind of war had to be fought, after all. But it is difficult to believe that if not for the political nous of Attlee and the rest it would have taken the form that it did. The outcome was that a party with little prospect of winning an election in 1939 now stood in a position of legitimacy and even esteem in the public eye. Moreover, the Labour ministers ensured that their party became aligned with the fleeting sense of 'national community' that developed during the war. They all understood it – think of Attlee's 'unity' campaign of 1941 – and were able to present Labour doctrines as conforming to the deeper inclinations of the British public.

With the collapse of the coalition, then, the 'Long Parliament' of 1935 entered its final phase. Up in Blackpool, the conference witnessed a ringing endorsement of the Morrison-crafted *Let Us Face the Future*.[170] For Attlee there were other warning signs as well. The Home Secretary – who through it all remained publicly uncommitted about his own strategy – delivered an aggressive address on socialism, nationalization and 'the most important general election of all time', which was a clear leadership kite.[171] Rousing the audience in a way that no one else could, Morrison received a thunderous standing ovation lasting several minutes.[172] Beaverbrook's *Daily Express*, as mischievous as ever, lauded him as 'the undoubted leader' of the Labour Party.[173]

But – equally importantly – Attlee's response to the defeat was impressively robust. Adapting quickly, at the executive meeting on 20 May he immediately gave his assent to the decision and did not seek to push the matter any further.[174] In the conference hall he then read out to the delegates, word for word, a new letter to Churchill, rejecting prolonged alliance and attacking the possibility of a khaki election. ('It appears to me that you are departing from your position of a national leader. ... Should you, however, decide to hold an election in July despite all the disadvantages to the electors ... the responsibility must and will ... be yours.')[175] With his favoured strategy foreclosed, Attlee thus tacked back towards the party. Just days later, Laski wrote to Attlee privately and forcefully requested him to stand down before the election:

I have been acutely aware for many months ... of the strong feeling that the continuance of your leadership is a grave handicap to our hopes of victory in the coming election. [This opinion] is felt by a majority of our own Executive. It is felt by the outstanding trade union leaders ... and the rank-and-file ... share this view profoundly. So ... do many of your parliamentary colleagues.[176]

The NEC chairman went on to say that Attlee's resignation would be a 'great service'.[177] This time, however, Attlee nonchalantly brushed it off in a famously dismissive response that has been frequently cited by scholars – 'Dear Laski, thank you for your letter, contents of which have been noted'[178] – and then simply carried on. It might be deemed significant that, even when left so precariously exposed as in May 1945, Attlee was able to survive.

The spoils of war

It seems unnecessary either to treat in depth the 1945 general election campaign or to consider the reasons for Churchill's defeat. All that has been done capably by others. But it is relevant to the current account that, after the disintegration of the alliance, Attlee smoothly resumed his place as leader of the Labour Party, and he and Morrison each occupied prominent places in the resultant work. The issue of the leadership was thus kicked into touch until after the election. It was an exceptionally bitter campaign. Masterminding the work from Transport House, the former Home Secretary gave dozens of speeches around the country and delivered the Labour Party's final election broadcast.[179] He was also one of only two ministers to have a pamphlet devoted to his duties in government,[180] and in January had signalled his intention to lead Labour's advance onto new ground by changing his constituency from blue-collar Hackney to contesting white-collar East Lewisham.[181] Meanwhile, Attlee himself – despite spending part of the time at Potsdam with Churchill – delivered around seventy addresses at public rallies and was, as always, concerned that one 'silly speech by Aneurin Bevan might easily be used to stampede the electors away'.[182] He strove to ensure that speakers at the hustings stuck to official policy. More importantly, in an election broadcast in response to Churchill's famously clumsy suggestion in early June that a Labour government would resemble the 'Gestapo',[183] Attlee was 'quietly devastating':[184]

> When I listened to the Prime Minister's speech last night in which he gave such a travesty of the policy of the Labour Party, I realised at once what was his object. He wanted the electors to understand how great the difference was between Winston Churchill, the great

leader in war of a united nation, and Mr Churchill, the party leader of the Conservatives. He feared that those who accepted his leadership in war might be tempted out of gratitude to follow him further. I thank him for having disillusioned them so thoroughly.[185]

It was probably his best-received foray onto the public stage. Jenkins called it 'the making' of Attlee as a figure in the election.[186] Though he was always eclipsed by Morrison as a speaker, his measured style was better suited to the medium of radio broadcasts by leading figures – which around half the British public tuned in to hear.[187] Attlee achieved the unlikely feat of getting the better of Churchill in the public arena. That his was a typically adept response to being compelled to follow a path he opposed was underlined when Attlee dealt with Laski's latest *faux pas* in a mature manner. The LSE maverick declared on 14 June that the Labour Party could not be bound by agreements reached between Churchill, Truman and Stalin at Potsdam, and also raised the spectre of unconstitutional control of Parliament by claiming that the peace settlement would have to be ratified by the NEC.[188] The scandal generated sensationalist headlines right up until polling day such as 'Obscure Laski Caucus Will Give Orders',[189] and even accusations that Laski fancied himself as head of a 'dictatorship'.[190] Though he was privately furious, Attlee met the hysteria by denying that the NEC would be allotted any unconstitutional powers in a public exchange of letters with Churchill.[191] The incident undoubtedly damaged the Labour Party, for public opinion swung sharply towards the Conservatives in the three weeks prior to the election when the episode dominated the news.[192] But it was Attlee, not Morrison, who contained the storm. In one of the few instances of enmity that made it into his memoirs, Attlee – with his habitual understatement – recalled that Laski's political judgement was 'not very good',[193] and plainly thought it odd that he imagined himself a 'leading figure' on the public stage.[194]

With the campaign over, Attlee and Churchill set off for three further weeks at the Potsdam peace conference. It was a glorious summer's day when the election results came in on 26 July; that made for a vivid contrast with the wet and grey summer of 1939 in which the Labour Party's journey through Hitler's war began. And, just as then, the weather paralleled the mood of its leaders. Even with the eruption of the Laski furore, the election results were certainly not what Attlee feared: far from being defeated, the Labour Party in fact swept home with its first landslide victory, seizing 393 seats to the Conservatives' 213. It was a rout. Attlee must have been astonished, for he had told Colville that, in his view, the best-case scenario was a Conservative majority of 40.[195] The Liberal Party, meanwhile, was reduced to just 12 MPs. This meant that, for the first time, Labour would be able to build a government with a majority in Parliament. It altered the entire mental landscape. Moreover, many of the newly won constituencies were located in middle-class areas. Some Cabinet ministers, including Beaverbrook and Macmillan, lost their seats. 'This is democracy', lamented Headlam.[196] Channon was 'stunned and shocked' at the country's 'treachery'.[197] But having survived under 'controls' and 'planning' for six years, the electorate discerned many features of *Let Us Face the Future* that hardly appeared all that new. And undoubtedly of most significance was that Labour tapped into the new style of democratic politics unleashed by the war; it was a stark contrast with the 'No Promises But Every Preparation' stance of the Conservatives.[198] Utopianism represented the key to what happened. That is not a mystery. But there is still an important point here. The unshackling of the democracy from the restraints imposed upon it by Baldwin a generation earlier was a systemic change within British political life, which has not been adequately understood by historians and needs proper study.

As events transpired, then, the Labour Party was out of office for barely two months. That rendered Attlee's initial calculations – and Morrison's for that matter – irrelevant. Their party was in no need of a coalition to govern. In turn, this presented important imperatives because what remained was not merely the issue of the Labour leadership but also – unexpectedly – the highest stakes of all, occupancy of 10 Downing Street. Once again, scholars have overlooked this problem. Exploring how it was resolved requires a second detailed analysis of elite decision-making, in this case the events of 25 to 28 July. Churchill's message to Attlee of 26 July, in which he conceded defeat, acted as the starting gun for a fresh series of plots and manoeuvres that at last brought the Attlee–Morrison competition into the open and determined the hierarchy of public life in the years following 1945. Some 24 hours earlier, on 25 July, Morrison wrote privately to Attlee as the election results came through and let loose the broadside he had waited ten years to fire:

> Whatever the result of the election may be, the new parliamentary
> party is bound to include many new members. They should, I

think, have the opportunity of deciding as to the type of leadership they want. … I have decided … I should accept nomination for the leadership of the party.[199]

Morrison insisted that 'I am animated solely by considerations of the interests of the party, and regard for their democratic rights, and not by any personal unfriendliness towards yourself, I need hardly assure you.'[200] He subsequently protested that he had been 'pressed' to seek the leadership by his supporters, implying that he would not have done so otherwise.[201] We might take that with a pinch of salt. Attlee immediately conveyed news of Morrison's intentions to Bevin, who was, characteristically, apoplectic: 'I won't have it. You leave him to me.'[202] The former Minister of Labour then spoke to Morrison by telephone and warned him that 'if you go on mucking about like this, you won't be in the bloody government at all.'[203] That was an empty threat, but it does show that Attlee and Bevin were ready to resist the ambitions of the heir apparent. Sure enough, the next day, when the letter from Churchill arrived at Transport House on the afternoon of 26 July, Attlee was holding preliminary discussions with Morrison, Bevin, Laski and Morgan Philips.[204] As soon as Attlee relayed the news of Churchill's message, Morrison struck. He declared that the king's commission should not be sought until Labour MPs had formally been offered an opportunity to decide on who they wanted to be the leader.[205] That was a veiled way of throwing his hat into the ring. Yet, Morrison's eagerness can be appreciated – if Attlee was to go to Buckingham Palace and accept an invitation to form a government, all would be lost. It was unlikely that a new Prime Minister could be ousted if the only reason for doing so was one's own thirst for his job.

In terms of the PLP rulebook, Morrison was, of course, technically correct: it was a long-standing ritual for the party leader to be formally endorsed on an annual basis, at the beginning of each new parliamentary session. But what he really wanted was – and is – obvious. It constituted a bid to exploit his political pre-eminence to remove Attlee and become head of the new regime himself. One more thing working in his favour was that an 'unusually large'[206] number of older MPs had retired at the 1945 election, many of whom were Attlee's original supporters; in a PLP swollen by a new intake, and less dominated by hostile union-sponsored figures, Morrison enjoyed markedly improved prospects in any ballot. In the discussions, Laski supported Morrison's appeal for delay before seeing the king.[207] He suggested that Attlee should advise the Palace that the party would require two more days to hold a contest.[208] Emanating from Attlee's other great adversary, it was hardly the most subtle of manoeuvres. Propriety had become a device through which to defend and advance personal ambitions. Even 15 years later, Morrison stuck resolutely to this line, entitling the relevant section of his memoirs 'The Rights of the Parliamentary Party'.[209] It was an ingenious way of finding a formula to legitimize an old-fashioned duel. Morrison later claimed, 'I was disturbed to learn that moves had begun to propose me as leader of the party in place of Attlee.' That seems difficult to accept. 'I promptly took steps to see these activities stopped.'[210] He insisted that 'the idea [of snatching the leadership] never entered my head.'[211] All of this would be hard enough to believe if Morrison had not proposed *himself* to Attlee as soon as the election results became clear on 25 July.

But forewarned is forearmed. Attlee and Bevin responded to Morrison's call for a leadership contest with vigorous resistance of their own. And their stance too was enshrined in constitutional nuance: Attlee purported that to delay would hardly be consistent with the constitution of the nation itself. 'If the King asks you to form a government, you say "Yes" or "No", not "I'll let you know later",' as he put it.[212] 'You either bring it off successfully or you don't. ... People like Laski who knew all about the theory of politics and nothing about its practice just didn't understand it.'[213] Their argument seems to have been that the electorate voted for Labour in the knowledge that Attlee was its leader and hence it would simply be improper to replace him after the fact.[214] In itself, it was a somewhat tendentious interpretation of constitutional propriety, given the age-old practice of identifying the candidate best placed to win the support of a majority in the House of Commons. For both candidates, though, the dispute over the competing constitutional imperatives of the Labour Party and the nation offered a useful fig leaf to cover a struggle for the highest office in British politics. As the argument at Transport House continued, Morrison was called out of the room to receive a telephone call from Cripps; when he returned, it was to announce that Cripps, too, backed the bid for a leadership election.[215] The erstwhile Home Secretary's momentum – building steadily for seven months and having accelerated rapidly with his victories since May – now appeared irresistible.

In reality, though, it was only a mirage. Attlee still held all the cards.

And he understood that perfectly. This book has worked to debunk the assumption – which still prevails, even if less explicitly stated than it once was – that Attlee was a weak leader, and contended that, on the contrary, he was endowed with a rare steel and tactical finesse. While Morrison was out of the room conferring with Cripps, Attlee and Bevin derailed his challenge with brutal efficiency. Bevin advised Attlee, 'Clem, you go to the Palace straight away.'[216] What that meant was that Attlee should unilaterally exercise his authority as leader and simply accept the sovereign's commission immediately – in other words, pre-empt any ballot and present Morrison with a *fait accompli*. But the truth is that Attlee probably needed little encouragement: he later recalled deciding, after receiving Morrison's initial communiqué of 25 July, simply to ignore it.[217] Although Bevin's formidable support must have confirmed Attlee in his inclinations, it seems implausible to hold – considering the style and character of his leadership in the preceding six years – that any other path would have recommended itself.

In consequence, when Morrison returned to the meeting with news of Cripps's backing, Attlee and Bevin relayed nothing of their private deliberations.[218] The meeting broke up and the former Home Secretary spent the rest of the day under the distinct impression that his bid to force Attlee into a corner had yielded success and that he was soon to assume the premiership.[219] One associate recorded that 'I have never seen Mr Morrison happier.'[220] Yet, Attlee had got the better of him without Morrison even realizing it. While the latter was at a Labour victory rally at Westminster Central Hall early that evening, sounding out MPs for support and declaring that 'we cannot have this man as our leader',[221] Attlee simply got into the family car and drove over to see King George VI at the Palace.[222] Once there, after a short audience, he accepted the invitation to take on the premiership. That was the end of the matter. To be certain, *acting*, rather than *talking*, was a less glamorous style of politicking; but Attlee's decision displayed a surer grasp of the fact that true authority was to be found at the top of the Mall, not at a party rally of MPs and apparatchiks. That Attlee had comprehensively outmanoeuvred his rival at the death is confirmed in that the first the stunned Morrison learned of any of this was when Attlee suddenly arrived at the rally.[223] He went up onto the platform to announce to the crowd that he had just returned from Buckingham Palace and was already, therefore, the new Prime Minister of Great Britain.[224]

It does not require a fertile imagination to conceive of the surprise that Morrison must have felt at that. After outflanking Attlee on all fronts, on 26 July he was bested by the oldest tactic of all – going to see the king. The crux of the matter was that Morrison's understanding of what transpired that afternoon was quite different from what Attlee and Bevin had decided ought to happen next. While Morrison's rise was a remarkable individual feat, for the same reason his defeat in July was a potent reminder of Attlee's gifts. Even one of the most dynamic politicians of the century, at the height of his powers, proved incapable of defeating a man commonly likened to a bank manager.

A brief postscript – and which gives the lie to Morrison's contemporary and subsequent protestations that he did not seek the leadership for himself – failed to alter the reality of what had occurred. On 27 July, Attlee refused to make any commitment when Morrison approached him about becoming Foreign Secretary, but he gladly acceded to him being informally the Deputy Prime Minister and the 'number two' in government.[225] What that meant, if anything, was left unclear. Likewise, when Morrison amazingly *again* raised the matter of a leadership ballot at the PLP executive that day, he was firmly rebuffed and the committee signalled its unanimous backing to Attlee's establishment of a Labour ministry.[226] As his biographers observed, Morrison emerged from this unrealistic bid to stop Attlee with little credit, for his private agenda was painfully obvious.[227] Unsurprisingly, given her personal relationship with Morrison, Wilkinson was the last to give up, continuing to press his case prior to the inaugural gathering of the PLP the next day.[228] That was even more unfeasible: by this point, several ministers had already accepted the seals of office. It never got off the ground. Bevin himself opened the PLP meeting on 28 July and brought the whole episode to an emphatic end with a speech about Attlee's 'unimpeachable personal integrity', followed by moving a motion of confidence in the Prime Minister.[229] That was passed with a lengthy ovation.[230] Ede recorded that 'no one could doubt that Attlee had come into his own,' and 'I have never heard such sustained cheering. ... [Attlee] was obviously very deeply moved.'[231] After giving a brief speech of his own, Attlee set off to Potsdam and, in a moment heavy with symbolism, handed the meeting over to his new deputy – Morrison.[232]

There was one final matter awaiting Attlee's attention; and it is from here that we must exit our account. He now had to build a government of his own.[233] Despite failing in his patient bid to bring the old political system to a soft landing, he still became the principal beneficiary of its crash. Ensconced in Downing Street, Attlee quickly, and ruthlessly, constructed what was akin to a spider's web of influence, with himself nestled at its centre. All his colleagues – adversary and ally alike – were bound to him. It was remarkable not only for containing the activities of Morrison during the next six years but also for getting the best out of those around him. Bevin went to the Foreign Office, Morrison became Lord President and Cripps returned to the fold. All three shone. Most importantly, Attlee placed those who might pose problems – Bevan, Shinwell, Cripps, Wilkinson and, especially, Morrison – in roles about which the Labour Party would be sensitive. Morrison, for instance, as Lord President became a domestic overlord tasked with guiding the implementation of Labour's reform programme.[234] True, no one would have been better suited to achieving Labour's grandiose plans. Yet, if the Prime Minister also calculated that if the schemes went awry Morrison might prove a useful fall guy, we cannot know; but he certainly *did* calculate in that way about other difficult individuals. Attlee hinted at this tactic in his memoirs when recalling the appointments of Shinwell and Bevan. 'There were two positions which would be of great importance in view of our legislative programme *and of the urgency in the problems to be faced by their occupants* – Fuel and Power and Health.'[235] Many of Attlee's long-standing opponents were given truly thankless tasks – the NHS, dealing with the mines, sorting out education and rescuing British trade.[236] But the only glimpse of vindictiveness was spared for Laski: 'a period of silence on your part would be welcome.'[237]

By the end of July, his adversaries' fortunes were linked irrevocably to those of the government. Collective responsibility – and having one's own reputation at stake – was the best guarantee of loyalty. It was a cunning way of building an administration. Where *Let Us Face the Future* had been quintessential Morrison, the Labour government was classic Attlee. Morrison was also made Leader of the Commons, in other words, the principal government spokesman in Parliament. Politically, at least, being appointed Attlee's right-hand man was a dubious reward. No longer would he be able to occupy the ground between the Prime Minister and the Labour Party. In his memoirs, Dalton recalled that Attlee 'reigned without challenge',[238] but it was Shinwell who got to the heart of the matter when summing up Attlee's style: 'It is not bad tactics to make one's enemies one's servants.'[239]

Conclusion

Although the Conservatives finally reasserted themselves in the last phase of the war, it was too little too late. What had happened since 1944 was that the political system as a whole had suffered a major wrench due to the prospect of military victory. The end of the war forced politicians to rethink their situation, specifically their futures, and created new options about what to do next. Despite the constant carping of backbenchers, as the main 'winners' of the war the Labour Party possessed obvious incentives to shed the restraints of alliance and advance into independence brandishing its new credentials. For many Conservatives, too, there was a similar sense that the party had to rediscover itself following its post-Chamberlain stasis. But these were not the inclinations of the party leaders. Those men had preferred to stay together; indeed, Attlee and Churchill fought for it until the last possible moment. Given the extent of elite backing for prolonging the alliance, the reasons for the coalition's dissolution pose problems that historians have not fully picked up on. To be sure, the mass parties were hostile to the idea; their voices had been silenced for long enough. But, whatever his other failings, Churchill was still able to hold his own party – the issue was never put to the Conservatives. That leaves Labour and, in the form that the eventual decision took, the key influence was the role assumed by Morrison. What this chapter has done is to explore properly Morrison's role in determining the shape of public life at the end of the war and integrate it within historical analysis of the period. Not only had he piloted the election campaign and written *Let Us Face the Future* but, more significantly still, Morrison played the principal role in torpedoing Attlee and Churchill's shared strategy. His performance in May 1945, of seeking over a fortnight to prevent the identical positions of Attlee and Churchill from coming together, and then engineering the possibility of guiding Labour into a new coalition prior to taking the lead in seeking the collapse of the existing government, was a masterful instance of the political arts at work.

Furthermore, Attlee's gambit to carry on until peace in the Pacific was not only the boldest of all his decisions since 1939; it was rejected overwhelmingly. How Attlee was able to hang on in these conditions, let alone preserve his credibility, is important. First, his bid to keep the alliance in being was the culmination of an incremental but continuous process of leadership since 1941. There is no evidence that Attlee took any clear views on the issue of the future at that premature stage. That was not his style. But what he did do was to nudge the party system, consistently, in one direction. Yet, paradoxically, that style of incremental politics, decisive in its own way but without the element of public confrontation that attends most major leadership decisions, was precisely how Attlee was able to reverse course so inconspicuously after 20 May. He never shed the image of being someone who listened and acted according to the wishes of his party – even if in practice there had been little evidence of such behaviour since 1939. That impression imbued Attlee with a durability that permitted him not only to sustain this blow but also to move out of it in such a way as to avoid an overt crisis centred on his own position. And when faced with Morrison's direct challenge in July 1945, those same antennae led Attlee to overcome it by simply pre-empting the whole debate and forming a ministry on his own authority. This was a man who in retirement maintained that 'I was never conscious of any intrigue against me.'[240]

The subsequent chapter will seek to draw conclusions about Attlee's leadership and his place within the ranks of British politicians, but for now it seems sufficient to propose that scholarly understanding of public life during the Second World War needs fresh thinking in order to build on Addison's pioneering original work. There can be little doubt that while historians have neglected many of the events considered here, the episodes of May and July 1945 were not only linked to all that had gone before but must be judged central to the reshaping of party and government politics. Certainly, they were treated them that way by the participants. The panoply of phraseology used to provide a structure to earlier writing – consensus, disunity, patriotism, public opinion, reform – needs much more vigorous scrutiny.

Having faced defeat and replacement in the spring of 1945, then, by the summer Attlee unexpectedly found himself in an unassailable position as the British Prime Minister. Where he stood did not simply *arise*; that does not happen in politics. Attlee had earned it. Tested under fire, his leadership, deeply nuanced since 1939, shaped and responded to events with greater consistency than that of any of his peers. There is something else. Attlee was not just a party leader during the war. This point is critical in properly conceptualizing what he had done. His sphere of activity would be best understood as comprehending the larger part of the political system as a whole. That was Attlee's 'secret'. A *News Chronicle* photograph of Attlee, Bevin and Morrison taken at the July 1945 victory rally captures the essence of what had occurred: depicting a proud-looking Attlee, it shows him, pipe in hand, flanked on either side by Bevin and Morrison.[241] Those two stare at one another. And, although Attlee and his deputies smile for the camera, Morrison looks almost shell-shocked. Such was his ordeal; and such was the new Prime Minister's enduring success.

Conclusion

In May 1940, a new government was born when Winston Churchill – breaking the habit of a lifetime – deliberately said little in a meeting with Chamberlain and Halifax. His silence at the critical moment enabled him to seize the crown. Five years later, Clement Attlee acquired the premiership in an uncannily similar fashion, namely by resolutely keeping quiet during a tense session with Bevin and Morrison at Transport House. If Churchill's tactics for once signalled a break with his penchant for theatrical behaviour, those of his successor in Downing Street were in line with Attlee's oldest habits. Attlee served as Prime Minister from 1945 to 1951, and thereafter as Labour leader until December 1955. But a strong case can be made that, in many respects, the critical period of his leadership was the war.

The key problem remaining before us is how we are properly to draw together the strands of his leadership and reconceptualize Attlee. Scholars know that they rate him, but cannot adequately explain why.[1] It has been the contention of this book that while successive generations of historians have tried, and failed, to come to grips with Attlee as a near-mythical figure – and being deeply disappointed with what they find – approaching him in that way is itself the problem. Rather, by studying him as a *public actor* instead, steadily tracing his impact on the political environment, a really convincing Attlee comes into view for the first time. He had led the Labour ministers' gradual, and adroit, exploration of the possibilities thrown up by Hitler's bid to dominate Europe; and he emerged from it all as Prime Minister. The purpose of this conclusion is not, then, to reiterate what he had done, but to try to achieve a richer understanding of his leadership. By extension, it also stresses the importance of studying 'leadership' more broadly as an explanatory instrument. One other goal of the book has been to rework our existing understandings of wartime politics itself. It makes no claim to exhaustiveness in that respect – more analysis, for instance, is needed of key areas of government policy, the role of other significant individuals, and the wartime evolution of political communication – but has focused instead on a series of neglected themes. As such, this chapter also dwells on the consequences of the advance for Labour Party doctrines that occurred during the war, briefly linking the implications of this new style of governing to the postwar era – the high watermark of 'democratic' politics.

Attlee: authority and reputation

It seems appropriate to develop some more general conclusions about Attlee's direction of the Labour Party in order to contextualize properly what we have seen. The same is true of his reputation as well. First, it might now be obvious why Attlee's name has never been 'a counter in the currency game of political cult'.[2] Although his government is frequently invoked, there is no great rush to lay claim to Attlee's mantle. There have been no proclaimed heirs, no political acolytes. There is no 'Attleeite', or 'Attleeism', in the political lexicon. The truth is that his leadership did not offer a ready example for others to emulate. One reason for this is that it was not clustered in a claim to moral authority; nor did Attlee enjoy a significant public persona. Indeed, these deficiencies were the cause of the most regular complaints directed against him. Lacking an appealing public face is unusual for a leader in a democratic system. Additionally, ambiguity was integral to Attlee's political character. That left a decidedly flat impression on contemporaries; and it persists in baffling scholars. But what needs to be fully appreciated is that such opaqueness was itself a tool. Think of his memoir, *As It Happened* – unrevealing yes, dull undoubtedly, but wholly consistent with a calculated style rooted in inscrutability. That is a start. Second, Attlee was not a shaper of public opinion, like a Baldwin or a Blair. Given that he was no master of the democratic arts, this leaves the basis for his ascendancy still more puzzling. Whereas most major leaders interact with the public and make that one of the bases of their power, Attlee was different: he clustered his leadership inside the regime. In a sense, he was simply – and utterly – out of step with the trends of politics in twentieth-century Britain, particularly the importance of 'personality' – a process begun many decades before he became leader – and of visually appealing imagery. To put it bluntly, Attlee fails to conform to what we expect of a modern politician. That makes him a source of deep frustration, but, in reality, he was perhaps the last great example of a much older style.

From 1939 onwards, Attlee was consistently able to dominate party and government politics in Britain. No one occupied more political space than he did; few of his peers enjoyed the sheer range of jobs he acquired; and none of his colleagues matched him as a strategist or tactician. It was he who managed the political system, created new opportunities for his party, restrained it when necessary, and took the lead in directing the under studied but vital area of electoral policy. Perhaps 'Capability' Attlee would be a better description than the 'little mouse' of lore. The key to it was that, rather than revealing his priorities on a public platform or in the press, Attlee's favourite implements were the committee system, the private meeting and, most of all, the simple memorandum. Of course, every politician relies on those tools, but it persists in being the *extent* of Attlee's mastery of such weaponry that stands out. Coupled with his limited profile in the public sphere, the combination is a striking one. There was another aspect too, best drawn out by Geoff Fry. Attlee's 'reputation as a man of few words' was itself a conscious pose.[3] Even his signature pipe became a political 'prop', encouraging an image of 'sagacity'.[4] 'The resort to the pipe [was] used to punctuate discussion on his own terms,' a means of slowing and controlling events.[5] Opposition was there to be dismissed. From Attlee's contemporaries there was only intermittent grasp of the significance of his actions between 1939 and 1945; he moved by stealth. But the record of his wartime pre-eminence speaks for itself. There is something else as well: Attlee had not only – or even principally – *interpreted* what was happening. He *moulded* it himself. While he did not shape public opinion, he did know how to run an institutional system. In a real sense, he was an English Stalin, and one imagines that Attlee would have thrived in the Byzantine politics of the Soviet Union. This account has been the first to study him in that sense and to establish his ascendancy in a specific period. To be sure, he was far too cunning to commit his real thoughts to paper; and he was an expert at maintaining 'legitimacy' for his decisions that even today make it difficult to see him as anything but a reluctant, loyal servant. The Labour leader proceeded carefully and covered his tracks every step of the way as he went. This – just as much as his impenetrable persona – might be why Attlee's success has been ill appreciated. But the direction in which he consistently headed is evident. Flexible about means of travel, he had a clear destination in mind.

With the exception of Beckett, recent observers seem to have given up the ghost on cracking the Attlee enigma. How, then, are we to conceptualize him? What were the key elements of his leadership? What is most striking from the events of the Second World War is that the hallmark of Attlee's approach to politics was an extraordinary, and even single-minded, determination. Though reciting bland, emollient phrases at every turn, he actually conceded remarkably little. That is important. He achieved his objectives in restrictive conditions against a party that was sceptical about the leap of faith he forced it to make. In addition, vital decisions were his to take – and he was by no means averse to taking them. Whether it was to bide time in 1939, to enter the coalition, to pressurize the Conservatives, or resist Labour, Attlee took the hard choices himself. And he did so with unusual decisiveness and lack of con-sultation. That said, he was also a master hedger, and this may be yet another reason for historical confusion; hedging, improperly understood, can appear as merely inconsistency and contradiction. But it was in fact a deliberate act of leadership that yielded regular harvests of political fruit. Attlee was concerned with the impact of particular decisions on the total situation; and it was that larger picture to which he devoted his attention.

Furthermore, he remained very much alive to the power of language and words in reshaping political moods and generating new options. Few were more adept at this than Attlee; not, to be certain, in terms of the grand oratorical flourishes of Churchill, or the public partisanship of Morrison, but merely the wording chosen for a memorandum or a press release. That was a crucial part of his armoury. As we saw in his memoirs, here was a man who always chose his words with extreme care. Attlee based his stewardship of difficult situations, none more so than electoral policy, on an appreciation of the value of incremental movement and cautious language. Because he had no real confidantes – as far as we know – his priorities and objectives generally did not leak out into either contemporary political circles or subsequent memoir.[6] Attlee concealed his thoughts and said little; and so, to study him properly, our only choice is to look to his observable activity instead.

The consequences of these characteristics for understanding Attlee's place in public life are important. He was definitely not a 'political teacher' or a 'public moralist'.[7] But he did possess unusual gifts. A short essay on Attlee by James Margach, written in 1979, gets closer to the heart of the man than any of the other literature: he was 'cold', 'ruthless as a butcher', had 'extraordinary bloody-mindedness', displayed 'callous indifference' when need be, and even 'cruelty and cynicism'.[8] All these characteristics were on display during the period examined here. We might go further. What was Attlee's own understanding of leadership? The man himself listed 'judgement, strength of character, experience of affairs, and an understanding of ordinary people' as the essentials.[9] One had to 'suffer fools gladly'.[10] A Prime Minister needed 'a sense of urgency, of dispatch ... you must have a sense of timing, judgement of what will go and what won't and when.'[11] Tellingly, Attlee invested much weight in the skill necessary to be able to 'sum up' decisions of the PLP and NEC in such a way as to get agreement and move forward ('that takes some doing') – and which he carried out consistently, to great effect, throughout the war.[12]

As Leader of the Opposition in conventional conditions, Attlee lacked the charisma and dynamism to offer much in the way of vision, and was unable to motivate his followers or really *lead* them anywhere. But when faced with a specific task to master, with the need for careful positioning and patience, and when he had access to power, Attlee was in his element. By explicitly addressing his elusiveness and studying him on his own terms, both Attlee and the politics of war are illuminated. Proceeding beyond biography in the current account, what has become evident is his recurrent centrality in instigating and directing significant political events between 1939 and 1945. The conventional interpretations of Attlee's role during the war –that he was not one of the 'big men', that he did not really make a 'mark', and that he had 'very little influence' – seem difficult to sustain. Moreover, given that it is now perhaps safe to judge that the larger structures of British politics after 1940 were less rigid – and bland – previous accounts would imply, and in fact were themselves at the centre of political attention, those who still doubt that Attlee was the major figure in strategy and tactics need to demonstrate who else was.

There is another point. This analysis of Attlee – attempting to discern problems as he encountered them during the war, and avoid engagement with him as a mythological figure – hints at the need for, and value of, further sustained study of 'leadership' as an explanatory force. Though elite studies are aplenty, few historians to date have recognized the usefulness of properly examining leadership. Yet, it might offer a vehicle for better appreciation of political activity in modern Britain, not least because it would highlight, in a more conceptualized manner, the true wealth and range of political life.

What is clear first – and this point would be objectionable to very few –

is that leadership is critical in shaping the contours of political life. Yet, it is equally apparent that the character of leadership is rarely studied as an activity in and of itself. Because each leader is an individual, there is ample scope for distinctive work. Men as diverse as Balfour and Ian Paisley await their interpreters. But another, more serious, difficulty remains the question of precisely *who* should be deemed significant and why. Surprisingly, this might not be self-evident. One starting point (and this is particularly relevant to Attlee) is to examine whether those individuals whom their peers deem 'important' are the actors upon whom we should concentrate our attention. The thinking goes that by being *seen* as significant, they are inevitably invested with a degree of authority and influence. In most cases, it is undoubtedly true. But, how does that impact on men like Attlee? Certainly, being leader of the Labour Party would make anyone important in the eyes of his or her contemporaries. Yet he was also treated dismissively by those people. As this account has contended, Attlee often operated beneath the radar of other politicians. Few would have judged Attlee one of the most significant figures in the country. Though he has not been the focus of this book, one could make a similar case for John Anderson. It seems that there is a need for additional exploration of the political roles performed by the uncharismatic, grey men in the Attlee mould. Think of Campbell-Bannerman and Bonar Law. Given the nature of democratic politics, we perhaps instinctively favour the charismatic, more obviously dynamic individuals; but in some cases that might impart very little about the workings of the political machine. Publicly saleable individuals (like Churchill in the war) often manage a team, or present a face to the wider world; but the precise role they play, and the importance of their individual work, needs to be investigated and might even be debatable.[13] All of this is an indirect way of saying that there is a category of significant political actors that stands in sharp contrast to the glamorous stars of the democratic age – the administrators. These need better study. Attlee, for instance, lived his entire life in a mental universe firmly pre-1914 in orientation. What might be most important about Attlee was that, in him, the features of the administrator combined with someone who also actually held the position of leader – generating a kind of politician unique in the public life of modern Britain.

The problems highlighted here – and grasped in different contexts by scholars like John Charmley, Jeremy Smith and Philip Williamson – would appear to necessitate far more extensive attention to 'leadership' across a broad range of fronts. Leaders are what make politics tick; achieving a richer and better-conceptualized appreciation of that role remains an urgent task.

The new democratic politics

Since 1939, politicians in these islands had waged a competition to channel – and harness – the impact of a major global event – the war – to their own advantage. Some succeeded; others failed. In its overriding concern with the business of politics, rather than ideologies, social changes or other ineluctable forces, this book is one of a series of linked pieces that I have published elsewhere.[14] As historians seek inexorably to expand the boundaries of what is deemed 'politics' and range ever further into areas like 'culture' (and frequently ever further into gibberish masquerading as sophisticated thought), the case for refocusing attention on the realm of the elite is a powerful one. Founded upon a specific impression of public life, this account has deliberately excluded rank-and-file politics, social change, egalitarianism and the vague – though undoubtedly real – mood for 'reform'. Instead, it assumes the existence of a governing class, that its assumptions should be examined, and that parliamentary politics, through the worlds of Westminster and Whitehall, are, in most respects that matter, sealed off. This was especially true during the war, because the business of governing, and planning for the future, carried unusual urgency. As such, this book has contributed nothing to the debate about whether the war generated a 'consensus'. Such an argument requires an interaction with policy, where this book has concentrated on politics and also a longer perspective. Anyway, I am myself unsure as to whether there was a consensus. Given the gulf between intention and outcome in governing – and what that means for ascribing policy results to 'ideologies' – the issue becomes still more elusive. Perhaps understandings of British government as a whole need to be injected with greater sophistication, and scepticism, before it can be resolved.[15]

Moreover, the central problem with historical writing on this period has been, as Cowling put it, that 'identification with the regime that "won the war" made writing about its enthronement an act of self-congratulation.'[16] Part of this is the assumption that the war *had* to be fought. We might go further and suggest that most of the material written about British politics during the war is in fact really about July 1945. A 'high political' framework for this era might render it less agreeable to many. But – besides their ministerial duties – activity of that sort is what politicians were engaged in. And the impact of this was to engender far more fluidity in the total political situation than Addison and others have conveyed. To be sure, the widespread preference at the end of the war for a prolonged alliance was a temporary expedient; there was none of the hostility to the party system as the ordering concept of politics expressed in earlier periods of systemic instability. But conditions, and possibilities, led leaders to consider maintenance of the current coalition-based system for a time. And while Addison and others talk up the winds of change sweeping the country, the weather vanes of the political world itself give more nuanced indication of those phenomena. Social strife was remarkable in its absence. There was no class tension, or upheaval, to produce a basis for political troubles. Historians of the war might have exaggerated the degree to which the moods of society should be seen as driving its politics – a product, perhaps, of Calder's linkage of the two in *The People's War*. Likewise, economic and industrial issues, or imperial ones for that matter, failed to exert the influence they might have. The conflicts that mattered – besides the war, of course – were in the political system itself.

If the party's leaders had come to enjoy such a dominant position in the polity, what had Labour advanced in the realm of ideas? The truth is that, throughout its history, the Labour Party's traditions in terms of ideological sophistication are largely fictitious. The party has produced little in the way of detailed programmes for breathing life into its doctrines. Given that socialists like nothing more than informing the world of their plans, this will rightly be thought a significant problem. Consider Dalton's 1935 *Practical Socialism for Britain*. Its author was one of the few Labour politicians whom we might expect to have come up with more than gesture; but, in fact, it contained no coherent programme for how a socialist society was to function. Morrison's *Socialization and Transport* was often fêted as offering a detailed plan for nationalized industry; but actually Morrison's 'solution' was simply to stress the merits of the public corporations model. There was little discussion of what to do *next*. This problem has recurred throughout Labour's history. The passage of legislation, of nationalizing areas of the economy, or of creating new administrative structures, is too often deemed to itself be the solution. But getting programmes on the statute book is one thing. The real issue was, and is, how to *run* them effectively thereafter, and at working that out Labour has been poor. To pass a new law and then go home satisfied with one's virtue is nothing more than a gesture, the instinct of the exhibitionist. Of course, intellectuals and commentators – most of whom have never run anything in their lives – do not spot this, and so mistake shadow for substance. These criticisms can be made of the Attlee government's legislative programme, Bevan's *In Place of Fear*, Crosland's *The Future of Socialism*, Wilson's fetish for creating new departments and Blair's fixation with press releases. The war was no exception. The only idea that Attlee and his colleagues seem to have shared was an instinctive conviction of the merits of 'planning' and of using the bureaucracies of Whitehall to achieve this. On its own terms, that worked well enough. Perhaps the most one can say in terms of 'ideas' is that Labour leaders have traditionally been able to use the power of the state as a means of muddling through. If that is an unfavourable record from one perspective, it has still proven sufficient to satisfy the ambitions of several generations of politicians.

Indeed, the main legacy of the period remains the advance of this doctrine of state power to a position of absolute primacy in the public sphere. That created a wholly new political style; and, with the partial exception of Elie Kedourie's scathing critique of the 1960s, some of its implications have not been properly appreciated by historians. What mattered most about Attlee, Bevin and Morrison was that they grasped – far better than others of their generation – the uses to which 'democratic' politics could be put. National unity and weariness were potent weapons in the right hands. To be sure, the reinvigorated Conservative Party proved rather more cunning than Labour over the subsequent decades at conducting the game according to these different rules. Both Labour and Conservatives were to recognize that Keynes provided a language ideal for playing snakes-and-ladders in a democracy. None has bettered it since. But the fact that political life had changed in terms of *how* politicians could now expect to generate support from the public, and that this was to be predicated upon a convergence between the deeper instincts of Labour doctrine and the imperatives of democratic politics, remains the most important lesson to draw. Think of the Conservatives' later electoral platform of 'the property-owning democracy'. The revolution – that is the right word – wrought by Attlee and the rest – both during the war and after it – was not principally about policy; the new system perhaps lay in a *method* of governing, a series of vocabularies and a way of thinking in

237

public life. Certainly, collectivism was already a growing trend – to say the very least – during the interwar period. The point, though, is that Attlee and his senior colleagues took advantage of this; and, in 1945 the chips fell where they did in large part because Labour's leaders responded with as much skill as the Conservatives lacked. The changes can be detected in the new mental framework and tools with which Britain was run, and the assumptions that underpinned government. It all centred on encouraging the idea that the state – that is the politicians – could now act as the 'Universal Provider'.[17]

This condition was not *only* a product of decisions taken in government. It was more complex than that. The miseries of wartime austerity gave birth to a new common culture that encouraged ordinary citizens to demand gratification – and the quicker the better, too.[18] Profound changes were occurring in social mores; religion and respectability were among the casualties. A culture of hedonism took hold in Britain. It has never let go. The problem – and it *was* a problem – lay in the connection between the democratic regime and the society that fed it. Recall Alexis de Tocqueville.[19] But, regardless, leading politicians were deeply conscious of the novelty of this situation. Even if historians typically consider the years immediately following 1918 to represent the triumph of democracy, at the level of the elite the changing of the guard only came about at the end of the Second World War. Yet all of that, in turn, sprang not from the tracts of an intellectual clerisy but the imperatives of electoral politics and the prizes to be gained from acquiring and retaining support. In their own way, men like Keynes and Beveridge, or Archbishop Frederick Temple, had been just as important to this new mood. In terms of politics though – the subject of this book – it was the Labour leaders, under Attlee's direction, who were central, who exploited it and who entrenched it.

The political sociology of Joseph Schumpeter remained as durable as ever.[20] Political actors still ran their system. However, the way in which politics was conducted and the tools that public actors used, was much changed. A process of 'modernization' begun in 1828, never inevitable but driven inexorably along by the short-term conveniences of individual politicians, finally ran its course in the years after 1945. Addison chose to close his own account of the war with a rather uplifting statement about postwar politics.[21] Perhaps a contrary perspective is in order here. In the 1920s and 1930s, the Conservatives employed the imagery of national identity, constitutionalism and citizenship to potent effect, contrasting that with Labour's supposedly sectional appeal. By the end of the war, however, Labour claimed to represent 'the public' just as completely as its rivals. Over the next few years they were to establish on that ground a new politics, with different totems – of the welfare state, egalitarianism and promises of 'affluence'. This paradigmatic shift meant that, for decades, promising to do better, to do more, in these areas constituted a politician's principal claim to power.[22]

It might have been the logical endpoint of a democratic polity, but it was also employed as a tool. Enoch Powell saw that in 1958. Mrs Thatcher did as well, but just what she did about it is another matter. All parties recognized the potential of appealing to the 'greed and envy' of the electorate – reinforcing the 'Robin Hood' character of successful social democratic politics.[23] If Cowling was correct, and 'the salient feature of the political system since 1832 was not the attempt of popular feeling to make itself felt in Parliament but the attempts of parliamentary politicians to find ways of securing support from extra-parliamentary opinion,'[24] then the aftermath of the war was a turning point in ways that are yet to be explored. The full effects of democracy were staved off throughout the interwar period. But from 1945 things changed in important ways. Due to the decisions taken by the Labour leaders to exploit public exhaustion and win power with promises of Shangri La, politics in Britain would henceforth be marked not only by the struggle between elites to mount the greasy pole but by the need for those same men to wage that competition by constantly devising fresh initiatives to pass down to the tens of millions situated at the bottom of the pole. Kedourie's 'politics of "how much"' had its origins in the war.[25] That it chimed with conventional wisdom in parts of the clerisy does not detract from what it meant. The 'High Politics' of Economic Policy and The 'High Politics' of the Welfare State remain to be written. But postwar policy cannot be understood except as part of an old contest that now took on new forms.

One story had thus come to an end. That said, it was not *the* end. 'Truth' had not been spotted on a radar screen monitoring the skies of southern England, or dug up in the sands of El Alamein. Still less was a 'new Jerusalem' built. There was no land of milk and honey; nor even one 'fit for heroes'. Politicians had simply reshuffled the cards in the deck. Their game was still afoot.

Appendix
The Adventurers

Career details provided are those relevant to the war.

Leo Amery (1873–1955): Secretary of State for India, 1940–45. A far more consistent Tory hardliner than Churchill ever managed; the two did not get on, especially over India. Endured the ignominy of his son being hanged as a traitor.

John Anderson (1882–1958): National MP for Scottish Universities, 1938–50; Home Secretary, 1939–40; Lord President of the Council, 1940–43; Chancellor of the Exchequer, 1943–45. A nonentity in party politics, but he proved that, occasionally, party is not everything. Some rated him the most powerful man in the realm.

Clement Richard Attlee (1883–1967): Leader of the Labour Party, 1935–55; Leader of the Opposition, 1935–40; Lord Privy Seal, 1940–42; Secretary of State for the Dominions, 1942–43; Lord President of the Council, 1943–45; Deputy Prime Minister, 1942–45; Leader of the Opposition, 1945; Prime Minister, 1945–51. He was a bureaucratic operator *par excellence* or a mouse, rabbit or sheep, depending on your perspective.

Max Beaverbrook (1879–1964): Minister of Aircraft Production, 1940–41; Minister of State, 1941; Minister of Supply, 1941–42; Minister of Production, 1942; Lord Privy Seal, 1943–45. Canadian, newspaper magnate and 'anti-appeaser' who in fact opposed war with Hitler – perhaps the only man who was a bigger rogue than Winston Churchill .

Aneurin Bevan (1897–1960): Labour MP for Ebbw Vale; *Tribune* editor, 1941–45. Welsh miner turned bon viveur and social climber. Often invested with the status of a left-wing demigod, but actually the era's biggest hypocrite. Later played the central role in wrecking the Labour Party while trying to succeed Attlee as its leader.

William Beveridge (1879–1963): social policy planner, 1941–43; Liberal MP, 1944–45. Another of those 1940s' progressives made a secular saint, but actually a cunning and cynical operator – supreme egotist and liked pretty girls.

Ernest Bevin (1881–1951): Minister of Labour and National Service, 1940–45. Of the big beasts, surely the biggest. Quite possibly started the cold war. And, in tying down the United States so adeptly, let all Britons be glad he did.

Brendan Bracken (1901–58): Parliamentary Private Secretary to Churchill, 1939–41; Minister of Information, 1941; First Lord of the Admiralty, 1945. Rumoured to be Churchill's illegitimate son, but actually just another Churchillian crank. 'Audacious' is perhaps the best description.

Rab Butler (1902–82): Under-Secretary of State for Foreign Affairs, 1938–41; President of the Board of Education, 1941; Minister of Labour, 1945. Highly intelligent educational reformer, long picked as a future Conservative leader – but never quite got there.

Neville Chamberlain (1869–1940): Conservative Party leader, 1937–40; Prime Minister, 1937–40; Lord President of the Council, 1940. Scholarly reassessment has not corrected his popular demonization. A plausible grand strategy – and with it Britain's standing as a world power – was broken on the rocks of Churchill and Labour's ambition.

Henry 'Chips' Channon (1897–1958): Parliamentary Private Secretary to Butler, 1938–41. Chamberlain loyalist, flamboyant diarist and political nonentity.

Winston Spencer Churchill (1874–1965): First Lord of the Admiralty, 1939–40; Prime Minister and Minister of Defence, 1940–45; Leader of the Conservative Party, 1940–55. Look up 'adventurer' in any reputable dictionary and his photograph will surely be there.

Stafford Cripps (1889–1952): Ambassador to Moscow, 1940–42; Lord Privy Seal and Leader of the House of Commons, 1942; Minister of Aircraft Production, 1942–45. Committed Christian and former lawyer; exploiting the erroneous belief that it was he who brought Russia into the war, Cripps briefly became a threat to Churchill but he soon fizzled out.

William Crozier (1879–1944): Editor of the *Manchester Guardian*, 1932–44. A favoured journalist for intriguers.

Hugh Dalton (1887–1962): Minister of Economic Warfare, 1940–42; President of the Board of Trade, 1942–45. Amateurish plotter but first-class diarist.

James Chuter Ede (1882–1965): Parliamentary Secretary at the Board of Education, 1940–45. Skilled administrator and educational reformer.

Anthony Eden (1897–1977): Secretary of State for the Dominions, 1939–40; Secretary of State for War, 1940; Foreign Secretary, 1940–45; Leader of the House of Commons, 1942–45. 'Glamour boy' and fond of the romantic gesture. Spent most of his career as Churchill's designated successor.

Arthur Greenwood (1880–1954): Deputy Leader of the Labour Party, 1935–45; Minister without Portfolio, 1940–42. Notorious drunk.

James Griffiths (1890–1975): Labour MP for Llanelli. Considered one of the Labour Party's bright young men. Attlee ensured that he was kept in his place during the war.

Cuthbert Headlam (1876–1964): Conservative MP for Newcastle North. Frustrated politician, shrewd diarist and doom merchant.

John Maynard Keynes (1883–1946): enjoyed a roving brief within government during the war. Economist of the Bloomsbury Set. Wrote *The Economic Consequences of the Peace*, which made the reading classes feel sorry for poor old Germany. Hugely entertaining personal life.

Harold Laski (1883–1950): Chairman of the Labour Party National Executive Committee, 1945–46. One of the century's most influential public intellectuals. Prolific writer and trouble causer.

Hastings Bertrand Lees-Smith (1878–1941): Leader of the Opposition, 1940–41; Acting Leader of the Labour Party, 1940–41. Usually described as elderly and decrepit, but actually younger than Churchill. Highly competent parliamentarian. Attlee relied on him.

Harold Macmillan (1894–1986): Parliamentary Secretary at the Ministry of Supply, 1940–42; Under-Secretary at the Colonial Office, 1942; Minister Resident at Allied headquarters in NW Africa, 1942–45; Secretary of State for Air, 1945. Aristocratic rogue, a man who would seemingly do or say anything. Flirted with every political position imaginable.

Herbert Morrison (1888–1965): Minister of Supply, 1940; Home Secretary and Minister of Home Security, 1940–45. Conscientious objector during the First World War, but was more comfortable the second time around. A man of flair, administrative expertise and burning ambition. His grandson Peter Mandelson has inherited Morrison's skills in the dark arts.

Frederick William Pethick-Lawrence (1871–1961): Leader of the Opposition, 1941–42; Acting Leader of the Labour Party, 1941–42. A capable deputy to Lees-Smith and then Greenwood.

Emanuel Shinwell (1884–1986): Labour MP for Seaham Harbour. Frustrated troublemaker who fancied himself as acting leader. At one point he compared his own military judgement with that of Moses. Like Laski, he brought out Bevin's casual anti-Semitism.

Ellen Wilkinson (1891–1947): Parliamentary Secretary at the Ministry of Pensions, 1940; Parliamentary Secretary at the Home Office, 1940–45; Chairman of the Labour Party National Executive Committee, 1944–45. Morrison's biggest fan. Quite possibly his mistress.

Edward Wood, first Earl of Halifax (1881–1959): Foreign Secretary, 1938–40; Leader of the House of Lords, 1940; Ambassador to Washington, 1941–46. Could have stopped Churchill's rise, but failed – because of either too little stomach or too much cunning.

Kingsley Wood (1888–1943): Secretary of State for Air, 1938–40; Lord Privy Seal, 1940; Chancellor of the Exchequer, 1940–43. A neglected figure at the forefront of the battle with Attlee and the other Labour ministers.

Notes

Introduction

1. Kevin Theakston and Mark Gill, 'Rating 20th-century British prime ministers', *British Journal of Politics and International Relations*, 8 (2006) pp. 193–213.

2. K. O. Morgan, *Labour in Power, 1945–1951* (Oxford, 1985) pp. 47–8.

3. Paul Addison, *The Road to 1945: British Politics and the Second World War* (London, 1994 edition); Angus Calder, *The People's War: Britain, 1939–45* (London, 1969); Kevin Jefferys, *The Churchill Coalition and Wartime Politics, 1940–1945* (Manchester, 1991). J. M. Lee, *The Churchill Coalition, 1940–1945* (Connecticut, 1980) is also significant.

4. Stephen Brooke, *Labour's War: The Labour Party during the Second World War* (Oxford, 1992).

5. For example, Stephen Fielding, 'What did "the people" want? The meaning of the 1945 general election', *Historical Journal*, 35 (1992) pp. 623–39; Henry Pelling, 'The 1945 general election reconsidered', *Historical Journal*, 23 (1980) pp. 399–414; Richard Sibley, 'Essays in Labour statistics: the swing to Labour during the Second World War: when and why?', *Labour History Review*, 55 (1990) pp. 23–34.

6. That is not to denigrate studies of political culture *per se*, merely the faddish language and *faux* sophistication of much of the work. It is a tendency absorbed from cultural studies, and which Roger Scruton bemoans as now constituting 'the lingua franca of the humanities: gibberish', an 'armoured nonsense' to protect 'fraudulence', a 'gobbledygook' in which 'words are cast as spells rather than used as arguments' resulting only in 'intellectual disaster' – Roger Scruton, *The Uses of Pessimism* (London, 2010) pp. 183–5. For an example of what can be done with genuine sophistication in political culture, read James Vernon, *Politics and the People: A study in English Political Culture, c. 1815–1867* (Cambridge, 1993); and in cultural history (with not a trace of gobbledygook throughout) David Hackett Fischer, *Albion's Seed: Four British Folkways in America* (Oxford, 1989).

7. Consult my essay '"High politics", political practice and the Labour Party', in Robert Crowcroft, S. J. D. Green and Richard Whiting (eds) *The Philosophy, Politics and Religion of British Democracy: Maurice Cowling and Conservatism* (London, 2010) pp. 153–85. Observe too John Charmley's glorious statement that 'I am not much concerned with theories of discourse, masculinities, feminism, or any of the other modish things that have come along in the last twenty-five years' – *Conservative History Journal*, 5 (2005)

pp. 2–6, at 2: a wonderful two-fingered salute to the absurdities of the contemporary university.

8. Maurice Cowling, *1867: Disraeli, Gladstone and Revolution. The Passing of the Second Reform Bill* (Cambridge, 1967); *The Impact of Labour 1920–1924: The Beginning of Modern British Politics* (Cambridge, 1971); and *The Impact of Hitler: British Politics and British Policy 1933–1940* (Cambridge, 1975). Also, Michael Bentley, *Politics Without Democracy 1815–1914* (London, 1984); A. B. Cooke and John Vincent, *The Governing Passion: Cabinet Government and Party Politics in Britain 1885–86* (Sussex, 1974).

9. For example: J. C. D. Clark, *English Society 1688–1832: Ideology, Social Structure, and Political Practice during the Ancien Regime* (Cambridge, 1985); Lewis Namier, *The Structure of Politics at the Accession of George III* (London, 1963, one volume edition) and his *England in the Age of the American Revolution* (second edition, London, 1966).

10. Augustine, *The City of God against the Pagans*, translated by R. W. Dyson (Cambridge, 1998).

11. The best recent edition being John Calvin, *Institutes of the Christian Religion*, translated by Henry Beveridge (Massachusetts, 2008).

12. Psalm 94:11.

13. Genesis 6:5.

14. Consult the papers in Crowcroft et al., *The Philosophy, Politics and Religion of British Democracy*.

15. Alexander Hamilton, James Madison and John Jay, *The Federalist*, edited by Terence Ball (Cambridge, 2003).

16. Richard Shannon, *The Age of Salisbury, 1881–1902: Unionism and Empire* (London, 1996); Jeremy Smith, *The Tories and Ireland, 1910–1914: Conservative Party Politics and the Home Rule Crisis* (Dublin, 2000).

17. For one of the more interesting analyses sympathetic to WSC, consult Sheila Lawlor, *Churchill and the Politics of War, 1940–1941* (Cambridge 1994): it is an experimental analysis linking party politics and military strategy.

18. Besides *The Road to 1945*, see Paul Addison, 'Journey to the centre: Churchill and Labour in coalition, 1940–5', in Alan Sked and Chris Cook (eds) *Crisis and Controversy: Essays in Honour of A. J. P. Taylor* (London, 1976) pp. 165–93.

19. Besides *The Churchill Coalition*, see Kevin Jefferys, 'British politics and social policy during the Second World War', *The Historical Journal*, 30 (1987) pp. 123–44.

20. Jefferys, *Churchill Coalition and Wartime Politics*, p. 36.

21. See note 4 above, as well as Paul Addison, 'By-elections of the Second World War', in Chris Cook and John Ramsden (eds) *By-Elections in British Politics* (London, 1973) pp. 165–90; R. B. McCallum and Alison Readman, *The British General Election of 1945* (London, 1947).

22. Trevor Burridge, *British Labour and Hitler's War* (London, 1976).

23. Andrew Thorpe, *Parties at War: Political Organization in Second World War Britain* (Oxford, 2009).

24. See also Daniel Ritschel, 'The making of consensus: the Nuffield College conferences during the Second World War', *Twentieth Century British History*, 6 (1995) pp. 267–301.

25. Cowling, *Impact of Hitler*, Chapters 11–13.

26. Addison, *Road to 1945*, p. 294.

27. Ben Pimlott, *Labour and the Left in the 1930s* (Cambridge, 1977) p. 25.

28. Ibid.

29. Most obviously Philip Williamson, *Stanley Baldwin: Conservative Leadership and National Values* (Cambridge, 1999).

30. For instance, George L. Bernstein, 'Sir Henry Campbell-Bannerman and the Liberal imperialists', *Journal of British Studies*, 23 (1983) pp. 105–24; Jeremy Smith, 'Bluff, bluster and brinkmanship: Andrew Bonar Law and the third Home Rule Bill', *Historical Journal*, 36 (1993) pp. 161–78.

31. Richard Toye and Julie Gottlieb (eds) *Making Reputations: Power, Persuasion and the Individual in Modern British Politics* (London, 2005).

32. Tony Shaw, *Eden, Suez and the Mass Media: Propaganda and Persuasion during the Suez Crisis* (London, 1995).

33. Most notably Jon Lawrence and Miles Taylor, *Party, State and Society: Electoral Behaviour in Britain since 1820* (Aldershot, 1997).

34. See my essay '"High politics", political practice and the Labour Party', in Crowcroft et al., *The Philosophy, Politics and Religion of British Democracy*.

35. Shannon, *The Age of Salisbury*, p. 3.

36. For example, Hugh Dalton, *The Fateful Years: Memoirs 1931–1945* (London, 1957) (hereafter *FY*); Herbert Morrison, *An Autobiography* (London, 1960).

37. Dalton, *FY*, p. 19.

38. Dalton, *FY*, p. 70.

39. Kenneth Minogue, *Politics: A Very Short Introduction* (Oxford, 1995) p. 64.

40. Clement Attlee, *As It Happened* (London, 1965).

41. Kenneth Harris, *Attlee* (London, 1982).

42. Trevor Burridge, *Clement Attlee: A Political Biography* (London, 1985).

43. Burridge, *Attlee*, pp. 315–7.

44. Jerry H. Brookshire, *Clement Attlee* (Manchester, 1995); David Howell, *Attlee* (London, 2006); Robert Pearce, *Attlee* (London, 1997); Nicklaus Thomas-Symonds, *Attlee: A Life in Politics* (London, 2010).

45. Giles Radice, *The Tortoise and the Hares: Attlee, Bevin, Cripps, Dalton, Morrison* (London, 2008).

46. Francis Beckett, *Clem Attlee* (London, 2007 edition).

47. John Swift, *Labour in Crisis: Clement Attlee and the Labour Party in Opposition, 1931–1939* (Basingstoke, 2001).

48. Harris, *Attlee*, pp. 252, 317.

49. Harris, *Attlee*, pp. 565–9.

50. Richard Whiting, 'Clement Richard Attlee', in H. C. G. Matthew and Brian Harrison (eds) *Oxford Dictionary of National Biography*, 2 (Oxford, 2004) pp. 875–85, at 878–9.

51. Whiting, 'Clement Richard Attlee', pp. 878.

52. Burridge, *Attlee*, Chapters 8 and 9.
53. Burridge, *Hitler's War*, p. 125.
54. Ralph Miliband, *Parliamentary Socialism: A Study in the Politics of Labour* (second edition, London, 1975) pp. 272–85.
55. Swift, *Labour in Crisis*, p. 4.
56. Addison, *Road to 1945*, p. 47.
57. Addison, *Road to 1945*, p. 104.
58. Addison, *Road to 1945*, p. 113.
59. Addison, *Road to 1945*, p. 294.
60. Ibid.
61. Ibid.
62. Beckett, *Clem Attlee*, pp. 159–65.
63. Burridge, *Hitler's War*, pp. 49, 53.
64. Most obviously the debates surrounding the changing fortunes of the political parties: for instance, Peter Clarke, *Lancashire and the New Liberalism* (Cambridge, 1971); E. H. H. Green, *The Crisis of Conservatism* (London, 1995); Ross McKibbin, *The Evolution of the Labour Party, 1910–1924* (Oxford, 1974); Duncan Tanner, *Political Change and the Labour Party, 1910–1918* (Cambridge, 1990). I could go on, but won't.

Chapter 1. Capturing the Language of Patriotism

1. This is true of Addison, Jefferys and even Brooke. All were critical of Labour's role in this period. For other instances of neglect or criticism, see Cowling, *Impact of Hitler*; N. J. Crowson, *Facing Fascism: The Conservative Party and the European Dictators 1935–1940* (London, 1997); David Dilks, 'The twilight war and the fall of France: Chamberlain and Churchill in 1940', in David Dilks (ed.) *Retreat from Power – Studies in Britain's Foreign Policy of the Twentieth-Century, Volume Two: After 1939* (London, 1981) pp. 36–65; D. J. Dutton, 'Power brokers or just "glamour boys"? The Eden group, September 1939–May 1940', *English Historical Review*, 118 (2003) pp. 412–24; Kevin Jefferys, 'May 1940: the downfall of Neville Chamberlain', *Parliamentary History*, 10 (1991) pp. 363–78; Lynne Olson, *Troublesome Young Men: The Churchill Conspiracy of 1940* (London, 2007); Nick Smart, *The National Government, 1931–40* (Basingstoke, 1999); and 'Four days in May: the Norway debate and the downfall of Neville Chamberlain', *Parliamentary History*, 17 (1998) pp. 215–43; Larry L. Witherell, 'Lord Salisbury's "Watching Committee" and the fall of Neville Chamberlain, May 1940', *English Historical Review*, 116 (2001) pp. 1134–66.
2. Cowling, *Impact of Hitler*, p. 372.
3. For an exception, consult the entertaining account in John Charmley, *Chamberlain and the Lost Peace* (London, 1989).
4. Owen A. Hartley, 'Winston Churchill', in Richard Kelly and John Cantrell (eds) *Modern British Statesmen, 1867–1945* (Manchester, 1998) pp. 193–204, at 197.
5. The 1939 *Labour Party Annual Conference Report* (the conference reports are hereafter cited as *LPACR*) pp. 330–1.

6. Ibid.

7. British Library of Political and Economic Science, London, Hugh Dalton papers, diary, 24 August 1939 (reprinted in Ben Pimlott (ed.) *The Political Diary of Hugh Dalton, 1918–40, 1945–60* (London, 1986) p. 283). Subsequent references contain a page reference to the printed diary if it appears in the published version. People's History Museum, Manchester, Labour Party Archive, NEC minutes, 2 September 1939. The PLP minutes for 1938 to 1941 were destroyed during the war. See also *London News*, October 1939.

8. NEC minutes, 2 September 1939.

9. House of Commons Debates, Fifth Series (hereafter HC Debates) 351, 24 August 1939, cols 10–14.

10. Ibid.

11. NCL minutes, 25 August 1939.

12. Ibid.

13. Ibid.

14. Swift, *Labour in Crisis*, p. 119.

15. HC Debates, 351, 29 August 1939, cols 110–16 (emphasis mine).

16. NEC minutes, 1 September 1939.

17. Attlee interview, cited Harris, *Attlee*, p. 166.

18. Dalton Diary, 6 September 1939 (p. 297).

19. Ibid.

20. Attlee interview, cited Harris, *Attlee*, p. 165.

21. Birmingham University Library, Neville Chamberlain papers, Chamberlain to Ida Chamberlain, 26 February 1939, and to Hilda Chamberlain, 14 March and 29 April 1939.

22. C. R. Attlee, *Clem Attlee: The Granada Historical Records Interview* (London, 1967) p. 17.

23. For instance, *The Times*, 25 February 1939 and 25 March 1939.

24. NEC minutes, 2 September 1939.

25. Ibid.

26. Richard Whiting, 'Arthur Greenwood', in Keith Gildart, David Howell and Neville Kirk (eds) *Dictionary of Labour Biography*, 11 (London, 2004) p. 89.

27. HC Debates, 351, 2 September 1939, col. 282; Cowling, *Impact of Hitler*, p. 345.

28. HC Debates, 351, 2 Sept. 1939, col. 282.

29. *The Times*, 11 September 1939.

30. Dalton Diary, 22 August 1939 (pp. 282–3).

31. HC Debates, 351, 3 September, cols 292–4; see also 1 September 1939, col. 133–5.

32. *The Times*, 4 September 1939.

33. Smart, *National Government*, p. 209.

34. Witherell, 'Watching Committee', p. 1141.

35. Duff Cooper, *Old Men Forget* (London, 1953) p. 260.

36. Churchill College, Cambridge, Leopold Amery papers, diary, AMEL 7 (hereafter Amery diary) box 33, 3 September 1939; Robert Pearce (ed.)

Patrick Gordon Walker: Political Diaries, 1932–1971 (London, 1991) 3 September 1939, p. 96; J. Harvey, *The Diplomatic Diaries of John Harvey, 1937–40* (London, 1970) 5 October 1939, pp. 324–4; N. Rose (ed.) *Baffy: The Diaries of Blanche Dugdale, 1936–47* (London, 1973) 3 September 1939, p. 150.

37. Cooper, *Old Men Forget*, p. 263.
38. Witherell, 'Watching Committee', p. 1135.
39. HC Debates, 351, 3 September 1939, cols 293–4.
40. NEC Election Committee minutes, 5 September 1939.
41. NEC minutes, 22 September 1939.
42. Ibid.
43. Bodleian Library, Oxford, Clement Attlee papers, box 8, Attlee to James Middleton, January 1940 (n.d.).
44. *Tribune*, 26 January 1940.
45. Attlee papers, box 2, 'Your constituencies in wartime: an interview with the Rt Hon. C. R. Attlee', *The Labour Candidate: Journal of the Society of Labour Candidates*, winter 1939.
46. The best treatment of this is Brooke, *Labour's War*, Chapter 2.
47. 'Politicus', 'Labour and the war', *Political Quarterly*, 10 (1939) pp. 477–88.
48. Ibid.
49. HC Debates, 351, 21 September 1939, col. 1103.
50. *New Statesman*, 4 May 1940.
51. Brooke, *Labour's War*, p. 37.
52. He chaired the NEC meeting on the 29th – NEC minutes, 29 September 1939.
53. *Sunday Express*, 1 January 1939; *Daily Herald*, 9 June 1939.
54. Dalton Diary, entries for 26 May to 2 June 1939 (p. 267).
55. Ibid.
56. For analysis of Freemasons within the PLP, see John Hamill and Andrew Prescott, 'The Mason's candidate: new welcome lodge no. 5139 and the Parliamentary Labour Party', *Labour History Review*, 71 (2006) pp. 9–41.
57. *Daily Herald*, 3 June 1939.
58. Ibid.
59. *Sunday Referee*, 4 June 1939.
60. Ibid.
61. Dalton Diary, 14 June 1939 (pp. 268–70).
62. Ibid.
63. Ibid.
64. Ibid.
65. Brooke, *Labour's War*, p. 40.
66. Dalton Diary, 18 September 1939 (pp. 301–2).
67. Ibid.
68. Ibid.
69. NEC minutes, 15 September 1939.
70. Ibid.
71. HC Debates, 351, 3 October 1939, cols 1862.

72. HC Debates, 352, 12 October 1939, cols 568–70.
73. Ibid.
74. Warwick University Archive, Trades Union Council papers, Trades Union General Council minutes, 12 October 1939.
75. NCL minutes, 20 October 1939.
76. NEC minutes, 25 October 1939.
77. Ibid.
78. Burridge, *Hitler's War*, p. 33.
79. Ibid.
80. C. R. Attlee, *Labour's Peace Aims* (London, 1939).
81. *LPACR*, 1939, p. 274; Harold Laski, *The Labour Party, the War and the Future* (London, 1939).
82. Ibid.
83. Isaac Kramnick and Barry Sheerman, *Harold Laski: A Life on the Left* (London, 1993) p. 416.
84. NEC minutes, 15 September 1939.
85. See, for example, *News Review*, 19 October 1939.
86. Dalton Diary, entries for November 1939 (pp. 311–13).
87. Ibid.
88. Bernard Donoughue and G. W. Jones, *Herbert Morrison: Portrait of a Politician* (London, 2001 edn) p. 245.
89. Ibid.
90. Dalton Diary, entries for November 1939 (pp. 311–13).
91. Ibid.
92. Ibid.
93. Dalton papers, 5/6 (3) (5) Alfred Edwards letter to Dalton, 9 November 1939.
94. Dalton papers, copy of Morrison letter to Alfred Edwards, 11 November 1939.
95. Dalton Diary, entries for November 1939 (pp. 312–13).
96. Ibid.
97. Dalton, *FY*, p. 281.
98. Dalton Diary, entries for November 1939 (pp. 312–13).
99. Ibid.
100. Morrison's position in the poll fell from first place (which he had retained since 1936) to eighth, while Dalton fell from third to tenth – David Butler and Gareth Butler, *Twentieth Century British Political Facts, 1900–2000* (8th edn) (London, 2000) p. 152.
101. Dalton immediately scurried to try and repair his relations with Morrison, sending him a note that stated: 'The way of earth shifters is hard in this political allotment and I am not inclined to do any more digging at present. Yours, with undiminished regard' – Dalton Diary, entries for November 1939 (p. 313).
102. HC Debates, 353, 16 November 1939, cols 876–8.
103. Cowling, *Impact of Hitler*, p. 373.

104. HC Debates, 355, 5 December 1939, cols 499–506.

105. Ibid.

106. Ibid.

107. Chamberlain papers, Chamberlain to Ida Chamberlain, 23 September 1939.

108. Ibid.

109. Chamberlain papers, Chamberlain to Hilda Chamberlain, 24 October 1939.

110. HC Debates, 352, 17 October 1939, cols 725–7.

111. See, particularly *Daily Mirror*, 30 March 1940.

112. *The Listener*, 18 January and 8 February 1940.

113. See, for example, HC Debates, 355, 28 November 1939, cols 16–25, and 29 November 1939, cols 98–9; 356, 16 January 1940, cols 43–50, 31 January 1940, cols 1221–5, and 1 February 1940, cols 1414–22; 359, 2 April 1940, cols 44–7 and 9 April 1940, cols 509–10.

114. *The Times*, 18 January 1940.

115. Ibid.; *The Times*, 11 December 1939.

116. For instance, HC Debates, 352, 18 October 1939, cols 963–5; 351, 26 September 1939, cols 1246–50, and 356, 16 January 1940, cols 49–50.

117. HC Debates, 356, 1 February 1940, cols 1414–22.

118. HC Debates, 355, 28 November 1939, col. 19; 356, 1 February 1940, cols 1415–22.

119. HC Debates, 358, 19 March 1940, cols 1845–53.

120. HC Debates, 355, 16 November 1939, cols 876–8; 355, 28 November 1939, cols 16–25. Attlee called peace aims an issue of 'vital importance' for it represented the 'master weapon' that would win the war.

121. For instance, HC Debates, 351, 26 September 1939, cols 1246–50; 352, 18 October 1939, cols 963–5; 356, 16 January 1940, cols 49–50.

122. HC Debates, 356, 1 February 1940, col. 1414.

123. HC Debates, 356, 16 January 1940, cols 43–44.

124. Alan Bullock, *The Life and Times of Ernest Bevin*, 1, *Trade Union Leader, 1881–1940* (London, 1960) p. 644.

125. See HC Debates, 358, between 21 February and 4 March 1940.

126. NEC minutes, 6 and 7 February 1940; for the full text, see *LPACR*, 1940, pp. 188–90.

127. Labour Party, *Labour, the War and the Peace* (London, 1940).

128. *LPACR*, 1940, p. 24.

129. Attlee papers, 2/63, Attlee to Grant McKenzie, March 1940.

130. NEC minutes, 20 March 1940.

131. *LPACR*, 1940, pp. 191–5.

132. Attlee Papers, 2/63, Attlee to Grant McKenzie, March 1940.

133. Arthur Greenwood, *Why We Fight: Labour's Case* (London, 1940).

134. Hugh Dalton, *Hitler's War: Before and After* (London, 1940).

135. *Daily Herald*, 16 January 1940, 8 February 1940, 7 and 16 March 1940, 8 April 1940.

136. Harold Laski, *Is This an Imperialist War?* (London, 1940).

137. Harold Laski, 'The war and the future', in C. R. Attlee (ed.) *Labour's Aims in War and Peace* (London, 1940).

138. For example, HC Debates, 356, 1 February 1940, cols 1309–25; 357, 12 March 1940, cols 621–33; 358, 15 March 1940, cols 1523–41.

139. For the weight given to these activities, see *LPACR*, 1940, appendices II and III, pp. 188–95.

140. Ibid.

141. *Manchester Guardian*, 28 March 1940.

142. Dalton Diary, 9 April 1940.

143. Ibid.

144. Ibid.

145. Dalton, *FY*, p. 297; Dalton Diary, 9 April 1940.

146. Ibid.

147. Charles Peake to Sir Alexander Cadogan, 2 December 1939, cited in Donoughue and Jones, *Herbert Morrison*, p. 269.

148. Ibid.

149. Harris, *Attlee*, p. 173.

150. Amery diary, box 34, 1 and 2 May 1940; Robert Rhodes James (ed.) *'Chips': The Diaries of Sir Henry Channon* (London, 1993) 26 and 30 April 1940, pp. 242–3; *The Times*, 4 May 1940.

151. *Daily Herald*, 3, 9, 16, 23 and 27 April 1940.

152. Dalton Diary, 1 May 1940.

153. James, *Diaries of Sir Henry Channon*, 25 April 1940, p. 242; Attlee, *As It Happened*, p. iii; Dalton, *FY*, pp. 311–12.

154. HC Debates, 356, 1 February 1940, col. 1422.

155. Attlee interview in Francis Williams, *A Prime Minister Remembers: The War and Post-war Memoirs of the Rt Hon. Earl Attlee* (London, 1961) pp. 20–1, 28.

156. Ibid., Attlee, *As It Happened*, p. iii.

157. Witherell, 'Watching Committee', p. 1165.

158. Nuffield College, Oxford, Herbert Morrison papers, draft autobiography.

159. Durham County Record Office, Cuthbert Headlam papers, diary (hereafter Headlam diary) 5 and 6 May 1940.

160. *Daily Herald*, 6 May 1940; *The Times*, 7 May 1940; *Daily Mirror*, 9 May 1940 (Morrison's article was entitled 'I Say Get Out' and warned that Britain would be defeated unless Chamberlain were removed).

161. The debate appears in HC Debates, 360, 7–8 May 1940. For Attlee's speech, see 7 May, cols 1086–94.

162. Ibid.

163. Ibid.

164. HC Debates, 360, 7 May 1940, cols 1086–94; 8 May 1940, cols 1251–65; *Sunday Post*, 15 March 1959; Donoughue and Jones, *Herbert Morrison*, p. 271.

165. Williams, *A Prime Minister Remembers*, p. 30; Herbert Morrison, *An Autobiography* (London, 1960) pp. 172–3.

166. Addison, *Road to 1945*, pp. 95–6.

167. Williams, *A Prime Minister Remembers*, p. 30; Morrison papers, 'draft autobiography'.

168. Dalton Diary, 8 May 1940 (p. 340).

169. Morrison papers, 'draft autobiography'.

170. Harris, *Attlee*, p. 173. It has been suggested that Attlee wavered and may have been willing to serve under Chamberlain after all around this time, if not for a 'talking-to' by Greenwood. While such a possibility cannot be wholly discount, and there is the possibility that Attlee's later vocal denunciations of Chamberlain were a case of selective memory, nonetheless, this assertion is not consistent with the available evidence about Attlee's behaviour beforehand. Perhaps more likely is that the possibility was simply discussed, and the leader's non-committal personality gave a misimpression to someone. See Laurence Thompson, *1940* (London, 1966) p. 86; also Smart, *National Government*, p. 222.

171. Attlee later recalled his pleasure at seeing 'Conservative MP after Conservative MP' abandon Chamberlain and vote with Labour (Williams, *A Prime Minister Remembers*, p. 32).

172. Dalton Diary, 9 May 1940 (pp. 343–4).

173. Attlee, *Granada Records Interview*, p. 21.

174. University of York, 1st Earl of Halifax papers, Halifax diary, 9 May 1940.

175. Smart, *National Government*, p. 221.

176. Attlee papers, 1/16, autobiographical notes.

177. Attlee interview, cited in Harris, *Attlee*, p. 174.

178. NEC papers, 'Resolutions for annual conference 1940'; Attlee papers, James Middleton to Attlee, 15 March 1940, box 7.

179. NEC minutes, 10 May 1940.

180. Smart, 'Four days in May', p. 240.

181. NEC minutes, 10 May 1940 (my emphasis).

182. Ibid.

183. NEC minutes, 11 May 1940.

184. Ibid.

185. M. Webb, 'The Rt. Hon. Herbert Morrison, MP', in H. Tracey (ed.) *The British Labour Party* (London, 1948) 3, pp. 37–8.

186. NEC minutes, 11 May 1940; Dalton Diary, 11 May 1940 (p. 345).

187. Ibid.

188. Ibid.

189. Ibid.

190. Interview with Grant McKenzie in Donoughue and Jones, *Herbert Morrison*, p. 274.

191. Donoughue and Jones, *Herbert Morrison*, p. 275.

192. Morrison, *Autobiography*, pp. 178, 211.
193. Morrison, *Autobiography*, pp. 201–3.
194. NEC minutes, 11 May 1940; *LPACR*, 1940, pp. 128–33.
195. Ibid.; *Daily Herald*, 14 May 1940.
196. *The Times*, 14 May 1940.
197. Addison, *Road to 1945*, p. 106.
198. Addison, *Road to 1945*, p. 60.
199. Swift, *Labour in Crisis*, p. 158.
200. Jefferys, 'May 1940', p. 368.

Chapter 2. Capturing the Home Front

1. James, *Diaries of Sir Henry Channon*, 18 May 1940, p. 254; and 21 July 1940, p. 262.
2. For useful essays see Brian Harrison, 'Frederick William Pethick-Lawrence', in H. C. G. Matthew and Brian Harrison (eds) *Oxford Dictionary of National Biography*, 2 (Oxford, 2004) pp. 809–14; David Martin, 'Hastings Bertrand Lees-Smith', in John Saville and Joyce Bellamy (eds) *Dictionary of Labour Biography IX* (London, 1993) pp. 175–81.
3. Dalton Diary, 18 May 1940 (pp. 12–13). Until the break-up of the coalition in 1945, the relevant published edition is the second volume of Ben Pimlott's work, *The Second World War Diary of Hugh Dalton, 1940–1945* (London, 1986).
4. Dalton Diary, 20 May 1940 (p. 14); and 21 May 1940 (p. 17).
5. Ibid. Lees-Smith, interestingly, was a titular Leader of the Opposition only; though having to transact the business of the Commons and oversee the PLP, he did not receive the salary that came with the post. NEC minutes, 21 August and 25 September 1940.
6. Dalton Diary, 21 May 1940 (p. 17).
7. James Griffiths, *Pages from Memory* (London, 1969) p. 69.
8. See R. M. Punnett, *Front-Bench Opposition: The Role of the Leader of the Opposition, the Shadow Cabinet and Shadow Government in British Politics* (London, 1973) pp. 410–11.
9. Brooke, *Labour's War*, pp. 73–4.
10. See R. T. McKenzie, *British Political Parties: The Distribution of Power within the Conservative and Labour Parties* (London, 1967) Appendix D, pp. 664–5.
11. For a full list, see McKenzie, *British Political Parties*, pp. 664–5.
12. Pethick-Lawrence topped the poll in the first election held in November (Lees-Smith, along with Attlee, was an ex-officio member) an indication of his strong position. Dalton came second, with Morrison, Alexander and Griffiths tying for third.
13. Dalton Diary, 21 May 1940 (p. 15).
14. Ibid.
15. Ibid.; Dalton Diary, 23 May 1940 (p. 19).
16. Attlee, *As It Happened*, p. 116.
17. Dalton Diary, 23 May 1940 (p. 19).
18. Ibid.

19. Amery diary, box 34, 18 June 1940.

20. HC Debates, 361, 22 May 1940, col. 152.

21. For instance, HC Debates, 362, 18 June 1940, col. 61; 363, 23 July 1940, cols 667–71.

22. HC Debates, 361, 23 May 1940, cols 345–7.

23. Headlam diary, 12 June 1940.

24. Dalton Diary, 15 and 16 July 1940 (pp. 59–60).

25. Most obviously, Addison, *Road to 1945*, p. 294 and the neglect evident through Jefferys, 'May 1940', as well as Brooke, *Labour's War*. Lee, *The Churchill Coalition*, p. 32, endorses negative views of Attlee. Ben Pimlott, *Hugh Dalton* (London, 1985) p. 367, sees Attlee as 'still with little of the aura of a "Leader" about him' and 'barely altered' by war, while Donoughue and Jones, *Herbert Morrison*, pp. 323–4, also subscribe to a jaundiced view of Attlee and criticize him for his inability 'to inspire the mass of the people'. Even Bullock did not see Attlee as a central figure. See Bullock, *Life and Times*, 1, p. 113.

26. Roy Jenkins, *Mr Attlee: An Interim Biography* (London, 1948) p. 226.

27. See the National Archives, London (all government records used are located here) CAB 65 (conclusions of the War Cabinet) 66 and 67 (War Cabinet memoranda) 68 (reports by government departments) for evidence of Attlee's role.

28. See CAB 69 (Defence Committee Operations minutes) and 70 (Defence Committee Supply minutes).

29. See CAB 71 (Lord President's Committee minutes and papers) and 132 (subordinate committees minutes and papers).

30. Harris, *Attlee*, p. 180.

31. CAB 118 (Attlee's files as Deputy Prime Minister) as well as PREM 3 are particularly useful.

32. Addison, *Road to 1945*, p. 294.

33. Cited Beckett, *Clem Attlee*, p. 165.

34. Harris, *Attlee*, p. 180.

35. CAB 67, WP (G) 275, 24 May 1940, and CAB 65/5, WM (40) 64, 19 June 1940.

36. Lee, *The Churchill Coalition*, p. 84.

37. See CAB 71 (34 volumes) for evidence of Attlee's role in running and directing the activities of the committee. For instances of Anderson's lack of stature, see Headlam diary, 30 March 1939, 4 October 1940, and 3 July 1942.

38. CAB 67, WP (G) 380, 12 October 1940.

39. Ibid.

40. Lee, *The Churchill Coalition*, p. 34.

41. See CAB 74 (Food) CAB 75 (Home Policy) and CAB 72 (Production and Economic Policy).

42. Beckett, *Clem Attlee*, p. 160.

43. Beckett, *Clem Attlee*, pp. 159–65.

44. Peter Clarke, *A Question of Leadership* (London, 1999) pp. 196–7.

45. He did this through the Lord President's Committee over the summer and autumn of 1940. See CAB 71.

46. Churchill College, Cambridge, Attlee papers, notes on draft autobiography, 1/16 folio 3.

47. Beckett, *Clem Attlee*, p. 164.

48. Dalton Diary, 27 May 1940 (p. 23).

49. All quotes from Morgan, *Labour in Power*, pp. 47–8.

50. Ibid.

51. Morgan, *Labour in Power*, pp. 48–9.

52. Charmley, *Chamberlain and the Lost Peace*, p. 248.

53. Beckett, *Clem Attlee*, p. 164.

54. Churchill College, Cambridge, Attlee papers, notes on draft autobiography, 1/16 folio 3.

55. HC Debates, 362, 18 June 1940, col. 61; NEC Emergency Subcommittee minutes, 18 June 1940.

56. Amery diary, box 34, 11 May 1940.

57. Ibid.

58. For example, *Daily Herald*, 27, 28 May and 1, 3, 5 June 1940; *Daily Mirror*, 26, 27 May and 5, 6 June 1940; *Tribune*, 3, 7 June 1940.

59. Chamberlain papers, Chamberlain to Ida Chamberlain, 11 May 1940.

60. *The Times*, 21 July.

61. *New Statesman*, 13 July 1940; *News Chronicle*, 8 July 1940. One opinion poll showed that 77 per cent of respondents wanted Chamberlain sacked.

62. Headlam diary, 31 July 1940.

63. *The Times*, 10 June 1940.

64. James, *Diaries of Sir Henry Channon*, 4 June 1940, p. 256.

65. Headlam diary, 12 June 1940.

66. Headlam diary, 1 July 1940.

67. Headlam diary, 31 July 1940.

68. Addison, *Road to 1945*, p. 108.

69. Chamberlain papers, Chamberlain diary, 5, 6 June 1940; University of York, Halifax papers, Halifax diary, 6 June 1940.

70. Cato (Michael Foot, Peter Howard and Frank Owen) *Guilty Men* (London, 1940).

71. Michael Foot, *Aneurin Bevan: A Biography*, 1, *1897–1945* (London, 1962) pp. 319–20.

72. Consult the important revisionist works: Charmley, *Chamberlain and the Lost Peace*; and, by the same author, *Churchill: the End of Glory* (London, 1993), and *Churchill's Grand Alliance: The Anglo-American Special Relationship, 1940–1957* (London, 1996).

73. Hartley, 'Winston Churchill', p. 199.

74. I am grateful to John Charmley for discussions on this point, and to Professor Eric Grove for reading a paper by Professor Charmley at the Imperial War Museum North in May 2010. Charmley suggested that Halifax stood aside for Churchill principally to permit the gung-ho WSC to fatally

discredit the idea of continuing the war through a few months of stalemate. If Halifax had taken the job at the outset, as he easily could have done, then WSC might well have spent the summer of 1940 outflanking him publicly and in Cabinet. With war discredited, Halifax could safely topple and replace WSC. If that interpretation is correct, Charmley contends, Halifax had forgotten Churchill's rhetorical abilities – the new Prime Minister delivered his 'we will fight them on the beaches' speeches to line 'the people' up behind him, render the idea of parley unthinkable, and thus neuter his political rivals. Or, as Professor Charmley summarizes it, Churchill and Labour alike depended 'upon the continuance of the war for their positions'.

75. Cowling, *Impact of Hitler*, p. 3.

76. John Colville, *The Fringes of Power: Downing Street Diaries 1939–1955* (London, 1985) 10 May 1940, p. 122.

77. See, for instance, John Charmley, *Splendid Isolation? Britain, the Balance of Power, and the Origins of the First World War* (London, 1999). I am also grateful to Dr Jeremy Smith for interesting observations on the connections between the decision to declare war in 1914 and the situation in Ireland.

78. Nigel Nicolson (ed.) *Harold Nicolson: Diaries and Letters, 1939–1945* (London, 1960) pp. 99–101; INF I/849, minutes of the Home Policy Committee, 18 June 1940.

79. CAB 65/4, WM (40) 220, 23 August 1940.

80. Ibid.

81. CAB 121 contains the War Aims Committee records, 4 October 1940.

82. For instance, HC Debates, 361, 30 May 1940, cols 724–30; 363, 16 July 1940, cols 116–21, 144–48; *Tribune*, 24 May 1940; *New Statesman*, 14 December 1940.

83. Trinity College, Cambridge, Pethick-Lawrence papers, 1/71/ Pethick-Lawrence to Attlee, 21 August 1940.

84. CAB 65/3, WM (40) 270, 18 October 1940.

85. Dalton Diary, 9 July 1940 (p. 56).

86. These records are in CAB 87 (Committees on Reconstruction, Supply and other matters).

87. Churchill College, Cambridge, Viscount Halifax papers, Londonderry to Halifax, 23 November 1940.

88. Ibid.

89. Andrew Roberts, *Eminent Churchillians* (London, 1995) p. 137. Also, for example, Bodleian Library, Oxford, Geoffrey Dawson papers, diary, 13 May 1940; Bodleian Library, Oxford, Lord Woolmer papers, Richard Law to Woolmer, 23 May 1940.

90. Geoffrey K. Fry, *The Politics of Decline: An Interpretation of British Politics from the 1940s to the 1970s* (London, 2005) p. 113.

91. Fry, *The Politics of Decline*, p. 71.

92. *Economist*, 25 May 1940; *News Chronicle*, 22 May 1940.

93. See Hugh Armstrong Clegg, *A History of British Trade Unions since 1889*, 3, *1934–1951* (Oxford, 1994) Chapter 3.

94. For different perspectives, see Addison, *Road to 1945*, p. 120 and Jefferys, *Churchill Coalition and Wartime Politics*, p. 63.

95. Alan Bullock, *The Life and Times of Ernest Bevin*, 2, *Minister of Labour* (London, 1967) p. 113.

96. Ibid.

97. Williams, *A Prime Minister Remembers*, p. 150.

98. Bullock, *Life and Times*, 2, pp. 117–18.

99. Lord Avon interview, cited in Donoughue and Jones, *Herbert Morrison*, p. 314.

100. Williams, *A Prime Minister Remembers*, p. 150.

101. Ibid.

102. CAB 65/7, WM (40) 135, 23 May 1940.

103. HC Debates, 361, 22 May 1940, cols 154–85.

104. Ibid.

105. Clegg, *History of British Trade Unions*, p. 177.

106. *The Times*, 25 May 1940.

107. *1940 TUC Conference Report*, pp. 269–70.

108. Ibid.; Harris, *Attlee*, p. 183.

109. *Manchester Guardian*, 4 October 1940.

110. A. J. P. Taylor interview with Beaverbrook, 24 August 1940, cited in Kevin Jefferys (ed.) *Documents in Contemporary History: War and Reform – British Politics during the Second World War* (Manchester, 1994) pp. 57–8.

111. *Daily Telegraph*, 25 June, 22 July, 29 July 1940.

112. CAB 66/11 WP (40) 339, Morrison memorandum on the Munitions Situation, 29 August 1940.

113. Dalton Diary, 14 August 1940 (pp. 73–4).

114. Morrison attended ten of twelve meetings of the main NEC between May 1940 and May 1941, compared with just seven meetings by Attlee. *LPACR*, 1941, p. 46.

115. Dalton Diary, 13 December 1940 (p. 119).

116. Simon Ball, *The Guardsmen* (London, 2004) p. 221.

117. CAB 65/7, WM (40) 235, 2 October 1940; *The Times*, 3 October 1940.

118. Herbert Morrison, *Socialization and Transport* (London, 1933). Note Geoff Fry's observation that, in Morrison, 'Labour had a form of answer to Mosley, to the extent that fascism was concerned with public policy.' See Geoffrey K. Fry, *The Politics of Crisis: An Interpretation of British Politics, 1931–1945* (London, 2001) p. 46.

119. *Manchester Guardian*, 7 January 1941.

120. Dalton Diary, 8 August 1940 (p. 72); 24 August 1940 (p. 77); and 13 December 1940 (p. 119).

121. *The Times*, 11 September 1939; Whiting, 'Arthur Greenwood', p. 89.

122. Dalton Diary, 14 December 1940 (p. 121).

123. CAB 65/10, WM (40) 308, 31 December 1940.

124. *Manchester Guardian*, 7 January 1941.

125. See PREM 4 100/4 for Churchill's persistent obfuscation.

126. CAB 65/10, WM (40) 308, 31 December 1940.

127. Most famously Hugh Gaitskell, Harold Wilson, Douglas Jay and Evan Durbin.

128. Jefferys, *Churchill Coalition and Wartime Politics*, p. 38.

129. For examples of Shinwell's attacks, see, for instance, HC Debates, 364, 7 August 1940, cols 300–9, 367; 27 November 1940, cols 231–50; and 371, 6 May 1941, cols 784–92; also examine Emanuel Shinwell, *Conflict Without Malice* (London, 1955) p. 150; and Peter Slowe, *Manny Shinwell: An Authorised Biography* (London, 1993) p. 203.

130. For instance, HC Debates, 361, 30 May 1940, cols 724–30.

131. See, for example, *Tribune*, 24 May 1940.

132. *Tribune*, 11 October 1940, and HC Debates, 363, 16 July 1940, cols 116–21, 144–8.

133. *Tribune*, 11 October 1940; Foot, *Bevan*, p. 317.

134. Addison and Jefferys, for example, neglect his role; Brooke depicts Laski as a troublemaker but fails to identify either his importance to wartime politics or his challenge to Attlee.

135. University of Hull, Harold Laski papers, Laski to Alfred Cohn, 12 April 1940.

136. *LPACR*, 1939, p. 274; *LPACR*, 1940, p. 156; *LPACR*, 1941, p. 154; *LPACR*, 1942, p. 125; *LPACR*, 1943, p. 137; *LPACR*, 1944, p. 131; *LPACR*, 1945, p. 89.

137. NEC minutes, 26 June 1940.

138. Ibid.

139. NEC Campaign Committee minutes, 16 July 1940; NEC minutes, 23 July 1940.

140. NEC Policy Committee minutes, 16 August 1940.

141. Ibid.

142. NEC minutes, 27 August 1940.

143. *Daily Herald*, 21 October 1940.

144. Ibid.

145. Ibid.

146. NEC minutes, 23 October 1940; Dalton Diary, 5 November 1940 (unpublished).

147. NEC Emergency Committee minutes, 5 November 1940.

148. Ibid.; Dalton Diary, 5 November 1940.

149. Hull University, Laski papers, Laski to Alfred Cohn, 12 April 1940.

150. *New Statesman*, 14 December 1940.

151. CAB 65/10, WM (40) 310, 27 December 1940

152. CAB 65/21 WM (41) 5, 13 January 1941; CAB 67, WP (G) (41) 7, 11 January 1941.

153. Dalton Diary, 22 January 1941 (p. 144).

154. Ibid.
155. Ibid.
156. HC Debates, 368, 28 January 1941, cols 491–4.
157. HC Debates, 368, 28 January 1941, cols 465–79.
158. HC Debates, 368, 28 January 1941, col. 516.
159. HC Debates, 368, 28 January 1941, cols 528–30.
160. NEC minutes, 4 February 1941.
161. *Tribune*, 3 January 1941.
162. See *Tribune*, 7 February 1941. His article was under the inflammatory title 'Choose How to Live or Die'.
163. Attlee papers, 2/100, Chuter Ede to Attlee, 14 February 1941.
164. Foot, *Bevan*, p. 331.
165. *Tribune*, 18 April 1941.
166. NEC minutes, 21 January 1941.
167. Ibid.
168. Ibid.
169. Ibid.
170. Ibid.
171. NEC papers, Laski memorandum, 27 January 1941.
172. Ibid.
173. Ibid.
174. Ibid.
175. Ibid.
176. Ibid.
177. Ibid.
178. Ibid.
179. Ibid.
180. Hull University, Laski papers, Attlee to Laski, 29 January 1941.
181. Ibid.
182. NEC minutes, 26 February 1941.
183. After being referred to the Policy Committee in late February, when that body finally met on 21 March, Greenwood objected to Laski's proposed policy Various drafts and redrafts for a statement on reconstruction to the conference were then written. It was, in the words of Newman, 'painfully slow'. See Michael Newman, *Harold Laski: A Political Biography* (London, 1993) p. 217. See also NEC, Policy Committee minutes, 21 March 1941 and 10 April 1941.
184. Hull University, Laski Papers, Attlee to Laski, 1 April 1941.
185. NEC minutes, 21, 22 and 26 April 1941; Newman, *Laski*, p. 218.
186. NEC papers, Morrison to Middleton, 21 April 1941.
187. NEC papers, Middleton to Morrison, 22 April 1941 and Morrison to Middleton, 26 April 1941. Middleton and Morrison had been enemies since the former defeated Morrison in the contest for the position of general secretary following the retirement of Arthur Henderson.

188. NEC minutes, 7 May 1941.
189. Ibid.
190. NEC Policy Committee minutes, 23 May 1941.
191. NEC minutes, 30 May 1941.
192. This quote appears in Clarke, *A Question of Leadership*, p. 207, but the source is unclear.
193. Jefferys, *Churchill Coalition and Wartime Politics*, p. 55.
194. *Tribune*, 6 June 1941.

Chapter 3. Remoulding the State and Defending the Alliance

1. While in my experience of 'progressives' the characterization of Hitler as a fellow leftist usually provokes splenetic denials, one must remember that family feuds are always the most bitter.
2. *Labour in the Government: A Record of Social Legislation in War Time* (Labour Party, 1941).
3. Brooke, *Labour's War*, p. 57.
4. *The Times*, 17 February 1941.
5. *The Times*, 31 March 1941.
6. *The Labour Party, the War and the Peace* (Labour Party, 1941).
7. Ibid.
8. Ibid.
9. *Labour in the Government*.
10. Ibid.
11. Ibid.
12. Ibid.
13. Ibid.
14. Ibid.
15. *LPACR*, 1941, pp. 131–4, 143–7. A majority of 120 to 1 approved the former, and 2,413,000 votes to 30,000 the latter.
16. Addison, *Road to 1945*, p. 129.
17. For observations, see H. C. G. Matthew, 'Rhetoric and Politics in Great Britain, 1860–1950', in P. J. Waller (ed.) *Politics and Social Change in Modern Britain: Essays Presented to A. F. Thompson* (Sussex, 1987) pp. 34–58.
18. *LPACR*, 1941, pp. 131–4.
19. Ibid.
20. S. J. D. Green, 'From Puritanism to Pantheism: reflections on the degeneration of English life since 1945', *The Machray Review: A Publication of the Prayer Book Society of Canada*, 7 (1997) pp. 1–16.
21. Headlines in *The Times* about Attlee's speeches provide an impression of this: 'Liberty of the Spirit' (16 January 1941); 'The People's Spirit' (31 March 1941); and 'Unity of Free Men' (12 May 1941).
22. *The Times*, 16 January 1941.
23. *LPACR*, 1941, pp. 6–7.
24. For hints, see Thorpe, *Parties at War*, pp. 62–4.

25. *The Times*, 4 June 1941.
26. Ibid.
27. Newman, *Laski*, p. 218.
28. NEC minutes, 25 June 1941; NEC Policy Committee minutes, 4 July 1941.
29. NEC minutes, 25 June 1941.
30. Ibid.
31. Addison, *Road to 1945*, pp. 127–89; Jefferys, *Churchill Coalition and Wartime Politics*, pp. 61–84.
32. Churchill College, Cambridge, Attlee papers, 2/2 folio 11, Attlee to Churchill, n.d., but probably April 1941 (subsequent references to the Attlee papers denote the larger Bodleian collection unless otherwise noted).
33. CAB 71/2, LP (41) 26, 3 July 1941; CAB 71/2, LP (41) 29, 8 July 1941.
34. CAB 71/3, LP (41) 104, 'The Railways and the War: Memorandum by the Lord Privy Seal', 1 July 1941.
35. CAB 66/17/31, WP (41) 158, 'The Future of the Railways', 11 July 1941.
36. Ibid.
37. CAB 65/19, WM (41) 70, War Cabinet conclusions, 15 July 1941.
38. Attlee papers, 4/4, Middleton to Attlee, 3 October 1941.
39. HC Debates, 374, 22 October 1941, cols 1805–12.
40. Ibid.
41. Addison, *Road to 1945*, p. 167.
42. Ibid.
43. This story can be traced throughout the year, but reached a culmination in CAB 71/2, LP (41) 68, 8 December 1941, and CAB 71/3, LP (41) 69, 24 December 1941.
44. Richard Whiting, *The Labour Party and Taxation: Party Identity and Political Purpose in Twentieth-century Britain* (Cambridge, 2001) p. 52.
45. See Robert Skidelsky, *John Maynard Keynes: Fighting for Freedom, 1937–1946* (London, 2001). Wood lacks a published biography, but G. C. Peden's *DNB* essay, 'Wood, Sir (Howard) Kingsley (1881–1943)' is perceptive.
46. W. Wheeler-Bennett, *John Anderson, Viscount Waverley* (London, 1962) is helpful.
47. Churchill to Anderson, 28 January 1941, memorandum cited W. Churchill, *The Second World War, III, The Grand Alliance* (London, 1950) p. 102 (emphasis added).
48. Ibid.
49. J. M. Keynes, *How to Pay for the War* (London, 1940).
50. ED 138/21, Butler to Churchill, 12 September 1941.
51. Colville, *Diaries*, 10 May 1944, p. 122.
52. Amery diary, box 35, 18 December 1941.
53. Headlam diary, 16 July 1941.
54. Headlam diary, 7 July 1941.
55. Ibid., 7 July 1941.
56. Colville, *Diaries*, 4 August 1941, p. 424.
57. Whiting, *Labour Party and Taxation*, p. 61.

58. Whiting, *Labour Party and Taxation*, p. 62.
59. Superb accounts of mobilization issues are provided in Bullock, *Life and Times*, 2; and in W. K. Hancock and M. M. Gowing, *History of the Second World War: United Kingdom Civil Series – British War Economy* (London, 1949).
60. Bullock, *Life and Times*, 2, p. 92.
61. HC Debates, 370, 26 March 1941, cols 603–14.
62. Hancock and Gowing, *British War Economy*, p. 283.
63. Bullock, *Life and Times*, 2, p. 64.
64. HC Debates, 376, 4 December 1941, col. 1342.
65. Hancock and Gowing, *British War Economy*, p. 298.
66. Interview with Sir Godfrey Ince, cited in Bullock, *Life and Times*, 2, p. 124.
67. Attlee in the *Observer*, 13 March 1960.
68. See Bullock, *Life and Times*, 2, pp. 114–17.
69. Hancock and Gowing, *British War Economy*, p. 313. For a more critical view, see Headlam diary, 27 October 1941.
70. Headlam diary, 4 December 1941.
71. *The Times*, 24 November 1940.
72. *Manchester Guardian*, 21 October 1940.
73. Bullock, *Life and Times*, 2, p. 42.
74. Headlam diary, 25 July 1941 and 11 December 1941.
75. The Rt. Hon. The Earl of Avon, *The Reckoning: The Memoirs of the Rt. Hon. Sir Anthony Eden* (London, 1965) diary entry for 18 February 1942, p. 321.
76. Addison, *Road to 1945*, p. 167.
77. Ibid.
78. Ibid.
79. Lord Beveridge, *Power and Influence* (London, 1953) p. 298.
80. See HC Debates, 376, 4 December 1941.
81. Hancock and Gowing, *British War Economy*, p. 314.
82. See *The Times*, 21 October 1941, 1 November 1941 and 16 November 1941; *Economist*, 29 November 1941.
83. Consider CAB 71/2 over October and November 1941 for the act's gestation.
84. CAB 65/20, WM (41) 119, 25 November 1941.
85. Bullock, *Life and Times*, 2, p. 110.
86. Brooke, *Labour's War*, pp. 72, 80.
87. INF 1/292, Home Intelligence Weekly Reports, 7 January 1942 to 4 February 1942.
88. Jefferys, *Churchill Coalition and Wartime Politics*, p. 79.
89 HC Debates, 373, 5 August 1941, col. 1844.
90. HC Debates, 376, 18 December 1941, cols 2202–6; *Tribune*, 5 December 1941.
91. HC Debates, 374, 23 October 1941, col. 1972–82.
92. For example, *Tribune*, 9 May 1941; *Nation*, 22 March 1941; Harold Laski, *Great Britain, Russia and the Labour Party* (London, 1941); NEC Reconstruction

Committee minutes, 17 September 1941. For Attlee's comments on some of Laski's literature, see Attlee papers, Attlee to J. Chamberlain, 2 December 1941.

93. British Library, London, Baron Chuter Ede papers, diary (hereafter Ede diary) 1 October 1941.

94. Ede diary, 14 February 1941.

95. *TUC Annual Report*, 1941, pp. 110–12.

96. Ibid.

97. HC Debates, 374, 9 September 1941, cols 151–2.

98. Evidence of complaints from the rank and file about the policy is plentiful in the NEC papers. See, for example, NEC minutes, 30 May 1941; NEC Organisation Committee minutes, 9 September 1941.

99. Attlee papers, 2/125, Attlee to Churchill, 24 September 1941.

100. Ibid.

101. Ibid.

102. NEC minutes, 24 September 1941.

103. Ibid.; Dalton Diary, 24 September 1941 (p. 286).

104. Ibid.

105. PLP minutes, 2 December 1941.

106. CAB 65/20, WM (41) 122, 3 December 1941.

107. PLP minutes, 2 December 1941.

108. Ibid.; Ede diary, 3 December 1941.

109. PLP minutes, 2 December 1941.

110. Ede diary, 3 December 1941.

111. Ibid.; PLP Administrative Committee minutes, 3 December 1941; PLP minutes, 3 December 1941.

112. Ede diary, 4 December 1941.

113. HC Debates, 376, 4 December 1941, cols 1348–50.

114. Ede diary, 4 December 1941.

115. Ede diary, 19 December 1941.

116. Amery diary, box 35, 18 December 1941.

117. James, *Diaries of Sir Henry Channon*, 17 February 1942, p. 322 and 21 May 1942, p. 331.

118. For comments on his performance as acting leader, see Ede diary, 19 December 1941; Dalton Diary, 18 December 1941 (p. 226). The Lees-Smith press cuttings file at the Labour Party archive contains useful material. Attlee said he was someone 'we could ill spare'.

119. NEC minutes, 8 December 1941; PLP Administrative Committee minutes, 11 December 1941; PLP Administrative Committee papers, 'Confidential Memorandum on Party Policy', n.d., but mid-December 1941; PLP minutes, 17 December 1941 and 21 January 1942; Ede diary, 19 December 1941; Dalton Diary, 8 December 1941 (p. 331).

120. There is no evidence to suggest that Attlee tried to save Greenwood, a conclusion the leader's biographer shared. See Harris, *Attlee*, p. 195.

121. PLP Administrative Committee minutes, 26 February 1942; Ede diary, 26 February 1942.

122. See also CAB 65, 66, and 67 from December 1941 to March 1942 for evidence of Attlee's greatly increased role.

123. See CAB 91 minutes and papers, November 1941 to March 1942. Also Attlee to Churchill, 9 January 1942, in CAB 65/25 WM (42) 8, 12 January 1942; CAB 66/21 WP (42) 59, Attlee memorandum, 'The Indian political situation', 2 February 1942; Churchill College, Attlee papers, 1/13, folio 7, autobiographical notes; Amery diary, box 36, 27 February 1942; Robin James Moore, *Churchill, Cripps and India, 1939–45* (Oxford, 1979) pp. 54–5.

124. A. J. P. Taylor, *Beaverbrook* (London, 1972) p. 612; Attlee interview, cited in Harris, *Attlee*, p. 194.

125. Laski papers, Laski to Frida Laski, n.d. but late 1941.

126. Laski papers, Laski to Frida Laski, 1, 2, 3, and 4 March 1942.

127. Dalton Diary, 21 April 1942 (p. 413).

128. Laski papers, Laski to Bevin, March 1942.

129. NEC minutes, 6 March 1942.

130. Laski papers, Laski to Frida Laski, 1, 2, 3, and 4 March 1942.

131 *New Statesman*, 21 March 1942.

132. Ruskin College, Oxford, Jim Middleton papers, 67/26, Laski manuscript speech, n.d. but March 1942.

133. Churchill College, Cambridge, Ernest Bevin papers, 3/1/43, Laski to Attlee, March 1942.

134. NEC papers, Laski memorandum, 'The Party and the Future', early April 1942.

135. Ibid.

136. Ibid.

137. Ibid.

138. Ibid.

139. Ibid.

140. Ibid (Laski's emphasis).

141. Ibid.

142. NEC minutes, 9 April 1942.

143. Ibid.

144. Ibid.

145. Ibid.

146. Ibid.

147. Ibid.

148. Ibid.

149. Laski papers, Laski to Frida Laski, 23 June 1942.

150. Headlam diary, 26 July 1941 and 3 May 1942.

151. Samuel H. Beer, *Modern British Politics* (London, 1969) p. 215.

152. *News Chronicle*, 23 June 1941 (emphasis added).

153. Winston S. Churchill, *The Unrelenting Struggle* (London, 1943) p. 85.

154. Cited in Taylor, *Beaverbrook*, pp. 494–5.

Chapter 4. 'Parliament is Given over to Intrigue': The Political System under Siege

1. Cowling, *Impact of Labour*, p. 9.

2. Philip Williamson, *National Crisis and National Government: British Politics, the Economy and Empire, 1926–1932* (Cambridge, 1992) p. 133.

3. Cowling, *Impact of Labour*, p. 10.

4. Addison, *Road to 1945*, pp. 154–8, remains the best account.

5. NEC Elections Committee minutes, 27 March 1942.

6. And by early March 1943 there had been 108 – *The Times*, 2 March 1943.

7. NEC papers, Attlee memorandum, 'Platform Propaganda', January 1942.

8. *New Statesman*, 4 April 1942; INF 1/292, Appendix on 'Home Made Socialism', 24 March 1942.

9. NEC minutes, 9 April 1942.

10. *Daily Herald*, 15 April 1942; *Tribune*, 14 and 21 April 1942; Dalton Diary, 9 April 1942 (p. 408).

11. NEC minutes, 9 April 1942.

12. Ibid.

13. Dalton Diary, 9 April 1942 (p. 408).

14. *The Times*, 10 April 1942.

15. Ibid.

16. *The Times*, 25 April, 26 April, 28 April, 7 May and 14 May 1942.

17. For example, NEC papers, letter from South Wales Regional Council of Labour, 14 April 1942.

18. NEC Elections Committee minutes, 13 May 1942.

19. Ibid.

20. Ibid.

21. *The Times*, 13 May 1942.

22. NEC Elections Committee minutes, 13 May 1942.

23. Ibid.

24. Ede diary, 21 and 22 January 1942.

25. PLP Administrative Committee minutes, 22 and 27 January 1942, 12 and 24 February 1942; PLP minutes, 12 and 25 February 1942; Ede diary, 27 January 1942.

26. Ede diary, 25 February 1942.

27. For instance, *Tribune*, 5 December 1941, 29 May 1942, 5 June 1942.

28. *Tribune*, 5 December 1941.

29. Ibid.

30. Churchill College, Cambridge, Bevin papers, 3/1/43, Laski to Attlee, n.d. March 1942.

31. For instance, Ede diary, 4 March 1942.

32. For instance, Ede diary, 7 August 1942; *New Statesman*, 17 October 1942.

33. Ede diary, 18 February 1942.

34. PLP Administrative Committee papers, Greenwood memorandum, 'The Labour Party and the future', March 1942.
35. NEC minutes, 22 May 1942.
36. Ibid.
37. NEC minutes, 25 May 1942.
38. Ibid.
39. Thorpe, *Parties at War*, especially pp. 1–14, 277–88.
40. *LPACR*, 1942, pp. 142–50.
41. Ibid.
42. *Daily Herald*, 25 May 1942.
43. *LPACR*, 1942, pp. 142–50.
44. Ibid.
45. Ibid.
46. *Daily Herald*, 28 May 1942.
47. *LPACR*, 1942, pp. 102–4.
48. CAB 65/25, WM 32 (42) 9 March 1942; CAB 65/25, WM 35 (42) 18 March 1942.
49. Morrison was denounced by *The Times, Manchester Guardian, News Chronicle*, and even the *Daily Herald*; see also PLP Administrative Committee minutes, 24 March 1942; Ede diary, 25 March 1942.
50. *Daily Express*, 12 April 1942.
51. PLP Administrative Committee minutes, 24 March 1942; PLP minutes, 25 March 1942; Ede diary, 25 March 1942.
52. HC Debates, 378, 20 March 1942, cols 2247–92. Bevan stayed away from a party meeting; when his clash with Morrison came, it was in Parliament rather than behind closed doors – Ede diary, 25 March 1942.
53. Ibid.
54. Attlee was compelled to help protect his rival, snapping at Bevan during a PLP meeting in February that those who railed against Morrison's suppression of the press would be living under the Nazis in Europe – PLP minutes, 11 February 1942; Ede diary, 11 February 1942.
55. Morrison interview with W. P. Crozier, 28 May 1942, in A. J. P. Taylor (ed.) *W. P. Crozier: Off the Record – Political Interviews, 1933–1943* (London, 1973) p. 322.
56. Ibid.
57. Ibid.
58. *LPACR*, 1942, pp. 99–100.
59. *LPACR*, 1942, pp. 122–30.
60. NEC papers, 'Result of Conference ballot', May 1942.
61. NEC minutes, 27 May 1942.
62. NEC minutes, 7 July 1942.
63. Ibid.
64. See Williamson, *National Crisis*, Chapter 4.
65. Dalton Diary, 12 May 1942 (p. 435).
66. Dalton Diary, 15 June 1943 (p. 607).

67. *Tribune*, 22 May 1942.

68. *LPACR*, 1942, pp. 118–20.

69. Ibid.

70. HC Debates, 379, 7 May 1942, cols, 1475–85.

71. Dalton Diary, 27 May 1942 (pp. 446–7).

72. NCL Coal Committee minutes, 5 June 1942; NCL minutes, 6 June 1942; NEC minutes, 8 June 1942.

73. Administrative Committee papers, minutes of joint meeting of NCL and Administrative Committee, 8 June 1942; PLP minutes, 10 June 1942; HC Debates, 380, 11 June 1942, cols 1269–1302, 1346–50.

74. HC Debates, 381, 1 and 2 July 1942; for the speeches that undermined the challenge, see 1 July, cols 224–47; PLP minutes, 24 and 25 June 1942; HC Debates, 381, 1 July 1942, cols 224–47; Ede diary, 24 and 25 June 1942.

75. PLP minutes, 23 July 1942; PLP Administrative Committee minutes, 28 July 1942; Ede diary, 23 and 29 July 1942; HC Debates, 382, 29 July 1942, cols 641–61.

76. Ede diary, 30 July 1942.

77 Ede diary, 30 June 1942.

78. Churchill College, Cambridge, A. V. Alexander papers, 6/1/3, Bevin to Alexander, 21 June 1942.

79. Ede diary, 26 October 1942.

80. NEC Press, Publicity and Campaign Committee minutes, 16 June 1942.

81. Ibid.

82. NEC Press, Publicity and Campaign Committee minutes, 14 July 1942.

83. Ibid.

84. NEC Press, Publicity and Campaign Committee minutes, 16 June 1942.

85. NEC Press, Publicity and Campaign Committee minutes, 14 July 1942.

86. NEC Press, Publicity and Campaign Committee minutes, 16 June 1942.

87. *Reynold's News*, 12 July 1942.

88. *Reynold's News*, 9 August 1942.

89. *Reynold's News*, 26 July 1942.

90. Maurice Cowling, *Religion and Public Doctrine in Modern England*, 3 (Cambridge, 2001) p. 527.

91. Ibid.

92. Cowling, *Religion and Public Doctrine*, 3, p. 522.

93. Cowling, *Religion and Public Doctrine*, 3, p. 519.

94. NEC Organisation Committee minutes, 18 August 1942.

95. *Reynold's News*, 6 September 1942.

96. NEC minutes, 23 September 1942.

97. Ibid.; Dalton Diary, 23 September 1942 (p. 494).

98. NEC minutes, 23 September 1942.

99. Dalton Diary, 23 September 1942 (p. 494).

100. NEC minutes, 23 September 1942.

101. Dalton Diary, 12 October 1942 (pp. 500–1).

102. NEC minutes, 12 October 1942; Kramnick and Sheerman, *Laski*, p. 444.

103. NEC minutes, 12 October 1942.

104. Ibid.; Dalton Diary, 12 October 1942 (pp. 500–1).

105. Ibid.

106. Ibid.

107. NEC minutes, 12 October 1942; Dalton Diary, 23 September 1942 (p. 494) and 12 October 1942 (pp. 500–1).

108. NEC minutes, 28 October 1942.

109. Ibid.

110. Ibid.

111. Ibid.; Dalton Diary, 28 October 1942 (p. 509).

112. NEC minutes, 28 October 1942.

113. Ibid. The other was probably F. J. Burrows; Burrows seconded Watson's attempt to consider expulsion.

114. Ibid.

115. Brooke, *Labour's War*, p. 98.

116. Dalton Diary, 28 October 1942 (p. 510).

117. Ibid.

118. PLP papers, 'Results of Ballot for Administrative Committee', 21 October 1942.

119. Donoughue and Jones, *Herbert Morrison*, p. 313.

120. For example, *Daily Express*, 23 November 1943; *Reynold's News* (which called him 'about the best administrator we have discovered ... since Lord Haldane'), 29 November 1943; and *The Times*, 26 November 1943.

121. Herbert Morrison, *The Spearhead of Humanity* (London, 1942).

122. Ede diary, 23 and 24 March 1943; James, *Diaries of Sir Henry Channon*, 18 February 1943, p. 351.

123. Consult Jose Harris, 'William Henry Beveridge', in the *DNB*.

124. Fry, *The Politics of Decline*, p. 29. The Beveridge Report episode illustrates rather vividly – for those who care to look anyway – the problem of whether we should adhere to Whiggish visions of the war, or, alternatively, see the events of the period as a series of self-advertisements and machinations. Few, after all, were more egotistical than the saintly Beveridge; the most enjoyable part of his sudden fame was the fact that, according to the man himself, pretty girls used to sketch his portrait surreptitiously. Naturally, 'if I liked the looks of the young woman, as I generally did, I ... autographed it for her' – Beveridge, *Power and Influence* (London, 1953) pp. 319–20.

125. For instance, TUC Social Insurance Committee minutes, 3 December 1942.

126. Within three hours of its publication, 70,000 copies had been sold – Harriet Jones, 'The Conservative Party and the welfare state, 1942–1955' (unpublished Ph.D. thesis, University of London, 1992) p. 70.

127. Ibid.

128. HC Debates, 385, 1 December 1942, cols 1043–54.

129. Hull University, Laski Papers, Laski to Frida Laski, 11 November 1942.

130. *Tribune*, 4 December 1942.

131. Ibid.

132. *Tribune*, 11 December 1942.

133. CAB 118/33, PR (43) 5, 'The Financial Aspects of Reconstruction: A Memorandum by the Chancellor of the Exchequer', 11 January 1943.

134. Harmut Kopsch, 'The approach of the Conservative Party to social policy during the Second World War' (unpublished Ph.D. thesis, University of London, 1970) p. 109.

135. Ede diary, 12 November 1942.

136. Ede diary, 31 December 1942.

137. CAB 65, WM (42) 150, 4 November 1942; CAB 65, WM (42) 19 November 1942; CAB 67, WM (42) 159, 26 November 1942.

138. PLP papers, minutes of joint meeting of NEC and PLP Administrative Committee, 15 December 1942.

139. NCL minutes, 17 December 1942.

140. Ibid.

141. Ibid (my emphasis).

142. NEC papers, 'Suggested centres for conferences and demonstrations on Beveridge Report', December 1942.

143. Ede diary, 3 December 1942.

144. PLP papers, minutes of joint meeting of NEC and PLP Administrative Committee, 15 December 1942.

145. Administrative Committee papers, untitled memorandum, *circa* mid-January 1943.

146. *Reynold's News*, 10 January 1943.

147. Kramnick and Sheerman, *Laski*, p. 445.

148. Ibid.

149. HC Debates, 386, 9 February 1943, cols 1278–86.

150. PLP Administrative Committee minutes, 10 February 1943.

151. PLP minutes, 27 January 1943; Ede diary, 27 January 1943, and 17 February 1943.

152. For instance, study CAB 65, WM (43) 28, 12 February 1943.

153. Addison, *Road to 1945*, pp. 222–3.

154. RP (43) 5, 'The Financial Aspects of the Social Security Plan: Memorandum by the Chancellor of the Exchequer', 11 January 1943.

155. CAB 76/13, PR (43) 2, 'Memorandum by the Home Secretary', 20 January 1943.

156. Ede diary, 12 November 1942.

157. Churchill College, Cambridge, Attlee papers, 2/2/7–8, Attlee to Churchill, n.d., but mid-February 1943.

158. Ibid.

159. CAB 65, WM (43) 28, 12 February 1943; CAB 65/35, WM (43) 29, 15 February 1943; HC Debates, 386, 16 February 1943, col. 1678.

160. Bodleian Library, Conservative Party archive, Box 600/01, Secret Conservation Committee, 'Report on the Beveridge proposals', 19 January 1943.

161. HC Debates, 386, 16 February 1943, cols 1615–29; Dalton Diary, 16 February 1943 (p. 553).

162. Dalton Diary, 17 February 1943 (p. 553).

163. PLP Administrative Committee minutes, 16 February 1943; PLP minutes, 17 February 1943; Ede diary, 17 February 1943.

164. National Library of Wales, Griffiths papers, D3/20-1, draft autobiography.

165. Dalton Diary, 18 February 1943 (p. 554).

166. Dalton Diary, 17 February 1943 (pp. 553–4).

167. CAB 195, WM (43) 31, 17 February 1943.

168. Ibid.

169. Ibid.

170. HC Debates, 386, 18 February 1943, cols 1964–75.

171. HC Debates, 386, 18 February 1943, cols 2030–50.

172. Ede diary, 18 February 1943; CAB 97, WM (43) 31, 17 February 1943.

173. Bodleian Library, Oxford, Attlee letters to Tom Attlee (this collection was acquired subsequently to, and is kept separate from, the main Attlee papers), Attlee to Tom Attlee, 22 February 1943.

174. *The Times*, 19 February 1943.

175. HC Debates, 386, 18 February 1943, cols 2030–50.

176. Ibid.

177. Ede diary, 18 February 1943.

178. Dalton Diary, 18 February 1943 (p. 555). For other comments, see *Daily Telegraph*, 19 February 1943.

179. HC Debates, 386, 18 February 1943, cols 2050–54.

180. Ibid.; Ede diary, 18 February 1943.

181. Attlee letters to Tom Attlee, Attlee to Tom Attlee, 22 February 1943.

182. Ibid.

183. CAB 66/33, WP 18 (43) 'Promises about Post-war Conditions: Note by the Prime Minister', 12 January 1943.

184. Ede diary, 19 February 1943.

185. Dalton Diary, 22 February 1943 (p. 557).

186. Bullock, *Life and Times*, 2, p. 232.

187. Dalton Diary, 22 February 1943 (p. 557).

188. Ede diary, 22 February 1943.

189. Dalton Diary, 22 February 1943 (p. 557).

190. Ibid.

191. PLP Administrative Committee minutes, 23 February 1943; Ede diary, 23 February 1943; Dalton Diary, 24 February 1943 (p. 559).

192. Ibid.

193. Ede diary, 18 February 1943.

194. Ede diary, 23 February 1943.

195. Ede diary, 24 February 1943.
196. NEC papers, report of meetings between NEC Elections Committee and representatives from TUC, 5 January and 23 February 1943.
197. Dalton Diary, 24 February 1943 (p. 559).
198. NEC papers, 'Report of the Committee on Electoral Machinery', 27 January 1942.
199. Ibid.
200. NEC minutes, 24 February 1943.
201. Ibid.
202. Ibid.
203. Ibid.
204. Ibid.
205. Ibid.
206. Ede diary, 22 February 1943.
207. Bullock, *Life and Times*, 2, pp. 231–2; John Parker, *Father of the House: Fifty Years in Politics* (London, 1982) p. 81.
208. TUC General Council minutes, 24 February 1943.
209. Ibid.; Ede diary, 24 February 1943.
210. NCL minutes, 23 February 1943; Dalton Diary, 24 February 1943 (p. 559).
211. Ede diary, 25 February 1943; LPA, General Secretary papers, Attlee to Middleton, 25 February 1943.
212. Dalton Diary, 25 February 1942 (p. 560).
213. Ede diary, 25 February 1943.
214. Dalton Diary, 25 February 1942 (p. 560).
215. Ibid.
216. Ibid.
217. PLP papers, joint meeting of NEC, PLP Administrative Committee and Labour ministers, 21 April 1943.
218. For example, there were six in February alone.
219. By 1945, the Common Wealth Party had won three parliamentary seats at by-elections, and won a substantial proportion of the vote at others.
220. Addison, *Road to 1945*, p. 225.
221. *The Times*, 22 March 1943.
222. Ibid.
223. *The Times*, 26 March 1943.
224. Dalton Diary, 22 March 1943 (p. 569).
225. Ibid.
226. Dalton's account gives the impression that he suggested the idea, and Morrison agreed. However, it should be noted that this was the precise plan advocated by Morrison subsequently, while Dalton was to prove flexible. Perhaps they were both thinking along the same lines, or perhaps one appropriated the proposition.
227. Ibid.

228. Dalton Diary, 24 March 1943 (p. 570).

229. Dalton Diary, 26 March 1943 (p. 571).

230. Ibid.

231. *The Times*, 5 April 1943.

232. James, *Diaries of Sir Henry Channon*, 26 March 1942, p. 354.

233. *The Times*, 5 April 1943.

234. Dalton Diary, 24 March 1943 (p. 570).

235. *The Times*, 29 June 1942.

236. Ede diary, 6 April 1943, p.132.

237. NEC minutes, 24 March 1943; PLP minutes, 24 March 1943; Dalton Diary, 24 March 1943 (pp. 569–70).

238. PLP minutes, 24 March 1943; Ede diary, 24 March 1943.

239. PLP minutes, 7 April 1943.

240. Ibid.; Dalton Diary, 7 April 1943 (pp. 575–6).

241. PLP minutes, 7 April 1943.

242. Ibid.; Dalton Diary, 7 April 1943 (pp. 575–6).

243. Ibid.; PLP minutes, 7 April 1943.

244. Dalton Diary, 7 April 1943 (pp. 575–6); *The Times*, 8 April 1943.

245. There remains a subtle, teleological, narrative that the politics of the 1914–18 war were, in common with that conflict, a destructive and negative force (messy, for want of a better word) while those of the 1939–45 war were, like the war itself, a just, positive and constructive politics. This is perhaps founded on an intention to tie party politics into a politicized statement about the outcome of the wars themselves. That may be an attractive literary device, but the cross-party alignments of the two wars were not in fact as different as it would imply. The best analysis of the concept of cross-party government is G. R. Searle, *Country Before Party: Coalition and the Idea of 'National Government' in Modern Britain, 1885–1987* (London, 1995).

246. Cowling, *Impact of Labour*, p. 8.

247. Ibid.

248. HC Debates, 378, 12 March 1942, cols 1300–2.

249. Ibid.

250. HC Debates, 381, 1 July 1942, cols 224–47.

251. Cited in Bullock, *Life and Times*, 2, p. 177.

252. Headlam diary, 23 June 1942. Also 30 July 1942.

253. Malcolm MacDonald, *Titans and Others* (London, 1972) pp. 109–10; Cripps memorandum to Churchill, 2 July 1942, cited in Winston S. Churchill, *The Second World War, IV: The Hinge of Fate* (London, 1951) pp. 354–6.

254. Headlam diary, 14 and 30 July 1942, 22 November 1942.

255. For instance, Headlam diary, 16 and 17 March 1942.

256. Ede diary, 23, 24 and 26 March 1943.

257. James, *Diaries of Sir Henry Channon*, 18 February 1943, p. 351.

258. Headlam diary, 28 September 1942.

Chapter 5. Future Uncertain

1. For instance: *Evening Standard*, 18 December 1942; *Daily Herald*, 21 December 1942; *London News*, January and February 1943; *The Times*, 25 February 1943. The list goes on.
2. *The Times*, 21 December 1942.
3. Ibid.
4. *Daily Herald*, 21 December 1942.
5. *Manchester Guardian*, 12 January 1943.
6. *The Times*, 25 February 1943.
7. Jefferys, *Churchill Coalition and Wartime Politics*, p. 122.
8. Interviews with S. C. Leslie and Sir Austin Strutt, cited Donoughue and Jones, *Herbert Morrison*, p. 325.
9. *The Times*, 13 January 1943.
10. Donoughue and Jones, *Herbert Morrison*, p. 324.
11 Morrison interview with Crozier, 22 October 1943, cited in Taylor, *Off the Record*, p. 383.
12. Beaverbrook to Morrison, 23 November 1943, cited Donoughue and Jones, *Herbert Morrison*, p. 313.
13. Consult the attendances at NEC meetings. Also, Pimlott, *Dalton*, p. 371; Dalton Diary, 22 March 1943 (p. 569).
14. London Labour Party papers, 9177, 25 February 1943, cited Donoughue and Jones, *Herbert Morrison*, p. 327.
15. Donoughue and Jones, *Herbert Morrison*, p. 327.
16. NEC minutes, 24 March 1943; also see NEC minutes and Policy Committee minutes, January–June 1943, for the development of *The Labour Party and the Future*.
17. CAB 66 WP (43) 255, Cabinet memorandum 'The Need for Decisions', 26 June 1943.
18. Attlee was busy attempting to restrict postwar Jewish immigration into Palestine at this point – see his memorandum 'Palestine', CAB 66 WP (43) 266, 23 June 1943.
19. Ibid.
20. Trinity College, Cambridge, Rab Butler papers, G15, f.37, notes by Butler, 25 May 1943, cited in Jefferys, *Churchill Coalition and Wartime Politics*, p. 135, fn. 31.
21. Ibid.
22. Morrison interview with Crozier, 28 May 1943, cited in Taylor, *Off the Record*, pp. 359–60.
23. Ibid.
24. Ibid.
25. Ibid.
26. Ibid.
27. Morrison interview with Crozier, 2 July 1943, cited Taylor, *Off the Record*, p. 371.
28. Morrison, *Autobiography*, p. 231.
29. Morrison, *Autobiography*, p. 231.

30. Dalton Diary, 11 and 13 June 1943 (pp. 601–4).
31. Dalton Diary, 13 June 1943 (pp. 603–4).
32. Dalton Diary, 11 June 1943 (p. 602); Morrison interview with Crozier, 2 July 1943, cited in Taylor, *Off the Record*, p. 370.
33. Harris, *Attlee*, pp. 224–5.
34. Dalton Diary, 13 June 1943 (pp. 603–4).
35. NEC minutes, 14 June 1943.
36. Dalton Diary, 13 June 1943 (pp. 603–4).
37. Dalton Diary, 14 June 1943 (pp. 604–6).
38. NEC minutes, 14 June 1943.
39. Ibid.; Dalton Diary, 14 June 1943 (pp. 604–6).
40. NEC minutes, 14 June 1943.
41. *LPACR*, 1943, pp. 120–2 and pp. 125–7.
42. Ibid. (emphasis mine).
43. *Evening Standard*, 14 June 1943.
44. Donoughue and Jones, *Herbert Morrison*, p. 327.
45. *LPACR*, 1943, p.140.
46. Dalton Diary, 13 June 1943 (p. 604), and 15 June 1943 (pp. 606–7).
47. Morrison interview with Crozier, 2 July 1943, cited Taylor, *Off the Record*, p. 370.
48. Ede diary, 17 June 1943.
49. Headlam diary, 15 June 1943.
50. Dalton Diary, 14 June 1943 (pp. 604–6).
51. Ibid.
52. Harris, *Attlee*, p. 224.
53. *LPACR*, 1943, p. 142.
54. NEC papers, Central Committee on Reconstruction Problems, 'Labour's Plan for Reconstruction', for presentation to 1943 conference.
55. NEC minutes, 13 June 1943; *LPACR*, 1943, p. 127.
56. Ibid.
57. *LPACR*, 1943, pp. 7–9.
58. *LPACR*, 1943, p. 127.
59. Ibid.
60. *LPACR*, 1943, p. 134.
61. Predictably enough, Bevan immediately complained that the union bloc vote was 'bovine' and the party a 'farce' – *Tribune*, 18 June 1943.
62. NEC minutes, 23 June 1943; NEC Policy Committee minutes, 21 July 1943.
63. NEC papers, joint meeting of the NEC, TUC General Council and PLP Administrative Committee, 8 June 1943.
64. NEC Policy Committee minutes, 21 July 1943.
65. Ibid.
66. Dalton Diary, 5 August 1943 (p. 624).
67. For instance, NEC Policy Committee minutes, 21 July 1943; Dalton Diary, 11 January 1944 (p. 698), and 'Saturday 4th to Sunday 5th' March 1944 (p. 718). See also the minutes of the NEC Postwar Finance Committee. The

unpublished version of Dalton's diary contains references to informal meetings in restaurants.

68. Hugh Dalton, *Full Employment and Financial Policy* (Labour Party, 1943).

69. This phrase is Cowling's – *Impact of Labour*, p. 4.

70. NEC papers, 'Policy Campaign' memorandum, 28 July 1943.

71. Ibid.

72. For an excellent recent instance of this approach, revealing a great deal (and implying even more) about Sinn Fein leaders Gerry Adams and Martin McGuiness, see Ed Moloney, *A Secret History of the IRA* (London, 2007, second edn). Try not to laugh too hard at Perfidious Albion at work.

73. Dalton Diary, 14 September 1943 (p. 638).

74. Dalton Diary, 16 September 1943 (p. 640); CAB 65/40 WM (43) 140, confidential annexe to War Cabinet minutes of a meeting of ministers (Churchill, Attlee and Bevin), 13 October 1943. Bevin was fiercely loyal to Churchill, and the latter later attributed Bevin's willingness to continue the coalition to their relationship – Winston S. Churchill, *The Second World War, VI: Triumph and Tragedy* (London, 1954) p. 514.

75. Dalton Diary, 16 September 1943 (p. 640).

76. Dalton Diary, 14 September 1943 (p. 638).

77. Consult Thorpe, *Parties at War*, most obviously.

78. *Tribune*, 22 October 1943.

79. Headlam diary, 6 September 1943.

80. *The Times*, 18 March 1943.

81. Headlam diary, 25 September 1943.

82. James, *Diaries of Sir Henry Channon*, 15 January 1944, p. 385.

83. James, *Diaries of Sir Henry Channon*, 28 September 1943, pp. 376–7.

84. James, *Diaries of Sir Henry Channon*, 16 November 1943, p. 380.

85. James, *Diaries of Sir Henry Channon*, 28 September 1943, pp. 376–7.

86. CAB 65/40, WM (43) 140, 14 October 1943.

87. Ibid.

88. CAB 65/40, WM (43) 140, confidential annexe to War Cabinet minutes, 14 October 1943.

89. Ibid.

90. Ibid.

91. Ibid.

92. Ibid.

93. Ibid.

94. Ibid. The three took it in turns to attack government policy.

95. Ibid.

96. Ibid.

97. Churchill interview with Crozier, 22 October 1943, cited in Taylor, *Off the Record*, pp. 379–80.

98. Churchill 'had never excelled' in the realm of party politics, 'preferring instead a people-based approach'. Hartley, 'Winston Churchill', p. 200.

99. Hartley, 'Winston Churchill', p. 193.

100. CAB 65 WM (43) 144, 21 October 1943.

101. Ibid.

102. Examine CAB 87 for the work of the Reconstruction Committee. See also Lord Woolton, *The Memoirs of the Rt Hon. the Earl of Woolton* (London, 1959) pp. 259–72.

103. Argued most gloriously in the title essay of Elie Kedourie, *The Crossman Confessions* (London, 1984).

104. Dalton Diary, 2 November 1943 (p. 662).

105. Lord Attlee, 'The Churchill I Knew', in *Churchill by his Contemporaries: An 'Observer' Appreciation* (London, 1965) pp. 19–20.

106. Dalton Diary, 1 November 1943 (p. 662), 2 November 1943 (p. 662), and 3 November 1943 (p. 663).

107. Ibid.

108. Dalton Diary, 10 November 1943 (p. 667).

109. But he was annoyed at what he considered a barefaced lie on Churchill's part (ibid.).

110. Addison, *Road to 1945*, p. 230.

111. Amery diary, box 38, 28 February and 5 April 1944. See Charmley, *Churchill's Grand Alliance*, especially Chapters 7 and 8, for the definitive analysis. Owen Hartley offers a subtle, if brief (and, given the remarkable cynicism of its author, uncharacteristically Whiggish) contrast with this interpretation of Churchill's management of the United States: Hartley, 'Winston Churchill', p. 199.

112. James, *Diaries of Sir Henry Channon*, 16 December 1943, pp. 382–3.

113. Ian Harris, 'Religion, authority and politics: the thought of Maurice Cowling', *The Political Science Reviewer* (1997), pp. 434–81, at 467.

114. PREM 4/88/1, unsent note to Attlee, 20 November 1944.

115. Dalton Diary, 10 November 1943 (p. 667).

116. There is considerable evidence for this in the Dalton papers: examples include Dalton Diary, 9 September 1943 (p. 637), and 6 July 1944 (p. 764).

117. Morrison interview with Crozier, 2 July 1943, cited Taylor, *Off the Record*, p. 370.

118. See, for example, *The Times*, 28 June 1943; *London News*, August 1943; Morrison interview with Crozier, 22 October 1943, cited in Taylor, *Off the Record*, p. 383; *The Times*, 15 November 1943.

119. Headlam diary, 14 November 1943.

120. Morrison, *Autobiography*, pp. 232–3; Dalton Diary, 2 November 1943 (p. 663).

121. PLP papers, 'Ballot for Administrative Committee', 10 November 1943.

122. See the Morrison press cuttings file at the Labour Party Archive.

123. An example of this is HC Debates, 391, 15 July 1943, cols 452–6, 489–508.

124. Ede diary, 15 June 1943.

125. *Daily Express*, 15 October 1943.

126. CAB 65/35, WM 156 (43) 17 November 1943; Annexe CAB 65/36, WM 163 (43) 29 November 1943.

127. Bevin papers, Brendan Bracken to Bevin, 30 November 1943. Bevin briefly considered resigning from the government in protest. Bracken managed to talk him around by appealing to Bevin's strong personal loyalty to the Prime Minister.

128. Bullock, *Life and Times*, 2, p. 287.

129. Donoughue and Jones, *Herbert Morrison*, p. 304.

130. *Daily Express*, 19 November 1943; HC Debates, 393, 23 November 1943, cols 1428–33; Foot, *Bevan*, p. 461.

131. *Daily Express*, 24 November 1943; *The Times*, 24 November 1943; *Evening Standard*, 23 November 1943.

132. *Daily Express*, 19 November 1943 and 24 November 1943; *The Times*, 20 November 1943; *Manchester Guardian*, 22 and 26 November 1943, *Daily Telegraph*, 23 November 1943, *Daily Mail*, 25 November 1943.

133. NCL minutes, 24 November 1943.

134. NEC minutes, 24 November 1943.

135. TUC General Council minutes, 24 November 1943.

136. Attlee avoided any involvement in party or NEC meetings, as well as in the Commons.

137. PLP Administrative Committee minutes, 25 November 1943.

138. PLP minutes, 25 November 1943; Ede diary, 25 November 1943.

139. PLP minutes, 25 November 1943.

140. *Manchester Guardian*, 25 November 1943.

141. PLP minutes, 25 November 1943.

142. Ede diary, 25 November 1943.

143. Ibid.

144. PLP minutes, 25 November 1943.

145. Ibid.

146. PLP Administrative Committee minutes, 30 November 1943. See the debate in HC Debates, 395, 1 December 1943.

147. *Daily Express*, 26 November 1943.

148. Ibid.

149. Dalton Diary, 30 November 1943 (p. 677).

150. PLP minutes, 1 December 1943; Ede diary, 1 December 1943.

151. Ibid.

152. PLP minutes, 1 December 1943.

153. HC Debates, 395, 1 December 1943, cols 456–76.

154. Ibid.

155. *Evening Standard*, 2 December 1943.

156. HC Debates, 395, 1 December 1943, cols 475–8.

157. HC Debates, 395, 1 December 1943, cols 475–8.

158. Ede diary, 31 December 1943.

159. Tom Attlee papers, Attlee to Tom Attlee, December 1943, n.d.

160. CAB 65, WM (43) 163, 29 November 1943.

161. NEC papers, copy of Attlee flyer, February 1944.

162. Ibid., my emphasis.

163. NEC minutes, 25 February 1944.

164. NEC papers, minutes of NEC meeting together with Herbert Morrison, 26 and 27 February 1944.

165. Ibid.

166. Ibid.

167. Ibid.

168. Ibid.

169. Ibid.

170. Dalton Diary, 'Saturday 26th to Sunday 27th' February 1944 (pp. 712–15).

171. Addison, *Road to 1945*, p. 230.

172. See Laura Beers, 'Whose opinion? Changing attitudes towards opinion polling in British politics, 1937–1964', *Twentieth Century British History*, 17 (2006) pp. 177–205.

173. James, *Diaries of Sir Henry Channon*, 23 February 1944, p. 387.

174. Addison, *Road to 1945*, p. 241.

175. Dalton Diary, 'Saturday 26th to Sunday 27th' February 1944 (pp. 712–15).

176. Ibid.

177. Ibid.; NEC papers, minutes of NEC meeting together with Herbert Morrison, 26 and 27 February 1944.

178. Ibid.; Dalton Diary, 'Saturday 26th to Sunday 27th' February 1944 (pp. 712–15).

179. Ibid.; Attlee papers, Morrison to Attlee, 9 March 1944.

180. Ibid.

181. Ibid.

182. NEC papers, minutes of NEC meeting together with Herbert Morrison, 26 and 27 February 1944. It is unclear whether there was a vote on this decision, or how widely supported or disputed it was.

183. NEC papers, Attlee memorandum, 1 March 1944.

184. Ibid.

185. Ibid.

186. Addison, *Road to 1945*, p. 251.

187. Attlee papers, Attlee to Bevin, 1 March 1944.

188. NEC papers, minutes of NEC meeting together with Herbert Morrison, 26 and 27 February 1944.

189. Ibid.

190. James, *Diaries of Sir Henry Channon*, 23 March 1944, p. 389.

Chapter 6. Politics in the Shadow of Victory

1. Hugh Trevor-Roper, *The Last Days of Hitler* (London, 1947).

2. *The Times*, 3 April 1944.

3. *The Times*, 13 April 1944.

4. Headlam diary, 28 March 1944; James, *Diaries of Sir Henry Channon*, 28 March, p. 390.
5. *The Times*, 24 April 1944.
6. Ibid.
7. See the debate in HC Debates, 399, 28 April 1944, cols 1061–1126.
8. Ibid.
9. *Tribune*, 5 May 1944.
10. HC Debates, 399, 28 April 1944, cols 1061–1126.
11. PLP Administrative Committee minutes, 2 May 1944; PLP minutes, 3 May and 10 May 1944 1944; Ede diary 3 May 1944.
12. Ede diary, 10 May 1944.
13. Dalton Diary, 18 July 1944 (p. 770).
14. Ibid.
15. Ibid.
16. Ibid.
17. Minutes of the special PLP meetings, 8 and 12 July 1944.
18. NEC minutes, 26 July 1944.
19. Noted in *The Times*, 7 October 1944.
20. Consult CAB 78/28, General Series 49, for the records.
21. *The Times*, 30 March 1944.
22. Dalton Diary, 22 August 1944 (pp. 779–80).
23. Ibid.
24. Ibid.
25. Ibid.
26. NEC papers, Attlee memorandum, n.d.; Bevin was furious that Attlee did not discuss it with him first – see Attlee papers, Bevin to Attlee, 13 September 1944.
27. *The Times*, 14 September 1944.
28. Ibid.
29. Ibid.; NEC papers, Attlee memorandum, n.d.; NEC minutes, 13 September 1944.
30. Tom Attlee papers, Attlee to Tom Attlee, 16 October 1944.
31. Harris, *Attlee*, p. 235.
32. *The Times*, 14 September 1944.
33. NEC papers, press release, 'Labour and the General Election', 5 October 1944 (my emphasis).
34. Ibid.
35. Ibid.
36. Ede diary, 7 October 1944.
37. NEC papers, press release, 'Labour and the General Election', 5 October 1944.
38. Ede diary, 11 October 1944.
39. *Observer*, 5 May 1944.
40. CAB 124/214, Memoranda on the Employment Policy White Paper, March 1944.

41. See for instance CAB 87/5, R (44) 34, confidential annexe, 24 April 1944.

42. Rodney Lowe, 'The Second World War, consensus, and the foundation of the welfare state', *Twentieth Century British History*, 1 (1990) pp. 152–82, at 168.

43. Addison, *Road to 1945*, p. 252.

44. Jefferys, *Churchill Coalition and Wartime Politics*, p. 171 ('a compromise on every level').

45. Brooke, *Labour's War*, p. 227.

46. Lord Butler, *The Art of the Possible: The Memoirs of Lord Butler* (London, 1971) p. 125.

47. HC Debates, 401, 23 June 1944, cols 525–32.

48. Oliver Lyttelton, *Seven Points of Conservative Policy* (London, 1944).

49. Addison, *Road to 1945*, p. 246.

50. Headlam diary, 16 March 1944.

51. Headlam diary, 11 July 1944.

52. Addison, *Road to 1945*, p. 238. It was also a cunning means to consolidate the conservative basis of the British state: see S. J. D. Green, 'The 1944 Education Act: a church–state perspective', *Parliamentary History*, 19 (2000) pp. 148–64.

53. CAB 66/52, 'Post-War Financial Commitments: Memorandum by the Chancellor of the Exchequer', 28 June 1944.

54. Headlam diary, 25 April 1944.

55. PREM 4 89/5, Woolton to Churchill, 27 June 1944.

56. PREM 4 89/5, Anderson to Churchill, 27 June 1944.

57. CAB, 66/52, 'Post-War Financial Commitments: Memorandum by the Chancellor of the Exchequer', 28 June 1944.

58. Ibid.

59. Jefferys, *Churchill Coalition and Wartime Politics*, p. 176.

60. *The Times*, 22 March 1943.

61. *The Times*, 3 October 1944.

62. *Manchester Guardian*, 9 October 1944.

63. Churchill College, Attlee papers, Attlee to Churchill, n.d.; Churchill to Attlee, 19 January 1945.

64. Bevin papers, Bevin to Attlee, 18 May 1944.

65. Morrison papers, Morrison to Bevin, 17 October 1944.

66. Ibid.

67. Ibid.

68. Bevin papers, Bevin to Morrison, 24 October 1944; Morrison papers, Morrison to Bevin, 25 October 1944.

69. NEC minutes, 29 October 1944.

70. Ibid.

71. Ibid.

72. Ibid.

73. CAB 87/9, R (44) 196, 'The Future of the Electricity Industry: Memorandum by the Home Secretary', 24 November 1944.

74. Butler, *Art of the Possible*, p. 125.

75. The executive's flagship economic policy document, *Full Employment and Financial Policy* – 1944 *LPACR*, pp. 161–8. For the contents, consult pp. 50–2. Moreover, there was great bitterness over Britain's intervention against the Greek communists – examined by Andrew Thorpe, "In a rather emotional state'? The Labour Party and British intervention in Greece, 1944–5', *English Historical Review*, (2006) pp. 1075–105.

76. *LPACR*, 1944, p. 131; NEC minutes, 10 January 1945.

77. A glance at the sheer range of matters the Campaign Committee covered gives a sense of Morrison's influence.

78. NEC Campaign Committee minutes, 19 February 1945.

79. NEC minutes 28 February 1945; NEC Policy Committee minutes, 23 January 1945; Donoughue and Jones, *Herbert Morrison*, p. 331.

80. Labour Research Department papers, 282, 'First Draft Declaration of Policy for the 1945 Annual Conference', February 1945; NEC Campaign Committee minutes, 19 February 1945.

81. Donoughue and Jones, *Herbert Morrison*, p. 324.

82. Butler, *Art of the Possible*, p. 129.

83. *Labour Organiser*, March 1945, pp. 8–9.

84. *The Times*, 30 April 1945.

85. *LPACR*, 1944, pp. 161–8.

86. Warwick University, TUC papers, minutes of special General Council meeting, 23 May 1945.

87. Dalton Diary, 18 October 1944 (p. 795).

88. Ibid.

89. Consult the relevant record of attendees in the PLP papers.

90. Donoughue and Jones, *Herbert Morrison*, pp. 340–1.

91. Labour lost a seat in Motherwell to the Scottish Nationalists, while the Conservatives lost the seat for the Scottish Universities to an Independent, and Chelmsford to Common Wealth – Butler and Butler, *British Political Facts*, p. 255.

92. Headlam diary, 18 January 1945.

93. CAB 65, WM (45) 38, 3 April 1945.

94. *Tribune*, 30 March 1945.

95. See, for instance, Bevan in *Tribune*, 19 January 1945, where he proposed an alliance with Common Wealth and CPGB instead.

96. Bevin papers, Attlee to Bevin, n.d. Attlee drew up the note during a Cabinet meeting and passed it to Bevin.

97. Attlee, *Granada Records Interview*, p. 53.

98. PLP Administrative Committee minutes, 18 April 1945.

99. *The Times*, 9 April 1945. Angered by Churchill's speech to the Conservative conference, Bevin labelled the party a 'one-man show' and suggested the Prime Minister was not suited to peacetime leadership.

100. *The Times*, 10 April 1945.

101. Dalton Diary, 10 May 1945 (p. 858).

102. NEC papers, minutes of a joint meeting of the NEC, TUC and PLP Administrative Committee, 9 May 1945.

103. Brooke, *Labour's War*, p. 317. Reinforced in Bullock, *Life and Times*, 2, p. 375.

104. Morrison, *Autobiography*, p. 235.

105. Morrison, *Autobiography*, p. 233.

106. PREM 4/65/4, Churchill to Eden, 13 May 1945.

107. Ibid.

108. PREM 4/65/4, Eden to Churchill, 12 May 1945.

109. Headlam diary, 4 May 1945.

110. Amery diary, 4 September 1944.

111. H.C. Debs, 31 October 1944 col. 667.

112. Churchill to Randolph Churchill, 23 November 1944, cited in Martin Gilbert, *Winston S. Churchill, 7: Road to Victory 1941–1945* (London, 1986) p. 1072.

113. Headlam diary, 20 July 1944.

114. Headlam diary, 15 March 1945.

115. Addison, *Road to 1945*, p. 230.

116. Churchill, *Second World War: VI*, p. Churchill, *Second World War: VI*, p. 511. It is unclear when this occurred.

117. Churchill, *Second World War: VI*, p. 512.

118. Dalton Diary, 11 May 1945 (pp. 858–9).

119. Morrison, *Autobiography*, p. 234.

120. Dalton Diary, 11 May 1945 (pp. 858–9).

121. Ibid.

122. Ibid.

123. Ibid.

124. Morrison, *Autobiography*, p. 234.

125. Bevin papers, copy of Attlee letter to Morrison, 12 May 1945.

126. Ibid.

127. Attlee, *As It Happened*, p. 157.

128. Dalton Diary, 11 May 1945 (pp. 858–9).

129. Louis Morton, 'The decision to use the atomic bomb', in Robert J. Art and Kenneth Waltz (eds) *The Use of Force* (London, 1988, third edn) pp. 198–219, at 214.

130. Consult Churchill, *Second World War: VI*, Chapter 35, which contains extensive documentation on politics at the end of the war, but, revealingly, excludes this episode. Attlee distorts the sequence of events in *As It Happened*, Chapter 16; and see Dalton, *FY*, Chapter 30.

131. PREM 4/65/4, Churchill to Attlee, 18 May 1945.

132. Williams, *A Prime Minister Remembers*, p. 63.

133. PREM 4/65/4, Churchill to the Chief Whip, 18 May 1945.

134. It began 'My dear Attlee'.

135. PREM 4/65/4, Churchill to Attlee, 18 May 1945.

136. PREM 4/65/4, Churchill to the Chief Whip, 18 May 1945.

137. Colville, *Diaries*, 18 May 1945, p. 600; Dalton Diary, 18 May 1945 (p. 861). Jefferys's (*Churchill Coalition and Wartime Politics*, p. 183) suggestion that Bevin 'had long ago rejected any such possibility' seems difficult to uphold.

138. Brooke, *Labour's War*, p. 304.

139. Foot, *Bevan*, p. 500. In a review of Foot's book (*Observer*, 21 October 1962), Attlee rejected the charge. Intriguingly, he commented that 'we were advised' that the defeat of Japan would take only 'another six months'. Most serious military opinion in fact reckoned on at least another year. Perhaps Attlee was still working to avoid the official version of events reflecting unfavourably.

140. Of course, Dalton may have misconstrued Attlee's assent the previous July. That was not the first time the leader's laconic manner gave others a – probably deliberate – misimpression.

141. Cited Andrew Roberts, *Salisbury: Victorian Titan* (London, 1999) p. 610.

142. PREM 4/65/4, Churchill to the Chief Whip, 18 May 1945. The letter is reproduced in full in Churchill, *Second World War, VI*, pp. 515–16.

143. *Tribune*, 19 January 1945.

144. G. R. Strauss interview, cited in Donoughue and Jones, *Herbert Morrison*, p. 340; *Tribune*, 19 January 1945; Betty D. Vernon, *Ellen Wilkinson, 1891–1947* (London, 1982) p. 197. Bevan was staying with Strauss at this time and participated in several telephone discussions (it is unclear with whom) on the leadership issue, making apparent his preference for Morrison.

145. Shinwell, *Conflict Without Malice*, p. 169.

146. Donoughue and Jones, *Herbert Morrison*, p. 341.

147. Dalton Diary, 19 May 1945 (p. 862).

148. NEC minutes, 20 May 1945; Dalton Diary, 19–22 May 1945 (pp. 861–2).

149. NEC minutes, 20 May 1945; Morrison, *Autobiography*, p. 235; Dalton Diary, 18 and 19 May 1945 (pp. 861–2); Addison, *Road to 1945*, p. 257.

150. NEC minutes, 20 May 1945; Slowe, *Shinwell*, p. 203.

151. NEC minutes, 20 May 1945.

152. A glimpse of the lack of centrality afforded to the issue of postwar coalition is offered by scrutinizing earlier work. Though Addison (*Road to 1945*, p. 252) acknowledged that it is hard to tell if the ministers differed in their 'heart of hearts' or were forced to break up the alliance by their parties, his analysis does not explore the problem. He deals with it only fleetingly (see *Road to 1945*, pp. 234–5, 241–2, 252). Brooke's lone coverage is in *Labour's War*, p. 304, where he suggests that 'it is doubtful' that a postwar coalition was ever 'considered seriously'. Jefferys (*Churchill Coalition and Wartime Politics*, pp. 167–8, 174–5) offers the best discussion, but that is also limited. For instance, he devotes only half a paragraph (pp. 183–4) to the Attlee–Churchill letter exchange and the breaking of the government.

153. Unsurprisingly, he did not recount this in his memoirs either – Attlee, *As It Happened*, pp. 157–60.

154. NEC minutes, 18 May 1945. Why Attlee was absent remains a mystery. Having arrived from San Francisco the previous evening and then been at a meeting with Churchill into the small hours, it is possible that he was sleeping off the trip. But it is still odd.

155. For examples – and there are many – see 'Churchill has won the election already' in James, *Diaries of Sir Henry Channon*, 15 and 16 March 1945, pp. 399–400; 'Conservative pundits' were 'blind', and their 'faith' in 'Winston's name' 'pathetic', in Headlam diary, 27 April 1945; Ede believed Churchill would 'attract an overwhelming majority' fighting on 'party lines', and 'speculations based on by-elections … notoriously … turn out badly', in Ede diary, 2 January and 21 May 1945.

156. Williams, *A Prime Minister Remembers*, p. 3.

157. NEC minutes, 18 May 1945.

158. *The Times*, 22 May 1945.

159. Colville, *Diaries*, 21–23 May 1945, pp. 601–2.

160. *The Times*, 25 May 1945.

161. Colville, *Diaries*, 21 May 1945, p. 601.

162. Butler and Butler, *British Political Facts*, pp. 20–1 contains a full list of ministers.

163. Colville, *Diaries*, 22 May 1945, p. 601.

164. Colville, *Diaries*, 21 May 1945, p. 601.

165. Butler, *Art of the Possible*, pp. 126–7.

166. Ibid.

167. Headlam diary, 22 May 1945.

168. Butler, *Art of the Possible*, p. 128.

169. Although Corelli Barnett, *The Audit of War: The Illusion and Reality of Britain as a Great Nation* (London, 1986) brutally exposes the flaws in Britain's performance.

170. *LPACR*, 1945, pp. 81–2.

171. *LPACR*, 1945, pp. 89–92.

172. *The Times*, 23 May 1945; *News Chronicle*, 23 May 1945.

173. *Daily Express*, 23 May 1945.

174. NEC minutes, 20 May 1945.

175. *LPACR*, 1945, p. 88. Morrison helped draft this.

176. Hull University, Laski papers, Laski to Attlee 29 May 1945.

177. Ibid.

178. Hull University, Laski papers, Attlee to Laski, 30 May 1945.

179. NEC papers, 'Broadcasting', n.d.

180. NEC Campaign Committee minutes, 19 March 1945 and 11 April 1945. The other was Bevin.

181. *The Times*, 10 January 1945.

182. Attlee, *As It Happened*, p. 167; Attlee papers, 1/24, undated memorandum.

183. David Cannadine (ed.) *Blood, Toil, Tears and Sweat: Winston Churchill's Famous Speeches* (London, 1989) pp. 270–7.

184. Roy Jenkins, *Churchill: A Biography* (London, 2001) p. 793.

185. Roy Jenkins (ed.) *Purpose and Policy: Selected Speeches by the Prime Minister, the Rt. Hon. C. R. Attlee* (London, 1947) p. 3.

186. Jenkins, *Churchill*, p. 793. Echoed in Headlam diary, 5 June 1944.

187. McCallum and Readman, *The British General Election of 1945*, p. 175.

188. *Daily Herald*, 15 June 1945.

189. *Daily Express*, 16 June 1945; see also 23 and 25 June.

190. *Daily Express*, 16 June 1945; and consult 20 June and 4 July, 'Shall the Laski 25 Rule Great Britain?'

191. See *The Times*, 21, 22, 23 and 24 June 1945.

192. Addison, *Road to 1945*, p. 266.

193. Attlee, *As It Happened*, p. 168.

194. Attlee, *As It Happened*, p. 161.

195. Colville, *Diaries*, p. 611.

196. Headlam diary, 26 July 1945.

197. James, *Diaries of Sir Henry Channon*, 28 July 1945, p. 409.

198. W. S. Churchill, 'No promises but every preparation', *The Listener*, 25 March 1943.

199. Morrison papers, Morrison to Attlee, 25 July 1945.

200. Ibid.

201. Morrison, *Autobiography*, p. 245.

202. Dalton, *FY*, p. 468.

203. Ibid. For his part, Morrison denied that Bevin made any such threat (Morrison, *Autobiography*, p. 246).

204. Williams, *A Prime Minister Remembers*, p. 3; Bullock, *Life and Times*, 2, pp. 391–2; Harris, *Attlee*, p. 262. That this critical meeting was not minuted hinders our understanding; consequently, we have to reconstruct the account from various subsequent recollections, interviews and memoirs. Helpfully, there does not appear to be controversy about what occurred. Following the established pattern of these events, Attlee failed to mention the meeting in his memoirs (Attlee, *As It Happened*, p. 171).

205. Morrison, *Autobiography*, p. 245; Williams, *A Prime Minister Remembers*, pp. 3–4.

206. PLP papers, Carol Johnson letter to PLP, 14 June 1945.

207. Morrison, *Autobiography*, p. 245; Williams, *A Prime Minister Remembers*, pp. 3–4; Granville Eastwood, *Harold Laski* (London, 1977) pp. 341–2.

208. Morrison, *Autobiography*, p. 245; Williams, *A Prime Minister Remembers*, pp. 3–4.

209. Morrison, *Autobiography*, p. 245.

210. Morrison, *Autobiography*, p. 236.

211. Morrison, *Autobiography*, p. 245.

212. Attlee interview, cited in Harris, *Attlee*, p. 263.

213. Williams, *A Prime Minister Remembers*, pp. 3–4.

214. Ibid.

215. Ibid.

216. Attlee interview, cited in Harris, *Attlee*, p. 263.

217. Ibid.; Williams, *A Prime Minister Remembers*, pp. 3–4.

218. Attlee interview, cited in Harris, *Attlee*, p. 263.

219. Donoughue and Jones, *Herbert Morrison*, pp. 341–2.

220. *Star*, 27 July 1945, cited in Donoughue and Jones, *Herbert Morrison*, pp. 341–2.

221. R. Boon, G. Isaacs and J. Parker interviews, cited in Donoughue and Jones, *Herbert Morrison*, pp. 341–2.

222. Williams, *A Prime Minister Remembers*, p. 3.

223. Donoughue and Jones, *Herbert Morrison*, p. 342.

224. Confirmed by McKenzie, *British Political Parties*, p. 331. McKenzie was present as an observer.

225. Churchill College, Cambridge, Attlee papers, 1/17, draft autobiography; Dalton, *FY*, p. 474.

226. PLP Executive Committee minutes, 27 July 1945; Dalton Diary, 27 July 1945 (unpublished).

227. Donoughue and Jones, *Herbert Morrison*, p. 343. Despite this, Morrison purported it was 'untrue' that 'I tried to obtain the premiership for myself'. Indeed, if there had been a ballot, 'I myself had no doubt that the party would confirm Attlee's position as leader' (Morrison, *Autobiography*, p. 245). Such is the stuff of which political memoirs are made.

228. Wilkinson waited at a railway station to meet new MPs travelling to London and tried to get their backing for a motion demanding a contest (Vernon, *Wilkinson*, p. 197). Also, Summerskill, Manning and Roben interviews, cited Donoughue and Jones, *Herbert Morrison*, p. 346.

229. PLP minutes, 28 July 1945; Ede diary, 28 July 1945.

230. Ibid.

231. Ibid.

232. Ibid.

233. For Attlee's own observations on running a government, consult his essay 'In the driver's seat', *Observer*, 18 October 1964.

234. Churchill College, Cambridge, Attlee papers, 1/17, draft autobiography.

235. Attlee, *As It Happened*, pp. 154, 178 (my emphasis).

236. 'If I'd known what it was going to be like, I'd have asked for something easier,' Shinwell confessed – Shinwell's notes on 1945, cited in Slowe, *Shinwell*, pp. 206.

237. Hull University, Laski papers, Attlee to Laski, 20 August 1945. Attlee also ignored Laski's surreal request to be appointed British ambassador to Washington.

238. Hugh Dalton, *High Tide and After: Memoirs, 1945–1960* (London, 1962) p. 237.

239. Shinwell, *Conflict Without Malice*, p. 134.

240. *Observer*, 7 February 1960.

241. Reproduced in J. T. Murphy, *Labour's Big Three: A Biographical Study of Clement Attlee, Herbert Morrison and Ernest Bevin* (London, 1948) inside cover.

Conclusion

1. We might speculate that one reason why historians typically do not 'get' Attlee is because he was alien to two of the most important traditions in shaping how modern British politics has been conceptualized. The first is the LSE tradition – influenced initially by Laski, through him to Miliband, and diffused into a wider consciousness – of 'ideas'. The second is the Oxford tradition – so centred first on Cole, who picked it up in part from Morrison – of 'organization'. Both exercised, and still do, a major influence on political science and history. Most scholars, consciously or otherwise, descend from one of these two larger schools of thought. But Attlee does not conform to what these two approaches held about public life. Neither school had much sympathy for the technical side of political skill. Even the 'organization' approach fails to comprehend Attlee. This, it must be said, indicates that, for all the scholars who profess to understand the 'fixers' and 'machine politicians', painfully few actually grasp the type; the proof is in the pudding.

2. Shannon, *The Age of Salisbury*, p. 3.

3. Fry, *The Politics of Decline*, pp. 57–8.

4. Ibid.

5. Ibid.

6. Tom Attlee might be an obvious exception, but, even in their correspondence, Attlee largely refrained from writing about the political arts.

7. Williamson, *Baldwin*, p. 155.

8. James Margach, *The Anatomy of Power: An Enquiry into the Personality of Leadership* (London, 1979) pp. 4, 11, 25.

9. *Observer*, 18 October 1964.

10. *Observer*, 6 November 1960.

11. Williams, *A Prime Minister Remembers*, p. 83.

12. *Observer*, 18 October 1964.

13. I am indebted to Owen Hartley on this point.

14. See my essays '"High politics", political practice and the Labour Party', in Crowcroft et al., *The Philosophy, Politics and Religion of British Democracy*; 'The "high politics" of Labour Party factionalism, 1950–5', *Historical Research*, 81 (2008) pp. 679–709; 'Maurice Cowling and the writing of British political history', *Contemporary British History*, 22 (2008) pp. 279–86.

15. But for a starting point, consult the exemplary statement: Kedourie, *The Crossman Confessions* – easily the most stimulating thing written about British politics for decades. Also, Whiting, *The Labour Party and Taxation*, is excellent on the difficulties of translating instincts into policy – let alone into outcomes.

16. Cowling, *Impact of Hitler*, p. 2.

17. Fry, *The Politics of Decline*, p. 53.

18. S. J. D. Green, 'The strange death of Puritan England, 1914–1945', in Wm. Roger Louis (ed.) *Yet More Adventures with Britannia: Personalities, Politics and Culture in Britain* (London, 2005) pp. 185–210, expresses this view powerfully.

19. Alexis de Tocqueville, *Democracy in America*, translated by Gerald Bevan (London, 2003).

20. Joseph A. Schumpeter, *Capitalism, Socialism, and Democracy* (London, 1943) Chapter 22.

21. Addison, *Road to 1945*, p. 278.

22. And if any evidence is needed that this was never about politicians *listening* to the people, then their contempt in the subsequent decades for the opinions of the public on capital punishment, immigration, terrorism and Europe is surely conclusive.

23. Fry, *The Politics of Crisis*, p. 26.

24. Cowling, *Impact of Labour*, p. 6.

25. Kedourie, *The Crossman Confessions*, p. 23.

Extended Bibliography

Primary sources

Government material

CAB 65, War Cabinet minutes, 1939–45

CAB 66/67, War Cabinet and Cabinet Memoranda, 1939–45

CAB 68, War Cabinet: Reports by Government Departments, 1939–42

CAB 69, War Cabinet and Cabinet: Defence Committee minutes and papers, 1940–45

CAB 70, War Cabinet and Cabinet: Defence Committee (Supply) minutes and papers, 1940–45

CAB 71, War Cabinet and Cabinet: Lord President's Committees, minutes and papers, 1940–45

CAB 72, War Cabinet: Committees on Economic Policy: Minutes and Papers, 1940–45

CAB 74, War Cabinet: Food Policy Committees: Minutes and Papers, 1940–43

CAB 75, War Cabinet: Home Policy Committee, later Legislation Committee, and Sub-Committees: Minutes and Papers, 1940–45

CAB 87, War Cabinet and Cabinet: Committees on Reconstruction, Supply and other matters: Minutes and Papers, 1941–45

CAB 118, War Cabinet and Cabinet: Various Ministers – Private Office Files: Clement Attlee correspondence and papers, 1940–45

CAB 118, War Cabinet and Cabinet: Various Ministers – Private Office Files: Arthur Greenwood correspondence and papers, 1940–42

CAB 127, Private collections of Ministers' and Officials' papers, Hugh Dalton correspondence, 1940–51

CAB 127/209, Private collections of Ministers' and Officials' papers, Ernest Bevin-Hugh Dalton correspondence 1940–41

CAB 132, Cabinet: Lord President's Committee and Subordinate Committees and Home Affairs Committee, minutes and papers, 1940–45

INF 1/177, Problems of peace aims and reconstruction, suggestion by Richard Rapier Stokes

PREM 3, Prime Minister's Office: Operational Correspondence and Papers, 1939–45

Party papers (People's History Museum, Labour Party Archive, Manchester)

Labour Party, Annual Conference Resolutions, 1939–45

Labour Party, National Executive Committee (NEC) papers, 1939–45

Labour Party Annual Conference Reports, 1939–45

National Council of Labour papers, 1939–45

Parliamentary Labour Party papers, 1939–45

Parliamentary Labour Party Administrative Committee papers, 1940–45

Personal papers

Christopher Addison papers, Bodleian Library, Oxford

A. V. Alexander papers, Churchill College, Cambridge

Leopold Amery papers, Churchill College, Cambridge

Clement Attlee papers, Bodleian Library, Oxford and Churchill College, Cambridge

Ernest Bevin papers, Churchill College, Cambridge

Rab Butler papers, Trinity College, Cambridge

Neville Chamberlain papers, Birmingham University Library

Walter Citrine papers, British Library of Political and Economic Science

Hugh Dalton papers, British Library of Political and Economic Science

Geoffrey Dawson papers, Bodleian Library, Oxford

James Chuter Ede papers, British Library

James Griffiths papers, National Library of Wales

1st Earl of Halifax papers, Churchill College, Cambridge, and University of York

Cuthbert Headlam papers, Durham County Record Office

Harold Laski papers, Hull University Archive, and Labour Party Archive, Manchester

H. B. Lees-Smith papers, Hull University Archive

James Middleton papers, Ruskin College, Oxford

Herbert Morrison papers, Nuffield College, Oxford

Frederick William Pethick-Lawrence papers, Trinity College, Cambridge

Emanuel Shinwell, British Library of Political and Economic Science

Richard Stokes papers, Bodleian Library, Oxford
Patrick Gordon Walker papers, Churchill College, Cambridge
Lord Woolmer papers, Bodleian Library, Oxford

Trade Unions
Trade Union Congress papers, 1939–45, Warwick University Archive
Trades Union Annual Conference Reports, 1939–1945

Newspapers and journals

Daily Herald	*Daily Telegraph*
Evening Standard	*London News*
Manchester Guardian	*New Statesman*
Political Quarterly	*Reynold's News*
The Economist	*The Times*
Tribune	

Parliament
Parliamentary Debates (Commons) Fifth Series, 1939 to 1945

Contemporary publications by relevant individuals
Attlee, Clement, *Labour's Peace Aims*, pamphlet (London, 1939)
__ (ed.) *Labour's Aims in War and Peace* (London, 1940)
Cato, *Guilty Men* (London, 1940)
Churchill, Winston S., *The Unrelenting Struggle* (London, 1943)
__ 'No promises but every preparation', *The Listener*, 25 March 1943
Dalton, Hugh, *Hitler's War: Before and After* (London, 1940)
__ *Full Employment and Financial Policy* (London, 1943)
Greenwood, Arthur, *Why We Fight: Labour's Case*, pamphlet (London, 1940)
Keynes, J. M., *How to Pay for the War* (London, 1940)
Labour Party, *Labour, the War and the Peace* (London, 1940)
__ *Labour in the Government: A Record of Social Legislation in War Time* (London, 1941)
__ *The Labour Party, the War and the Peace* (London, 1941)
Laski, Harold, *The Labour Party, the War and the Future* (London, 1939)
__ *Is This an Imperialist War?*, pamphlet (London, 1940)
__ 'The war and the future', in C. R. Attlee (ed.) *Labour's Aims in War and Peace* (London, 1940)

__ *Great Britain, Russia and the Labour Party* (London, 1941)

Lyttelton, Oliver, *Seven Points of Conservative Policy* (London, 1944)

Morrison, Herbert, *Socialization and Transport* (London, 1933)

__ *What Are We Fighting For?* (London, 1939)

__ *The Spearhead of Humanity* (London, 1942)

__ *Looking Ahead: Wartime Speeches* (London, 1943)

Politicus, 'Labour and the war', *Political Quarterly*, 10 (1939) pp. 477–88

Printed sources

Attlee, Clement, *Clem Attlee: The Granada Historical Records Interview* (London, 1967)

Channon, Sir Henry, *'Chips': The Diaries of Sir Henry Channon*, edited by Robert Rhodes James (London, 1996 edition)

Colville, John, *The Fringes of Power: Downing Street Diaries 1939–1955* (London, 1985)

Crozier, W. P., *W. P. Crozier: Off the Record – Political Interviews, 1933–1943*, edited by A. J. P. Taylor (London, 1973)

Dugdale, Blanche, *Baffy: The Diaries of Blanche Dugdale, 1936–47*, edited by N. Rose (London, 1973)

Gordon Walker, Patrick, *Patrick Gordon Walker: Political Diaries, 1932–1971*, edited by Robert Pearce (London, 1991)

Harvey, J. (ed.) *The Diplomatic Diaries of John Harvey, 1937–40* (London, 1970)

Jefferys, Kevin (ed.) *Documents in Contemporary History: War and Reform – British Politics during the Second World War* (Manchester, 1994)

Jenkins, Roy (ed.) *Purpose and Policy: Selected Speeches by the Prime Minister, the Rt. Hon. C. R. Attlee* (London, 1947)

Nicolson, Nigel (ed.) *Harold Nicolson: Diaries and Letters, 1939–1945* (London, 1960)

Autobiographies and memoirs

Attlee, Clement, *As It Happened* (London, 1956)

Avon, The Rt. Hon. The Earl of, *The Reckoning: The Memoirs of the Rt Hon. Sir Anthony Eden* (London, 1965)

Beveridge, William, *Power and Influence* (London, 1953)

Butler, David Butler, David *The Art of the Possible: The Memoirs of Lord Butler* (London, 1971)

Churchill, Winston S., *The Second World War*, 6 vols (London, 1948–64)

Cooper, Duff, *Old Men Forget* (London, 1953)

Dalton, Hugh, *The Fateful Years: Memoirs, 1931–1945* (London, 1957)

__ *High Tide and After: Memoirs, 1945–1960* (London, 1962)

Griffiths, James, *Pages from Memory* (London, 1969)

Mallaby, George, *From My Level: Unwritten Minutes* (London, 1965)

Morrison, Herbert, *An Autobiography* (London, 1960)

Parker, John, *Father of the House: Fifty Years in Politics* (London, 1982)

Pethick-Lawrence, Frederick William, *Fate Has Been Kind* (London, n.d. but 1943)

Shinwell, Emanuel, *Conflict Without Malice* (London, 1955)

__ *I've Lived Through It All* (London, 1973)

__ *Lead With the Left* (London, 1981)

Williams, Francis, *A Prime Minister Remembers: The War and Post-war Memoirs of the Rt Hon. Earl Attlee* (London, 1961)

Secondary sources
Books

Addison, Paul, *The Road to 1945: British Politics and the Second World War* (London, 1975)

Augustine, *The City of God against the Pagans*, translated by R. W. Dyson (Cambridge, 1998)

Ball, Simon, *The Guardsmen* (London, 2004)

Barnett, Correlli, *The Audit of War: The Illusion and Reality of Britain as a Great Nation* (London, 1986)

Beckett, Francis, *Clem Attlee* (London, 2007)

Beer, Samuel H., *Modern British Politics* (London, 1969)

Bentley, Michael, *Politics Without Democracy 1815–1914* (London, 1984)

Bentley, Michael and John Stevenson (eds) *High and Low Politics in Modern Britain: Ten Studies* (Oxford, 1983)

Brivati, Brian and Harriet Jones (eds) *What Difference Did the War Make?* (London, 1993)

Brooke, Stephen, *Labour's War: The Labour Party during the Second World War* (Oxford, 1992)

Brookshire, Jerry H., *Clement Attlee* (Manchester, 1995)

Bullock, Alan, *The Life and Times of Ernest Bevin*, 1, *Trade Union Leader, 1881–1940* (London, 1960)

__ *The Life and Times of Ernest Bevin*, 2, *Minister of Labour* (London, 1967)

Burridge, Trevor, *British Labour and Hitler's War* (London, 1976)

__ *Clement Attlee: A Political Biography* (London, 1985)

Butler, David (ed.) *Coalitions in British Politics* (London, 1978)

Butler, David and Gareth Butler, *Twentieth Century British Political Facts, 1900–2000* (London, 2000)

Calder, Angus, *The People's War: Britain, 1939–45* (London, 1969)

Callaghan, John, Steven Fielding and Steve Ludlam (eds) *Interpreting the Labour Party: Approaches to Labour Politics and History* (Manchester 2003)

Calvin, John, *Institutes of the Christian Religion*, translated by Henry Beveridge (Massachusetts, 2008)

Campbell, John, *Nye Bevan: A Biography* (London, 1987)

Cannadine, David (ed.) *Blood, Toil, Tears and Sweat: Winston Churchill's Famous Speeches* (London, 1989)

Charmley, John, *Chamberlain and the Lost Peace* (London, 1989)

__ *Churchill: the End of Glory* (London, 1993)

__ *Churchill's Grand Alliance: The Anglo-American Special Relationship, 1940–1957* (London, 1996)

__ *Splendid Isolation? Britain, the Balance of Power, and the Origins of the First World War* (London, 1999)

Charteris-Black, Jonathan, *Politicians and Rhetoric: The Persuasive Power of Metaphor* (Basingstoke, 2005)

Clark, J. C. D., *English Society 1688–1832: Ideology, Social Structure, and Political Practice during the Ancien Regime* (Cambridge, 1985)

Clarke, Peter, *Lancashire and the New Liberalism* (Cambridge, 1971)

__ *A Question of Leadership* (London, 1999)

Clegg, Hugh Armstrong, *A History of British Trade Unions since 1889*, 3, *1934–1951* (Oxford, 1994)

Cooke, A. B. and John Vincent, *The Governing Passion: Cabinet Government and Party Politics in Britain 1885–86* (Sussex, 1974)

Cowling, Maurice, *1867: Disraeli, Gladstone and Revolution. The Passing of the Second Reform Bill* (Cambridge, 1967)

__ *The Impact of Labour 1920–1924: The Beginning of Modern British Politics* (Cambridge, 1971)

__ *The Impact of Hitler: British Politics and British Policy 1933–1940* (Cambridge, 1975)

__ *Religion and Public Doctrine in Modern England*, 3 (Cambridge, 2001)

Crowcroft, Robert, S. J. D. Green and Richard Whiting (eds) *The Philosophy, Politics and Religion of British Democracy: Maurice Cowling and Conservatism* (London, 2010)

Crowson, N. J., *Facing Fascism: The Conservative Party and the European Dictators 1935–1940* (London, 1997)

Dellar, Geoffrey, *Attlee As I Knew Him* (London, 1983)

Donoughue, Bernard and G. W. Jones, *Herbert Morrison: Portrait of a Politician* (London, 1973)

Drucker, H. M., *Doctrine and Ethos in the Labour Party* (London, 1979)

Eastwood, Granville, *Harold Laski* (London, 1977)

Foot, Michael, *Aneurin Bevan: A Biography, 1, 1897–1945* (London, 1962)

Fry, Geoffrey K., *The Politics of Crisis: An interpretation of British Politics, 1931–1945* (Basingstoke, 2001)

__ *The Politics of Decline: An Interpretation of British Politics from the 1940s to the 1970s* (London, 2005)

Green, E. H. H., *The Crisis of Conservatism* (London, 1995)

Goodhart, Philip and Ursula Branston, *The 1922: The Story of the Conservative Backbenchers' Parliamentary Committee* (London, 1973)

Gorst, Anthony, Lewis Johnman and W. Scott Lucas (eds) *Contemporary British History, 1931–1961: Politics and the Limits of Party* (London, 1991)

Guttsman, W. L., *The British Political Elite* (London, 1963)

Hackett Fischer, David, *Albion's Seed: Four British Folkways in America* (Oxford, 1989)

Hamilton, Alexander, James Madison and John Jay, *The Federalist*, edited by Terence Ball (Cambridge, 2003)

Hancock, W. K. and M. M. Gowing, *History of the Second World War: United Kingdom Civil Series – British War Economy* (London, 1949)

Harris, Kenneth, *Attlee* (London, 1982)

Howell, David, *Attlee* (London, 2006)

Hughes, Emrys, *Sydney Silverman: Rebel in Parliament – A Biography* (London, 1969)

Jackson, Robert J., *Rebels and Whips: An Analysis of Dissension, Discipline and Cohesion in British Political Parties* (London, 1968)

Jefferys, Kevin, *The Churchill Coalition and Wartime Politics, 1940–1945* (Manchester, 1991)

Jenkins, Roy (ed.) *Mr Attlee: An Interim Biography* (London, 1948)

__ (ed.) *Churchill: A Biography* (London, 2001)

Kavanagh, Dennis (ed.) *The Politics of the Labour Party* (London, 1982)

__ *Politics and Personalities* (London, 1990)

Kavanagh, Dennis and Peter Morris, *Consensus Politics from Attlee to Major* (Oxford, 1994)

Kedourie, Elie, *The Crossman Confessions* (London, 1984)

Kramnick, Isaac and Barry Sheerman, *Harold Laski: A Life on the Left* (London, 1993)

Krug, Mark M., *Aneurin Bevan: Cautious Rebel* (London, 1961)

Lawlor, Sheila, *Churchill and the Politics of War, 1940–1941* (Cambridge 1994)

Lawrence, Jon and Miles Taylor, *Party, State and Society: Electoral Behaviour in Britain since 1820* (Aldershot, 1997)

Lee, J. M., *The Churchill Coalition, 1940–1945* (Connecticut, 1980)

McCallum, R. B. and Alison Readman, *The British General Election of 1945* (London, 1947)

MacDonald, Malcolm, *Titans and Others* (London, 1972)

McKenzie, R. T., *British Political Parties: The Distribution of Power within the Conservative and Labour Parties* (London, 1967)

McKibbin, Ross, *The Evolution of the Labour Party, 1910–1924* (Oxford, 1974)

McLean, Iain, *Rational Choice and British Politics: An Analysis of Rhetoric and Manipulation from Peel to Blair* (Oxford, 2001)

Margach, James, *The Anatomy of Power: An Enquiry into the Personality of Leadership* (London, 1979)

Martin, Kingsley, *Harold Laski, 1893–1950: A Biographical Memoir* (London, 1953)

Miliband, Ralph, *Parliamentary Socialism: A Study in the Politics of Labour* (London, 1975)

Minkin, Lewis, *The Contentious Alliance: Trade Unions and the Labour Party* (Edinburgh, 1991)

Minogue, Kenneth, *Politics: A Very Short Introduction* (Oxford, 1995)

Moloney, Ed, *A Secret History of the IRA* (2nd edn) (London, 2007)

Moore, Robin James, *Churchill, Cripps and India, 1939–45* (Oxford, 1979)

Morgan, K. O., *Labour in Power, 1945–1951* (Oxford, 1985)

Murphy, J. T., *Labour's Big Three: A Biographical Study of Clement Attlee, Herbert Morrison and Ernest Bevin* (London, 1948)

Namier, Lewis, *The Structure of Politics at the Accession of George III* (London, 1963)

__ *England in the Age of the American Revolution* (London, 1966)

Newman, Michael, *Harold Laski: A Political Biography* (London, 1993)

Olson, Lynne, *Troublesome Young Men: The Churchill Conspiracy of 1940* (London, 2007)

Pearce, Robert (ed.) *Attlee* (London, 1997)

Pelling, Henry, *A Short History of the Labour Party* (London, 1961)

__ *The Origins of the Labour Party, 1880–1900* (Oxford, 1965)

Pimlott, Ben, *Labour and the Left in the 1930s* (Cambridge, 1977)

__ (ed.) *The Political Diary of Hugh Dalton, 1918–40, 1945–60* (London, 1986)

__ *Hugh Dalton* (London, 1985)

__ (ed.) *The Second World War Diary of Hugh Dalton, 1940–1945* (London, 1986)

Punnett, R. M., *Front-Bench Opposition: The Role of the Leader of the Opposition, the Shadow Cabinet and Shadow Government in British Politics* (London, 1973)

Radice, Giles, *The Tortoise and the Hares: Attlee, Bevin, Cripps, Dalton, Morrison* (London, 2008)

Ramsden, John, *A History of the Conservative Party*, 5, *The Age of Churchill and Eden, 1940–1957* (London, 1995)

Roberts, Andrew, *'The Holy Fox': The Life of Lord Halifax* (London, 1991)

__ *Eminent Churchillians* (London, 1994)

__ *Salisbury: Victorian Titan* (London, 1999)

Schoenfeld, Maxwell Philip, *The War Ministry of Winston Churchill* (Iowa, 1972)

Schumpeter, Joseph A., *Capitalism, Socialism, and Democracy* (London, 1943)

Scruton, Roger, *The Uses of Pessimism* (London, 2010)

Searle, G. R., *Country Before Party: Coalition and the Idea of 'National Government' in Modern Britain, 1885–1987* (London, 1995)

Shannon, Richard, *The Age of Salisbury, 1881–1902: Unionism and Empire* (London, 1996)

Shaw, Tony, *Eden, Suez and the Mass Media: Propaganda and Persuasion during the Suez Crisis* (London, 1995)

Shepherd, John, *George Lansbury: At the Heart of Old Labour* (Oxford, 2002)

Skidelsky, Robert, *John Maynard Keynes: Fighting for Freedom, 1937–1946* (London, 2001)

Slowe, Peter, *Manny Shinwell: An Authorised Biography* (London, 1993)

Smart, Nick, *The National Government, 1931–40* (Basingstoke, 1999)

Smith, Jeremy, *The Tories and Ireland, 1910–1914: Conservative Party Politics and the Home Rule Crisis* (Dublin, 2000)

Stewart, Graham, *Burying Caesar: Churchill, Chamberlain and the Battle for the Tory Party* (London, 1999)

Swift, John, *Labour in Crisis: Clement Attlee and the Labour Party in Opposition, 1931–40* (Basingstoke, 2001)

Tanner, Duncan, *Political Change and the Labour Party, 1910–1918* (Cambridge, 1990)

Taylor, A. J. P. (ed.) *Lloyd George: Twelve Essays* (London, 1971)

__ *Beaverbrook* (London, 1972)

Thomas-Symonds, Nicklaus, *Attlee: A Life in Politics* (London, 2010)

Thompson, Laurence, *1940* (London, 1966)

Tiratsoo, Nick (ed.) *The Attlee Years* (London, 1991)

Thorpe, Andrew, *Parties at War: Political Organization in Second World War Britain* (Oxford, 2009)

Tocqueville, Alexis de, *Democracy in America*, translated by Gerald Bevan (London, 2003)

Toye, Richard and Julie Gottlieb (eds) *Making Reputations: Power, Persuasion and the Individual in Modern British Politics* (London, 2005)

Vernon, Betty D., *Ellen Wilkinson, 1891–1947* (London, 1982)

Vernon, James, *Politics and the People: A study in English Political Culture, c.1815–1867* (Cambridge, 1993)

Wheeler-Bennett, W., *John Anderson, Viscount Waverley* (London, 1962)

Whiting, Richard, *The Labour Party and Taxation: Party Identity and Political Purpose in Twentieth-century Britain* (Cambridge, 2001)

Williamson, Philip, *National Crisis and National Government: British Politics, the Economy and Empire, 1926–1932* (Cambridge, 1992)

__ *Stanley Baldwin: Conservative Leadership and National Values* (Cambridge, 1999)

Woolton, Lord, *The Memoirs of the Rt Hon. the Earl of Woolton* (London, 1959)

Worley, Matthew, *Labour Inside the Gate: A History of the British Labour Party between the Wars* (London, 2005)

Articles and essays

Addison, Paul, 'By-elections of the Second World War', in Chris Cook and John Ramsden (eds) *By-Elections in British Politics* (London, 1973) pp. 165–90

__ 'Journey to the centre: Churchill and Labour in coalition, 1940–5', in Alan Sked and Chris Cook (eds) *Crisis and Controversy: Essays in Honour of A. J. P. Taylor* (London, 1976) pp. 165–93

Beers, Laura, 'Whose opinion? Changing attitudes towards opinion polling in British politics, 1937–1964', *Twentieth Century British History*, 17 (2006) pp. 177–205

Bernstein, George L., 'Sir Henry Campbell-Bannerman and the Liberal imperialists', *Journal of British Studies*, 23 (1983) pp. 105–24

Brent, Richard, 'Butterfield's Tories: 'High Politics' and the writing of modern British political history', *The Historical Journal*, 30 (1987) pp. 943–54

Crowcroft, Robert, 'Maurice Cowling and the writing of British political history', *Contemporary British History*, 22 (2008) pp. 279–86

__ 'The "high politics" of Labour Party factionalism, 1950–5', *Historical Research*, 81 (2008) pp. 679–709

__ '"What is happening in Europe?": Sir Richard Stokes, fascism, and the anti-war movement in the British Labour Party during the Second World War and after', *History*, 93 (2008) pp. 514–30

__ '"High politics", political practice and the Labour Party', in Robert Crowcroft, S. J. D. Green and Richard Whiting (eds) *The Philosophy, Politics and Religion of British Democracy: Maurice Cowling and Conservatism* (London, 2010) pp. 153–85

Dilks, David, 'The twilight war and the fall of France: Chamberlain and Churchill in 1940', in Dilks, David (ed.) *Retreat from Power – Studies in Britain's Foreign Policy of the Twentieth Century, Volume Two: After 1939* (London, 1981) pp. 36–65

Dutton, D. J., 'Power-brokers or just "glamour boys"? The Eden Group, September 1939–May 1940', *English Historical Review*, 118 (2003) pp. 412–24

Fielding, Steven, 'What did 'the people' want? The meaning of the 1945 general election', *The Historical Journal*, 35 (1992) pp. 623–39

__ 'The Second World War and popular radicalism: the significance of the movement away from party', *History*, 80 (1995) pp. 123–44

Green, S. J. D., 'From Puritanism to Pantheism: reflections on the degeneration of English life since 1945', *The Machray Review: A Publication of the Prayer Book Society of Canada*, 7 (1997) pp. 1–16

__ 'The 1944 Education Act: a church–state perspective', *Parliamentary History*, 19 (2000) pp. 148–64

__ 'The strange death of Puritan England, 1914–1945', in Louis, Wm. Roger (ed.) *Yet More Adventures with Britannia: Personalities, Politics and Culture in Britain* (London, 2005) pp. 185–209

Hamill, John and Andrew Prescott, 'The Mason's candidate: new welcome lodge no. 5139 and the Parliamentary Labour Party', *Labour History Review*, 71 (2006) pp. 9–41

Hanak, H., 'Sir Stafford Cripps as ambassador in Moscow, June 1941–January 1942', *English Historical Review*, 97 (1982) pp. 332–44

Harris, Ian, 'Religion, authority and politics: the thought of Maurice Cowling', *The Political Science Reviewer* (1997) pp. 434–81

Harrison, Brian, 'Frederick William Pethick-Lawrence', in H. C. G. Matthew and Brian Harrison (eds) *Oxford Dictionary of National Biography*, 2 (Oxford, 2004) pp. 809–14

Hartley, Owen A. 'Winston Churchill', in Richard Kelly and John Cantrell (eds) *Modern British Statesmen, 1867–1945* (Manchester, 1998) pp. 193–204

Harvie, Christopher, 'Labour in Scotland during the Second World War', *The Historical Journal*, 26 (1983) pp. 921–44

Imley, Talbot, 'From villain to partner: British Labour Party leaders, France and international policy during the phoney war, 1939–40', *Journal of Contemporary History*, 38 (2003) pp. 579–96

Jefferys, Kevin, 'British politics and social policy during the Second World War', *The Historical Journal*, 30 (1987) pp. 123–44

___ 'May 1940: the downfall of Neville Chamberlain', *Parliamentary History*, 10 (1991) pp. 363–78

Lowe, Rodney, 'The Second World War, consensus, and the foundation of the welfare state', *Twentieth Century British History*, 1 (1990) pp. 152–82

Martin, David, 'Hastings Bertrand Lees-Smith', in John Saville and Joyce Bellamy (eds) *Dictionary of Labour Biography*, 9 (London, 1993) pp. 175–81

Matthew, H. C. G., 'Rhetoric and politics in Great Britain, 1860–1950', in P. J. Waller (ed.) *Politics and Social Change in Modern Britain: Essays Presented to A. F. Thompson* (Sussex, 1987) pp. 34–58

Morton, Louis, 'The decision to use the atomic bomb', in Robert J. Art and Kenneth Waltz (eds) *The Use of Force* (London, 1988) pp. 198–219

Peden, G. C., 'Wood, Sir (Howard) Kingsley (1881–1943)', *Oxford Dictionary of National Biography* (Oxford, 2004)

Pelling, Henry, 'The 1945 general election reconsidered', *The Historical Journal*, 23 (1980) pp. 399–414

Ritschel, Daniel, 'The making of consensus: the Nuffield College conferences during the Second World War', *Twentieth Century British History*, 6 (1995) pp. 267–301

Sibley, Richard, 'Essays in Labour statistics: the swing to Labour during the Second World War: when and why?', *Labour History Review*, 55 (1990) pp. 23–34

Smart, Nick, 'Four days in May: the Norway debate and the downfall of Neville Chamberlain', *Parliamentary History*, 17 (1998) pp. 215–43

Smith, Jeremy, 'Bluff, bluster and brinkmanship: Andrew Bonar law and the third Home Rule Bill', *Historical Journal*, 36 (1993) pp. 161–78

__ 'Sir Edward Carson and the myth of partition', in R. Swift and C. Kinealy, *Power and Authority in Victorian Ireland* (Dublin, 2006)

Theakston, Kevin and Mark Gill, 'Rating 20th-century British prime ministers', *British Journal of Politics and International Relations*, 8 (2006) pp. 193–213

Thorpe, Andrew, '"In a rather emotional state"? The Labour Party and British intervention in Greece, 1944–5', *English Historical Review*, 121 (2006) pp. 1075–105

Tombs, Isabelle, 'The Victory of Socialist 'Vansittartism': Labour and the German Question, 1941–5', *Twentieth Century British History*, 7 (1996) pp.287–309

Webb, M., 'The Rt. Hon. Herbert Morrison, MP', in H. Tracey (ed.) *The British Labour Party* (London, 1948), 3, pp. 37–8

Whiting, Richard, 'Arthur Greenwood', in Keith Gildart, David Howell and Neville Kirk (eds) *Dictionary of Labour Biography*, 11 (London, 2004) pp. 83–91

__ 'Clement Richard Attlee', in H. C. G. Matthew and Brian Harrison (eds) *Oxford Dictionary of National Biography*, 2 (Oxford, 2004) pp. 875–85

Witherell, Larry L., 'Lord Salisbury's "Watching Committee" and the fall of Neville Chamberlain, May 1940', *English Historical Review*, 116 (2001) pp. 1134–66

Theses

Addison, Paul, 'Political change in Britain, September 1939–May 1940' (unpublished D.Phil. thesis, Oxford, 1972)

Calder, Angus, 'The Common Wealth Party, 1942–45', 2 vols (unpublished Ph.D. thesis, University of Sussex, 1968)

Jones, Harriet, 'The Conservative Party and the welfare state, 1942–1955' (unpublished Ph.D. thesis, University of London, 1992)

Kopsch, Harmut, 'The approach of the Conservative Party to social policy during the Second World War' (unpublished Ph.D. thesis, University of London, 1970)

Index